Value Added Tax Fraud

Serving as an introduction to one of the 'hottest' topics in financial crime, the Value Added Tax (VAT) fraud, this new and original book aims to analyze and decrypt the fraud and explore multidisciplinary avenues, thereby exposing nuances and shades that remain concealed by traditional taxation-oriented researches. Quantifying the impact of the fraud on the real economy underlines the structural damages propagated by this crime in the European Union. The 'fraudsters' benefit when policy changes are inflicted in an economic space without a fully fledged legal framework. Geopolitical events like the creation of the Eurasian Union and 'Brexit' are analyzed from the perspective of the VAT fraud, thereby underlining the foreseeable risks of such historical turnrounds. In addition, this book provides a unique collection of case studies that depict the main characteristics of VAT fraud.

Introduction to VAT Fraud will be of interest to students at an advanced level, academics and reflective practitioners. It addresses the topics with regards to banking and finance law, international law, criminal law, taxation, accounting and financial crime. It will be of value to researchers, academics, professionals and students in the fields of law, financial crime, technology, accounting and taxation.

Marius-Cristian Frunza is a Director with Schwarzthal Kapital, United Kingdom, and an Associate Researcher with the Laboratory of Excellence for Financial Regulation (LABEX ReFI) in Paris, France.

Routledge Research in Finance and Banking Law

Available:

Financial Stability and Prudential Regulation
A Comparative Approach to the UK, US, Canada, Australia and Germany
Alison Lui

Law and Finance after the Financial Crisis
The Untold Stories of the UK Financial Market
Abdul Karim Aldohni

Microfinance and Financial Inclusion
The Challenge of Regulating Alternative Forms of Finance
Eugenia Macchiavello

Law and Regulation of Mobile Payment Systems
Issues Arising 'Post' Financial Inclusion in Kenya
Joy Malala

Management and Regulation of Pension Scheme
Australia: A Cautionary Tale
Nicholas Morris

The Regulation and Supervision of Banks
The Post Crisis Regulatory Responses of the EU
Chen Chen Hu

Regulation and Supervision of the OTC Derivatives Market
Ligia Catherine Arias-Barrera

Value Added Tax Fraud
Marius-Cristian Frunza

For more information about this series, please visit: www.routledge.com/Routledge-Research-in-Finance-and-Banking-Law/book-series/FINANCIALLAW

Value Added Tax Fraud

Marius-Cristian Frunza

Routledge
Taylor & Francis Group

LONDON AND NEW YORK

First published 2019
by Routledge
2 Park Square, Milton Park, Abingdon, Oxon OX14 4RN

and by Routledge
52 Vanderbilt Avenue, New York, NY 10017

First issued in paperback 2020

Routledge is an imprint of the Taylor & Francis Group, an informa business

British Library Cataloguing-in-Publication Data
A catalogue record for this book is available from the British Library

Library of Congress Cataloging-in-Publication Data
A catalog record has been requested for this book

ISBN 13: 978-0-367-58260-9 (pbk)
ISBN 13: 978-1-138-29829-3 (hbk)

DOI: 10.4324/9781315098722

Typeset in Galliard
by codeMantra

This book is dedicated in memoriam of Ignacio Echeverría Miralles de Imperial, a Spanish financial crime expert, cowardly killed on 3 June 2017, during the London Bridge terrorist attacks.

Contents

List of figures   ix
List of tables   xi
Acknowledgements   xiii

1 Introduction to the mechanisms of VAT fraud   1

2 Markets and VAT fraud   14

3 Impact of the VAT fraud on the EU's economy   31

4 Brexit effect on the VAT fraud   77

5 VAT: a modern economic weapon   85

6 How the VAT fraud proceeds are laundered   94

7 Perspectives upon the VAT fraud in the Eurasian
  Economic Union   103

8 The economy of terror: VAT fraud and terrorism financing   113

9 Technology: a real leverage for the VAT fraudsters   129

10 Who is who in the VAT milieu?   178

11 How the VAT fraud reshaped the criminal underworld   247

12 Investigating the VAT fraud   258

13 Avenues of countering VAT fraud   265

Appendix   279
  - Interview: Chris Perryman, Europol *279*
  - Interview: Bo Elkjaer, a pioneer journalist in
    VAT investigation *288*
  - Interview: Dr Mike Cheetham, VAT fraud expert *292*

Bibliography   301
Index   307

Figures

1.1 Basic mechanism of the VAT fraud 7
1.2 Carousel version of the MTIC fraud 8
1.3 Cross-invoicing is an enhanced version of the MTIC 9
1.4 Contra-trading aims to hinder the detection of MTIC fraud 10
1.5 VAT fraud with countertrades or barter trades 11
3.1 Evolution of the total tax receipts for the EU countries 32
3.2 Total level of taxation and the breakdown of the tax revenue for each country of the EU expressed in percentage of the national GDP 33
3.3 Evolution of total VAT receipts in European Union since 1999 34
3.4 Geographical distribution of the VAT share in the total tax receipts in 2016 35
3.5 Evolution between 1999 and 2019 of the VAT share in the national tax receipts for each member country 37
3.6 Estimates of the VAT gap for 28 EU member states between 2012 and 2015 44
3.7 Evolution of the relative VAT gap for the 28 EU member states between 2012 and 2015 (expressed in percentage of the collected VAT) 45
3.8 Breakdown of the VAT loss due to the shadow economy in 2015 55
3.9 Evolution of the VAT losses due to the shadow economy for the 28 countries of the EU between 2013 and 2015 56
3.10 VAT loss due to the shadow economy compared to VAT loss on formal economy (VAT gap) in 2015 56
3.11 Framework for modelling the VAT gap related to MTIC fraud 60
3.12 MTIC VAT loss/Total VAT gap (%) for 2013 65
3.13 2014 MTIC VAT gap breakdown (million euros) 66
3.14 Breakdown of the VAT loss due to the MTIC fraud in 2014 (%) 68
3.15 Evolution of EU's Imports from other member countries and from non-members between 1999 and 2017 72
3.16 2015 Snapshot of the benchmark of the EU Imports and Exports with respect to the origin of the counterparts 73
5.1 Alteration of the supply demand equilibrium in a market affected by VAT fraud 86

x   *Figures*

5.2	Evolution of the traded volumes on the Paris-based CO_2 allowance exchange: BlueNext	87
5.3	Structural breaks in the relationship of EUA prices to its fundamental drivers	89
5.4	Observed prices on the spot market and theoretical prices	90
5.5	Evolution of the number of cars produced in France and Germany between 2002 and 2016	92
8.1	MTIC fraud and terrorism funding	119
8.2	VAT fraud involving SF Energy Trading	122
8.3	Q-Transport case	125
8.4	Q-Transport account with BRFKredit	127
8.5	The evolution of Q-Transport bank's account balance with BRFkredit	127
8.6	Q-Transport account with BRFKredit	128
9.1	VAT fraud on CO_2 emissions exchange	131
9.2	VAT evasion through online marketplace	136
9.3	Structure of an MLM pyramidal scheme	141
9.4	Evolution of the most popular cryptocurrency prices over the past four years	162
9.5	Mechanism of a mixer/tumbler	165
10.1	Main players in Operation *Phuncards-Broker*	216
10.2	Operation *Traffico Telefonico* scheme involving I-Globe Srl and Telefox Srl	226
10.3	Operation *Traffico Telefonico* scheme involving Planetarium Srl and Globe Phone Network	227

Tables

1.1	2016 snapshot of the most cashless countries in Europe	5
2.1	Example of VAT fraud cases with trades of technology products	17
2.2	Summary of Spanish operation against VAT evaders specializing in alcoholic beverages	28
3.1	Evolution of the VAT rates (%) across the EU members since 1999	36
3.2	VAT gap estimates in EU member states between 2011 and 2015	43
3.3	Estimation of the shadow economy of EU countries, 2003–2016	50
3.4	Regression results for the model specified in Equation (3.1)	52
3.5	Regression results for the parameters specified in model from Equation (3.2)	53
3.6	Impact of the changes in the VAT rate on the intra-EU trade gap	61
3.7	Model estimation with raw and normalized VAT figures and trade gap and GDP as drivers	62
3.8	Model estimation with raw and normalized VAT figures and Imports, Exports and GDP as drivers	63
3.9	Model estimation with VAT, Imports and Exports normalized by the GDP	64
3.10	Estimates of the MTIC VAT fraud in 2013	67
3.11	Estimates of the MTIC VAT fraud in 2014	69
3.12	Breakdown of the estimated losses from the MTIC fraud in 2015	69
3.13	Evolution of the losses due to MTIC scams between 2013 and 2015	70
3.14	Estimates of the losses due to the MTEC fraud in the EU between 2013 and 2015	74
3.15	Breakdown of the total losses from VAT fraud in the EU between 2013 and 2014	75
3.16	Total VAT fraud losses compared to the VAT gap, the collected VAT amount and the EU GDP	75
4.1	Brexit scenarios and issues with the VAT fraud	79
6.1	List of territories categorized as 'No man's land' from a tax perspective	101

7.1   Estimates of the VAT fraud losses to the national treasuries
in the EAEU   112

8.1   Snapshot of VAT fraud cases with alleged links to the
terrorist financing   120

8.2   Companies that had direct and indirect trades with SF
Energy Trading between 2008 and 2010   122

8.3   Summary of companies that defrauded the Danish tax office
in the Q-Transport case   126

9.1   Top online retailers in 2017   134

9.2   Percentage of parcels where VAT and customs tax are collected 138

9.3   Estimates of the VAT loss due to non-compliant sellers
trading through online marketplaces   139

9.4   Legal status of Bitcoin and Altcoin in different jurisdictions,
with a focus on the VAT treatment   167

10.1 Snapshot of the three major operations targeting the Stoke-
on-Trent gangs   185

10.2 Fastweb recovered 33.39 million euros of VAT from the
Italian tax office and sent it to Web Wizard and CMC Italia   222

10.3 Financing loans of Fulcrum and LBB Trading from
Web Wizard Srl   222

10.4 Operational margins of TIS S.p.A. between 2005 and 2007   228

10.5 Operational margins of Fastweb S.p.A. between 2005 and 2007 229

10.6 Main financial flows between the companies involved in
Operation *Traffico Telefonico*   231

10.7 Cash outflows from Fastweb and TIS towards Planetarium Srl
and I-Globe between 2005 and 2007   232

10.8 Financial flows of Broker Management S.A.   232

10.9 Synthesis of the VAT inflows and outflows made towards the
company involved in the fraud   233

10.10 Sentences for the persons charged in Operation *Phuncards-Broker* 234

11.1 Summary of main operations of Italian law enforcement
against VAT fraudsters   249

12.1 Name versions in several languages for some individuals
investigated in the *Carbon Connection*   263

Acknowledgements

The author would like to express his very great appreciation to the three persons who agreed to be interviewed for this textbook:

- Bo Elkjaer, journalist at Danish national television [Danmarks Radio-1 (DR1)], a pioneer in the investigation of the VAT fraud on the CO_2 market and a pioneer in connecting the dots between VAT and terrorism
- Dr Mike Cheettham, VAT expert
- Chris Perryman, head of VAT investigation at Europol.

This work would not have been possible without the guidance of the following people:

- Prof. Dominique Guegan, professor of econometrics at Pantheon-Sorbonne Paris I University.
- Prof. Richard Ainsworth from New York University, the main scholar producing high-quality avant-garde research in the area of the VAT fraud.
- Prof. Didier Marteau, professor of economics at Paris European Business School (ESCP Europe), and his comprehensive inputs on taxation.

I would like to thank Ilgiz Mustafin from Kazan Innopolis University for his substantial help and expertise on the text mining and name matching. My special gratitude goes to my friends Petr Ryzhenkov, Evgueny Kurinin, Bogdan Donisa, Evgueny Shurmanov and Thomas Alderweireld.

1 Introduction to the mechanisms of VAT fraud

VAT: a European concept

> VAT rules are a quarter of a century old and no longer fit for purpose. Fraud today is not something citizens can accept any more, particularly when it finances organised crime and terrorists.
>
> Pierre Moscovici, European Union Commissioner, 2017[1]

Tax can be defined as a financial liability established and collected by a government or an equivalent agency. The government of a country can apply tax levies to income, capital, resources, labour, goods and services. Tax concerns all physical and moral persons encompassed by the jurisdiction of a government.

Taxes are the main source of revenue for the national budget of a country or region. They are classified as direct taxes and indirect taxes. Direct taxes are charged directly on the income or wealth of the person, while indirect taxes are imposed on the price of goods and services. The computation of tax levy has, in general, two main components:

- the tax levy base, representing the nominal value upon which the assessment of tax liability is made, and
- the tax rate, which is presented generally as a percentage.

Value Added Tax (VAT) is an indirect consumption tax, charged on most trades of goods and services. The base of the VAT is the *value added* by the economic agent. For example an industrial company purchasing raw materials for 100 euros and transforming them into a finite product sold for 130 euros has a VAT liability on the 30 euros of value added in the production process.

A wholesaler buying clothes for 1,000 euros and selling them to retailers for 1,500 euros is liable on the 500 euros of commercial value added. VAT is charged to registered businesses and final non-business customers. Final clients do not pay the VAT directly to the government but to B-to-C (business to client) companies.

---

1 www.ft.com/content/a6cdc2d4-a8bc-11e7-ab55-27219df83c97.

DOI: 10.4324/9781315098722-1

B-to-C companies registered for VAT pay their liability periodically (generally quarterly) to the tax office of the country where the product is consumed. B-2-B (business to business) companies are also liable for VAT, depending on the difference between VAT charged to clients and the VAT paid for purchases. If the balance is negative the company can claim a refund from the tax office. If the balance is positive the business is required to pay the tax levy to the concerned national treasury.

The concept of VAT was fathered in the 1950s by Maurice Lauré (Laure, 1955). He was the head of the French Tax Authority. VAT was introduced in France through a law on 10 April 1954.

VAT (TVA, *Taxe sur la valeur ajoutée*) was first tested in Ivory Coast (Côte d'Ivoire), a French colony, in 1954. After the Ivorian experiment, VAT was extended to the entire French territory in 1958. Rapidly, the concept of VAT spread to other European countries.

After the collapse of the former communist bloc and the dismantlement of the Soviet Union in August 1991, major policy reforms were immediately implemented in the former Eastern Bloc, aiming to regulate the exponentially rising economic activities.

VAT (НДС, налог на добавленную) was introduced in Russia in 1992. It is administered by the Federal Tax Service, with a rate of 18% for most goods and services. In 1993, VAT was also introduced in Romania (TVA, Taxa pe Valoare Adaugata), while Bulgaria adopted VAT (ДДС, Данък върху добавената стойност) in 1994. China started to implement VAT gradually between 1984 and 1993, when the State Council promulgated a dedicated policy. The United Arab Emirates and Saudi Arabia adopted VAT as of 2018, with a small rate of 5% that is supposed to increase over time.

Goods and Services Tax (GST) is an equivalent of the VAT implemented in countries like India, Canada, Australia and New Zealand. By the early 2000s, VAT had become the key component of the indirect taxation systems in more than 120 countries, with tax rates varying from 5% to 27%.

Interestingly, the VAT failed to find acceptance in the United States, despite numerous attempts by various politicians to bring momentum around the introduction of the VAT as a Federal tax. Michigan adopted a modified VAT, named a Business Activities Tax, and used the system for 14 years. The United States is, along with a few financial paradises (i.e., the British Virgin Islands, the Cayman Islands, Gibraltar and Guernsey), amongst the only states in the world without a VAT system.

Tax fraud

The separation line between tax compliance and tax fraud is very murky. When a company or an individual looks for leeways from the normal avenue of being fully compliant with all tax liabilities, few legal options are available.

1   Tax optimization consists of adjusting the various financial metrics comprising a base for tax levies in order to minimize the total tax liability. A simple example is using debt in corporate as a means to reduce the corporate tax bill.

2   Tax arbitrage profits from the way a given transaction is taxed in different countries or different regions of a country. VAT for example has various rates in different countries. Within the same country a region (i.e., Livigno in Italy) could be exempted of tax.

3   Tax avoidance is the practice that employs legal methods in order to aggressively reduce tax liability by claiming deduction or refunds. Tax avoidance can employ sophisticated structures like offshore holdings and structured financial products, like insurance or derivatives, designed to enhance tax avoidance.

Tax evasion is employing illegal methods to reduce partially or totally the tax liability or to access fraudulently tax reimbursement from the national tax office.

By its very nature, VAT's effectiveness relies on the integrity and loyalty of various intermediaries that collect and pay the tax along the economic chain. On the one hand, economies with 'black markets' involving undeclared trades are not submitted to VAT, thereby reducing its base and constituting a source of tax evasion. On the other hand, defecting intermediaries in distressed financial situations or unfaithful (missing) traders vis-à-vis a tax discipline represent a second source of evasion.

VAT evasion touches all countries having indirect taxation systems, including both VAT and GST. If most often the cases from the European Union (EU) or the United Kingdom are reported, VAT fraud occurs also in Australia or the Russian Federation. Countries from the African continent like South Africa were also touched. In 2018,[2] the South African Revenue Service and crime intelligence officers arrested eight men and a woman in connection with a scam with a potential loss to the taxpayer of more than 90 million rans (5.7 million euros). The gang was also associated with violent crimes.

In January 2018 the United Arabs Emirates and Saudi Arabia introduced VAT in their taxation systems. Despite being a source of structural risk for the global trade, VAT is definitely a stable source of income for the national budget. Dubai is already an international hub for financial crime, and the introduction of VAT will most likely make the Emirates more attractive for crooks.

VAT fraud typologies

Tax fraud appears in many forms and shapes, touching multiple markets and sectors of the economy. As pointed out before the borderline between tax fraud, tax avoidance and tax optimization is not well defined and can swing, depending on the interpretation of national laws and regulations. Therefore, any classification of VAT fraud typologies needs to be apprehended cautiously and might not be consistent in regards to both legislation and economic reasoning. Without loss of generality, one can split the economy of a country into two major silos:

*   The *formal economy*, represented by those economic activities governed by the national law and with observable and quantifiable turnover figures.

---

2   www.enca.com/south-africa/police-bust-large-vat-fraud-syndicate.

Traditionally, the formal economy is established on organized commercial entities registered with the national business registries. The size of the formal economy is measured from compulsory reports required by governments from businesses, including tax fillings, financial annual statements, etc.

- The informal or the *shadow economy*, encompassing all trades of goods and services taking place outside the perimeter of national laws. The volumes and the values of the trades for the shadow economy are in most of the cases not directly observable. The output of the shadow economy is not included in the base of any national tax.

Based on these considerations, the following empirical classification of VAT fraud typologies is proposed:

1   *Shadow economy*-related VAT fraud encompasses the undeclared domestic and cross-border trades of goods and services not submitted to VAT.
2   Dissimulation of trades from formal economy is known as *Missing trader* fraud. The *Missing trader*'s aim of concealing the totality or part of the turnover is to underestimate the base of the VAT and to pay less or not to pay the full value of the liability towards the national treasury. The missing trader 'disappears' after a relatively short period of time by closing, abandoning or bankrupting the business.
3   Misrepresenting the figures from the trading book of an organization by employing *Accounting shenanigans* aim to artificially reduce the amount of VAT liabilities, without altering the rest of the accounting figures. The accounting shenanigans can be used over an extended period of time, without ceasing the business, as in the case of the missing trader.
4   Misrepresenting the type of traded goods or services aims to reduce the VAT liability by applying an inappropriate VAT rate lower than required. *Misrepresentation of goods and services* entails declaring for taxation purposes an item in a category different from the correct one in order to arbitrate the VAT rate percentage.

The shadow economy

The base of the value added taxation is represented by the formal economy. Thus, the shadow economy is inevitably linked to tax fraud and especially to VAT fraud. The trades taking place within the shadow economy are not declared for any tax purpose, thereby the government is not able to tax these trades.

The base of the VAT is directly proportional to the turnover of the formal economy. The observability and the accuracy of the figures reported within the formal economy rely on the robustness of the collection processes of accounting data from the organizations included in the national business registry. If the figures related to the taxation base or to the appropriate tax rate of a given company are not accurate, the amount of the collected tax will not be genuine.

Some traders from the formal economy may choose to dissimulate or to mis-represent trades, thereby including them de facto in the shadow economy. Thus, these trades are not included in the compulsory reporting and the respective tax bases are not accurate.

The shadow economy, known as the black market, refers to economic activities that are invisible to the national statistics. Therefore, these activities are not included in the national Gross Domestic Product (GDP) figure. The informal economy can include activities which are both legal and illegal in nature. Traditionally the shadow economy involves trades of services and goods for which the customer pays in cash.

In recent years, with the increasing scrutiny of the cash transactions and with the zero cash policy of some European countries,[3] the assumption of a cash-only shadow economy needs to be reconsidered. Table 1.1 shows a few relevant statistics for three European countries that have a clear policy to move towards a cashless economy. In countries like Sweden or France, the percentage of transactions using a non-cash method was almost 60% in 2016. Many innovative payment methods proposed by the Fintech companies are as invisible to the tax collector as cash payments.

Therefore, in the current context, the shadow economy encompasses non-cash transactions, including:

- Transactions with digital currencies, including cryptocurrencies. Bitcoin and the altcoins have a very heterogeneous legal status across the world. Most crypto-transactions are not submitted to any form of taxation.
- Barter transactions. Exchange of goods and services for other goods or services is very difficult to tax.
- Shadow banking. With the financial crisis many alternative methods of financing saw the light of day. Non-banking financial institutions have a significant share of the market. Many of those liquidity providers are not monitored by regulators or tax authorities. Therefore, their clients are able to operate outside the formal economy.

Table 1.1 2016 snapshot of the most cashless countries in Europe

Country	Sweden	The United Kingdom	France
Proportion of cards in issue with contactless functionality	25	41	39
Debit cards per capita	0.98	1.48	0.65
Credit cards per capita	1.04	0.88	0.1
Percentage of transactions using non-cash methods	59	52	59

Source: Telegraph, Forex Bonuses.

3 www.telegraph.co.uk/money/future-of-money/10-cashless-countries-world-does-uk-rank/.

- Hawala-type systems encompass money transfers without money movement. In a Hawala transfer the sender and the receiver of the money cannot be linked. The transfer does not require any physical or electronic transfer of money. Hawala-type transfers bypass the traditional avenues of the banking services.

Evading VAT in the shadow economy can take many forms. Most frequently, the VAT loss is caused by unregistered traders that exert an economic activity, without being registered with the respective tax office. Thus, all the underlying trades of an unregistered trader are liable to VAT.

Another source of VAT loss is the undeclared sales of registered traders. In the retail sector, for instance, a small shopkeeper has a discretionary option to keep some sales undeclared, thereby diminishing the base for the VAT levy. This illegal action would also entail an underestimation of the corporate tax or revenue tax of the trader. In the accounts, these undeclared sales are declared as damaged stocks and are thereby written off.

Missing trader

Missing trader fraud is taking advantage of the VAT rules on cross-border transactions of goods and services. VAT is not applicable on cross-border transactions, especially within the EU. A trader can buy a product from another country VAT-free, sell it domestically with VAT and never pay the VAT liability. Missing trader encompasses a wide panel of VAT fraud typologies, including Missing Trader Extra-Community (MTEC) fraud, carousel fraud, cross-invoicing, contra-trading and barter trading.

Missing Trader Intra-Community

The Missing Trader Intra-Community (MTIC) scam is one of the most frequent and damaging VAT fraud types. Its underlying mechanism is based on the fact that intra-Community trades are not submitted to VAT. The basic form of the MTIC fraud is depicted in Figure 1.1. An item is bought from a different country of the EU without VAT and sold domestically with VAT. The VAT is not paid to the local tax authority.

As shown in the investigation of the Hungarian[4] VAT fraud the bigger the difference between the domestic VAT rate and the VAT rates of neighbouring countries, the stronger the incentive to commit fraud. The wide range of VAT rates across the EU (Barbone, 2013), juxtaposed with the frequent rate changes over time, represents a real incentive for fraud and makes it more difficult to track and investigate.

4 Hungary has the biggest VAT rate in the EU.

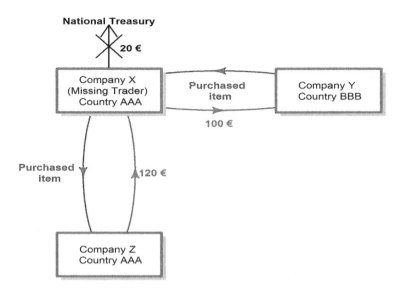

Figure 1.1 Basic mechanism of the VAT fraud. An item is bought from a different country of the EU without VAT and sold domestically with VAT. The VAT is not paid to the local tax authority.

In MTIC fraud's most simple form, a trader collects tax on sales and then fails to remit it to the government, for example, by engineering bankruptcy. It is not a fraud against the Community itself and does not come about because of mismanagement by European institutions but instead is an attack upon the measures that Member States have introduced to promote cross-border trade in the Community. Growth in the fraud is driven by four factors:

a   The increase in high-value/low-weight goods, which make it easy and inexpensive to transport valuable consignments.
b   The zero rate of taxation on intra-Community cross-border trade, which allows purchasers of goods from other EU countries not to pay VAT on purchases, although they charge VAT on sales normally.
c   At the same time, exporters of goods are still able to reclaim VAT that they have paid to other traders, thus crystallizing the loss as the revenue authority refunds a payment for which it had not received a remittance earlier in the transaction chain.
d   The abolition of frontier formalities within the EU, which prevents Member States from operating procedures which could impede the free flow of goods within the EU. This means that the verification of the zero-rated goods imported could only be based on an audit of the traders' transaction records – a process which at present is normally only undertaken when VAT receipts are remitted, sometimes after the transactions.

Carousel fraud

The most complex and damaging form of MTIC fraud, the VAT carousel is depicted in Figure 1.2. The same item circulates many times through a chain of companies situated in at least two countries. One of the companies (the Missing Trader) fails to pay the VAT liability to its local tax authority. The amount of the pocketed tax is proportional to the number of times the goods turn in the carousel. For this form of fraud the items with low physical volume and high value are preferred in order to reduce the cost of storage and transportation. Precious metals, mobile phones, laptops and clothes are traditionally the preferred targets for the carousel. Nevertheless, the investigators observed in many cases that the items never got out of the country, and forged paper and invoices were used.

The growth of the cyber-based economy moved the carousel fraud to a new dimension. Immaterial items, like cloud memory, software, Voice over Internet Protocol (VoIP) and some financial instruments (carbon emissions allowances), amplified the damaging effects of the carousel fraud. For these items there is no storage and virtually no cost of transfer. The items can change ownership across countries almost instantly, and a carousel tour can be executed in terms of minutes.

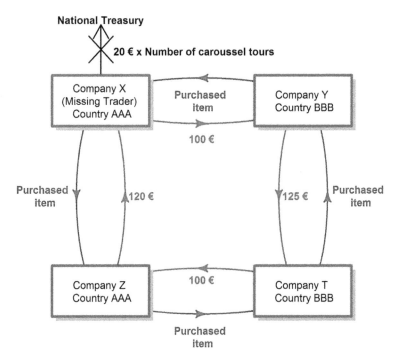

Figure 1.2 Carousel version of the MTIC fraud. The same item circulates many times through a chain of companies situated in at least two countries. One of the companies (the Missing Trader) fails to pay the VAT liability to its local tax authority. The amount of the pocketed tax is proportional to the number of times the goods go through the carousel.

Cross invoicing

One of the main issues with classic MTIC fraud depicted in Figure 1.1 is the fact that the lifespan of the Missing trader is short. In fact the fraudulent company would not be able to justify unpaid VAT liability and thereby is exposed to the risk of being detected by a control of the tax authority. A solution to this issue is to obtain invoices from different legal entities that would match the trades entailing the VAT fraud.

Cross-invoicing is a mechanism aiming to enhance the MTIC and to hinder a potential audit by providing with face invoices that would give the impression that the missing trader is a VAT complaint. A simple control would not be able to discover the reality behind the scam, and the missing trader could continue to steal tax for a longer period. As depicted in Figure 1.3, the missing trader (Company X) buys a good or a service from Company T, based in another country, and resells it domestically to Company Y with VAT. At the same time, Company X engages in bogus trades with two companies, one domestic and another from overseas. These bogus trades are backed by invoices that will match the two other trades, thereby implying in theory a zero VAT liability for Company.

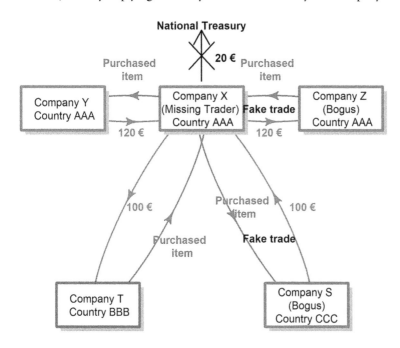

Figure 1.3 Cross-invoicing is an enhanced version of the MTIC. The missing trader (Company X) buys a good or a service from Company T, based in another country, and resells it domestically to Company Y with VAT. At the same time Company X engages in bogus trades with two companies, one domestic and another from overseas. This bogus trades have invoices that will match the two other trades, thereby implying, in theory, a zero VAT liability for Company X.

Double carousel – contra-trading

Another solution that could hamper the detection of MTIC fraud is the use o 'contra-trading'. A 'contra-trader' is a registered company engaged in two differ ent streams of transactions at the same time. The VAT charges of two streams can cel each other out, thereby generating a null total liability for the contra-trader. The two streams of transactions are depicted in Figure 1.4:[5]

- The first stream entails a VAT credit for the contra-trader (Company T) Company T buys a product domestically from Company Z (which is the missing trader) with VAT, sells it abroad to Company X without VAT. I benefits from a VAT credit of 20 euros.
- The second stream generates a VAT liability to Company T. The contra-trade buys a product (it can be different from the product of the first stream) from abroad (Company Q) without VAT and resells it domestically to Compan S at a price, including 21 euros of VAT. Company S will export the product abroad to Company Y without VAT.

Thus, the contra-trader is liable for 1 euro of VAT because the input tax offset the output tax liability. In this scheme, the counter-trader has a very small lia bility towards the national tax office. The missing trader will not pay the VAT

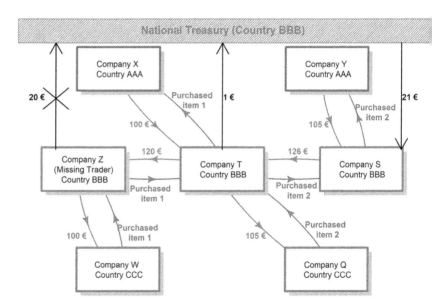

Figure 1.4 Contra-trading aims to hinder the detection of MTIC fraud. It consists of two streams of MTIC frauds or two carousel.

---

5 www.gov.uk/hmrc-internal-manuals/vat-fraud/vatf23550.

liability, while Company S will be refunded for its VAT credit. The contra-trader benefits from a refund act on a legal basis. Therefore, an audit from the customs department will not reveal any abnormality. In general between the missing trader and the contra-trader there are a few buffers involved that would make the detection even more complex.

In Great Britain, contra-trading was signalled by Her Majesty's Revenue and Customs (HMRC) in VAT fraud cases with mobile phones and computer components.

Countertrade (barter) fraud

The transfer of funds in an MTIC fraud is generally done through the banking system. This represents a big source of risk for the fraudster as bank transactions are an audit trail in the eventuality of an investigation. Bypassing totally or partially the banking system would confer a big advantage to MTIC scammers. One way of achieving this is by using countertrades. Countertrade or barter is a form of international trade in which goods or services are exchanged for other goods or services without involving any transfer of currency or cash settlement. The products exchanged should therefore have the same value.

Figure 1.5 shows the mechanism of MTIC based on countertrades. Two MTIC companies import different products from other countries without VAT. Instead of selling the products domestically Companies Z and S swap the products and resell them in their respective countries with VAT. The collected VAT is never

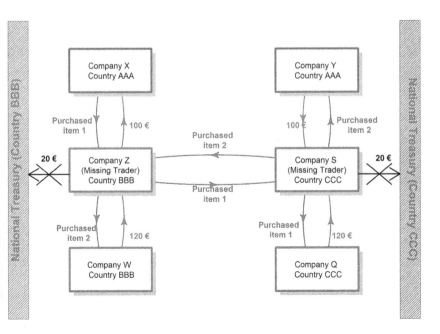

Figure 1.5 VAT fraud with countertrades or barter trades.

paid to their national tax office. The advantage of barter transactions is that between the Companies Z and S there is no fund transfer. The missing traders are not defrauding VAT on the products Company Y bought with currency from other countries but on other products. For example Company Z could import mobile phones, while Company S could import computer components and swap the products afterwards. This type of fraud would raise less suspicion, thereby being less likely to be detected.

Missing Trader Extra-Community

MTEC fraud is a version of MTIC, whereas the supplier of goods is outside the EU. This fraud works well for services and digital products. The development of online marketplaces showed that MTEC can also occur for physical goods.

With the increase of global trade, the expansion of MTEC fraud can become a real threat, and understanding its particularities becomes crucial for both investigators and customs services.

Accounting shenanigans

VAT fraud can be achieved in more subtle ways, without involving undeclared trades or missing companies. Accounting shenanigans encompass a set of techniques aimed at manipulating the financial statement and fillings of a company in a way that would present the firm in a different light from its real situation. Accounting shenanigans are often used in financial crime to abuse the confidence of investors in a company.

VAT levy is computed from accounting inputs relative to sales and acquisitions. Thus, by altering the accounting values of purchases and sales, a firm can reduce the VAT base, thereby diminishing the VAT liability. The manipulation can entail:

- an overestimation of purchases and
- an underestimation of sales.

For misestimating the purchases/sales two variables can be manipulated: the volume of purchase/sales and the price of purchases/sales. Theoretically, the volume and price are predetermined and are well described in contract invoices or delivery agreements. That might be true for most products and services, but there are cases when the price is the result of a valuation process or the result of subjective opinion. Acquisition or sale of items for which the fair value is difficult to establish can easily be misrepresented in accounting. Examples can include infrastructure, real estate, forestry, mining, resources, etc.

The energy markets have some specificities in the way that contracts are established. Swing contracts, which are popular in gas and energy markets, do not indicate a fixed volume and price for the transactions. They indicate a minimum and maximum volume and a minimum and maximum price. The valuation of these contracts is relatively complicated. The actual volume and price are difficult to establish, even when the trade is executed. Moreover, what is sold through these contracts is capacity, and checking the actual delivered volume of the trade would be a very complex task. Therefore, energy markets are targeted by fraudsters that would want to use accounting shenanigans to evade VAT.

Misrepresentation of product type

In most countries, the VAT system has different rates for different types of products. Some goods and services benefit from a reduced-rate VAT and even of VAT exception in some cases. Misrepresentation of product type consists in buying a product with a given VAT rate and rebranding the product in such a way that a different VAT rate is applied. From the difference, a profit can be made as no tax liability is entailed in theory by misrepresenting the product. The misrepresentation of product type is often presented by the fraudster as production or transformation process. The fraudulent company claims buying raw materials and transforming them into end-products, which have a different VAT rate. Two cases can arise:

- If the VAT of the mislabelled product is higher than the VAT rate of the original product, the profit is realized immediately when the mislabelled product is sold.
- If the VAT of the mislabelled product is lower than the VAT rate of the original product, the profit is unrealized, and the trader will require a VAT refund from the tax office.

2 Markets and VAT fraud

Overview

I do not care about revenues.

Jack Ma, Alibaba founder

A first risk assessment of the markets most susceptible to missing trader fraud was proposed by Ainsworth R. (2010). Virtual goods and services like CO_2 emissions and Voice over Internet Protocol (VoIP), along with energy supplies (gas and electricity), were underlined as bearing the biggest risks concerning Value Added Tax (VAT) fraud. These markets follow *the low-volume/high-value* postulate, which states that products requiring low storage space and being sold at big prices are a priority for Missing Trader Intra-Community (MTIC) fraudsters. The postulate was true, especially in the early years of VAT fraud, when the object of the scam were physical products, which needed to be stored and transported several times abroad in order to be able to claim the VAT. Therefore, items with low volume would reduce the cost of the fraud, while high price would increase its profit.

MTIC fraud on services was a game changer because services have virtually no costs of storage and transportation. Experts included these products in the same category of low volume/high value. Nevertheless, there is a big difference between the real and the virtual products. For the former there is an actual demand; thereby at the end of the MTIC chain the product is being sold to real customers. For the virtual products and services, there is no real demand for the artificial supply created by fraudsters. The particular feature of these markets is that the demand can be created artificially through bogus companies.

Markets of high-value products are also concerned by VAT fraud. Such fraud networks work at a lower speed than in the case of items with low volume. These markets encompass luxury goods and industrial equipment. The demand for these products is highly elastic with respect to price.

Another category of items bearing the risk of tax evasion is the market with an inelastic demand, whereas the consumption changes less, depending on the price. This category includes basic products like food, petrol, alcohol, tobacco and technology gadgets.

DOI: 10.4324/9781315098722-2

Low-volume, high-value products

The basic postulate of the MTIC fraud underscored the fact that tax evaders aim to maximize the profit of the crime while minimizing the execution costs. Therefore, criminals are prioritizing the products with high value that will generate a big loss to tax offices and those with low volume, which will require low cost of storage and transportation. Low physical volume products, including precious metals, electronic devices and clothes, are ideal for carousel-type frauds.

Precious metals and stones

Historically, precious metals were reported in the very first cases of VAT fraud in the 1970s in the United Kingdom. The sale of Krugerrand[1] was exempted from VAT, while gold bullions were not. Therefore, criminals found an ingenious method in which they would buy Krugerrands, melt them, sell the bars with VAT and never pay the tax back. In the 1990s, with the birth of the European Common Market, the VAT fraud with metal and precious stones increased exponentially in the United Kingdom. Gangs specializing in VAT fraud imported gold from Benelux countries VAT-free and resold it in Britain, without clearing their tax liability. That era established the foundation of the criminal networks that grew over time and entered into new markets and areas of crime.

Despite being heavily curtailed by law enforcement, VAT fraud with precious and non-precious metals is a persisting phenomenon in the European Union (EU). In Spain, Operation *Fenix* started in 2006 and revealed a network of 102 individuals and 45 companies based in Andalusia. Between 2002 and 2016 the Spanish gang defrauded more than 150 million euros from the Spanish tax-payers.[2] The main company of the network based in Barcelona imported 24 carat gold VAT-free from Switzerland, which it sold to wholesalers and jewellery manufacturers, most of them residents in Andalusia. The VAT collected through the domestic sale was never reimbursed. The court trial ended in 2017, and the recovery of the tax loss was limited.

VAT fraud with gold is not anymore a European or British phenomenon. It expanded to the other regions of the world that apply indirect taxes in one form or another. In early 2015, Australian prosecutors[3] realized that since 2012 the Australian gold industry had been heavily hit by tax fraud, representing more than 350 million euros of loss for the taxpayers. When a trader buys investment-grade gold bullion that has been stamped into bars and coins, he does not pay the Goods and Services Tax (GST).[4] When the same trader sells 'scrap' gold, which can be anything from cheap jewellery to fragments of pure

1 South African gold coin, first sold in 1967.
2 www.europapress.es/andalucia/noticia-juicio-cordoba-102-acusados-fiscal-caso-fenix-fraude-joyeria-20170323140106.html.
3 www.smh.com.au/business/gold-fraud-550m-tax-scam-hits-gold-industry-20160707-gq0s5f.html.
4 Goods and Services Tax, similar to VAT.

gold, a 10% GST does apply. A trader can collect potentially between 1,000 and 1,500 euros of tax for each kilogram of gold. Moreover, no licence is required in Australia to trade in gold bullion. The scam is thus simple and is similar to that from the 'Hatton Garden' days in the 1970s. As a result, the demand for gold in Australia became so intense that traders started to use fake transaction paperwork for gold trades that never happened.

The Australian Crime Commission cracked down on multiple GST fraud groups through Operation *Nosean*, which started in 2012. One of the indicted Brisbane precious metals trader Robert Bourke, involved with a GST fraud syndicate, was a known figure in the criminal world. Despite his criminal record Bourke was still able to act as a gold buyer on behalf of self-managed super funds. His business generated a loss in tax of 15 million euros.

Gold is not the only target of tax fraudsters. Other metals, like silver, copper or aluminium, and even rare metals like palladium and rhodium attract tax evaders. In 2017, British investigators discovered a criminal enterprise organized by Tony Bond, a scrap metal dealer[5] who has been accused of evading 17.5 million pounds in VAT. The fraud took place between 2008 and 2017 through a set of companies, including Bullion Bond, Eco Logic Solutions, Precious Waste Recovery, Dentalloy and Stewart Nicol Solutions Ltd.

In 2012, the Dutch authorities became aware of VAT fraud in the trade of copper cathodes.[6] The fraud was reported to be connected to the United Kingdom and Germany.

VAT fraud with aluminium resale was reported in Italy in 2004. Enzo Cibaldi, a businessman from Brescia, was a leader of a 23-strong group involved in fraud, accounting for 12 million euros in unpaid VAT.[7] Raw metal was bought from abroad and sold in Italy as semi-finished products, with VAT through two companies, Deral Spa and Acciaieria Riva, the latter being the missing trader.

Technology products

During the 1990s, VAT fraud was under the sign of the precious metals and stones. With the development of consumer electronic gadgets, including mobile phones, laptops, memory discs, TV screens and smartphones, tax evaders embraced new opportunities. Trading electronic gadgets was less suspicious than precious metals and at least as profitable. Examples showed in Table 2.1 are not the biggest cases of VAT fraud with electronic devices, but they aim to mark the timeline of the evolution of this scam from the late 1990s throughout the 2000s.

---

5 www.dailymail.co.uk/news/article-4802972/Scrap-metal-dealer-accused-17-5million-VAT-fraud.html.

6 www.tax-news.com/news/Netherlands_Tackles_VAT_Carousel_Fraud_In_Metal_Industry____58281.html.

7 www.siderweb.com/articoli/industry/686026-frode-sui-metalli-12-mln-di-euro-truffati-all-iva.

Table 2.1 Example of VAT fraud cases with trades of technology products

Fraud/operation	Country	Year	Amount of VAT fraud
Memory units	France	1996	10 million euros
Badajoz case	Spain-Portugal	1997–2002	36 million euros
Carré & Ribeiro	Portugal	2005	34 million euros
Operation *Medina*	Spain	2006	400 million euros
Forli group	Italy	2017	60 million euros
Operation *Sith*	Spain-Portugal	2017	25 million euros

The emergence of tax evasion in the electronic supplies business was reported as early as 1996, when David Haccoun, co-chairman of Dane Elec,[8] a French memory discs trading company, incriminated multinationals for evading VAT on memory units sale and hampering the competition. VAT loss from this fraud was estimated to be 10 million euros.

A case of VAT fraud of 36 million euros in computer equipment that occurred between 1997 and 2002[9] was investigated in 2008 in Badajoz, Spain. Companies involved in the fraud were based in Portugal and Spain.

Operation *Medina*[10] was one of the biggest busts from the 2000s in the VAT fraud groups. A total of 45 people have been arrested and charged for defrauding over 400 million euros between 2003 and 2006 on transactions of computer equipment and mobile phones. Few major retailers of electronic products were caught by the indictment. Thus, Bernabé Noya, the owner of the telecommunications business group Meflur, one of the most important companies in Northern Spain, was investigated for VAT evasion. Another company, Infinity System, a computer manufacturer with a turnover of 500 million, was also raided by prosecutors.

A massive case of VAT evasion in the resale of electronics was revealed in Portugal in 2005. The famous case of 'Carre & Ribeiro',[11] a company which generated a loss of 34 million euros to the Portuguese taxpayers, underlined the complexity of prosecuting and recovering stolen taxes in VAT fraud cases.

The VAT fraud with electronics got out of control in Great Britain, where it was estimated that in 2006, 10% of the country's exports were related to carousel fraud. Electronic products were turning in well-organized carousels up to 30 times, generating tens of millions of pounds in VAT refunds from Her Majesty's Revenue ad Customs (HMRC).[12]

In 2006, the British government asked permission from the European Commission to introduce reverse VAT on electronic products to curtail the fraud. This measure tackled the fraud only temporarily. New cases occurred later, following the same pattern.

---

8 www.channelweb.co.uk/crn-uk/news/1875763/memory-market-hit-huge-vat-fraud.
9 www.hoy.es/20080926/badajoz/condenado-anos-prision-principal-20080926.html.
10 www.elmundo.es/mundodinero/2006/11/30/economia/1164895173.html.
11 www.dn.pt/arquivo/2005/interior/quatro-empresarios-detidos-por-fraude-em-carrossel-no-iva-631893.html.
12 www.theguardian.com/uk/2006/aug/16/ukcrime.economy.

A 60 million euro[13] VAT fraud in the sector of the sale of electronic products, mobile phones and computers was reported in 2017 in Italy in the province of Forlì. The scam was organized around individuals who controlled 36 companies which imported and resold electronic products. In the same year, in Spain and Portugal the prosecutors dismantled as part of Operation *Sith*[14] a gang of 19 individuals, which had stolen 25 million euros of VAT over three years in trades of electronic products.

Clothes

Clothing business passed through massive mutation over the past two decades. Countries with a strong manufacturing sector in the EU – including France, Italy and Spain – saw the size of the industry shrinking, with factories moving into Eastern Europe, Northern Africa and Asia. The economic downturn put additional pressure on prices, and this made the clothing retail sector vulnerable to VAT fraud. Clothes fall into in the low-volume, high-value category, especially for luxury marks. Wholesalers play a crucial role in this market. They act like brokers between the manufacturers and the retailers. It is after going along the chain of wholesale that the end products see their markup increase compared to factory prices. Thus, in Europe, for clothes the retail price is 2.2 times higher than the factory price, and for shoes the prices are 2.8 times higher. Obviously, if the products come from cheap labour countries, the markups could be even higher. It was the case of an Italian investigation in a port in Agrigento in Southern Italy that found a network of missing traders specialized in importing clothes from China.[15] The fraud accounted for 2.6 million euros.

The mechanism of the VAT fraud in the clothing sector has some specific features entailed by the fact that buyers from outside the EU are entitled to refunds when shopping in Europe. A group of 146 Chinese nationals was busted in Italy as they were claiming illegally VAT refunds when shopping for clothes and shoes. An operation of Italian prosecutors called *Red Channel* showed that the group had stolen almost 1 million euros of VAT.[16]

Artificial demand

Throughout the 2000s, VAT fraud with low-volume/high-value products was massively hindered by the reversed charge introduced by different European governments and by the increased awareness of law enforcement. Thus, defrauding

13 www.ansa.it/emiliaromagna/notizie/2017/07/21/iva-60-mln-evasa-gdf-sequestra-ville_e759ea2a-b1ee-432a-88fc-3d6ae5775b44.html.
14 www.larazon.es/hacienda-desmonta-un-fraude-en-iva-de-25-millones-de-euros-DO15283642.
15 www.lasicilia.it/news/agrigento/154229/porto-empedocle-funzionari-adm-scoprono-frode-iva-per-oltre-2-6-mln.html.
16 www.pupia.tv/2017/07/canali/cronaca/merce-acquistata-italia-passaporti-stranieri-scoperta-frode-iva-denunciati-146-cinesi/391189.

VAT on traditional markets like precious metals, electronic products or clothes became a more complicated and less profitable crime. Moreover, these products need at the end of the trading chain a real demand from customers. The amount of the VAT fraud on low-volume/high-value products is capped by the capacity of the demand to absorb the merchandise.

Tax perpetrators who had gained experience with electronic products explored new fields where they could leverage their expertise with the VAT scam. The perfect scam would require a fast-circulating underlying, with low entry cost, and be sophisticated enough to make it hard to detect. Moreover, if the demand on the underlying could be artificially inflated, the pocketed VAT could reach, in theory, astronomic numbers. Three avenues seemed to be promising prospects for fraudsters: telecom services, CO_2 emissions allowances and energy markets.

Telecom services

With the liberalization of the telecom sector across the EU in the early 2000s a number of telecom retailers started the trading of broadband capacities. The supply of phone call cards was mainly for foreign workers, customers who were making calls to their home countries and were looking for a cheap price per minute. The companies dealing with this market were buying and selling broadband capacity across the continent. In a similar way to the physical items, broadband capacity was bought without VAT and sold with VAT, the tax never being reimbursed to the national treasuries. Detecting this scam is far more complicated as the broadband is not a physical item, and the demand can be artificially manipulated with premium tariff numbers or servers that automatically make calls. The contracts relative to broadband capacity are also complex as they imply various options and kickback fees. A broadband trader could buy, for instance, from a big national telecom company a massive amount of broadband capacity for a specific geographical area at a discount price. The contractual agreement could also include take-or-pay options similar to those in the energy markets (Frunza, 2015).

The complexity of telecom markets was the perfect financial shenanigan for covering potential fraud. Therefore, the number of cases investigated related to VAT fraud on telecom services was limited, the most prominent being the *Phuncards-Broker* operation in Italy.

In 2017, the French government became aware of the issues in the telecom service and decided to inflict a penalty on two main French telecom providers: SFR and Bouygues Telecom.

The practice pointed out by the French government is the misrepresentation of products linked to services such as SFR Presse or LeKiosk (Bouygues), integrated into the telecom subscriptions of SFR[17] or Bouygues Telecom. These services allow customers to read many newspapers in an unlimited way. However,

---

17 www.lemonde.fr/actualite-medias/article/2017/07/27/tva-le-gouvernement-cible-les-pratiques-de-sfr-et-bouygues-telecom_5165487_3236.html.

the press is subject to a 2.1% VAT rate, while telephony is subject to a 20% rate. Thus, the concerned operators apply a VAT rate of 2.1% on a part of the package, not 20% as they were doing previously. That allowed SFR to save 400 million euros per year, while Bouygues saved several hundred million euros.

Technology went a step further in the evolution process of telecommunication with the development of VoIP. VoIP designates a range of communication technologies that allow the transfer of voice and media data over the Internet.

In simple terms, VoIP describes a call that was initiated on Skype, Facebook, Slack or Google Voice. The calling party can start the call on the Internet, while the called party can be on Skype, on a mobile phone or on a landline. Thus, the call begins on the Internet but is rerouted on the public switched telephone network (PSTN). Technically, this is called VoIP call termination or VoIP termination. Telecom companies buying and selling VoIP termination are referred to as carriers. The demand for VoIP termination can be created artificially through buffer companies or through fake premium numbers. VAT fraud with VoIP services can be very disruptive, and its detection can be complex due to the technical aspects.

The massive case of VAT fraud with VoIP service was prosecuted in Italy in 2007 in Operation *Traffico Telefonico*. The fraud seems to have been revived in recent years, and few Member States introduced the Reverse Charge on telecommunication service, including the VoIP.

In February 2016, HMRC introduced a domestic VAT Reverse Charge in Great Britain to combat VAT fraud in the wholesale telecoms markets. The measure impacted business-to-business transactions between the telecommunications services wholesalers, including airtime carriers, network operators, message hubbing providers and short messaging service (SMS) and voice aggregators.[18, 19] The services encompassed by the measure are VoIP call termination, SMS and multimedia messaging service (MMS) services, value added services and SMS/voice aggregator services.

The measure did not concern all wholesale services, nor did it concern all companies. Companies buying VoIP for internal use are VAT liable. Carrier to carrier transactions of transport/capacity, access services, broadband and data transmission services continue to carry the VAT levy. These services have a physical proof of delivery (i.e., landline, cables, etc.), thereby making the MTIC scam more difficult to develop.

From June 2017, the Netherlands applied the same Reverse Charge as its British peers on certain telecommunication services,[20] following fears of an increase of carousel fraud. The Dutch Reverse Charge did not apply to sales to end consumers.

---

18 www.moorestephens.co.uk/news-views/january-2016/vat-anti-evasion-rules-wholesaling-telecom-service.

19 www.irglobal.com/article/vat-rule-changes-for-uk-wholesale-telecommunications-supplies-422d.

20 https://marosavat.com/en/dutch-reverse-charge-on-telecommunication-services/.

CO₂ emissions

The EU agreed under the Kyoto Protocol to reduce its greenhouse gas emissions for the period 2008–2012 by 8% with respect to the 1990 year levels. The adopted strategy was based on an environmental instrument called CO_2 emissions allowances. One CO_2 emissions allowance (European Union Allowance – EUA) confers the right to its owner to emit 1 tonne of CO_2.

The core members of the EU Emissions Trading System (EU ETS) were companies and installations emitting CO_2, resulting from industrial process or energy production. At its peak, the EU ETS included 11,000 installations, which submitted on a yearly basis at the end of April a compliance statement relative to the emissions balance.

The emissions of CO_2 and equivalent gases of each installation are measured and then reported to the national authority. At the end of the conformity period, each installation submitted a number of permits equivalent to the measured quantity of emitted greenhouse gases. A practical example would be a chemical refinery company's having a free allocation of 1,000,000 EUAs per year over a three-year period. If during the first year the installation emits 1,100,000 tonnes of CO_2, the company will need to buy 100,000 EUAs. If during the second year the refinery emits 900,000 tonnes of CO_2, it will use only a part of its free allocation in order to comply. Thus, in the third year the company will have a surplus of 100,000 EUAs. The company has the choice to sell the surplus on the market or to keep it in the books for the next year.

Under Directive 2003/87/EC, EU Member States were required to put in place a standardized, electronic national registry beginning in 2005, whilst parties to the Kyoto Protocol were required to put in place a national registry to allow international emissions trading beginning in 2008.

The national registries were in fact web-based interfaces, interconnected and acting as depositaries for the EUAs, each actor of the EU ETS having an account in one or a few registries. The traders of CO_2 emissions allowances could make transfers between registry accounts in a few minutes.

In the early 2000s an amalgam of new entrepreneurs seized the opportunities of the new markets via various enterprises, such as brokers, consulting, regulatory advisory, etc. The new rising 'green' tycoons were generally non-regulated companies, and their activities did not enter under any jurisdiction and did not bear any legal liability. Few national authorities were overseeing the sector; at the European level the European Commission was the only authority that had ruling ability over the EU ETS, but it did not have any means of imposing or controlling the application of its directive. It was supposed that the collaboration between the local authorities and the European Commission was to provide an adequate framework for overseeing the scheme.

These special circumstances allowed the development of the biggest VAT fraud in history between 2008 and 2010. The lack of regulation and control at all levels of the EU ETS was fertile ground for many criminals looking for quick profits. Indeed the CO_2 emissions market attracted criminals and adventurers

from all walks of life, some with experience in VAT evasion and others that de
buted in financial crime. The market allowed non-regulated brokers to registe
with exchanges and to trade EUAs. Moreover, the big market makers (i.e., bi
banks) and the exchanges were paying the VAT levy while trading domestically
the allowances. This fact amplified the size of the fraud because missing trader
did not need to require VAT refunds from the national treasuries.

The volumes traded in the market were much higher than the actual need to
hedge the environmental risk. In fact, there was no real demand from investors fo
EUAs. Fraudsters created an artificial demand which inflated in the short term the
volumes of allowances exchanged on the market without any fundamental value.

Gas and electricity

After the fraud on CO_2 emissions, the gas and power markets were suspected o
being corrupted by MTIC fraudsters.

The gas market has two types of contracts with physical delivery, thereby being potentially concerned by VAT levy:

- Short-term contracts, referring mainly to within-day and day-ahead contracts. Day-ahead contracts are made between seller and buyer for the delivery of gas the following day.
- Long-term contracts, referring mainly to 'swing' or 'take-or-pay' contracts.
  A swing contracts gives its holder the option to buy a predetermined quantity of gas at a predetermined price while offering some flexibility in the
  amount purchased and the price paid. A typical swing contract indicates:
  - the floor and the cap of gas volumes that can be bought in a given period
    (day, month, quarter, year),
  - time horizon of the contract,
  - the range of prices at which gas can be bought and
  - the frequency at which the buyer can change the gas quality he wants to buy.

If a decade ago long-term contracts were at the core of the gas market, in recent years, with the development of pipeline infrastructures and of the liquefied
natural gas (LNG) market, short-term contracts have become more popular. In
order to be able to trade on the gas markets a broker needs to be registered with
a natural gas hub terminal. The most popular hubs in Europe are based in Great
Britain, the Netherlands, France and Germany.

Electricity differs from other products in that it cannot be stored. Thus, electricity supply is either consumed or lost. Most electricity trades involve the 'physical' delivery of electricity at a given time.

Four type of contrast are:

- Futures and forwards are long-term contracts, with deliveries up to 20 years.
- Day-ahead contracts are short-term contracts, with deliveries in the following day.

- Intra-day contracts are spot contracts, with deliveries a given hour during the day.
- Balancing markets are the institutional arrangement that establishes market-based balance management in an unbundled electricity market. The sum of buys and sells on the contracts mentioned earlier should always be null. This is achieved through balance management. Balance management is a power system operation service vital for ensuring the security of supply through the continuous, real-time balancing of power demand and supply (van der Veen, 2016).

The parties involved in the electricity market, including producers, transmission system operators, retailers, providers of balancing and brokers, need to be connected to the power grid, which, in the EU, is in a strong process of transnational integration. Thus, a broker based in Poland could in theory buy electricity from Hungary and resell it to Germany.

Gas and electricity markets are vulnerable to VAT fraud. Some allegations were made in various media reports, but no case was prosecuted with regards to tax evasion on gas and electricity. European utilities have been involved and investigated in the VAT fraud in CO_2 emissions market, but the contagion in gas and power market is still weak. The main reason these markets are vulnerable is the structure of the optional contracts, which confer to the holder the right to dispose of a capacity. In the case of the swing contracts both price and volume are not exactly specified. The complexity of these contracts hampers the detection of a potential fraud. Moreover, the physical deliveries are difficult to 'track' as most settlements are done through the grid (power) or hubs (gas). Therefore, the delivery of a given quantity supplied as part of a contract cannot really be audited as it can in the case of other physical goods. The fraudsters can potentially use these 'flaws' in order to create fake deliveries, especially for the over-the-counter contracts. Therefore, the energy market, despite being regulated, can entail the creation of artificial demand, a fertile ground for MTIC fraud.

Services

The liberalization of the labour market in the EU as well as the mass migration of the workforce inside the EU, from the eastern and southern countries to the Nordic and western regions of the EU, changed the dynamic of services supply. A decade ago, services like freight and transport were mainly supplied by regional providers. In the current state of economy, a supplier based in a country of the EU can bid for a contract in other country and supply workforce from a third country of the EU. This structural change contributes to stronger European integration, but makes the services market more exposed to the risk of VAT evasion.

VAT fraud with a temporary workforce and construction labour was reported in a few member countries. Great Britain is particularly exposed, mainly in the construction sector, supplied massively by a non-domestic workforce, contracted through temporary staff agencies.

Freight and shipping also bear the risk of MTIC fraud. Shipping capacity is traded in the main European harbours through a close network of shipowners, charterers and brokers that sell the marginal transportation capacities on dry bulk carriers, tankers and containerships. The brokers are selling the freight capacity in many cases through over-the-counter trades. The service is liable for VAT, and therefore like other services, the market can be defrauded. Moreover, brokers can exchange contracts through online platforms, as in the case of CO_2 emissions permits.

Road freight transport is another sector which became liberalized within the EU. The trucking suppliers are mainly from Eastern Europe, due to lower costs of labour and social security. Therefore the geometry of contracts can be very complex, with a company based in Germany, for example, hiring a freight company from Poland, which will have Lithuanian-registered trucks and Romanian drivers. This market is concerned by not only VAT fraud but also the national insurance contribution and benefit frauds.

The main types of services susceptible to VAT fraud and the potential frequency and severity of the fraud are:

- temporary workforce (high frequency and low severity),
- constructions labour (high frequency and low severity),
- freight and shipping capacity (high frequency and medium severity),
- logistic and transport service (high frequency and medium severity),
- care services (high frequency and low severity),
- intermediation services in football transfers (low frequency and high severity) and
- TV rights of football games (medium frequency and high severity).

More sophisticated services like TV rights for football games or intermediation of footballers' transfers are exposed to VAT fraud. Given the huge size of these contracts the tax evaded can be significant.

Digital products

Online marketplaces accelerated the development and increased the turnover of digital products. Digital products are a multibillion-euro market, encompassing both web and mobile content. The sector boomed over the last decade, supported by the steady growth of the numeric economy. The Internet made the marketing of digital products much easier than that of physical products. Therefore, a supplier of digital products can potentially conclude a trade from anywhere either directly or through dedicated marketplaces.

When dealing with digitally monetized content the Missing Trader Extra-Community (MTEC) is as easy to implement as the MTIC. Some online platforms are required to check the tax liabilities of their register traders. But they represent only a small percentage of the total online marketplaces. The fact that digital products can be easily exchanged with less control from tax offices is a serious enabler for evasion.

A short list of digital products susceptible to VAT fraud and their associated risk includes:

- movies (high risk),
- music (medium risk),
- e-books (low risk),
- cloud/server memory (high risk),
- software licence (low risk),
- online advertising (high risk),
- photography (low risk),
- digital art (low risk),
- documents (medium risk),
- games (medium risk) and
- e-learning/coaching (low risk).

The strong expansion of online media platforms like YouTube and Instagram has incited content creators to sell ad space to various firms. Content providers with millions of followers charge very high prices for advertising space on their respective channels. Thus, a secondary market of online ads was born, where marketers, brokers and influencers trade huge volumes of advertising capacity. This deregulated market already reaches a few hundred million euros per year and exhibits strong growth. VAT evasion would not require much effort on these markets. A company could buy ads from overseas and sell them to a domestic company with VAT, a tax which would never be paid back. The control on such schemes would be in reality complex, and proving the fraud would necessitate facing many technical challenges. A company based in a European country can resell domestically advertising space from an Asian provider on an American platform. The question of whether VAT should be charged in the country of the company or in the country of the destination of the product would naturally bring a lot of debate, as in the case of VoIP and CO_2 emissions permits.

High-value products

The category of high-value products encompasses all types of goods carrying a high nominal value, regardless of their volume. Carousel fraud is less likely to occur on these items. Nevertheless, fraudsters often use fake invoices to build the carousel. The recurrent items are luxury cars, a few fraud circuits being already well documented within the EU. The demand for luxury cars is elastic, a price reduction entailing an increase in the number of cars sold. Southern European countries are popular marketplaces for luxury cars, and they obviously attract the tax fraudsters. Two representative cases are described in the following.

Italian economic police (Guardia di Finanza) dismantled in 2018 with the Operation *Car Jumping*[21] a group of 16 people and five companies specializing

---

21 http://roma.corriere.it/notizie/cronaca/18_febbraio_05/frosinone-vendevano-auto-lusso-frode-fisco-16-denunciati-704f0a7e-0a69-11e8-aeb9-f008c9e7034a.shtml?refresh_ce-cp.

in trading luxury cars. The group was buying luxury cars, such as Porsches and Ferraris, from Germany and registering them in Italy in the names of Bulgarian citizens, where they were also sold with VAT. The fraud generated a loss of 10 million euros to the Italian treasury.

The Spanish investigators dismantled in 2015 after the Operation *Wheels III*, a group that defrauded 15 million euros in VAT. The group had a network of 30 companies that imported luxury vehicles from Germany, Holland and Belgium.[22] The cars were registered in Spain in the names of Eastern European citizens and sold with VAT, which was never reimbursed.

But VAT fraud was also reported on Airbus engines, combine harvesters, mining equipment, steel products or concrete crushing machines. A 17-strong gang headed by Paul Hackney[23] from Stoke-on-Trent was dismantled by the HMRC in 2013. Hackney set up a chain of companies through which he defrauded 2.3 million pounds of VAT through the sale of fictitious concrete-crushing machines and construction equipment. Hackney's companies produced fake invoices in order to reclaim VAT on sales and exports.

The construction sector was also touched by VAT fraud in Poland in 2012. The Polish government was forced to introduce reverse-charge VAT for the steel sector to hamper the growing VAT evasion phenomena that touch that sector.[24] VAT for steel rebar in Poland was 23%, one of the highest in the EU, thereby being an incentive for tax evaders. In other European countries the demand for steel decreased, while in Poland it had a double digit increase. Poland organized with Ukraine the European Football Championship (Euro 2012), and many construction projects kicked off, thereby increasing the demand for steel rebar. Fraudsters used this opportunity to defraud VAT and to sell steel products at a lower price, thereby harming the honest producers. These VAT scams were so frequent in Poland prior to the Euro 2012 that more than half of 1.3 million tonnes of rebar used each year was linked to VAT fraud. The Polish case seemed to be related to another organized group of VAT scammers from the neighbouring country of Lithuania. The Lithuanian prosecutors stopped in 2017 a group of VAT scammers which was trading metals and precious stones with seven Polish companies. The group managed to steal 1.2 million euros in VAT.[25]

Inelastic demand

Goods and services with an inelastic demand like food and fuel do not abide by the low-volume/high-price rule. This does not make them safe from the VAT fraudsters. Goods of consumption with a structural demand can also be

---

22 www.rtve.es/noticias/20150826/diez-detenidos-red-importadores-vehiculos-lujo-fraude-iva/1206320.shtml.

23 www.accountancydaily.co/vat-fraud-gang-crushed-cement-scam.

24 www.metalbulletin.com/Article/3246173/Poland-cracks-down-on-steel-VAT-fraud.html.

25 www.vz.lt/verslo-aplinka/2017/10/24/prekybininkai-metalu-is-kaunosukosi-tarptautineje-pvm-sukciavimo-schemoje.

cargeted by VAT evaders. The main advantage of these markets is that there is always a sustainable demand, regardless of the price of the product. Therefore, the products will be consumed faster than high-value products, for instance. Cases reported in Spain and Italy showed that VAT fraud rings were linked with big retail chains, which were used by criminals as end points of distribution for the products, once the VAT was pocketed. For high-value goods with a more elastic demand, like luxury cars, the end customs would be more sensitive to price, thereby reducing the speed and the turnover of the VAT fraud chains.

VAT frauds using goods with inelastic demand span longer periods of time than the classic MTIC on low volume and high demand. In these cases, fraudsters cannot leverage the speed of a carousel and therefore choose to evade tax over a longer horizon. Investigation showed that VAT fraud on food or fuel often involved corrupting governmental or tax office representatives. Indeed, involving a governmental body in a fraud would guarantee the continuity of the criminal activity over a long period of time.

Food and beverages

Fraud on food and agricultural products has been reported since the early 2000s. These products are generally perishable and therefore need to be sold in a given time window. This, along with the storage costs, are the main limitations when defrauding VAT.

Such a case occurred in 2012, when Kaiser Matlub,[26] with nine other men, organized in the United Kingdom a fraudulent VAT refund of over 1.2 million euros. Matlub and his associates claimed that they were buying sheep carcasses and selling lamb chops. The enterprise was fictitious, and the scam was based in fact on fake invoices. Matlub helped the other gang members to get butcher licences in order to be able to trade meat with abattoirs and clients.

Tobacco and alcoholic beverages are another class of goods with inelastic demand which are of concern in regards to tax fraud. Both excise tax and VAT fraud were reported on these products. Tax fraud is often a byproduct of two other frauds relative to tobacco and alcohol: smuggling and counterfeiting. Organized crime groups control the traffic of these products in each country. The traffic of alcohol and tobacco is caused also by the aggressive policy of taxation in most Western countries, resulting in a higher price for consumers. This works in favour of VAT evaders who proposed products with lower prices, thereby managing to sell high qualities of alcoholic beverages in the retails market. For example, in early 2018 Spanish prosecutors[27] busted four networks of VAT fraud with alcoholic beverages. The groups (Table 2.2) sold more than 20 million litres of beverages, cumulating in a total of 150 million euros in stolen taxes.

26 www.mynewsdesk.com/uk/hm-revenue-customs-hmrc/pressreleases/fake-butchers-get-the-chop-in-ps1m-vat-fraud-919486.
27 www.20minutos.es/noticia/3328553/0/fraude-bebidas-alcoholicas-sofistica-eluden-pago-iva-cobran-cliente/.

Table 2.2 Summary of Spanish operation against VAT evaders specializing in alcoholic beverages

Operation	VAT defrauded/sold quantity	Observation
Bacia	20 million euros/3 million litres	20 arrested in Madrid, Ciudad Real, Badajoz Barcelona, Tarragona and Córdoba
Noticia	29 million euros/5 million litres	15 arrested in Madrid, Ciudad Real, Córdoba and Burgos
Spirit/Path	70 million euros	43 arrested, Castilla-La Mancha, La Rioja, Basque Country and Navarre
Spirit	25 million euros	43 detainees

Alcoholic products are the market where VAT fraud meets counterfeiting, as was shown by a recent operation called *Meeting*, which took place in 2017 in Italy.[28] Individuals from Rome, Romania and England were arrested and charged with VAT evasion accounting for 4 million euros. The fraud was financed by British Asians from London and intermediated by Romanian and Italian citizens. The alcoholic beverages sold in Italy were bootlegged abroad and smuggled.

Agricultural commodities are a preferred target for transnational MTIC fraudsters. Grains, sugar and rice are generally traded in high quantities, thereby enhancing the potential gain from tax evasion.

In 2013, the Bulgarian prosecutors dismantled a network of VAT fraud companies specializing in trading sugar and vegetable oil. The operation, called *Sweets*[29] targeted a group of four Bulgarian individuals, who managed to defraud taxpayers of over 1 million euro. The companies reported intra-Community acquisitions of sugar from companies based in Poland and the Czech Republic as well as intra-Community acquisitions of vegetable oil from Romanian companies and supplies of sugar and vegetable oil sold to Romanian companies. The reported intra-Community supplies to Romania were fictitious, and the sugar and vegetable oil had been sold in different places in Bulgaria.

Suspicions of massive VAT evasion in the EU using trades with soft commodities were raised beginning in the early 2000s. In 2003 the European Commission launched an investigation concerning a sharp increase in imports of sugar from Croatia, Serbia and Montenegro in the EU's member states.[30] The European authorities feared that the increase was fuelling a huge carousel fraud with soft commodities. Serbian media pointed out that the sugar supply to Europe was controlled by one of the richest Serbs, Miodrag Kostic, who had political connections. He owned three large sugar factories in the northern provinces of Serbia.

28 https://tuttoggi.info/frode-fiscale-internazionale-8-arresti-a-capo-uno-spoletino/416714/.
29 www.novinite.com/articles/147674/Bulgaria+Police+Bust+Crime+Ring+Involved+in+Massive+VAT+Fraud.
30 https://derstandard.at/1288603/Belgrad-dementiert-Karussellbetrug-mit-Zucker.

Fuel

Fuel is a crucial commodity for both consumers and industries, thereby having an inelastic demand. The fluctuations of the oil prices on the financial markets as well as the environmental taxes added by the EU on carburant increased prices for end-consumers. Moreover, the geographical heterogeneity level of fuel prices increased over the past years. These facts corroborated with the decreasing purchasing power in Southern and Eastern Europe, making fuel easy prey for professional MTIC scammers.

Thus, VAT fraud groups can sell cheaper fuel to gas stations, monopolizing the market and therefore putting the honest wholesalers out of business. Once the distribution business to retailers reaches a critical size, MTIC scammers attempt to monopolize direct sales to consumers by controlling or opening their own gas station networks.

Tax evasion on fuel is not a new scam and moreover is not only European. In the 1980s, the American-Italian crime syndicate operated a large-scale scam, defrauding the federal tax on fuel. The scam consisted in selling gas wholesale without paying tax on sales. Michael Franzese,[31] iconic figure and one-time rising star of the reputed New York-based Colombo mob family, was the architect and mastermind of the fraud (Franzese, 2009). Franzese's rise came in the early 1980s from infamous gasoline rackets, in which he was collecting the state and federal gas taxes but never paid them back. He started his operation in Florida with another mob member, Larry Iorizzo,[32] head of Vantage Petroleum, a large chain of unbranded gas stations on Long Island and in New Jersey. Iorizzo was shaken down by a rival crime syndicate who wanted to seize control of his business, and he called Franzese for help. The two went into business together in 1981, when Franzese became a silent partner in Vantage, a wholesale gasoline distribution company. The company entered into bankruptcy, and the two incorporated a new firm, Galleon Holdings, which within a few years comprised hundreds of stations, storage terminals and fleets of tankers in New York, Florida and New Jersey.

Gasoline wholesalers were supposed to pay state and federal excise taxes. In order to avoid the tax payments Iorizzo created a chain of shell companies, the last company in the chain being a 'missing trader'. By the time the Internal Revenue Service (IRS) started investigating the missing trader, the company was already bankrupt, and a new fraudulent chain was formed. Some of the buffer companies were incorporated in Panama, where Iorizzo had a residence and a fake passport; he even claimed a close friendship with Manuel Noriega, Panama's president at that time. Because Galleon paid no taxes, it was able to have very aggressive prices, thereby putting the competition out of business. In a short time, gas stations like Texaco, Chevron and Shell were dealing with Galleon tankers.

---

31 Member of Italian-American organized crime immortalized in Martin Scorsese's 1990 film *Goodfellas*.

32 www.vanityfair.com/news/1991/02/john-gotti-joe-columbo-fbi-investigation-witness.

By 1983, Franzese's operation collided with Russian organized crime, and he cut a deal and split profits with Michael Markowitz, a high-profile member of the Brighton Beach crime syndicate. The tax evasion scam generated around 6 million dollars per month, accounting for almost 100 million dollars over the entire period of the fraud. To launder the funds of the crime Franzese founded in Florida Miami Gold, a movie-production company.

Franzese's tax evasion by selling fuel occurred in many forms and in different countries. Recently, in 2016, a major case was reported by the Spanish prosecutors who dismantled through Operation *Burlao* a group led by an Italian fraudster, Estefano Cherici.[33] He led a 21-strong group that defrauded 25 million euros in VAT on carburant. The group had connections in Italy and Portugal. Cherici reinvested the proceeds of the crime in gold and was involved in two major operations related to precious metals. In one operation, Cherici's gang moved 34 tonnes of gold to Switzerland.

Another relevant case was reported in Spain in 2017, when the Spanish court prosecuted the owners of the Petromiralles group, José María and Pedro Torrens,[34] for alleged VAT fraud in gas stations in Catalonia, valued at 147 million euros, between 2011 and 2013. The funds were diverted to accounts in Hong Kong and Andorra through a network of companies, including Petromiralles SL, Petromiralles 3 SL, Bufete Orfisa, Fast Petrol Company, Advanced Petroleum Services, Giralda Oil Services, Scout Energy Petrol, Cian Plus and the Swiss company Willoil. José María Torrens, former mayor of Santa María de Miralles (Barcelona), was charged with money laundering, belonging to a criminal group, falsification of commercial documents and illegal possession of weapons. Petromiralles group had very low prices compared to the competition and managed in a few years to impose their trademark in Catalonia.

Italy was not spared by VAT fraud on carburant, as was revealed in 2018 by the Operation *Good Platts* in Northern Italy.[35] Fuel was imported from Croatia and Slovenia without VAT and sold in Italy in the province of Umbria with VAT without repaying tax to the Italian treasury. The scam was built around a company incorporated in Switzerland that managed to defraud 25 million euros in tax.

33 www.telemadrid.es/noticias/nacional/noticia/desmantelan-una-organizacion-criminal-dedicada-al-fraude-masivo-de-iva.

34 www.lavanguardia.com/vida/20170207/414100498874/el-juez-procesa-a-los-duenos-de-petromiralles-por-presunto-fraude-del-iva.html.

35 www.trasportoeuropa.it/index.php/home/archvio/9-autotrasporto/17955-frode-fiscale-sui-carburanti-in-umbria.

3   Impact of the VAT fraud on the EU's economy

Role of the collected VAT in the national budgets

> Always overpay your taxes. That way you'll get a refund.
>
> Meyer Lansky, American crime figure

The European Union (EU) finances itself from each of its members. The main source of revenue for each country is, without exception, the proceeds of taxation. The taxation structure exhibits a significant heterogeneity across the EU countries. Following the taxonomy of the European Commission,[1] tax revenues collected by the governments of European countries can be categorized as:

1   Taxes on income and capital, including corporate and personal income taxes; taxes on holding gains; payments by households for licences to own or use cars, hunt or fish; current taxes on capital that are paid periodically; etc.
2   Net social contribution, representing taxes paid on a compulsory or voluntary basis by employers, employees and self- and non-employed persons.
3   Taxes on production and imports, including mainly Value Added Tax (VAT), import duties, excise duties and consumption taxes, stamp taxes, payroll taxes, taxes on pollution, etc.

Taxes on income and capital are direct taxes, while taxes on production and imports are indirect taxes. The evolution since 1999 of the total tax receipts for the EU countries is depicted in Figure 3.1. The taxes collected by European governments represent almost 40% of the EU's gross domestic product (GDP). In nominal terms, the tax receipts increased from 35,000 billion euros in 2009 to almost 60,000 billion euros in 2016. This increase was marked by a significant contraction in 2009 during the economic crisis.

---

1   http://ec.europa.eu/eurostat/statistics-explained/index.php/Tax_revenue_statistics.

DOI: 10.4324/9781315098722-3

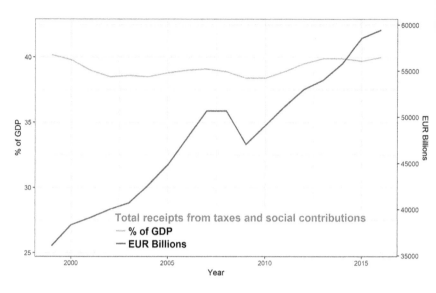

Figure 3.1 Evolution of the total tax receipts for the EU countries. The figures are presented in percentage points of GDP and in billion euros.
Source: Eurostat.

The total level of taxation and the breakdown of the tax revenue for each country are presented in Figure 3.2, the numbers corresponding to 2016. France, Denmark, Belgium and Sweden have the highest level of taxation, the total receipts representing around 45% of their national GDP. Ireland, Romania and Bulgaria have the lowest level of taxation. The shares of direct taxes, indirect taxes and social contributions vary significantly from one country to another. Sweden, for instance, has the highest level of indirect taxes, while Ireland has the lowest level.

The distribution of the share of the VAT in the total tax revenue for each member country depends on the total level of taxation and on the national tax structure. The VAT share of the total tax receipts, depicted in Figure 3.3, is stable over time, representing around 17%. The total VAT amount increased from 6,000 billion euros in 1999 to over 10,000 billion euros in 2016. Figure 3.4 shows a snapshot of the geographical distribution of the VAT share of the total tax receipts in 2016. Tax revenues of Bulgaria and Croatia relied heavily on VAT, which represented in 2016 around 30% of the total tax receipts. For Romania, Hungary and the Baltic countries the VAT was steadily above 20% of the tax receipts. The less VAT-dependent treasuries were those of France, Italy and Belgium.

The budgets of emerging economies in Central and Eastern Europe rely more on the VAT proceeds compared to their Western peers. Both the 2009 economic crisis and the 2011 Eurozone crisis impacted differently the developed and the emerging economies in the EU. The governmental measures to counter crisis's

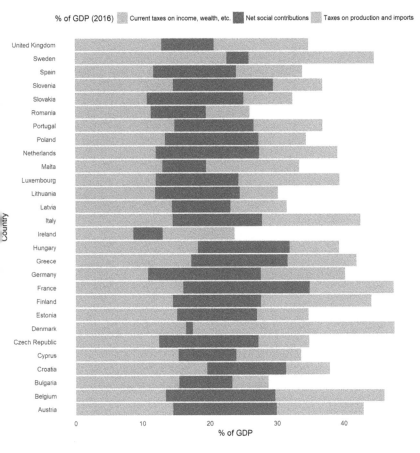

Figure 3.2 Total level of taxation and the breakdown of the tax revenue for each country of the EU expressed in percentage of the national GDP.

Source: Eurostat.

effects in terms of fiscal policies were different from one country to another. Thus, the figures presented earlier should be prudently interpreted. The historical evolution of the VAT share in the national tax receipts for each country of the EU brings additional evidence to this matter (Figure 3.4).

Figure 3.4 shows that the ratio between the collected VAT and the total tax revenue was stable over the past decade in Bulgaria, Croatia and the Baltic countries. The ratio had big swings in the case of Romania. The two core countries of the EU, Germany and France, observed different effects on the VAT share in the total tax bills. While Germany had an increase of the ratio with a big jump in 2006, in France the ratio followed a negative drift. Both Nordic countries, Sweden and Finland, had an increase in the VAT share over the past decade. Amongst the countries with status similar to a tax-haven, Ireland observed a

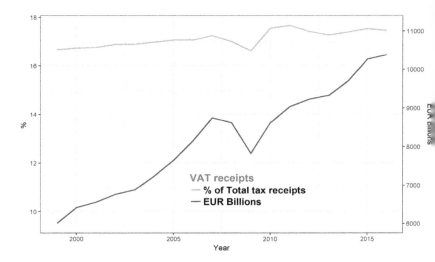

Figure 3.3 Evolution of total VAT receipts in European Union since 1999. The total VAT
amount is expressed as a percentage of the total tax receipts and in billion
euros.

Source: Eurostat.

steady decrease in the ratio between the collected VAT and the total tax receipts
while in Luxemburg the ratio increased, with a big jump in 2010.

These dynamics are consequences of many factors, including the changes in
the VAT rate and the changes in policy for direct taxes and social contribution.
The evolution of standard VAT rates for all members of the EU between 1999
and 2016 is presented in Table 3.1.

Additionally, countries have a reduced rate and a super-reduced VAT rate for
various types of goods and services. The level and the scope of this reduced rate
differ from one country to another.

As of 2016, Hungary has the highest standard VAT rate in the EU (27%), while
Luxemburg has the lowest (17%). Because of the 2009 crisis, few countries, including Hungary, Latvia and Lithuania, Romania and the Czech Republic, opted
to increase the standard level rate in order to increase the tax receipts (Figure 3.5).

Indirect taxes are one of the main sources of receipts for the national budgets
of the EU. On the one hand in the EU's developed economies, governments
have limited leverage in tuning the potential contribution of the VAT. On the
other hand, in the emerging economies of the EU, the VAT receipts represent
a bigger share in the tax bills. In addition, in these economies governments
may adjust the VAT rate in order to fill the gap in the national budgets. In
this picture, the case of Southern European countries is particular. While having increasing VAT rates since the crisis, the VAT receipts in these countries
influence the total tax bills to a lesser extent than in the case of their Eastern
European peers.

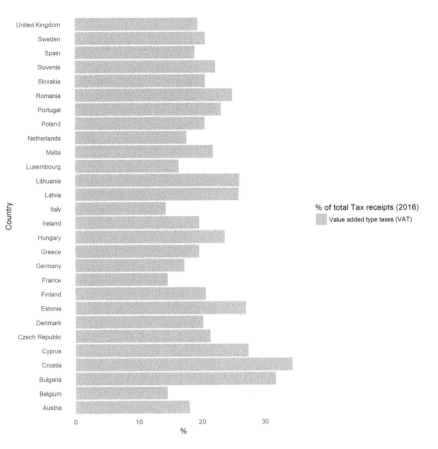

Figure 3.4 Geographical distribution of the VAT share in the total tax receipts in 2016.
Source: Eurostat.

VAT fraud as a drawback to the fully fledged EU integration

The crisis started in 2008 with financial problems on the American credit market and propagated rapidly to the European and Asian markets, and their respective economies. Within the EU, the impact of the crisis reflected the strong heterogeneity of the various economies and financial systems. The big differences between the tax and budgetary policies were emphasized by this crisis and played a major role in amplifying its consequences (Frunza, 2014).

The amplifications of disparities related to the economic and political integration followed the 1995, 2004 and 2007 enlargements of the EU. As shown by Campos (2014) there is strong evidence of positive pay-offs from EU membership, but there is also considerable heterogeneity across countries. Those heterogeneities became more pronounced during the crisis period and left the EU in

Table 3.1 Evolution of the VAT rates (%) across the EU members since 1999

Country/Year	1999	2000	2001	2002	2003	2004	2005	2006	2007	2008	2009	2010	2011	2012	2013	2014	2015	2016
Belgium	21	21	21	21	21	21	21	21	21	21	21	21	21	21	21	21	21	21
Bulgaria	20	20	20	20	20	20	20	20	20	20	20	20	20	20	20	20	20	20
The Czech Republic	22	22	22	22	22	21.5	19	19	19	19	19	20	20	20	21	21	21	21
Denmark	25	25	25	25	25	25	25	25	25	25	25	25	25	25	25	25	25	25
Germany	16	16	16	16	16	16	16	16	19	19	19	19	19	19	19	19	19	19
Estonia	18	18	18	18	18	18	18	18	18	18	18	20	20	20	20	20	20	20
Ireland	21	21	20	21	21	21	21	21	21	21	21.5	21	21	23	23	23	23	23
Greece	18	18	18	18	18	18	19	19	19	19	19	21	23	23	23	23	23	24
Spain	16	16	16	16	16	16	16	16	16	16	16	17	18	20	21	21	21	21
France	20.6	19.6	19.6	19.6	19.6	19.6	19.6	19.6	19.6	19.6	19.6	19.6	19.6	19.6	19.6	20	20	20
Croatia	22	22	22	22	22	22	22	22	22	22	23	23	23	25	25	25	25	25
Italy	20	20	20	20	20	20	20	20	20	20	20	20	21	21	22	22	22	22
Cyprus	8	9	10	11.5	15	15	15	15	15	15	15	15	15	17	18	19	19	19
Latvia	18	18	18	18	18	18	18	18	18	18	21	21	22	21	21	21	21	21
Lithuania	18	18	18	18	18	18	18	18	18	18	19	21	21	21	21	21	21	21
Luxembourg	15	15	15	15	15	15	15	15	15	15	15	15	15	15	15	15	17	17
Hungary	25	25	25	25	25	25	25	20	20	20	22.5	25	25	27	27	27	27	27
Malta	15	15	15	15	18	18	18	18	18	18	18	18	18	18	18	18	18	18
The Netherlands	17.5	17.5	19	19	19	19	19	19	19	19	19	19	19	19	21	21	21	21
Austria	20	20	20	20	20	20	20	20	20	20	20	20	20	20	20	20	20	20
Poland	22	22	22	22	22	22	22	22	22	22	22	22	23	23	23	23	23	23
Portugal	17	17	17	18	19	19	19	21	21	20.5	20	20.5	23	23	23	23	23	23
Romania	22	19	19	19	19	19	19	19	19	19	19	21.5	24	24	24	24	24	20
Slovenia	19	19	19	20	20	20	20	20	20	20	20	20	20	20	22	22	22	22
Slovakia	23	23	23	23	20	19	19	19	19	19	19	19	20	20	20	20	20	20
Finland	22	22	22	22	22	22	22	22	22	22	22	23	23	23	24	24	24	24
Sweden	25	25	25	25	25	25	25	25	25	25	25	25	25	25	25	25	25	25
The United Kingdom	17.5	17.5	17.5	17.5	17.5	17.5	17.5	17.5	17.5	17.5	15	17.5	20	20	20	20	20	20

1 https://ec.europa.eu/taxation_customs/sites/taxation/files/resources/documents/taxation/vat/how_vat_works/rates/vat_rates_en.pdf.

Source: European Commission.

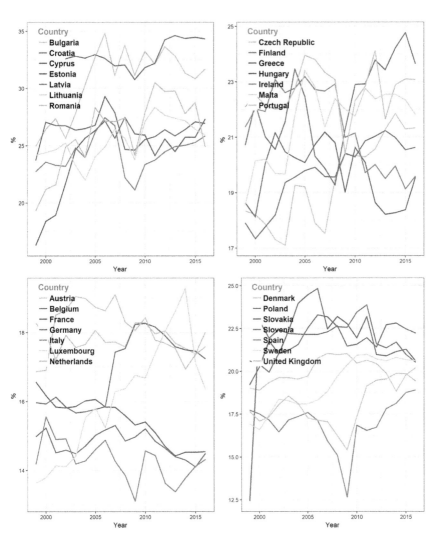

Figure 3.5 Evolution between 1999 and 2019 of the VAT share in the national tax receipts for each member country.

Source: Eurostat Countries listed in order of starting point on graph.

a multi-speed mode. The multi-speed Europe entails different regimes across countries in terms of financial and taxation policy.

In the midst of the crisis, one question became recurrent in Brussel's institutions. Why do certain countries have low credit ratings, and why do they need so much debt? The assessment of the tax structure from the previous section did not underline particular issues about those countries. Thus, it seems that some countries need a high level of debt to finance an economy which does not generate enough tax receipt for serving the debt.

The 2009 economic crisis and the 2011 Eurozone crisis sent out alarm signals that the Southern and Eastern European countries had serious problems with tax collection. As explained in the previous section, most of the distressed countries opted, amongst other measures, for an increase in the VAT rate in order to increase the tax receipts. The desired effect was not reached; *au contraire*, the inverse effect occurred, as will be revealed in the following sections.

Following the Eurozone crisis and historical record levels of sovereign debt, the European institutions launched two key assessments relevant for the VAT-related issues:

1   **The VAT gap:** For the first time, a study measured the effects of the inefficiencies of VAT collection within the EU, underlining a gap estimated to hundreds of billions of euros. The VAT gap is a term introduced by the European Commissions (Reckon, 2009) and defined as the difference between expected VAT revenue and the receipts actually collected by national tax authorities. The VAT gap includes also unpaid VAT resulting from bankruptcies, insolvencies, statistical errors, delayed payments and legal avoidance.

2   **'The cost of non-Europe':** The term was introduced by the European Parliament in the 1980s (Albert, 1983). It quantifies in terms of GDP points the potential efficiency gains in today's European economy by pursuing a series of policy initiatives recently advocated by EU's Parliament. 'The cost of non-Europe' is measured in relation to a large number of policy fields, from a wider and deeper digital Single Market to a more systematic coordination of national and European defence policies or increased cooperation to fight corporate tax avoidance.

In the recent report of the European Parliament (Hiller, 2017), a special section is dedicated to the impact of VAT-related policies on the cost of non-Europe and implicitly upon the European convergence.

The report mentions an extensive shortfall in VAT receipts, which is due in part to fraud. A stronger and better-coordinated EU VAT returns policy could result in additional VAT receipts of between 9 and 20 billion euros a year, depending on the level of harmonization. The harmonization of the VAT policy would include a European 'standard VAT return'. This standard VAT would be mandatory for Member States but optional for businesses registered in multiple member states.

The report mentions also an estimate of the EU's shadow economy at around 20% of official European GDP. A reduction of the informal economy would furthermore increase the efficiency of resource allocation in the European economy as a whole.

It is clear that both European bodies, the European Parliament and the European Commission, understood the critical role of the VAT in the post-crisis economy. Both reports pointed out some critical points, which included the VAT fraud, the heterogeneity of the VAT policies and the issues of uncollected non-fraud-related VAT.

The relationship between the European convergence and the shortfall in the VAT receipt is genuine. Yet the causality between the two phenomena is not clear. One could understand that the decrease of the VAT receipts hampers the road towards a fully fledged integrated EU. By looking at this problem from a different angle, a different scenario arises. What if the 'VAT gap' problem is not the cause but the consequence of the fast-paced European integration?

The first big issue in post-crisis Europe was the lack of banking financing to the real economy. With a more penalizing banking regulation, banks stopped to underwrite credits, especially to small and medium enterprises (SMEs).

Thus, many entrepreneurs resented strong challenges to financing the working capital of their business. Moreover, in order to be able to serve the huge amounts of public debt, many European countries (including the more developed ones, like France and Germany) opted to increase the budgetary burden upon businesses. Industries faced a double-edged effect:

- lack of financing and liquidity, and
- increased tax liabilities, including VAT.

With this scissor effect, SMEs ended up facing dilemmas in:

- ceasing the business by liquidation or bankruptcy, or
- continuing to operate and carrying on their balance sheet, increasing liabilities.

Therefore many small- and medium-size companies opted to continue operation with huge backlogs of unpaid VAT towards the national treasuries for many years. The VAT bill is in theory a short liability. In the post-crisis context, it became a long-term liability. A big part of what the European Commission assessed yearly under the 'VAT gap' corresponds to unpaid VAT due to delay in payments or bankruptcies. In addition to the VAT bill, the other short-term liabilities, especially the social contributions, followed the same pattern.

National authorities in the EU's countries also faced a dilemma with those enterprises that continued to exert their businesses, despite their huge tax liabilities. On the one hand, the taxman has the thorough option to inflict penalties to liable companies and to their directors respectively. If the targeted companies were going to be bankrupt, the due VAT would have been lost forever. On the other hand, the taxman also has the option to close his eyes and tolerate the huge VAT liabilities, hoping that once the economy does improve the collection of his tax arrears will ameliorate.

A study concerning the uncollected VAT in Greece (Tagkalakis, 2014) over a period between 2006 and 2011 showed that an increase in VAT-related tax arrears and uncollected (VAT-related) fines reduce tax compliance and consequently result in lower VAT revenue. The first option shows limited effect, especially in countries that underwent a severe crisis.

Therefore, in most countries, tax authorities opted to tolerate the struggling enterprises to carry over time the VAT backlogs. This was in fact a double-edged sword because, by allowing unpaid VAT liabilities to certain companies, it opened in fact the gate to VAT fraudsters.

The borderlines between the three concepts of VAT avoidance, VAT payment delays and VAT fraud are in some cases very thin and in some cases very thick grey zones. VAT fraudsters used this lax system in order to deploy VAT scam operations. The economic downturn became the perfect shelter for VAT frauds, the scammers being able to use the argument of a tough economy for not paying the VAT on time. This type of behaviour could exist for a long period of time and lead to a huge amount of pocketed funds, even for a small company.

An example[2] is that of a 60 million euro VAT fraud that was busted in 2017 in Forli in Northern Italy. The Italian economic crime police (Guardia di Finanza) and the Italian Customs Office identified a carousel fraud in the sector of the wholesale of electronic products, mobile phones and computers. The investigation originated following the verification of a company which systematically avoided paying VAT to the local tax authorities. In this specific case, 36 different companies were involved in the carousel. The companies were either fictitious or issued invoices for fictitious transactions. A third of the companies involved in this case have also been declared bankrupt or have ceased operations after having accumulated huge backlogs of unpaid VAT. This example of small companies that pocketed tens of millions of euros from the local taxman is not isolated. The fact that many businesses are ceasing operations or declaring bankruptcy is common even in the developed countries of the EU. Having huge liability towards the taxman does not automatically trigger a warning signal. Thus, many VAT scammers, even those with complex carousel schemes, can easily dissimulate their frauds.

The European crisis increased the level of awareness amongst authorities on the disruptive phenomena of the VAT fraud. Nevertheless, the impact of the crisis on the propagation of the fraud is ignored. The current policies are built around the postulate that a more homogenous VAT policy in the EU will increase the European integration and, implicitly, the economical recovery.

In October 2017 the European Commission[3] (European Commision, 2017) proposed a few directions for reforming the EU's VAT system. The final goal of the Commission is to achieve an integrated single EU VAT area. The policy reforms for achieving this goal include:

1   **Tackling fraud with temporary derogation**: The European Commission intends to apply temporarily the generalized Reverse Charge mechanism for trades of goods and services above a threshold of 10,000 euros per invoice. Under such a system, VAT would be 'suspended' along the whole economic chain (between businesses) and charged only to final clients. This measure targets the VAT carousel fraud.
2   **Adapting the VAT system to the digital economy**: This aims to improve the VAT system for e-commerce business.

2 www.ilrestodelcarlino.it/forl%C3%AC/cronaca/frode-fiscale-carosello-1.3283855.
3 https://ec.europa.eu/taxation_customs/sites/taxation/files/communication_-_towards_a_single_vat_area_en.pdf.

3   **Streamlining the VAT rate policy**: The destination principle of charging VAT will gradually replace the current system. The main idea of the destination principle is that the final amount of VAT is always paid to the country of the final consumer. Thus, providers of goods will obtain no VAT-related advantage from incorporating a lower-rate EU member.

4   **Simplifying the VAT system for SMEs**: A more flexible VAT framework for small- and medium-size business would reduce the compliance burden and would stimulate the cross-border trade.

In spite of all these reforms that target mainly the reduction of the VAT gap, the EU faces many structural challenges that will make the implementation of these measures more complicated than in reality.

The multi-speed Europe is an option which is still on Brussel's table. Each time there are serious deviations from the common fiscal policy or a populist party rise in national pools, the multi-speed Europe is cited as a solution by both politicians and bureaucrats. A multi-speed Europe would imply multi-regime taxation policies. Thus, tax arbitrages would be possible in that context. Obviously, the VAT system would be stricter in some parts of the EU and more lax in other parts.

The EU does not have a traditional leadership system or a hierarchical administrative structure. Unions similar to the EU, like the United States or the Russian Federation, have comparable levels of economic and fiscal heterogeneity. But they do have an integrated administrative and legislative system, thereby facilitating the implementation of new policies. The EU will face the challenges of delivering the righteous implementation of its policy, including those related to the VAT reform.

Many European institutions have seen their scope and role expanding over time. Thus, many administrators in these institutions do not have a proven track record for managing a transnational investment agenda. In addition to this, there are limited or no control entities at the European level in charge of overseeing the activities of European institutions. These facts can lead to decisions which are not backed by a genuine governance process. One of those decisions was the birth of the carbon emission markets, which led to one of the most disruptive tax frauds in history. A new market was created without proper governance and without supervision. The European commissioners in charge of the carbon emission markets were skilled neither in financial markets nor in market infrastructures. The outcome of this process was the biggest VAT fraud, which cost the European taxpayers at least 10 billion euros.

The VAT gap in the EU

Following a few major cases of carousel scams, the problem of the VAT fraud started to get proper attention from the EU. Over the past decade there have been few studies published by the various European institutions measuring the size of the missing VAT. In 2006, the European institutions gave a raw estimate of 100 billion euros a year. Previously, in May 2004 the European Federation of

Accountants (FEE) gave a similar figure for taxes missing.[4] Keen (2007) mentioned a few estimates of the missing VAT receipt for the United Kingdom, with a figure around 13.5% or, in a bad year, nearly 17%. Borselli (2011) indicates that within the EU-27, organized VAT fraud is estimated to amount to between 20 billion and 35 billion euros a year.

In 2011, it was estimated that 193[5] billion euros in VAT revenues (1.5% of EU's GDP) were lost due to non-compliance or non-collection, according to a study on the VAT gap in Member States (Barbone, 2013).[6] The study was the first quantitative assessment showing detailed data on the gap between the amount of VAT due and the amount actually collected in 26 Member States between 2000 and 2011. The main factors contributing to the VAT gap were also presented, along with an overview of the effect of the economic crisis on VAT revenues. The study is updated yearly and published by the European Commission as the official figure for the 'lost' VAT.

The figures published by the Commission and discussed in this section do not equate the amount corresponding to the VAT fraud. The 'missing' VAT, named the VAT gap, does not include only lost tax receipts for reasons other than crime.

A straightforward definition of the VAT gap measured by the Commission is simply the difference between the theoretical tax liability according to the tax law and the actual revenue collected. The theoretical tax liability, also known as the VAT Total Tax Liability (VTTL), is the result of an elaborate macroeconomic model built on the basis of national account aggregates and the actual structure of VAT rates and exemptions:

VAT GAP = VTTL – Actual collected VAT

VTTL has the following main components:

- **Household consumption liability:** the amount of VAT that is due on account of household consumption and calculated as the product of the appropriate VAT rates times the amount of consumption of individual products or services.
- **Unrecoverable VAT on intermediate consumption:** the amount of VAT paid on inputs by industries that cannot claim a credit because their sales are exempted from VAT.
- **Unrecoverable VAT on inputs to gross fixed capital formation (GFCF):** the amount of VAT paid on inputs to GFCF activities of industries that cannot claim a credit because their sales are exempted from VAT.
- **Unrecoverable VAT on government consumption:** amount of VAT on inputs on government consumption that cannot be recovered because most government activities are exempted from VAT. The VAT paid on such inputs is generally not recoverable and therefore included into the VTTL.

---

4 A tax net full of holes (www.economist.com/node/6923936).
5 This estimate was amended in the 2013 report, as presented in Table 3.2.
6 Fight against fraud: new study confirms billions lost in VAT gap http://europa.eu/rapid/press-release_IP-13-844_en.htm).

The VAT gap as computed with this framework encompasses four main causes of the 'missing' VAT:

1 VAT revenues 'lost' through legal avoidance,
2 VAT revenues 'lost' due to administrative 'gaps' with respect to registration, filing, under-reporting and payment issues,
3 VAT revenues 'lost' due to payment difficulties arising from bankruptcy and financial insolvency, and
4 VAT revenues 'lost' through tax fraud and evasion.

The Commission's study does not provide the breakdown of the VAT gap in the four mentioned components. Therefore, the share of the VAT fraud in the total gap should be apprehended cautiously. In some countries, like the United Kingdom (HMRC, 2010), the exercise of the VAT gap estimation came with additional bottom-up estimates for each component. The share of the tax avoidance in the United Kingdom was estimated in 2010 to represent 33% of the total VAT gap. The same study attributed 20% of the gap to companies in bankruptcy and financial insolvency.

At the aggregated level it is believed that almost 50% of the gap is non-fraud related. The estimates of the VAT gap breakdown should be cautiously interpreted. As shown in the previous section the borderline between tax avoidance and tax evasion is thin. Also bankruptcies and insolvencies are related in many cases to VAT fraud. Despite the fact that the VAT gap presented hereafter is different from the amount of the tax evasion, the estimate could be used for assessing the trend in VAT fraud. A customized approach aiming to provide an estimate of the fraud-related VAT gap is presented in the following section.

The studies published by the European Commission between 2013 and 2015 (Barbone, 2014, 2015; Poniatowski, 2016, 2017) underlined that the VAT revenue collection has failed to show significant improvement across the EU's countries. A summary of the yearly studies is presented in Table 3.2. The VAT gap expressed as a percentage of the VTTL decreases constantly between 2011 and 2015. The amount of the VAT gap cannot be easily compared, as the scope of the study encompassed gradually Cyprus and Croatia.

Table 3.2 VAT gap estimates in EU member states between 2011 and 2015 (EUR million)

Year/EUR millions	Total collected VAT	Total VTTL	VAT gap	VAT gap (%)
2015[EU-28]	1,035,339	1,186,869	151,530	12.77
2015[EU-27]	1,033,822	1,185,230	151,408	12.77
2014[EU-27]	977,121	1,137,342	160,220	14.09
2014[EU-26]	971,511	1,130,461	158,950	14.06
2013[EU-26]	934,094	1,094,837	161,442	14.75
2012[EU-26]	923,269	1,088,147	164,879	15.20
2011[EU-26]	903,848	1,075,015	171,167	16.00

1 EU-27 does not include Cyprus, and EU-26 does not include Croatia and Cyprus.

Source: European Commission studies.

The 2013 VAT gap was around 161 billion euros and equates to 15.2% of loss in tax receipts. The gap improvement compared to 2012 is for the 26 member states[7] considered in the study. Compared to the 2012 assessment, the 2013 number shows that 15 member states, including Latvia, Malta and Slovakia, saw improvement in their VAT gap figures, while 11 member states, such as Estonia and Poland, saw deterioration.

It should be noted that the amount of the VAT gap measured in 2015 on the full scope of the 28 Members State is 10 billion euros lower than the estimate for 2013 on a scope that excluded Cyprus and Croatia.

Figure 3.6 shows the evolution of the nominal VAT gap estimates (million euros) between 2012 and 2015. Italy, Germany, the United Kingdom and France exhibit consistently the biggest nominal gap over the whole mentioned

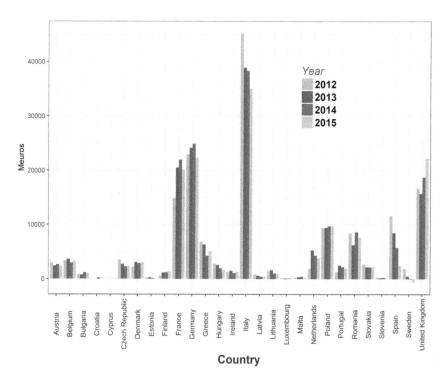

Figure 3.6 Estimates of the VAT gap for 28 EU member states between 2012 and 2015. Italy, Germany, the United Kingdom and France exhibit the biggest nominal gap. A negative gap figure is observed for Sweden in 2015. The United Kingdom's gap shows a positive trend over the studied period. Spain and Italy have a significant contraction in the size of the gap.

Source: European Commission reports.

7 EC, VAT Gap study: the total amount of VAT lost across the EU is estimated at €168 billion (http://codfiscal.net/43772/ec-vat-gap-study-the-total-amount-of-vat-lost-across-the-eu-is-estimated-at-e168-billion).

period. A negative gap figure is observed for Sweden in 2015. The United Kingdom's gap shows a positive trend over the studied period. France and Germany observed a similar positive trend in their gap between 2012 and 2014. A few southern members, like Greece, Spain and Italy, and Eastern European members, like Hungary and Latvia, have a significant contraction in the size of the gap between 2012 and 2015.

Figure 3.7 shows the evolution from 2012 to 2015 of the VAT gap for each member country. The VAT gap expressed in the percentage of the collected VAT exhibits the highest values for Romania in 2012 and 2014, when the VAT gap passed the 40% level. Slovakia, Lithuania, Malta and Greece exhibit a gap that is consistently above the 30% level. Slovakia, Spain, Lithuania, Hungary, Estonia and the Czech Republic show a diminishing trend for the relative VAT gap. The EU's biggest economies, France and Germany, have a relative gap above 10%, whilst Italy is above 25%. Thus, the country with the biggest impact of the VAT gap when taking into account both nominal and relative terms is Italy. Luxemburg, Sweden, Croatia and Finland have the smallest relative VAT gaps.

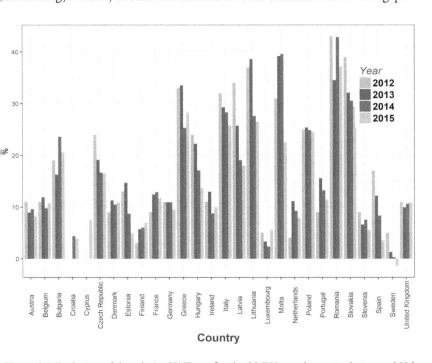

Figure 3.7 Evolution of the relative VAT gap for the 28 EU member states between 2012 and 2015 (expressed in percentage of the collected VAT). The highest values are observed for Romania in 2012 and 2014, when the VAT gap passed the 40% level. Slovakia, Lithuania, Malta and Greece exhibit a gap that is consistently above the 30% level. Slovakia, Spain, Lithuania, Hungary, Estonia and the Czech Republic show a diminishing trend for the relative VAT gap. The EU's biggest economies, France and Germany, have a relative gap above 10%, whilst Italy is above 25%.

The countries with the biggest relative VAT gap are also those with the biggest shares of VAT receipt in the national tax revenue.

The definition and the assumptions behind the VAT gap methodology are rather complex. Therefore the results presented earlier need to be interpreted in the context of the gap definition. The geographic distribution of the VAT gap and the evolution of the gap over time are consistent and robust. Nevertheless no conclusions can be made upon the factors that drive the gap. Concerning the defrauded amounts of VAT, the gap can provide only a high-level picture. The estimation of the share of the evaded tax in the total VAT gap is the object of the following section.

What is the real figure of the VAT fraud?

Introduced in the early1950s by Maurice Lauré, a former director of the French tax authority (Laure, 1955), the VAT is going through one of the most critical periods of its history. Over almost six decades the new tax spread very quickly across all members of the Common Market and was adopted by new members that joined the EU after the fall of the Berlin Wall in 1990. The VAT rate within the EU members ranges between 18% and 27% (European Commision, 2013).

Like any other type of tax, the VAT is the subject of fraud, the economic agents trying to avoid the full taxation. The way the VAT collection is implemented in the European countries is based on the self-assessment of each company. Thus a company subject to VAT fills periodically to the local tax authority its VAT balance. Afterwards the VAT liability (credit) is paid (reimbursed) to (by) the authority.

Despite being a major source of revenue for national treasuries, the VAT is more often associated with the organized fraud and criminal syndicates, and even terrorism. Investigation media was the first to trigger the alarm and to provide various guestimates of the size of the VAT fraud. Over the past decade many reports pointed out the magnitude of this fraud in various member countries and the various markets concerned by this scam.

Cars and automotive components are one of the most basic underlying targets of VAT fraudsters. Such fraudulent activity consisted of buying cars abroad VAT-free, and selling them in domestically with VAT. This fraud allowed dealers to sell high-end cars at greatly reduced prices by not charging VAT and represented in the case of the French car industry 5 billion euros per year in lost sales, while the state lost 1 billion euros in uncollected VAT on a total of 160,000 vehicles sold in the French market.[8]

VAT evasion on basic food products are probably the most common and easy to fraud. In 2012[9] a vast criminal investigation focussed on fraud involving tax

8 France moves to block fraudulent German car sales (www.euractiv.com/sections/euro-finance/france-moves-block-fraudulent-german-car-sales-310024).
9 Hungary losing 1 billion euros a year from food VAT fraud (www.reuters.com/article/2012/06/07/us-hungary-vat-fraud-idUSBRE85614B20120607).

evasion on Hungary's basic food products. A common approach was to import goods from other EU member states without paying import VAT and sell the products on to retailers via a series of buffer companies, adding VAT for each transaction and pocketing the difference. Other types of fraud involved buying goods in Hungary and exporting them on paper while applying for a VAT refund. The products remained in the country, however, and were sold with VAT. Fraudsters were attracted by Hungary's 27% VAT on most food products – the highest level in the EU – which was introduced in 2012 as a consequence of the country's large public debts. Thus, Hungary's food market became inaccessible for foreign companies that were playing by the rules. The VAT fraudsters were able to sell products domestically to lower prices compared to their legitimate counterparts. United States-based commodities firm Bunge Ltd. estimated at the time that tax fraud linked to the sale of goods such as edible oils, sugar, coffee and meat was worth up to 1 billion euros per year.

Another example is the VAT carousel (Frunza, 2015) on the CO_2 emissions market, which is qualified by specialists as the crime of the century. In the modern history of crime there is no example displaying more damage and disruption to financial markets than the VAT carousel on the carbon emission exchanges. The high-level architecture of the crime was exposed, but the impact on the market equilibrium is still a subject of study. A subsequent phenomenon occurred concomitantly to the VAT fraud: money laundering. This point was mentioned in almost all the indictments related to the VAT fraud on carbon markets. Nevertheless, its mechanism and consequences remained until today misapprehended. The money laundering on the carbon market had a severity probably even higher than the VAT fraud, accounting for a total of 9–10 billion euros.

For the purposes of assessing the amount of VAT receipts lost through criminal activities, the typologies of VAT fraud are categorized in three main types:

1   The first category is black market trading, where suppliers are not known to the tax authorities and do not fulfil their obligations to charge and remit VAT. This type of fraud takes place in many walks of life and concerns all types of products.
2   The second category is Missing Trader Intra-Community fraud (MTIC fraud). In such fraud there is a chain of transactions in which one company (Missing Trader) effectively charges VAT to another company from the chain but does not actually remit the VAT to the tax authorities. The Missing Trader disappears after a while, leaving the tax authorities empty-handed. The carousel fraud is a subtype of the MTIC fraud where the same item circulates a few times in a chain, and the corresponding VAT is pocketed.
3   The third category concerns the trade of goods and services with extra-EU countries (Missing Trader Extra-Community fraud or MTEC). In these cases, goods are imported from those countries and sold in the EU's member state, the VAT not being remitted to the concerned authorities.

The next sections present methodologies that attempt to measure the VAT gaps for each of the three categories mentioned earlier. The estimation methodologies are using as a benchmark the VAT gap showed in the previous sections. The method described hereafter assumes that the VAT gap estimated by the European Commissions has the following limitations:

- The VAT lost related to the shadow economy is partially or not considered at all in the VAT gap.
- Spillover effects[10] between the EU members are not modelled in the VAT gap.
- The borderline between the tax evasion and the other causes of the gap is very thin and shady.
- Collected VAT can be related to fraud, especially when fraudsters are counting on tax reimbursements.
- In carrousel VAT frauds the same item transits a few times across two or more countries. Therefore it is likely that the same item is to be counted a few times in the national statistic of a country and never counted in another country.
- VAT fraud via misclassification of goods cannot be accurately measured with the gap methodology. The gap estimate relies on national statistics. Once a good category is misrepresented in the national accounts it is rather complex to reverse-engineer the process.
- VAT losses from companies' liquidations, insolvencies and bankruptcies are part of the gap. Yet the recovery of the VAT liability in case of default is an opaque process, especially when companies operate in more than one country. Thus, the VAT gap figures should be cautiously apprehended as they depend massively on the recovery, given default hypothesis.

Despite these limitations, it is assumed that the gap provides relevant signals concerning the geographic distribution of the VAT fraud. For example, it is expected that countries with big VAT gaps are to exhibit also significant VAT losses due to fraud.

VAT gap due to the shadow economy

This section aims to provide an accurate estimate of the VAT gap due to the shadow economy in the EU. The shadow economy bypasses the formal taxation system, including the VAT system. The estimation is based on an econometric model that uses macroeconomic data. Macroeconomic data is used for quantifying the factor that drives potential VAT receipts if the shadow economy would become visible to the taxman.

The model uses as main input data the estimates of the size of the shadow economy, as measured by Williams 2016. The current literature deals mainly

---

10 For example a tax policy change in a country can influence the VAT gap in another Member State.

with the estimation of the lost VAT relative to the formal economy, focussing on the disruptive MTIC VAT fraud (Frunza, 2016). Less attention is given to the VAT loss linked to informal transactions, which are not captured in the national accounts. The black market, the underground economy or shadow economy is represented by those activities where taxes are not paid, and regulations are not strictly followed. Therefore the aim of this section is to assess the amount of VAT losses due to the unreported trades corresponding to the shadow economy trading. The methodology is built on the following components:

1 Schenider's estimations (Schneider, 2015) of the shadow economy in the EU are presented.
2 A statistical model is built for assessing the relationship between the observable VAT and the GDP.
3 A simplified model for estimating the VAT losses due to the shadow economy is discussed. The model uses as an input the GDP estimate of the informal economy.

Estimation of the shadow economy in the EU

The shadow economy, known as the black market, refers to economic activities that are invisible to the national statistics. Therefore, these activities are not included in the national GDP figure. The informal economy can include activities which are both legal and illegal in nature. Traditionally the shadow economy involves the trades of services and goods for which the customer pays in cash.

The increasing monitoring efforts of cash transactions in the banking system push the actors of the shadow economy to find transfer solutions that bypass completely the banking universe and the surveillance instruments of the governmental authorities.

The first attempt to estimate the size and development of the shadow economy for 158 countries over the period of 1991 to 2015 was proposed by Schneider through a series of studies (Schneider, 2000, 2002, 2003, 2005, 2010, 2011). His results, based on a robust statistical model, suggest that the average size of the shadow economy of these 158 countries over 1991 to 2015 is 32.5% of the official GDP, which was 34.82% in 1991 and decreased to 30.66% in 2015. The smallest size of the shadow economy is observed in East Asian countries, with 16.77% averaged over the period 1991 to 2015, followed by Organisation for Economic Co-operation and Development (OECD) countries with 18.7%; the Latin American and sub-Saharan African countries have the largest size, with values above 35%. A focus on the EU economy was published by Williams (2016), the size of the shadow economies being synthesized in Table 3.3.

The shadow economies of Eastern European countries exhibit the biggest size in terms of GDP, while the North-Western European countries have the smallest size. In 2016, Bulgaria was on the top of the list, the shadow economy representing almost 30% of the formal GDP. Croatia and Romania came close

Table 3.3 Estimation of the shadow economy of EU countries, 2003–2016 (in % of official GDP)

Year	2003	2004	2005	2006	2007	2008	2009	2010	2011	2012	2013	2014	2015	2016
Austria	10.8	11	10.3	9.7	9.4	8.1	8.5	8.2	7.9	7.6	7.5	7.8	8.2	7.8
Belgium	21.4	20.7	20.1	19.2	18.3	17.5	17.8	17.4	17.1	16.8	16.4	16.1	16.2	16.1
Bulgaria	35.9	35.3	34.4	34	32.7	32.1	32.5	32.6	32.3	31.9	31.2	31	30.6	30.2
Croatia	32.3	32.3	31.5	31.2	30.4	29.6	30.1	29.8	29.5	29	28.4	28	27.7	27.1
The Czech Republic	19.5	19.1	18.5	18.1	17	16.6	16.9	16.7	16.4	16	15.5	15.3	15.1	14.9
Denmark	17.4	17.1	16.5	15.4	14.8	13.9	14.3	14	13.8	13.4	13	12.8	12	11.6
Estonia	30.7	30.8	30.2	29.6	29.5	29	29.6	29.3	28.6	28.2	27.6	27.1	26.2	25.4
Finland	17.6	17.2	16.6	15.3	14.5	13.8	14.2	14	13.7	13.3	13	12.9	12.4	12
France	14.7	14.3	13.8	12.4	11.8	11.1	11.6	11.3	11	10.8	9.9	10.8	12.3	12.6
Germany	16.7	15.7	15	14.5	13.9	13.5	14.3	13.5	12.7	12.5	12.1	11.6	11.2	10.8
Greece	28.2	28.1	27.6	26.2	25.1	24.3	25	25.4	24.3	24	23.6	23.3	22.4	22
Hungary	25	24.7	24.5	24.4	23.7	23	23.5	23.3	22.8	22.5	22.1	21.6	21.9	22.2
Ireland	15.4	15.2	14.8	13.4	12.7	12.2	13.1	13	12.8	12.7	12.2	11.8	11.3	10.8
Italy	26.1	25.2	24.4	23.2	22.3	21.4	22	21.8	21.2	21.6	21.1	20.8	20.6	20.2
Latvia	30.4	30	29.5	29	27.5	26.5	27.1	27.3	26.5	26.1	25.5	24.7	23.6	22.9
Lithuania	32	31.7	31.1	30.6	29.7	29.1	29.6	29.7	29	28.5	28	27.1	25.8	24.9
Luxembourg	9.8	9.8	9.9	10	9.4	8.5	8.8	8.4	8.2	8.2	8	8.1	8.3	8.4
Malta	26.7	26.7	26.9	27.2	26.4	25.8	25.9	26	25.8	25.3	24.3	24	24.3	24
The Netherlands	12.7	12.5	12	10.9	10.1	9.6	10.2	10	9.8	9.5	9.1	9.2	9	8.8
Poland	27.7	27.4	27.1	26.8	26	25.3	25.9	25.4	25	24.4	23.8	23.5	23.3	23
Portugal	22.2	21.7	21.2	20.1	19.2	18.7	19.5	19.2	19.4	19.4	19	18.7	17.6	17.2
Romania	33.6	32.5	32.2	31.4	30.2	29.4	29.4	29.8	29.6	29.1	28.4	28.1	28	27.6
Slovakia	18.4	18.2	17.6	17.3	16.8	16	16.8	16.4	16	15.5	15	14.6	14.1	13.7
Slovenia	26.7	26.5	26	25.8	24.7	24	24.6	24.3	24.1	23.6	23.1	23.5	23.3	23.1
Cyprus	28.7	28.3	28.1	27.9	26.5	26	26.5	26.2	26	25.6	25.2	25.7	24.8	24.2
Spam	2	21.9	21.3	20.2	19.3	18.4	19.5	19.4	19.2	19.2	18.6	18.5	18.2	17.9
Sweden	18.6	18.1	17.5	16.2	15.6	14.9	15.4	15	14.7	14.3	13.9	13.6	13.2	12.6
The United Kingdom	12.2	12.3	12	11.1	10.6	10.1	10.9	10.7	10.5	10.1	9.7	9.6	9.4	9

Source: Estimating the size of the shadow economies of highly developed countries Schneider 2016.

to a 27% figure. While Bulgaria and Romania have big VAT gaps (as shown in Figure 3.7), Croatia has one of the smallest gaps in the EU.

Austria, Luxemburg and the Netherlands have the smallest informal economies, representing in 2016 less than 9% of the national GDP. The three countries also have a VAT gap below the European average. Sweden, the country that reached in 2015 a negative VAT gap, has a bigger shadow economy than France or Germany. Italy has the biggest informal economy, with 20% of the GDP, amongst the major EU economies.

The size of the shadow economy has a descending trend in most of the European countries. A notable exception is France, where the informal trades increased from 9.9% in 2013 to 12.6% in 2016.

Relationship between the VAT and the GDP

The basic mechanism of the VAT fraud is described in Figure 1.1. An item is bought from a different country of the EU without VAT and sold domestically with VAT. The VAT is not paid to the local tax authority. The VAT loss related to the shadow economy does not necessarily involve imports of services or goods from another country. With respect to VAT fraud, the shadow economy encompasses two types of good and services:

1   **Output products of the shadow economy:** Products are not registered and not declared to authorities, so no tax is paid on those transactions. This area of the shadow economy includes counterfeit products or services provided by non-registered workforce.
2   **Output products of the formal economy:** Products and services from the formal economy can be sold through the shadow economy. This can be the case for smuggled goods, stolen merchandise or embargoed items in a given country.

In order to assess the impact of the shadow economy on the VAT in the EU, it is necessary to determine the relationship between the temporal variation of the actual collected VAT and the variation of the GDP in a given country. This assessment would indicate whether the collected VAT is sensitive to the variation of the GDP. In normal economic conditions an increase in the GDP of a country would generate an increase in the VAT. If this hypothesis is not valid, it could signify that the additional economic output either is not reflected in the collectable VAT or is bypassing the formal economy.

A straightforward model is presented in the following equation:

$$\Delta \mathrm{VAT}_t^i = \mathrm{VAT}_t^i - \mathrm{VAT}_{t-1}^i = \alpha + \beta \cdot \Delta \mathrm{GDP}_t^i + \gamma \cdot \Delta R_t^i + \varepsilon$$
$$= \alpha + \beta \cdot (\mathrm{GDP}_t^i - \mathrm{GDP}_{t-1}^i) + \gamma \cdot (R_t^i - R_{t-1}^i) + \varepsilon \qquad (3.1)$$

where VAT_t^i is the amount of collected VAT in the country i during the fiscal year t, GDP_t^i is the GDP in the country i for the period t and R_t^i is the VAT rate in country i during year t.

Adding the level of the VAT rate as an independent variable in the regression specified aims to assess whether an increase in the tax rate is followed by an increase in the collected VAT. This would be a normal avenue as a government increases the VAT rate when it looks for additional receipts.

This regression is an estimate on a data set, sourced by Eurostat.[11] The data set includes collected VAT amounts, nominal GDP and VAT rates for the 28 countries[12] of the EU, between 2000 and 2015. The relationship between the VAT receipt and the independent variables requires a model fit for a cross-sectional data set. Therefore the regression specified in Equation (3.1) is estimated with a framework for panel data specified in the seminal book of Baltagi (2008) and implemented in a dedicated R package '*plm*' (Croissant, 2008).

The results of this multi-variate panel regression and the associated statistics are presented in Table 3.4. They indicate that the variation of the GDP and that of the VAT rate are significant independent explanatory variables. The R^2 is 69% and the intercept is not significant statistically at 95% confidence level.

The results exposed earlier should be carefully interpreted for two reasons:

- First, the VAT receipt increases with the increase of the VAT rate. This effect should not affect the dependence between the VAT receipts and the GDP.
- Second, a size effect is present in Equation (3.1). A country with a big GDP would surely have a bigger receipt of VAT.

Thus, the next step is to correct the VAT annual variation for the VAT rate variation. Therefore, a new variable is introduced: VAT_t^{*i}, as the amount of collected VAT in the country i during the fiscal year t, corrected by the variation of the VAT rate in that country.[13] Hereafter, it is considered that the reference year for the data set is 2006. Therefore, all rate variations compared to 2006 are imputed to the collected VAT figure:

$$\Delta VAT_t^{*i} = VAT_t^{*i} - VAT_{t-1}^{*i} = \alpha + \beta \cdot \Delta GDP_t^i + \varepsilon \qquad (3.2)$$

Table 3.4 Regression results for the model specified in Equation (3.1). The R^2 of the regression is 69%

Parameter	Estimates	Standard deviation	t-Value	p-Value
A	–1.200e+02	1.059e+02	–1.133	0.258
B	7.350e–02	2.561e–03	28.70	0.00
Γ	9.754e+02	1.455e+02	6.706	0.00

11 http://ec.europa.eu/eurostat.
12 The data for countries that entered the EU in 2005, 2007 and 2010 are gradually added to the data set. Thus, the data set has missing value for some countries for the years prior to joining the EU.
13 If in a country in year t the VAT rate increased from 15% in year $t-1$ to 20%, the collected VAT figure in year t is corrected by dividing it by 1.043 (1.043=1.2/1.15).

The results shown indicate that the positive relationship between the GDP variation and the adjusted collected VAT figure persists. The intercept of the regression is not statistically significant at a 95% confidence level. The R^2 is 51%, thereby highlighting the good performance of the model. The results underline the fact that when the GDP of a country increases, the amount of collected VAT in that country increases too.

Interestingly enough, if the model specified in Equation (3.1) is estimated with a new data set which includes the rate-corrected VAT amounts, then the γ parameter is statistically significant at 95% confidence level and is negative. This means that an increase of the VAT rate would induce a decrease of the base of the collectable VAT. This finding is in line with previous research (Gradeva, 2014), which showed empirically that, between 2004 and 2009, the trade gap is positively correlated with the VAT rate in a few Eastern European countries. This would mean that when the VAT rate increases, the amount of imports increases relatively to that of exports. This increase of the trade gap should be followed in theory by an increase in the VAT receipts, which is not always observed at the expected extent. The high levels of VAT can be one of the incentives for tax fraudsters, who look for quickly profitable scams. In a VAT scam the higher the VAT, the higher the pocketed amount. This aspect will be discussed in the following section concerning the MTIC fraud.

Going further the model needs to take into account the size effect that might be captured in Equation (3.2). Thus, if the model inputs are adjusted by the amount of the GDP, the resulting model will assess the dynamic of the VAT to GDP ratio in relation to the GDP growth. The dynamic of VAT to GDP ratio is the main input of interest for assessing the impact of the shadow economy upon the observable VAT:

$$\Delta\left(\frac{\mathrm{VAT}_t^{*i}}{\mathrm{GDP}_t^i}\right) = \frac{\mathrm{VAT}_t^{*i}}{\mathrm{GDP}_t^i} - \frac{\mathrm{VAT}_{t-1}^{*i}}{\mathrm{GDP}_{t-1}^i} = \alpha + \beta \cdot \frac{\Delta\mathrm{GDP}_t^i}{\mathrm{GDP}_t^i} + \varepsilon \qquad (3.3)$$

The results of the panel regression for Equation (3.3) are synthesized in Table 3.5. The slope is statistically relevant, indicating that a positive GDP growth will increase the VAT to GDP ratio with one basis point for each percent of growth. The R^2 of the regression is small, around 3%, underlining the lower explanatory power of the specified model.

Table 3.5 Regression results for the parameters specified in model from Equation (3.2) (variation of the corrected amount of collected VAT in relation to the variation of GDP, R^2 = 51%) and Equation (3.3) (the VAT to GDP ratio in relation to the GDP growth R^2 = 3%) between 2000 and 2015

Model	Parameter	Estimates	Std	t-Value	p-Value	R^2
Equation (3.2)	α	−24.817946	86.374422	−0.287	0.774	51%
	β	0.057310	0.002156	26.583	0.00	
Equation (3.3)	α	−0.0005983	0.0002314	−2.586	0.010063	3%
	β	0.0096497	0.0028295	3.410	0.00	

When applied to country level, the results of this regression show some heterogeneity, the slope not being statically relevant for all countries. Nevertheless, given the fact that the levels of GDP growth are not homogenous across the 28 countries, going forward, the results will be used for the estimation of the VAT loss from the shadow economy.

Size of the VAT loss due to the shadow economy

The VAT system is bypassed by the shadow economy. The output of the shadow economy does not enter in the base of the VAT receipts. For the purpose of VAT collection in a country the shadow economy is in fact invisible. If all the GDP from the shadow economy does enter the taxation base relevant to VAT, an additional VAT receipt would enter the government's accounts.

Hereafter the VAT loss from informal economy is computed based on the results from the previous section. The theoretical VAT (VAT^{SE}) denotes the amount that a country could collect if the shadow economy would be taxed, and GDP_t^{SEi} is the GDP from the shadow economy in country i and year t:

$$VAT^{SE} = \left(\frac{VAT_t^i}{GDP_t^i} + \beta \frac{GDP_t^{SEi}}{GDP_t^i} \right) \cdot GDP_t^{SEi} \tag{3.4}$$

Equation (3.3) is based on the assumption that there is a positive relationship between the VAT to GDP ratio and the GDP growth. Thus, a GDP increase will bolster the VAT collected as a percentage of the GDP. Basically, one could assume that the VAT to GDP ratio remains constant and does not depend on the GDP growth. The model specified in Equation (3.3) takes into account a spillover effect of the economic growth over the tax collection policy.

This effect could be explained by a few qualitative and behavioural factors:

- An increase in GDP would grant more resources to government for strengthening the controls and the collection of taxes.
- An increase of GDP would make business more confident, more compliant with respect to VAT liabilities.

Assuming this effect with a positive β makes the VAT loss estimate more conservative. The input data for Equation (3.4) is a share of the shadow economy in the formal economy national GDP. The data set corresponds to the estimates provided by Williams (2016) and discussed in Table 3.3.

Figure 3.8 shows the estimates of the VAT loss due to the shadow economy in 2015 for the 28 countries of the EU. The total amount of the VAT loss is around 131 billion euros. Germany, France, Italy and the United Kingdom account for more than 66% of the total gap due to the shadow economy. When analysing the ratio between the VAT loss and the VAT collected, the Eastern European countries rank on the top, with more than 25% of the collected VAT being lost due to the shadow economy.

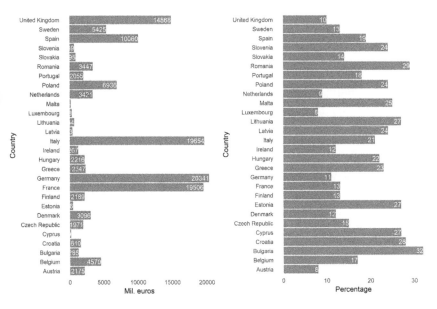

Figure 3.8 Breakdown of the VAT loss due to the shadow economy in 2015. Germany, France and Italy have the biggest VAT losses due to the shadow economies in the EU. The biggest VAT shares of the national GDP are observed in Bulgaria, Romania and Croatia.

Figure 3.9 shows the evolution of the VAT loss from the shadow economy between 2013 and 2015. In 2013 and 2014 the VAT losses linked to informal transactions accounted for 123 and 125 billion euros, respectively. The levels remained stable over the three years.

Few countries (the United Kingdom, Spain, Poland and France) exhibited an increase in the nominal size of the VAT loss due to the shadow economy between 2013 and 2015. The VAT loss to GDP ratio has followed a descending trend between 2013 and 2015 for most of the Eastern and Southern European countries (Croatia, Estonia, Denmark, Greece, Lithuania, Poland, Portugal and Sweden). The ratio increased in the case of France because of the increase in the size of the shadow economy.

Figure 3.10 shows the benchmark between the VAT loss due to the informal economy and the VAT loss (VAT gap) due to the formal economy. The figures for the VAT gap in the EU are those provided by the European Commission in the annual report for the VAT gap assessment (Poniatowski, Study and Reports on the VAT gap in the EU-28 member states: 2017 Final Report, 2017). The figures correspond to 2015.

The two nominal figures are relatively similar in terms of order of magnitude for the 28 countries. For most countries the VAT gap measured by the European Commission for the formal economy is higher than the VAT loss (gap) due to the shadow economy.

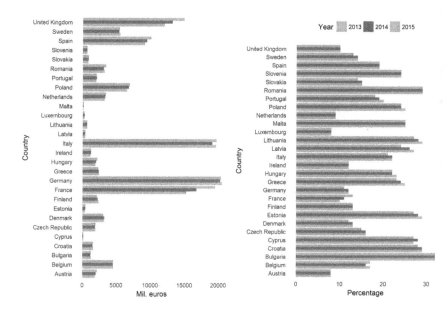

Figure 3.9 Evolution of the VAT losses due to the shadow economy for the 28 countries of the EU between 2013 and 2015.

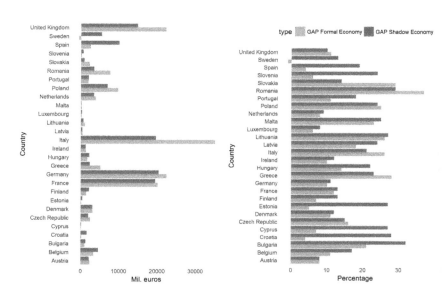

Figure 3.10 VAT loss due to the shadow economy compared to VAT loss on formal economy (VAT gap) in 2015. The left graph shows the nominal figures expressed in million euros. The right graph shows the percentage of the VAT loss out of the collected VAT.

In some cases (Spain, Portugal, Croatia, Hungary, Belgium, Bulgaria, Finland and Sweden) the VAT loss related to the shadow economy is lower than the gap related to the formal economy. This effect is mainly explained by two factors:

- Some countries have an aggressive policy for increasing the collection of VAT liabilities and tackling the VAT fraud (Sweden).
- Some countries have big shadow economies.

The VAT loss expressed as a percentage of the collected VAT receipts shows some massive disparities. Romania and Greece exhibit a much higher VAT loss from the formal economy than the gap from the shadow economy. For some countries, including Lithuania, Romania and Greece, the total VAT gap exceeds 50% of the observable VAT.

Estimation of the losses due to MTIC VAT fraud

The academic literature concerning the VAT fraud, and particularly the estimations of its negative externalities, is especially scarce. With the level of VAT fraud touching alarming levels few avenues of quantification were explored. For example Gradeva (2014) showed that the trade gap is positively correlated with the VAT rate in a few Eastern European countries. This research showed that a one-percentage-point increase in the VAT rate is associated with a 0.6% up to an around 3% increase in the trade gap.

The VAT gap estimated by the European Commission was presented and discussed in the previous section. The approach discussed in this section (Frunza, 2016) aims to explore the link between the trade gap and the MTIC gap. The MTIC fraud depends on the intra-Community cross-border inflow and the outflow of goods and services. This holds true also for the particular form of the carousel MTIC fraud described in Figure 1.2. Therefore, studying the correlation between the trade gap and the VAT collected in the EU's countries can reveal relevant information about the potential losses due to MTIC frauds.

The approach built in the following paragraphs attempts to estimate loss due to MTIC fraud and to benchmark it with the VAT gap. The methodology includes the followings steps:

- First, the link between the VAT amounts and the trade gap is modelled with a panel regression method.
- Second, based on this model the loss due to MTIC VAT fraud is assessed as the difference between the theoretical and the collected VAT for each EU member.

Econometric model

The use of econometric models for estimating the defrauded amount in a VAT scam is not new. Statistical models revealed valuable insights in the case of the fraud on carbon markets (Frunza, 2011). The particularity of the emission mar ket was the rich data set with daily prices and exchanged volumes, thereby mak ing easier the implementation of a multifactorial model.

This idea, leveraged for the wider case of the MTIC, is targeting the driver of the collected VAT in a country. The main goal is to assess the impact of the MTIC fraud on the drivers' behaviour. Therefore, the model developed here i not aimed at assessing the full picture of the VAT fraud and does not include the VAT fraud linked to the shadow economy (estimated in the previous section and to the extra-EU trades (discussed in the following section)).

Let's assume that the theoretical VAT denoted ($VAT_{Theoretical}$), which should be collected by a government if there was no fraud, is the sum of the actually collected VAT ($VAT_{Observed}$) and the pocketed VAT (VAT_{Lost}):

$$VAT_{Theoretical} = VAT_{Observed} + VAT_{Lost} \qquad (3.5)$$

The amount of VAT that should be collected in theory is an increasing func tion, depending on the amount of intra-EU imports. If a country observes an increasing trend in imports from other EU countries, then the VAT collected should increase accordingly. This is because VAT should be paid domestically by the importer upon resale. Simplifying the framework, one can assume that this relationship is linear, as expressed in the following equation:

$$VAT_{Theoretical} \sim \alpha \cdot Imports \qquad (3.6)$$

If a country observes a sudden increase in imports which is not explained by the economic trends, the phenomena can be linked to the presence of MTIC scammers or 'VAT carousel'. Indeed, when an MTIC scam occurs the big var iations in the levels of the trade gap do not have any justification based on the real demand of the economy. When MTIC fraud occurs, the imports overpass the normal economic level[14] ($Imports_{Normal}$), and the difference between the observed imports and the trigger level is the source of the MTIC VAT loss (VAT_{Loss}).

When analyzing the amount of VAT fraud figure on food products in Hungary,[15] it appears that the gap corresponds to a total of 4 billion euros worth of aliments. This is equivalent to an extra food consumption of 400 euros per habitant or an additional two months of supplies per year (reported to the average salary per capita). Indeed, these figures do not have any economic ex planation, and an increase in food trades can be explained only by MTIC VAT fraud. This is also sustained by the fact that Hungary had at that time and still has the highest VAT rate amongst the 28 countries of the EU.

14 The approach discussed here is based on the postulate that at any given time there is normal level of Imports, economically justified. All deviations from this normal level are related to an MTIC fraud pattern. The approach aims to estimate the normal level of the imports and consequently the share of, imports potentially related to the VAT fraud.

15 Hungary losing 1 billion euros a year from food VAT fraud (www.reuters.com/article/ 2012/06/07/us-hungary-vat-fraud-idUSBRE85614B20120607).

Thus, the VAT gap is proportional to the difference between the actual imports and the trigger level:

$$VAT_{Loss} \sim \kappa \cdot max\left(Imports - Imports_{Normal}, 0\right)$$
$$= \kappa \cdot Call\left(Imports, Imports_{Normal}\right) \tag{3.7}$$

Equation (3.7) is similar to the value of a vanilla call option, where the strike is the normal level of Imports $\left(Imports_{Normal}\right)$, and the sport price is the actual level of imports. This similarity to a well-known financial instrument is very useful for quantifying the sensitivity of the collected VAT to the trade gap and for estimating the VAT gap related to MTIC fraud.

If one measures the sensitivity of the VAT with respect to the level of imports by differentiating Equation (3.7), the obtained results is:

$$\frac{\partial VAT_{Theoreteical}}{\partial Imports} = \frac{\partial VAT_{Observed}}{\partial Imports} + \frac{\partial VAT_{Loss}}{\partial Imports} \tag{3.8}$$

From Equation (3.8) one can deduce that the sensitivity of the lost VAT to the variation of imports is proportional to the *Delta* of a vanilla call option. Thus, the sensitivity of the actual collected VAT $(VAT_{observed})$ can be expressed as:

$$\frac{\partial VAT_{Observed}}{\partial Imports} = \frac{\partial VAT_{Theoretical}}{\partial Imports} - \frac{\partial VAT_{Loss}}{\partial Imports}$$
$$\frac{\partial VAT_{Observed}}{\partial Imports} = \alpha - \kappa \cdot \Delta_{Call\left(Imports, Imports_{Normal}\right)} \tag{3.9}$$

where $\Delta_{Call(Imports, Imports_{Normal})}$ is the *Delta* of a European call with a spot equal to $Imports_{Normal}$, a strike equal to $Imports_{Normal}$ and a one-year maturity.

This framework for modelling the VAT gap related to MTIC fraud is depicted in Figure 3.11. In a VAT fraud-free world, the amount of VAT collected by a country would be an increasing function of Imports. The lost VAT or the amount pocketed by the MTIC fraudsters increases also with the amount of Imports in a country when this amount surpasses the thresholds of the Imports that fuel the normal (formal) economy ($Imports_{Normal}$). The observed VAT, the effective amount of VAT collected by a country, increases linearly until the level of Import is equal to $Imports_{Normal}$. When this threshold is surpassed the observed VAT remains almost constant. The sensitivity of the observed VAT goes towards zero when the value of Imports is much higher than the trigger value ($Imports_{Normal}$).

Thus, the main driver of the VAT amount with respect to intra-Community trades is without doubt the balance between the Imports and the exports, resumed in the trade gap. When the Imports increase relative to the exports in a country the collected VAT should increase in theory. If the reverse happens the VAT should decrease. Therefore, the VAT should have a dynamic negatively related to the trade gap variations.

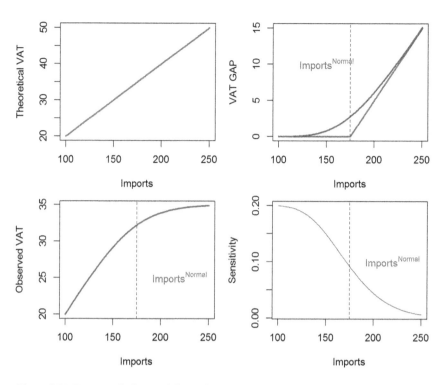

Figure 3.11 Framework for modelling the VAT gap related to MTIC fraud. Top left:
In a fraud-free world the amount of VAT collected by a country would be
an increasing function of Imports. Top right: The VAT gap or the amount
pocketed by the MTIC fraudsters increases also with the amount of Imports
in a country when this amount overpasses the thresholds of the Imports that
fuel the normal(legal) economy $(\text{Imports}_{\text{Normal}})$. Bottom left: The observed
VAT, the effective amount of VAT collected by a country, increases linearly
until the level of Import is equal to $(\text{Imports}_{\text{Normal}})$. When this threshold is
overpassed the observed VAT remains almost constant. Bottom right: The
sensitivity of the observed VAT goes towards zero when the value of Imports
is much higher than the trigger value $(\text{Imports}_{\text{Normal}})$.

Extending a set of models based on the trade gap and the GDP, we introduce
the following specification:

$$\Delta \text{VAT}^{it}_{\text{Observed}} = \beta_{\text{Trade}} \cdot \Delta \text{Trade Gap}^{it} + \beta_{\text{GDP}} \cdot \Delta \text{GDP}^{it} + \varepsilon^{it} \qquad (3.10)$$

where $\Delta \text{VAT}^{it}_{\text{Observed}}$ is the variation of the collected VAT in year t for the country
i, $\Delta \text{Trade Gap}^{it}$ is the variation of the trade gap, ΔGDP^{it} is the variation of the
GDP and ε^{it} is the noise.

The model is estimated with a special method fitted for panel data that might
exhibit cross-sectional variability, developed by Croissant (2008). The modelling
process has the following steps:

1   data preparation,
2   panel regression model and parameter estimation, and
3   estimation of the VAT loss related to MTIC fraud.

Data preparation

Using the Eurostat[16] public database, the time series from 1999 to 2014 of the collected VAT, Intra-EU trade gaps, Intra-EU imports[17] and Intra-EU exports are extracted for all EU countries. The frequency of the data set is yearly. From the official statements of the European Commission (Barbone, 2014, 2015) concerning the VAT rates across Europe, a set of time series is built (Table 3.1), showing the evolution of the VAT rates for each country from 1999 to 2016. Table 3.1 shows that the VAT rates exhibit a significant cross-sectional and temporal variability. In order to capture the impact of the trade gap volume on the collected VAT it is necessary to normalize the VAT data set in order to eliminate the variability induced by the changes in rates. The approach is similar to that used in the previous section. If a country increases the VAT rate, the collected VAT will increase, but this will bring no information concerning the relationship with the trade balance. Therefore, the normalization of the VAT figures aims to capture the effect of changes in the trade gap on the VAT collected independently of the change in the VAT rates. The VAT normalization factor is computed for each year and each country in order to eliminate the rate size effect. The normalization factor is obtained by dividing each column of Table 3.1 by the first column.

Panel regression model

Before analyzing the drivers of the collected VAT, one should look at the impact of the changes in the VAT rate on the Intra-EU flows of goods and services. This can be achieved by regressing the relative variations of trade gap over the changes of the VAT rate. The results of this panel regression are shown in Table 3.6, revealing that a 1% increase in the VAT rate can generate a 3.8% increase in the trade gap, with an adjusted R^2 value of 0.0166. These findings do confirm the results presented in the paper of Gradeva (2014) at the full EU space.

Table 3.6 Impact of the changes in the VAT rate on the intra-EU trade gap. A 1% increase in the VAT rate can generate a 3.8% increase in the trade gap. The adjusted R^2 is 1.7%

Factor	Estimate	Std. Error	t-Value	p-Value
VAT rate changes	0.038873	0.014833	2.6207	0.00913

16 http://ec.europa.eu/eurostat.
17 Over the rest of the chapter the figures concerning imports, exports and trade gaps are based on the Intra-EU flows.

Table 3.7 Model estimation with raw and normalized VAT figures and trade gap and GDP as drivers. The adjusted R^2 is 54% for the model with raw VAT figures and 59% for the normalized VAT figures

VAT figure	Factor	Estimate	Std. Error	t-Value	p-Value
Raw numbers	Trade gap (β_{Trade})	−0.0481308	0.0201621	−2.3872	0.01746
	GDP (β_{GDP})	0.0743925	0.0032614	22.8102	0.0
Normalized numbers	Trade gap (β_{Trade})	−0.126010	0.015302	−8.2349	0.0
	GDP (β_{GDP})	0.056853	0.002474	22.9795	0.0

The panel model introduced in Equation (3.10) is estimated for specification, assuming the raw VAT figures without including the effect of VAT rates change. The results exposed in Table 3.7 reveal an adjusted R^2 of 54%. The p-value of the Trade gap sensitivity (β_{Trade}) is 1.7%, and its value is negative, confirming that the VAT increases when the trade gap diminishes.

The current specification in Equation (3.10) assumes that the variation of imports accounts for the same as the variation of exports in the chain of the VAT. Nevertheless this model does not take into account the various regimes of VAT for various products and the specificity of each country in terms of the industrial transformation of goods and services. Thus, in some cases the Import and the Export might impact at a different scale the collected VAT. Based on this observation a second specification is tested:

$$\Delta \text{VAT}^{it}_{\text{Observed}} = \beta_{\text{Imports}} \cdot \Delta \text{Imports}^{it} + \beta_{\text{Exports}} \cdot \Delta \text{Exports}^{it}$$
$$+ \beta_{\text{GDP}} \cdot \Delta \text{GDP}^{it} + \varepsilon^{it} \tag{3.11}$$

where $\Delta \text{VAT}^{it}_{\text{Observed}}$ is the variation of the collected VAT in year t for the country i, $\Delta \text{Imports}^{it}$ is the variation of the Imports, $\Delta \text{Exports}^{it}$ is the variation of the Exports, ΔGDP^{it} is the variation of the GDP and ε^{it} is the noise.

The results exhibited in Table 3.8 synthesize the panel model introduced in Equation (3.11), estimated for the raw VAT figures. The adjusted R^2 is 55%, and the p-value improved compared to the previous model. As expected, the VAT increases with the increase in imports and decreases with the increase in exports.

These models are estimated with the normalized VAT figures filtered for the VAT rate changes. This way the increases of collected VAT due to an increase in the tax rate are filtered, and a corrected figure for the collected VAT enters the model. Table 3.7 (bottom rows) exhibits the new estimation results for the specification from Equation (3.10) and Table 3.8 (bottom rows) for Equation (3.11). The adjusted R^2 values are increasing, and the p-values of the parameters estimates improve for both model specifications.

The GDP appears as one of the main drivers of the collected VAT. This finding makes the task of assessing the VAT loss due to MTIC fraud more difficult as it introduces an additional variable. A straightforward way of reducing the dimensionality is considering the variables (VAT, Imports and Exports) as ratios to the GDP. Thus, the following variables are introduced:

Table 3.8 Model estimation with raw and normalized VAT figures and Imports, Exports and GDP as drivers. The Adjusted R^2 for the estimation using raw VAT numbers is 55% and 62% for normalized VAT numbers

VAT figures	Factor	Estimate	Std. Error	t-Value	p-Value
Raw numbers	Imports (β_{Imports})	0.0990150	0.0254769	3.8865	0.0001197
	Exports (β_{Exports})	-0.0610579	0.0203287	-3.0035	0.0028429
	GDP (β_{GDP})	0.0652438	0.0043053	15.1542	0.0
Normalized numbers	Imports (β_{Imports})	0.1930838	0.0187944	10.2735	0.0
	Exports (β_{Exports})	-0.1431040	0.0149933	-9.5446	0.0
	GDP (β_{GDP})	0.0448056	0.0031739	14.1169	0.0

$$\text{VAT}^{it}_{\text{GDP}} = \frac{\text{VAT}^{it}_{\text{Observed}}}{\text{GDP}^{it}}$$

$$\text{Imports}^{it}_{\text{GDP}} = \frac{\text{Imports}^{it}_{\text{Observed}}}{\text{GDP}^{it}}$$

$$\text{Exports}^{it}_{\text{GDP}} = \frac{\text{Exports}^{it}_{\text{Observed}}}{\text{GDP}^{it}}$$

Beyond the dimensionality reduction, the new specification resumed in Equation (3.12) has many advantages as it excludes the effect of the size of the country's economy as well as the effect of inflation:

$$\text{VAT}^{it}_{\text{GDP}} = \beta_{\text{Imports}} \cdot \text{Imports}^{it}_{\text{GDP}} + \beta_{\text{Exports}} \cdot \text{Exports}^{it}_{\text{GDP}} + \varepsilon^{it} \qquad (3.12)$$

The results of the parameters estimation on the full data panel are exhibited in Table 3.9. The adjusted R^2 is only 8%, thereby underlining the strong effect of the GDP from the previous models.

The introduction in 2006 of the European Directive relative to the intra-EU VAT regime for goods and services represented a crucial point in the dynamic of the intra-Community trade. The directive created a legal framework for the VAT exemption on intra-Community acquisitions and most likely was a headstone for the MTIC fraud. To assess further the dynamics of the trade and VAT, the model from Equation (3.12) is estimated on two different time subsamples: 2003 to 2009 and 2009 to 2014. Table 3.9 shows the results of the estimations for a period around the directive (2003–2009), and the R^2 is 23%, much higher compared to the full sample (Table 3.9).

The same model estimated on the period following the economic crush of 2009, shown in the two bottom rows of Table 3.9, exhibits less performance, with an adjusted R^2 of only 2.5% and p-values rejecting the statistical significance of the estimates for a 95% confidence level. After the economic crisis and the huge downturn in industrial production and consumption, juxtaposed with the Eurozone crisis in 2011, the authorities started to get more warnings about the increase of the VAT fraud within Europe. The prolonged recession could have been a trigger for the increase in the MTIC VAT fraud. The model for VAT gap

Table 3.9 Model estimation with VAT, Imports and Exports normalized by the GDP. For observations between 2003 and 2014 the adjusted R^2 is 8%. For observations between 2003 and 2009 the adjusted R^2 is 23%. For observations between 2009 and 2014 the adjusted R^2 is 2.5%

Period	Factor	Estimate	Std. Error	t-Value	p-Value
2003–2014	Imports (β_{Imports})	0.0565876	0.0098323	5.7553	1.718e-08
	Exports (β_{Exports})	−0.0329606	0.0107279	−3.0724	0.002268
2003–2009	Imports (β_{Imports})	0.097333	0.013986	6.9595	8.309e-11
	Exports (β_{Exports})	−0.082456	0.016934	−4.8692	2.670e-06
2009–2014	Imports (β_{Imports})	0.013669	0.012750	1.0721	0.2856
	Exports (β_{Exports})	−0.025047	0.013542	−1.8495	0.0666

described in the previous section is confirmed by the results from Table 3.9, which exhibits no sensitivity of the collected VAT with regards to the import numbers for the period 2009 to 2014. These results show that the EU might have witnessed a significant increase in the MTIC fraud since the beginning of the decade.

Model estimates

Based on the model specified in Equation (3.13) the VAT loss due to MTIC fraud can be estimated. The sensitivity of the observed VAT with respect to the Imports corresponds to estimates from the previous section. The figure reported in Table 3.9, obtained from the period prior to the economic crisis, is used. If the level of the Imports was in the range of the trigger level the delta could be approximated with the delta of an ATM (at-the-money option), which is around 0.5. In order to measure the VAT gap the κ and estimates are required as an entry in the following equation (Figure 3.12):

$$\text{VAT}_{\text{Loss}} = \kappa \cdot \text{Call}\left(\text{Imports}, \text{Imports}_{\text{Normal}}\right) \quad (3.13)$$

κ can be easily estimated from Equation (3.12) if α is approximated with the domestic VAT rate. For computing the trigger of normal economic levels of Imports ($\text{Imports}_{\text{Normal}}$) an initial proxy for the VAT MTIC loss can be the reported VAT gap for 2013 in the European Commission's study (Barbone, 2015). Let's assume that a proportion p_i or each of the 28 countries ($i \in \overline{1, 28}$) in the EU of the reported VAT gap corresponds to the lost VAT due to MTIC. Using a recursive optimization the implied trigger level of $\text{Imports}_{\text{Normal}}$ can be estimated in order to explain the VAT gap figure (Figure 3.13).

Thus the strike level is computed for each country, and this allows us to estimate the MTIC VAT loss. Using the Imports figures reported in 2013 the breakdown of the MTIC VAT loss is exhibited in Table 3.10. The estimation of the total pocketed funds through MTIC scams accounts for 82 billion euros, representing 0.5% of the EU's GDP in 2013. This figure represents 51% of the estimate of the total VAT gap across the 28 countries for the EU, as stated in the

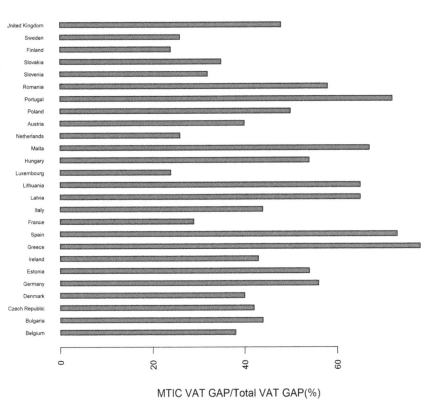

Figure 3.12 MTIC VAT loss/Total VAT gap (%) for 2013. MTIC VAT gap represents 49% of the estimate of the total VAT frauds across the EU, as stated by Barbone, 2015.

Commission's research (Barbone, 2014). Assuming the VAT gap encompasses the MTIC-related tax loss, the remaining 49% of the gap should correspond to other types of tax losses, including delays in payments, misestimating of tax liabilities, insolvencies and bankruptcies. The breakdown of the ration between the VAT lost due to MTIC scams and the total VAT gap for 2013 is exhibited in Figure 3.14.

In 2014, the losses due to MTIC VAT fraud accounted for 94 billion euros, as exhibited in Table 3.11 and Figure 3.13. It represents 0.67% of the GDP of the EU. The top countries in terms of MTIC VAT fraud are the United Kingdom, Germany, Italy, Spain and France, which are also in the top of all VAT frauds.

In 2014, the MTIC fraud represents 9.7% of the total collected VAT compared to only 8.8% in 2013. The geographical distribution of the VAT gap in percentage out of the total collected VAT is exhibited in Figure 3.16. The Eastern

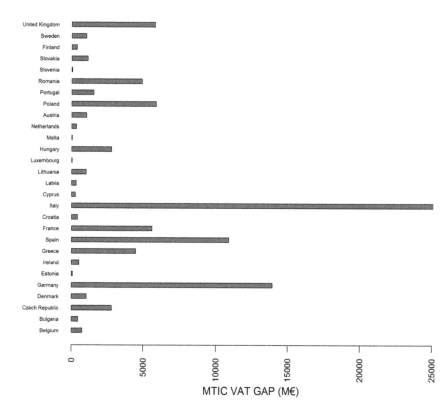

Figure 3.13 2014 MTIC VAT gap breakdown (million euros). In 2014, the loss due to MTIC VAT fraud represents 0.67% of the total EU's GDP. The top countries in terms of MTIC VAT fraud are the United Kingdom, Germany, Italy, Spain and France, which are also in the top of countries with VAT lost as a result of the shadow economy.

European countries, including Romania, Latvia, Poland, Slovakia and Hungary, are in the top, along with some Southern European countries, like Italy and Greece.

These estimates are in fact a lower boundary of the VAT lost because of the MTIC fraud. In reality, the global figure could be higher due to the fact that the models are depending at a certain extent upon the inputs of total VAT gap reported by the EU and on the assumption that the MTIC fraud was less endemic before 2009. Nevertheless, the results concerning the main countries of the MTIC fraud are robust and confirmed by other studies.

The estimates of the MTIC fraud in 2015 are detailed in Table 3.12. The total figure of the MTIC fraud in 2015 is 99 billion euros, representing 65% of the VAT gap estimated for 2015 (Poniatowski, 2017). For a few countries (the Czech Republic, Spain, Croatia, Cyprus, Lithuania and Hungary) the estimates of the MTIC fraud are bigger than the VAT gaps. This effect occurs

Table 3.10 Estimates of the MTIC VAT fraud in 2013. The size of MTIC VAT fraud
accounts for 82 billion euros

Country	MTIC VAT Loss (millions euro)	Total VAT gap (millions euro)	MTIC VAT loss/Total VAT gap (%)	MTIC VAT loss (% collected VAT)	Total VAT gap (% collected VAT)
Belgium	1,209	3,186	38	4	12
Bulgaria	348	785	44	9	20
The Czech Republic	1,412	3,375	42	12	29
Denmark	995	2,489	40	4	10
Germany	13,961	24,873	56	7	13
Estonia	171	315	54	11	20
Ireland	530	1,225	43	5	12
Greece	5,035	6,497	78	40	52
Spain	8,859	12,094	73	14	19
France	4,066	14,096	29	3	10
Croatia	78			1	
Italy	20,778	47,516	44	22	51
Cyprus	152			11	
Latvia	466	721	65	28	43
Lithuania	1,030	1,580	65	39	61
Luxembourg	45	187	24	1	6
Hungary	1,595	2,930	54	18	32
Malta	142	210	67	24	36
The Netherlands	473	1,852	26	1	4
Austria	1,288	3,217	40	5	13
Poland	5,093	10,131	50	18	36
Portugal	972	1,358	72	7	10
Romania	4,809	8,296	58	40	70
Slovenia	59	186	32	2	6
Slovakia	888	2,513	35	19	54
Finland	194	812	24	1	4
Sweden	463	1,776	26	1	5
The United Kingdom	7,374	15,431	48	5	11
Total	82,484	161,442	51.0	8.8	18

1 The original figures were adjusted with more recent reports.

for Eastern and Central European countries. The cases of Croatia and Cyprus should be addressed cautiously due to the fact that their national accents entered recently in the scope of Eurostat and therefore might not yet be fully harmonized with the other countries. Romania is on the top of the MTIC VAT fraud list, the pocketed funds representing almost 60% of the collected taxes in 2015. Greece, Italy, Slovakia and Lithuania also exhibit big figures, around 35%.

Table 3.13 depicts the evolution of the losses due to MTIC fraud between 2013 and 2015. A counter-intuitive effect is observed. On the one hand, the VAT gap reported by the Commission is decreasing in nominal terms and as a percentage of the collected VAT. On the other hand, the estimates of the defrauded VAT in MTIC scams is increasing in both nominal and relative terms.

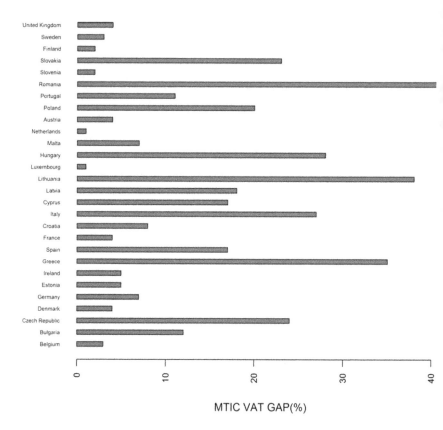

Figure 3.14 Breakdown of the VAT loss due to the MTIC fraud in 2014 (%). The Eastern
European countries, including Romania, Latvia, Poland, Slovakia and
Hungary, are in the top as are some Southern European countries, like Italy
and Greece.

Indeed, the nominal increase from 82 billion euros in 2013 to 99 billion euros in
2015 is partially explained by the increase in the total collected VAT. The share
of the MTIC estimates in the VAT gap increased from 51.1% in 2013 to 65.4%
in 2015. This effect can be explained by two causes:

• The model overestimates the MTIC loss.
• The VAT gap is underestimated.

The model can overestimate the MTIC losses for those cases when the imported
goods in a country are not sold domestically. The goods are only transiting
that country for being sold outside the EU. Nevertheless, the volume of exports
falling into this category would be small compared to the intra-EU imports.
Therefore, potential model overestimation is limited and does not challenge the
increasing trend of the MTIC fraud. The VAT gap is based on a theoretical

Table 3.11 Estimates of the MTIC VAT fraud in 2014. The size of MTIC VAT fraud accounts for 94 billion euros

Country	MTIC VAT loss (million euro)	Collected VAT (million euros)	MTIC VAT loss (%)
Belgium	764	27,518	2.8
Bulgaria	458	3,810	12.0
The Czech Republic	2,808	11,602	24.2
Denmark	1,070	24,950	4.3
Germany	13,934	203,081	6.9
Estonia	85	1,711	5.0
Ireland	540	11,521	4.7
Greece	4,481	12,676	35.4
Spain	10,893	63,643	17.1
France	5,610	148,454	3.8
Croatia	419	5,368	7.8
Italy	26,145	97,071	26.9
Cyprus	260	1,512	17.2
Latvia	315	1,787	17.6
Lithuania	1,040	2,764	37.6
Luxembourg	38	3,732	1.0
Hungary	2,775	9,754	28.4
Malta	42	642	6.5
The Netherlands	341	42,708	0.8
Austria	1,052	25,386	4.1
Poland	5,887	29,317	20.1
Portugal	1,554	14,682	10.6
Romania	4,898	11,496	42.6
Slovenia	52	3,155	1.6
Slovakia	1,136	5,021	22.6
Finland	361	18,948	1.9
Sweden	1,036	38,846	2.7
The United Kingdom	5,801	157,478	3.7
Total	93,531	978,633	9.6

Table 3.12 Breakdown of the estimated losses from the MTIC fraud in 2015. The total loss for the 28 countries accounts for 99 billion euros, which represents more than 65% of the VAT gap and 9.6% of the total collected VAT

Country	MTIC VAT loss (millions euros)	VAT gap (millions euros)	Collected VAT (millions euros)	MTIC VAT loss/ VAT gap (%)	MTIC VAT loss/collected VAT (%)	VAT gap/ collected VAT (%)
Belgium	765	3,323	27,547	12.1	2.8	23.0
Bulgaria	488	1,052	4,059	25.9	12.0	46.4
The Czech Republic	2,997	2,444	12,382	19.7	24.2	122.6
Denmark	1,092	3,092	25,470	12.1	4.3	35.3
Germany	14,520	22,366	211,616	10.6	6.9	64.9
Estonia	93	96	1,873	5.1	5.0	96.9
Ireland	560	1,319	11,955	11.0	4.7	42.5
Greece	4,555	5,079	12,885	39.4	35.4	89.7
Spain	11,740	2,503	68,589	3.6	17.1	469.0

(*Continued*)

Country	MTIC VAT loss (millions euros)	VAT gap (millions euros)	Collected VAT (millions euros)	MTIC VAT loss/ VAT gap (%)	MTIC VAT loss/collected VAT (%)	VAT gap/ collected VAT (%)
France	5,730	20,113	151,622	13.3	3.8	28.5
Croatia	444	232	5,689	4.1	7.8	191.4
Italy	27,212	35,093	101,034	34.7	26.9	77.5
Cyprus	262	122	1,517	8.0	17.3	214.8
Latvia	331	411	1,876	21.9	17.6	80.5
Lithuania	1,087	1,037	2,888	35.9	37.6	104.8
Luxembourg	35	202	3,432	5.9	1.0	17.3
Hungary	3,035	1,700	10,669	15.9	28.4	178.5
Malta	45	199	684	29.1	6.5	22.5
The Netherlands	358	3,872	44,879	8.6	0.8	9.3
Austria	1,087	2,357	26,232	9.0	4.1	46.1
Poland	6,039	9,765	30,075	32.5	20.1	61.8
Portugal	1,627	1,989	15,368	12.9	10.6	81.8
Romania	5,513	7,659	12,939	59.2	42.6	72.0
Slovenia	53	188	3,219	5.8	1.6	28.2
Slovakia	1,226	2,256	5,420	41.6	22.6	54.4
Finland	361	1,418	18,974	7.5	1.9	25.5
Sweden	1,080	–568	40,501	–1.4	2.7	–190.2
The United Kingdom	6,702	22,210	181,945	12.2	3.7	30.2
Total	99,037	151,529	1,035,339	14.6	9.6	65.4

Table 3.13 Evolution of the losses due to MTIC scams between 2013 and 2015. The VAT gap diminishes, while the losses due to MTIC increases

Year	MTIC VAT loss (millions euros)	VAT gap (millions euros)	Collected VAT (millions euros)	MTIC VAT loss/ VAT gap (%)	MTIC VAT loss/collected VAT (%)	VAT gap/ collected VAT (%)
2013	82,484	161,442	938,987	51.1	8.8	17.2
2014	93,531	160,221	978,633	58.4	9.6	16.4
2015	99,037	151,529	1,035,339	65.4	9.6	14.6

computation of the VAT liability (VTTL). This computation is based on observable data and is estimated for each country, given the domestic particularities. MTIC is not a country-specific fraud but a EU-specific fraud. Therefore, it is possible that aspects of the VAT liability due to intra-Community trades may not be captured by the Commission's framework.

Estimates of the MTEC VAT fraud

The term MTEC was first introduced by Ainsworth R. (2010). The big picture of the VAT fraud was incomplete, as revealed by scams, including services markets like the VAT fraud on CO_2 emissions and Voice over Internet Protocol (VoIP).

In those cases, many transactions that took place involved companies incorporated in countries which were not members of the EU. Carousel scams were able to function where parts of the carousel were based outside of the EU. Therefore, the concept of MTEC fraud was required to encompass those types of VAT scams involving counterparts based outside of the EU.

The initial description of MTEC in Ainsworth's view (Ainsworth R., 2010) stipulated that this type of fraud only occurs in tradable services, while MTIC focusses more on tradable goods.

This assumption was justified by the fact that VAT is collected by Customs as part of the Customs tax, when a good enters the territory of the EU. Indeed, when a European company imports goods from outside of the EU as part of the Customs Union clearance process a set of clearance taxes are applied, including the VAT equivalent, corresponding to the local rate of the country where the goods are delivered.

The same things apply when an EU-based company sells goods outside the EU. For example if a German company sells goods in the Eurasia Economic Union, VAT equivalent is paid as part of the Customs Union clearance process when the goods reach the border. Customs cannot do the same thing on imported service, thereby underlining the specificity of the MTEC to services.

Thus, the initial definition given by Ainsworth R. (2010) of MTEC is that of a scam occurring when an EU-based company[18] makes an international purchase outside of the EU of services without paying VAT. The company resells the services domestically, collects VAT and pockets the funds without paying the VAT liability towards the local national treasury.

A paradigm shift occurred[19] in 2017 when representatives of the British government pointed the finger at online marketplaces like Amazon and eBay. They were accused of facilitating the VAT evasion for their online sellers based outside of the EU. The sellers used the online marketplaces to sell mainly goods at a more advantageous price as they did not charge VAT. In April 2017 the British Audit Office published a report estimating that failure to declare and pay VAT from online retailers outside the EU inflicted a loss of 1.7 billion euros to Her Majesty's Revenue and Customs (HMRC).

In light of this recent evidence, goods need to be part of the scope of the possible targets of MTEC fraudsters. In fact, the online retailers are selling high volumes of low-value goods, delivered from offshore using the domestic postal services. Therefore, the postal delivery bypasses in many cases the Customs Union's clearance process, thereby avoiding the payment of the VAT.

Figure 3.15 shows the evolution of the Imports in the EU countries from other EU members and non-EU countries. The imports from the EU are constantly above those from outside non-EU countries. Both time series have a

---

18 Ainsworth's definition of the MTEC encompasses also VAT fraud resulting from a transaction between two non-member countries that have adopted the EU VAT as a model. This aspect will be discussed in Chapter 7 concerning the VAT fraud in the Eurasian Economic Union and in the Gulf countries.

19 Amazon and eBay turning blind eye to VAT evasion, say MPs (www.theguardian.com/technology/2017/sep/13/amazon-and-ebay-turning-blind-eye-to-vat-evasion-say-mps).

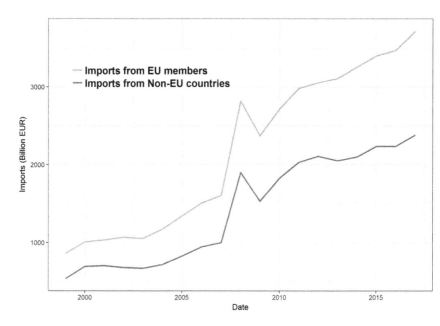

Figure 3.15 Evolution of EU's Imports from other member countries and from non-members between 1999 and 2017.

Source: Eurostat.

strong positive trend over time. The EU imports increased from 1,000 billion euros in 2000 to almost 3,000 billion euros in 2017. The non-EU imports in the EU area increased from 500 billion euros in 1999 to almost 2,500 billion euros in 2017. Nevertheless, the imports from other EU countries increased faster than those from outside the EU space.

Figure 3.16 depicts the evolution of the Exports from EU countries towards EU and non-EU jurisdictions between 1999 and 2017. The exports follow the same pattern as the imports, the exports towards the EU countries being bigger and increasing faster than the exports towards non-EU countries.

Based on these figures, the potential estimates of the MTEC fraud should be smaller than the estimates of the MTIC fraud presented in the previous section.

Figure 3.16[20] presents the breakdown of the imports (exports) depending on the country of destination (origin). Both imports (exports) numbers presented in Figure 3.16 indicate whether the country of origin (destination) is part of the EU or is a non-EU country.

Concerning the imports for most countries the imports from EU countries are bigger in value than those from non-EU countries. The exceptions are Malta and Ireland. The countries for which non-EU imports are close in value to the

20 2015 figures.

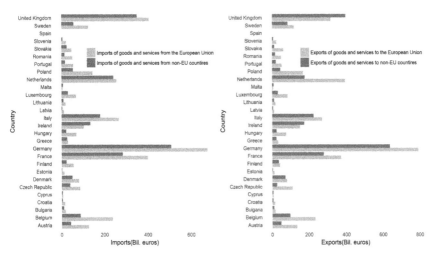

Figure 3.16 2015 Snapshot of the benchmark of the EU Imports and Exports with respect to the origin of the counterparts. Left: Benchmark of the EU Imports of goods and services from the EU with those from outside the EU. Right: Benchmark of the EU Exports of goods and services to the EU with those towards outside the EU.

Source: Eurostat.

EU imports are the United Kingdom, the Netherlands, Cyprus and Greece. The countries with more export towards non-EU destinations than towards EU destinations are Cyprus, Ireland, Malta and the United Kingdom.

The Netherlands, Cyprus, Malta and Greece have massive international harbour facilities and are major points of transit for global shipping. Thus, the breakdown trade gap between EU and non-EU trades can be justified for these cases.

The case of Ireland is particular and required a cautious interpretation. Ireland has a very aggressive taxation structure. Therefore, many marketplace companies, including Amazon and eBay, have their European and even global headquarters in Ireland. The online marketplaces monitored in the United Kingdom for VAT compliance issues are based in Ireland, and most likely the non-EU products sold in the EU enter the EU through Ireland before being dispatched to the member countries.

The United Kingdom traditionally has a lot of trade agreements with non-EU countries, a fact that could explain partially the findings from Figure 3.16. Additionally, companies based in the United Kingdom have been involved since the early 2000s in VAT scams involving non-EU countries (i.e., the Dubai Connection).

The estimation of the size of the MTEC fraud in the EU is more complex than that of the MTIC. The framework for estimating the MTIC was a purely quantitative top-down method. MTEC would require both quantitative and qualitative assumptions as well as a mix of top-down and bottom-up approaches.

In order to estimate the MTEC fraud, the framework and the results found in the previous section relative to the MTIC fraud can be leveraged. Estimating the amount of the lost VAT due to MTEC at the country level would require additional case studies that would provide additional intelligence concerning the various forms of this fraud. Thus, the framework proposed in this section leverages the approach from the previous section at a consolidated level for a cluster of countries that might be more likely to exhibit significant MTEC frauds. Based on the figures discussed previously for the purpose of estimating the MTEC the sample of 28 member countries is reduced to a subset of six countries, including the Netherlands, Cyprus, Ireland, Greece, Malta and the United Kingdom. The fact that only six countries are considered does not mean that MTEC does not exist in other countries of the EU or that the 22 remaining countries are ignored in this estimation. In fact, the six countries represent the entry point of the non-EU products.

The estimates discussed hereafter are the results of applying a method similar to that used to estimate the MTIC at an aggregate level for the six countries mentioned earlier. Table 3.14 shows the estimates of the VAT loss as a result of the MTEC fraud between 2013 and 2015. The estimate of the defrauded tax was 17 billion euros in 2013 and increased to 22 billion euros in 2015. It represents 2% of the collected VAT in the EU and between 11% and 15% of the VAT gap.

Table 3.14 shows also a benchmark between the estimates of the MTEC and the MTIC between 2013 and 2015. Both estimates increased during the considered period. The MTEC-related tax loss represents only 21–22% of the MTIC losses.

These estimates for the MTEC fraud should be interpreted carefully as the boundaries of the extra-Community schemes are murkier than those of the MTIC. Nevertheless, MTEC fraud in the EU is far from being a marginal phenomenon. The damages of this fraud inflicted to the governmental receipts and to the growth of the EU are significant.

The development of the e-commerce platforms and of online marketplaces like Amazon, eBay, Pinterest or Alibaba is an important growth factor for the global economy. And yet this development requires a cautious analysis in order to assess the potential relationship with the MTEC fraud.

The recent innovation in the area of blockchain technology is also a factor that needs special attention with respect to the MTEC. Blockchain technology

Table 3.14 Estimates of the losses due to the MTEC fraud in the EU between 2013 and 2015

Year	MTEC VAT loss (millions euros)	VAT gap (millions euros)	Collected VAT (millions euros)	MTEC VAT loss/VAT gap (%)	MTEC VAT loss/ collected VAT (%)	MTIC VAT loss (millions euros)	MTEC VAT loss/ MTIC VAT loss (%)
2013	17,304	161,442	938,987	10.72	1.84	82,484	21.0
2014	19,571	160,221	978,633	12.22	2.00	93,531	21.0
2015	22,317	151,529	1,035,339	14.73	2.16	99,037	22.5

facilitates massively the exchange of services, outside the radar of the taxman. Therefore, blockchain technology can be a facilitator of MTEC frauds on services. This aspect is discussed in a dedicated chapter.

Outlook

When adding up the different estimates from the previous section, the total amount of defrauded VAT equals more than 220 billion euros. The breakdown of the total VAT loss by fraud typology is presented in Table 3.15. The range of the total defrauded tax is between 222 billion euros in 2013 and 253 billion euros in 2015. The VAT evasion related to the shadow economy accounts for more than half of the total losses. MTEC-related fraud represents less than 10% of the grand total.

Table 3.16 provides further detail on the significance of the estimate in the context of the European economy. The total VAT fraud inflicts a loss to national budgets equating between 1.6% and 1.7% of EUs GDP. This loss is equivalent to the sum of Finland's and Estonia's GDPs. In addition, the total VAT loss represents between 23% and 25% of the actually collected VAT in all European countries. The total VAT losses are much bigger than the VAT gap estimated by the European Commission. This is justified by the fact that the assessment of the VAT gap does not encompass the same scope as the estimation process described in this chapter.

Table 3.15 Breakdown of the total losses from VAT fraud in the EU between 2013 and 2014

Year		MTEC VAT loss	MTIC VAT loss	Shadow economy VAT loss	Total VAT fraud loss
2013	(Millions euros)	17,304	82,484	122,849	222,637
	(%)	8	37	55	100
2014	(Millions euros)	19,571	93,531	125,332	238,434
	(%)	8	39	53	100
2015	(Millions euros	22,317	99,037	132,121	253,475
	(%)	9	39	52	100

Table 3.16 Total VAT fraud losses compared to the VAT gap, the collected VAT amount and the EU GDP

Year	Total VAT loss (millions euros)	VAT gap (millions euros)	Collected VAT (millions euros)	EU's GDP (millions euros)	VAT loss/ VAT gap (%)	VAT loss/ collected VAT (%)	VAT loss/EU's GDP (%)
2013	222,637	161,442	938,987	13,577,271	137.9	23.7	1.64
2014	238,434	160,221	978,633	14,044,690	148.8	24.4	1.70
2015	253,475	151,529	1,035,339	14,797,444	167.3	24.5	1.71

The Eastern and Southern European countries are more exposed to MTIC fraud, the losses representing a big percentage of the VAT collected in the respective countries. The big European economies (i.e., France, Germany, the United Kingdom) are less affected by the fraud, when comparing their VAT losses to their tax receipts. Nevertheless, due to the big size of their trading activities the VAT fraud in these countries accounts for more than half of the total VAT losses.

Therefore, the European economies are split into two categories with respect to the impact of the VAT fraud:

- the 'core' European economies, which are less affected relatively to their national budgets, and
- the 'peripheral' European economies, which bear significant losses in their national budgets due to the VAT fraud.

The 'leitmotif' of a multi-speed EU, criticized by many policymakers in Brussels, appears also as a conclusion of this deep dive into the VAT fraud phenomenon. The fraud affects the EU not only by reducing the receipts in the national budgets. A spillover effect occurs as the newer members that joined the EU after 2004 are more impacted than the rest. Thus, the endemic VAT fraud increases the gap between the 'core' and the 'peripheral' members, amplifying the political dichotomy of the Union.

The reform of the VAT system proposed by the EU will tackle only partially the fraud in the best-case scenario where the reforms are rapidly and homogenously implemented. The proposal of changing VAT for intra-Community trades is a double-edged policy. On the one hand, this can reduce the size of the MTIC frauds on goods. On the other hand, this could hamper the intra-EU commerce and could lead to an increase in prices.

4 Brexit effect on the VAT fraud

VAT and 'Brexit' negotiations

We don't need all these products from Europe. Let's buy our home made things.
Stas Baretsky, Russian artist

Before assessing the various Brexit scenarios with regards to the Value Added Tax (VAT), it should be underlined that VAT fraud already has a crucial place in the Brexit negotiations. In April 2017, some rumours from the negotiation room indicated that the European Commission considered the United Kingdom as liable for recent VAT evasion cases linked to online marketplaces like Amazon and eBay. Massive cases of VAT evasion were brought to the attention of the public in 2016, concerned with Chinese VAT fraudsters using British ports and warehouses to trade their items and avoid the payment of customs duties and VAT.

The rumours from the negotiation room suggested that the Brussels *eurocrats* tried to exploit the allegations that Her Majesty's Revenue and Customs (HMRC) is failing to tackle the tax fraud related to online marketplaces. The *eurocrats* allegedly tried to include in the divorce fee a 1.7 billion pound penalty concerning HMRC's inability to deal with that issue. Representatives of the European Commission denied immediately the rumours but did not exclude the likelihood that the topic might resurge during the talks of trading relationships beyond the spring of 2019. A previous investigation of the EU's anti-fraud unit (OLAF) brought evidence that goods imported from China are being deliberately undervalued in the British ports of Dover and Felixstowe in order to avoid the payment of VAT through the Low Value Customs Relief (LVCR). OLAF alleged that Chinese exporters used Great Britain as an entry gate in the European market, where they could inflow their merchandise at very aggressive prices.[1] The investigation gave some numbers related to the clothing sector, where the imports passing through the two main British ports doubled in volume between 2013 and 2016, and the prices of certain items were on average 3.5% lower than the European average.

---

1 Brussels says it WON'T make UK settle £1.7bn fraud case as part of Brexit negotiations www.express.co.uk/news/politics/796219/Brexit-news-EU-Commission-no-link-UK-fraud-probe-exit-deal.

DOI: 10.4324/9781315098722-4

Lower-end customer prices are a common effect that appears on markets touched by systemic VAT fraud. In this case it is the LVCR that is triggered by declaiming lower price. The European Commission decided in 2017 to stop this framework, which is massively abused by the exporters in non-member countries, mainly China. But the United Kingdom will have to make its own choice after Brexit. Given the crucial role of the online marketplaces in Britain's economy, the choice to repel the LVCR might not be so easy. The potential scenario of Britain keeping the LVCR is discussed in the following.

'Soft'-Brexit scenario

A 'Soft'-Brexit is generally associated with keeping some form of access to the Single Market and remaining in the Customs Union. Under the assumptions of a 'Soft'-Brexit the geometry of trade between the two sides of the channel will globally remain unchanged. One potential avenue for the United Kingdom to take would be to join the European Economic Area (EEA) or to lock a similar deal. The EEA agreement provides for the free movement of persons, goods, services and capital within the European Single Market. The EEA agreement does not encompass the European Customs Union. Thus, countries like Norway and Switzerland, which are part of the EEA, are not members of the Customs Union.

By reaching an EEA-like agreement, Britain would conserve much of the current situation with regards to goods, services, labour and capital flow. Yet it should be underlined that the European integration is an ongoing process, especially with regards to the fight against tax evasion. Thus, a 'Soft'-Brexit will move Britain apart from this incomplete process, thereby making the investigation of MTIC fraud more complex. Even a 'Soft'-Brexit would introduce more barriers in tackling the VAT fraud, mainly due to a foreseeable lower cooperation between investigating bodies in different member states.

The perspective of a lower cooperation between Britain and Europe is a serious issue in a global context where Gulf countries have opted to introduce VAT since 2018. This new threat will be faced by the European countries with a divided effort.

A relevant example is that of Norway, an EEA member, which secured only in February 2018[2] an agreement boosting VAT cooperation with the EU. The agreement provides a legal framework for administrative cooperation in preventing VAT fraud and assisting in the recovery of VAT claims. The EU-Norway agreement leverages the same structure and the same instruments used for cooperation between the member states.

Norway's example shows that even if access to the Single Market is granted, this does not solve the problem of VAT cooperation in fighting evasion. This problem revolves around the capacity of the member to exchange information. Membership in the EU's Customs Union answers this issue to a certain extent.

2 www.consilium.europa.eu/en/press/press-releases/2018/02/06/eu-norway-agreement-signed-strengthening-the-prevention-of-vat-fraud/.

Table 4.1 Brexit scenarios and issues with the VAT fraud

Single Market/ Customs Unions	In the Customs Union	Not in the Customs Union
Access to the Single Market	'Soft'-Brexit - Issues with the convergence of efforts to fight VAT fraud	'Soft'-Brexit - VAT cooperation issues- Issues with the convergence of efforts to fight VAT fraud
No access to the Single Market	'Hard'-Brexit - Issues with the convergence of efforts to fight VAT fraud - New forms of MTEC - Resurgence of old VAT frauds - Smuggling of goods - LVCR status	'Hard & Heavy'-Brexit - VAT cooperation issues - Issues with the convergence of efforts to fight VAT fraud - New forms of MTEC - Resurgence of old VAT frauds - Smuggling of goods - LVCR status

If the United Kingdom leaves the Customs Union while having access to the Single Market, it would put both parties in a delicate spot. In terms of flow of goods from outside the EU, some new threats could occur. Fraudsters from other countries could use the United Kingdom as a point of entry for their goods and services in the United Kingdom. The goods and services would be labelled as British-made and sold afterwards in the EU. This type of scam concerns mainly the LVCR products, which make most of the non-EU imports in the United Kingdom not liable for VAT.

The United Kingdom could also leave the full Customs Union and still negotiate membership similar to non-member countries which are part of the Customs Union. Indeed, some non-EU countries are part of the Customs Union for a set of products. For example, Turkey is part of the Customs Union for industrial goods. This would be an intermediary solution, which will bring some transparency in the exchange of goods and services but not reduce many issues of VAT evasion.

Table 4.1 presents a quick snapshot of various issues in relation to VAT that could occur under different Brexit scenarios.

'Hard'-Brexit scenario

The most extreme scenario of a 'Hard & Heavy'-Brexit is associated with Britain having no access to the Single Market and no relationship with the Customs Union. In that case, Britain would be faced with some major choices that could reshape its economy and its trading relationships:

- keep or scrap the VAT,
- tax the import through customs clearance and
- enforce or repeal the LVCR.

These are a few of the many choices Britain would need to make by itself with respect to taxation. For each of these choices the global picture of VAT fraud could be massively changed.

VAT scrapping scenario

In the eventuality of a 'Hard-Brexit', the British government has at least in theory the option to dismantle the VAT system. As described in Chapter 3, VAT accounts for 10–15% of the United Kingdom's tax receipts. Thus, the VAT scrapping scenario would be ex ante less plausible.

Nevertheless, if a 'Hard & Heavy'-Brexit occurs, Britain might face unique economic challenges, especially in the case where no trading agreement is reached with the EU. Exiting from the European Single Market would also entail less access to other non-European markets secured by the 56 free trading agreements that the EU has with its partners. Thus, for keeping its financial attractiveness the United Kingdom could opt to become a tax-haven. Scrapping the VAT could be part of the measures aimed at making Britain a new offshore hub.

Under this scenario, Britain would observe a massive reduction of losses due to VAT fraud. But, similar to Dubai before the introduction of VAT, Britain would face the threat of becoming a core centre of money laundering for crime proceeds, including VAT fraud on continental Europe.

Customs clearance

If the United Kingdom keeps its VAT system, the scenario that is most likely to happen, but cuts off abruptly the relations with the EU, a new set of financial challenges would appear for British importers.

While Britain is part of the EU, British imports of goods from other member countries paid no VAT to HMRC until the goods were sold to the final customer due to the fact that they were treated as intra-Community acquisitions for VAT purposes. When importing from a country outside the EU (i.e., China), currently, firms pay the VAT up front as part of the customs clearance. After a 'Hard'-Brexit, implying the exit from the current tax framework governed by the 2006 Directive, British importers would need to pay VAT or an equivalent Goods and Services Tax (GST) when acquiring goods from the EU.

In the eventuality of a 'Hard'-Brexit, the reintroduction of a separate British customs is more than probable. Therefore, the goods imported from outside Britain's territory would need to pass the customs clearance process. This process will imply the payment of the VAT/ GST up front by the importers, when goods would reach the British ports or hubs.[3] Moreover, this process would introduce delays in the transit time of products. The resulting cost for the British firms will be transferred to the final clients, thereby entailing an inflation of prices for goods imported from the EU. Firms will need to support the burden of financing the working capital due to the upfront payment of VAT/GST. The potential consequences are numerous and would surely hamper Britain's trade deficit with the EU.

The upfront payment of VAT upon the importation of European goods might seem a small piece of the puzzle, but its final results could be more serious.

---

3 Firms face cash VAT demand on European goods after Brexit (www.thetimes.co.uk/article/firms-face-cash-vat-demand-on-european-goods-after-brexit-m5slxww29).

An increase in prices can lead to an inflation which will result in a higher cost of the governmental debt for the United Kingdom. It should be underlined that Britain has 16% of its national debt indexed to inflation, thereby making it vulnerable to the rise of prices.

With regards to VAT fraud, new types of scam will appear in order to bypass the VAT/CSG payment. Britain will secure eventually some free trade agreements with non-EU countries or with some countries of the EU or on some products. The new fraud will aim to smuggle goods through Britain's customs. The smuggling would consist in physically bypassing the goods through the British customs or in labelling them as coming from a region/country that has a free trading agreement with Great Britain.

Another aspect of the VAT system that would be stressed is the LVCR, which exempts low-value goods from payment of tax upon importation. Upon a 'Hard'-Brexit and if the LVCR is kept, importers will try to max this leeway in order to avoid the upfront payment.

This will lead to lower declared prices of imported goods and consequently would be the cradle of a new type of VAT fraud. Goods could be imported through LVCR, but VAT would never be paid to HMRC. This issue was already signalled by the British media and OLAF concerning the online marketplaces based on Chinese VAT scammers.

The VAT paid up front by British firms will also result in a reduction of the Missing Trader Intra-Community (MTIC)/Missing Trader Extra-Community (MTEC) fraud. If goods cannot flow freely across the Channel, the missing trader frauds in the form currently known will have less space for manoeuvre.

MOSS scheme and MTEC

The sale of goods through online platforms comes along with the supply of digital products and services. This aspect is currently covered by a scheme proper to the EU called Mini One-Stop-Shop (MOSS), which allows a trader to supply telecommunication services, television and radio broadcasting services, and electronically supplied services within the EU without the need to register in each member State.

The scheme is available also for businesses based outside the EU for products with values inferior to 150 euros, the company needing to register in one Member state for VAT purposes.[4] Currently, British businesses can sell digital products in other member states without registering in that country for VAT purposes, using the MOSS framework. When Britain leaves the EU all those suppliers benefitting from MOSS as member states will need to opt for MOSS as businesses based in a non-Member country. Thus they will need to apply for a VAT number in one Member state.

A potential consequence of this change of regime for British firms could be an explosion of MTEC fraud on services. British-based fraudsters could export services like Voice over Internet Protocol (VoIP) termination to companies

4 https://europa.eu/youreurope/business/vat-customs/moss-scheme/index_en.htm.

benefitting from MOSS at a price without VAT. VAT would be collected in the member country where the MOSS is registered for VAT and pocketed afterwards. If Britain opts for an equivalent MOSS scheme for European firms that would want to supply digital products to Britain, the MTEC fraud could also affect the British taxpayers.

The threat of MTEC frauds on services has been highlighted since the early 2010s (Ainsworth R., 2010). MTEC on services had already had a few major episodes in Europe (see the VoIP connection). They were nevertheless co mingled with MTIC frauds. Brexit could provide a fertile ground for a new wave of MTEC fraudsters through the MOSS scheme.

Enforcing the LVCR

In a post-Brexit situation, one of the most stringent questions that the British government would need to answer is whether the LVCR should be kept or not. As of 2018, HMRC announced that goods with an intrinsic value of 15 pounds or less are not liable for import VAT. This does not include commercial consignments sent to the United Kingdom from the Channel Islands. The gift allowance is established to 39 pounds (also not liable to VAT) for products with a noncommercial nature.[5] LVCR concerns mainly products delivered through e-commerce platforms.

In December 2017, the European Commission extended the MOSS scheme, previously available for digital services, to distance sales of goods. This amendment comes after the decision to repeal the LVCR. Thus, sellers of small-value goods from non-EU countries are liable for VAT and need to register in EU's member states as a MOSS. Moreover, the online marketplaces are also liable for VAT on distance sales of goods if the seller is not registered as a MOSS in a member country. This new rule adopted by the European Commission adds more uncertainty to LVCR's future in the United Kingdom. The British Parliament became aware of the potential issues, and its Business, Energy & Industrial Strategy Committee issued in January 2018 a note concerning the tax implication on e-commerce after Brexit, encompassing the topics of LVCR and MOSS.[6] The Committee raised in 2017 a number of concerns to the British government about the implications of the United Kingdom's leaving the EU's common VAT. In response the government indicated that it is 'unable to provide any detail of a possible UK-EU VAT arrangement that would mitigate some of the consequences of the UK leaving the common VAT area'.

The reply also mentioned that in the eventuality of 'Hard'-Brexit British retailers can access the EU market as non-EU MOSSes and that the LVCR will be dismantled following the decision of the European Commission.[7] Indeed LVCR

---

5 www.gov.uk/guidance/gift-allowance-and-low-value-consignment-relief-limit-in-2018-cip24.
6 https://publications.parliament.uk/pa/cm201719/cmselect/cmeuleg/301-xi/30116.htm.
7 *12.34: The Minister does confirm that:*
   UK businesses, if reliant only on the VAT Directive and absent a special UK-EU arrangement, could access the non-EU MOSS scheme for both services and goods from January 2021.171
   However, to access the MOSS they will need to register for VAT in an EU country; moreover,

is a European setup, so it will be repealed once Britain exits the EU. But the reply of the British government did not mention whether or not the LVCR will be replaced with similar relief after Brexit.

Given the turnover and business generated by online marketplaces in the United Kingdom, the British government would have enough of an argument to keep the LVCR after Brexit and to bring an even higher inflow of goods from non-EU sellers, which would obviously choose Britain over the EU. This option would become even more realistic if Britain's objective to secure a 'deep and special partnership with the EU, based on free and frictionless trade in goods and services',[8] would not be reached.

A dedicated campaign (http://www.vatfraud.org/) against the companies committing VAT fraud through online marketplaces advocates the suppression of LVCR in the United Kingdom. A detailed analysis[9] published by the campaigners shows the negative impact of keeping the LVCR after Brexit. The report underlines the competitive advantage that overseas retailer would have over the British retailers.[10] It also points to the fact that the postal services would became a VAT collector, responsibility for which they are not prepared.

The Public Accounts Committee of the House of Commons also published in October 2017 a report[11] regarding VAT fraud on marketplaces. Their analysis emphasized that Brexit could actually aggravate the VAT fraud from overseas sellers and LVCR. Thus, if currently it is mainly the Chinese sellers that exploit the LVCR loophole, after Brexit sellers from Continental Europe could also exploit these flows at an even bigger intensity.

VAT fraud after Brexit

Whether the Brexit will be hard or not, a major consequence would most likely be a lower cooperation with customs offices and law enforcements in the EU. The VAT fraud is currently one of the main areas where European cooperation is crucial. Europol, for instance, is the main European agency for sharing information and expertise in the fight against tax evasion. Its role was crucial in

---

to use the scheme for sales of goods into the EU, they will have to appoint an EU-based intermediary until the UK has agreed a treaty on VAT cooperation with the EU;

the Government believes that the recent EU-Norway agreement on cooperation in VAT matters "could provide a useful precedent for a similar EU-UK agreement", although "any such agreement would of course be the subject of individual negotiations"; and

UK consumers will no longer benefit from LVCR on goods coming into the UK. Conversely, UK exports to the EU would also not benefit from the VAT exemption when the UK becomes a "third country". (Source: https://publications.parliament.uk/pa/cm201719/cmselect/cmeuleg/301-xi/30116.htm).

8 https://publications.parliament.uk/pa/cm201719/cmselect/cmeuleg/301-xi/30116.htm.

9 www.vatfraud.org/blog/brexit-vat-overseas-retailers/.

10 'If the UK government don't scrap LVCR post Brexit, every European & overseas business will have a 20% price advantage right on our door step' (Source: www.vatfraud.org/blog/brexit-vat-overseas-retailers/).

11 https://publications.parliament.uk/pa/cm201719/cmselect/cmpubacc/312/312.pdf.

investigating the few major cases of MTIC operating in a few Member states that overcame the competences of the local law enforcement. Therefore, a lower level of collaboration between the British customs officers and the European law enforcements would reduce the capacity necessary for tackling VAT fraud on both sides of the channel.

This aspect will touch mainly the MTIC fraud, which is by nature a transnational crime. A Brexit involving less exchange of tax-related information across the channel would hamper the capacity of investigating the MTIC case.

Moreover, VAT fraud typologies from the pre-Common Market era would resurge in order to exploit the weaknesses of lose the domestic version of VAT. Those frauds are less damaging from an economic point of view compared to MTIC, which is a low-frequency, high-severity fraud. But it could potentially lead to an increase in the frequency of small-scale frauds, which would explore flaws in the domestic VAT system. If the United Kingdom is opting out from the Customs Union, and products and services cannot flow freely across the border anymore, smuggling of goods could come back in force.

The role of LVCR and MOSS schemes after the Brexit and the way Britain will position itself on these topics will play a major role in defining the spectrum of VAT evasion.

Also, the VAT scammers will find new fraud opportunities in the turmoil that will follow the Brexit. With Gulf countries opting for VAT since 2018, the dimensionality of VAT fraud in the United Kingdom will increase after Brexit. The Dubai Connection is a recurrent pattern in many VAT fraud cases, and with the current perspective it will require more effort to take this connection down. Law enforcements from the United Kingdom, Continental Europe and the Gulf area are far from being prepared to face this potential complexification of the VAT fraud typologies.

The post-Brexit transitional period, during which Great Britain would rely on the European legal framework or VAT purposes, would be critical in regards to VAT fraud. Criminals will most likely try to exploit the legal vacuum to accelerate the current MTIC frauds.

In the scenario in which the United Kingdom keeps the VAT system, the amount of collected VAT will most likely follow a 'J-curve' in the post-Brexit years. Under all hypotheses presented here, in the short run the losses due to VAT fraud will increase in the years after Brexit. Spillover effects could eventually occur in the European countries that will keep a high trading balance with the United Kingdom. Those countries could also observe in the short run a decrease in the collected VAT.

In the long run, the flaws in the VAT system generated by Brexit will be progressively corrected, and the gates opened to fraudsters will gradually be closed. Thus, the opportunities for VAT fraud will be reduced. Moreover, if the goods are not able to circulate freely after Brexit, then there is a good chance that the size of the MTIC will decrease in the long term.

5 VAT

A modern economic weapon

VAT fraud: a negative externality for markets

> The world is changing and there are new opportunities for those who are ready
> to join forces with those who are stronger and more experienced.
>
> Salvatore Maranzano, Boss of the New York crime syndicate in the 1920s

Value Added Tax (VAT) fraud is not anymore a byproduct of a commercial activity. It should be seen as a main activity. Therefore, a negative externality is induced to the rest of the formal economy. An externality occurs when the activity of one entity affects a third party in a way that is outside of the market mechanism. Externalities are referred to in the macroeconomic jargon as spillover effects. Negative externalities are external costs that are supported by a third party because of an economic transaction. In a transaction, the producer and consumer are the first and second parties, and third parties include any individual, organization, property owner or resource that is indirectly affected.

When a massive MTIC fraud affects a market, the supply-demand equilibrium is impacted. One of the characteristics of the MTIC and particularly of the carousel fraud is that the amount of the illicit gains does not depend on the price of the product but on the number of times the product turns in the carousel. Empirical assessment showed that in markets harbouring carousels the price of the product disconnects from its real economic value. The prices in market affected by VAT are lower than those in an efficient market. In many cases, it was observed that retailers were selling high-end products at a lower price. The explanation is that those products had previously generated fraudulent gains from VAT scams. The criminals used the retailers as the exit points of the carousel, and their intention was not to make profits but to get rid of the stocks as fast as possible.

Figure 5.1 shows how the supply-demand equilibrium is affected by the VAT fraud. The normal supply-demand conditions are characterized by an equilibrium price P_0 and a supply volume Q_0. When carousel fraud occurs the supply curve shifts to the right, and a new price/volume is reached (P^*/Q^*). This equilibrium is not stable and is temporary; the size of the negative externality is

DOI: 10.4324/9781315098722-5

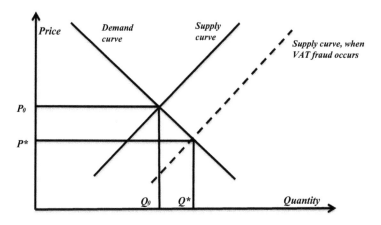

Figure 5.1 Alteration of the supply demand equilibrium in a market affected by VAT fraud.

$$E = \left(P_0 - P^*\right) \cdot \left(Q^* - Q_0\right)/2$$

The damage entailed by the MTIC fraud targets the suppliers in that market or the suppliers of similar products. If a supplier cannot fabricate a good or a service to a marginal price P_0, and he cannot switch at least temporary to a marginal cost P^*, he will face the scenario of bankruptcy.

Moreover, the low price of a product will attract the consumers of similar products, thereby affecting the markets of substitute products. One example is the car industry. Due to the lower price of German cars imported in France and sold by VAT evaders, the purchase of French cars was seriously affected. This effect was also observed on clothes, mobile phones, CO_2 emissions allowances, food products, etc.

As shown earlier negative externalities generate inefficiency in markets. VAT fraud makes no exception. Two common solutions are proposed by economists in order to bend the outcome of negative externalities and to restore efficiency:

- Private solutions based on market mechanisms. These types of solutions are based on Coase's theorem (Coase, 1974) concerning the distribution of rights to generate negative externalities.
- Public solutions based on taxation mechanisms employ the concept introduced by Pigou (1912).

The two solutions are not applicable in the case of the VAT fraud. In fact, in some countries where the VAT fraud (i.e., Hungary and Romania) generated big losses, the government opted to increase the VAT rate, which could be more or less assimilated to a Pigou tax. However, this resulted only in an increase in the intensity of the VAT fraud (Gradeva, 2014).

Three markets where the supply-demand equilibrium was affected by VAT fraud are discussed:

- CO_2 emissions allowances,
- cars and
- food markets.

Impact on the CO_2 emissions allowances

Tax fraud and securities fraud are generally distinctive issues which rarely intersect (Frunza, 2015). A case which involved a tax scam in an organized financial market was the VAT fraud on CO_2 emissions allowance markets. The fact that the fraud occurred on an organized exchange facilitates the study of the MTIC scam on the price of the allowances. The VAT fraud leveraging the CO_2 emissions allowance exchanges is explained in Figure 5.2 (Frunza, 2011)

The market infrastructure affected by the VAT fraud was the French-based exchange BlueNext.

The trading companies implied in the scheme allegedly imported large volumes of CO_2 emissions allowances VAT-free from other countries, then sold the credits on French carbon market BlueNext, having already marked up the price with the corresponding amount of VAT. The market players purchasing the permits were paid by BlueNext the price and the VAT, and did not reimburse this back to the French government.

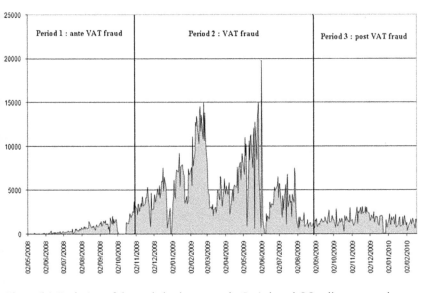

Figure 5.2 Evolution of the traded volumes on the Paris-based CO_2 allowance exchange: BlueNext.

Figure 5.2 depicts the evolutions of the traded volumes on BlueNext between 2008 and 2010, including the period of the fraud. During the summer of 2009 a number of suspected cases of fraud were detected in several European Union (EU) Member States and led different EU governments to take swift action by including greenhouse gas emission allowances in the list of supplies to which a (domestic) Reverse Charge system could be applied. Therefore, in June 2009 the governments of France, Great Britain and the Netherlands removed the VAT from carbon permits.

Given the rapid gains and the low market surveillance the VAT carousel would emphasize a bullish tendency of volumes traded on the exchange, as shown in Figure 5.2. In February 2009 the prices touched an historical low of 7 euros per tonne, which is significantly less than the minimal estimated economic price of depollution, which is around 10 euros per tonne (Figure 5.4). Moreover, the prices of the CO_2 allowances would cease to respond to fundamental driving factors.

A statistical study (Frunza, 2010) identifies the main fundamentals for CO_2 allowance prices through an Arbitrage Price Theory (APT)-like model. It appeared that Brent oil, German Dark Spread, German Spark Spread and French equity index (CAC40) explain more than 75% of the CO_2 prices behaviour between 2008 and 2010. These findings are used to demonstrate that during the VAT carousel the carbon prices ceased to respond to fundamental driving factors but recovered promptly after the VAT ban.

Structural breaks in market behaviour

The market of CO_2 emissions allowances (EUA) was mainly driven by power producers, which neutralize the carbon emission of their production on a regular basis. Hence, the carbon market is structurally linked to the power and fossils fuel markets. On the one hand, the assumption that the CO_2 permits prices are driven by a quasi-stationary supply/demand equilibrium on energy exchanges might fit well in an efficient market hypothesis (EMH) framework. On the other hand, the regulated status of the market and the heterogeneous information spread are serious reasons for EMH violations and for occurrences of correlated patterns of behaviour. It is well known that in the absence of market fundamentals, prices are driven more by behavioural biases and by psychological trading effects. In fact, the EMH breach and the behavioural effect were determined by the opportunity of high returns via the VAT fraud.

The APT model (Frunza, 2010) developed for the CO_2 emissions prices with the fundamental drivers mentioned earlier exhibits some fluctuations during the period of the VAT fraud. The explanatory power of the model decreases significantly at the end of 2008 and regains after the summer of 2009. In fact, the APT model quantifies to a certain extent the link between the EUA returns and the fundamental factors. If at a certain moment the EUA price is influenced by some new factors, the accuracy of the model diminishes. This situation occurred during the VAT carousel when prices were driven mainly by fraudsters, thereby responding less to fundamentals.

One could justify this downfall in model quality with the global, bearish tendency in commodities markets and high volatility that occurred between the end of 2008 and the beginning of 2009. The previous results underline that a trading 'epiphenomena' occurred between August 2008 and June 2009. This 'hidden trading' modified significantly the behaviour of the EUA market; its price level; and its relationship to other commodities, such as oil and energy. The epiphenomena was pushed by high trading volumes, which ceased after the VAT ban on carbon allowances.

The structural break test of Bai and Perron (Bai, 1998) shows that in the relationship between the carbon prices and the loading factor presented earlier two structural breaks occurred in August 2008 and September 2009. Figure 5.3 reflects the evolution of the empirical fluctuation process computed from the multivariate regression of the EUA returns on the fundamental drivers, as described by Zeileis (2002). These dates correspond to the period when the carbon fraud was acute on the market.

The VAT fraud on the carbon permits market that occurred between 2008 and 2009 represented a breach in the regulatory system. Beyond the VAT pocketing, the fraudulent scheme had a strong effect on market manipulation by pushing away the carbon price from its fundamental state. This situation reversed immediately after the French government banned the VAT trade. If the influence of the VAT fraud on markets volume is an undisputed finding, the impact upon

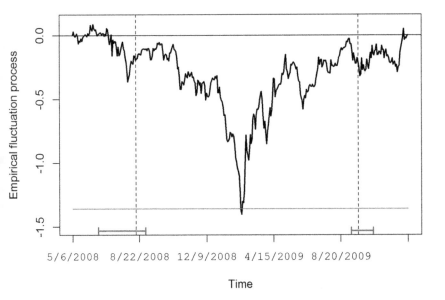

Figure 5.3 Structural breaks in the relationship of EUA prices to its fundamental drivers. The evolution of the empirical fluctuation process is computed from the multivariate regression of the EUA returns on the fundamental drivers, as described by Zeileis (2002). The lower the empirical fluctuation process, the higher the likelihood of a structural break.

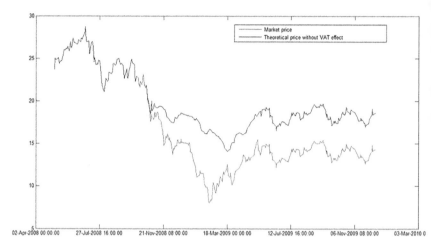

Figure 5.4 Observed prices on the spot market and theoretical prices. Due to excessive VAT-related transactions the price of the EUA did not reflect anymore the supply-demand equilibrium for an emission permit. Instead the market quoted an instrument generating a 19.6% return. Thus, the prices were significantly driven away from their fundamental value.

the market prices is still argued by regulators and exchanges. Obviously when an exchange clears massively both physical and cash flow trades based upon a rogue strategy, the market price tends to be very different from the fundamental level. Thus, the exchange does not quote anymore an underlying representing the marginal depollution cost but most likely the price of fraud instrument.

Based on previous research that assessed the link between the carbon prices and their drivers (power, oil, gas and equity) the influence of the VAT fraud on the carbon price is assessed. Assuming that the EUA price would follow the energy-equity complex, the theoretical price from the end of October 2008 to 2009 is simulated in Figure 5.4. It can be observed that the theoretic price is significantly higher than the market price, and the spread widens with the increase in fraud volumes. The difference between the modelled and observed prices remains around a level of 2–3 euros, even after June 2009, when the volumes decreased, and BlueNext banned the VAT.

The invisible dividend

The fact that the market price fell below the fundamental level is explained by the change in the intrinsic nature of the underlying exchanged on the market. EUA were in theory an emissions reduction instrument and became in practice a systematic fraud vehicle. Obviously, the amount of VAT pocketed by the rogue traders is independent of the EUA price and is only a function of the number of tours in the carousel, as shown previously. Thus, the VAT-pocketed amount is similar to an 'invisible dividend' provided by the EUA to its owner. In the same way, when a stock liberates a dividend, its value diminishes; in the case of the carbon the EUA diminishes in price as the VAT is extorted through the organized exchange or through the over-the-counter (OTC) mechanism. The VAT fraud might move the market into a low-price clustered region, away from the fundamental level, as given by the APT model calibrated previously, with 2–3 euros of spread. This finding could be interpreted suspiciously as the market price represents the equilibrium of offering and demand, thereby implying a comeback of the carbon prices at the equilibrium level before the fraud period.

Thus, the spread implied by the model should fall towards zero after the VAT was banned from the organized exchanges. This outcome is explained by the fact that EUA prices became highly uncertain after 2009 and dependent on the views of post-2012 future. The CO_2 emissions market was designed to create an increasing shortage in EUA compared to the free allocations for each phase, thereby driving the prices to around 30 euros per tonne. With the double-dip economic recession and the industrial slowdown the emission diminished by more than 10% in 2009, and thus the European depollution scheme (EU-ETS) became oversupplied with EUAs, putting pressure on the EUA price. Due to the portability of the EUA beyond 2012, the market began to price the expected deficit for post-2012, thereby making the very nature of the market incomplete. Without developing these particularities, it appears that an incomplete market can have theoretically few levels of equilibrium (Peter, 2001), the market more likely establishing an acceptance price. Under these conditions, a shock in the supply/demand equilibrium could alter irreversibly the market price by pushing it to a different level. Therefore, the spread between the theoretic and the observed price remained persistent, even after the end of the VAT fraud on the spot exchange (Frunza, 2013).

Impact on the car production in France

VAT fraud leveraging the imports of cars from Germany to France has been reported since the 2000s. Nevertheless, this fraud reached critical levels in 2014,[1] when the French Ministry of Finances pointed out that the VAT fraud affects the French car manufacturers and car dealers. The German cars brought in France by tax evaders were sold for a lower price than domestic cars.

The French National Federation of Automobile Workers solicited the French government to pass some quick measures that would introduce stricter controls on VAT declarations concerning imported cars. The Committee of French Automobile Manufacturers estimated that in 2012 the size of the market touched by VAT fraud was around 1.1 billion euros; the fraud rates represented between 20% and 40%, which would entail a loss for the French treasury of 45–90 million euros. But the estimates of the French National Federation of

---

1 www.euractiv.com/section/euro-finance/news/france-moves-to-block-fraudulent-german-car-sales/.

Automobile Workers (FNAA) were quite pessimistic as they accounted for the opportunity costs of the French car industry that lost market share in favour of German cars. In fact, second-hand luxury German cars, sold without VAT in France, were more attractive than medium-range French cars. Thus, the French second-hand market was flooded with German cars at good prices.

FNAA estimated that the German cars sold without VAT in France inflicted a loss of 5 billion euros to the French car industry per year, while the taxpayers lost 1 billion euros in uncollected VAT for a total of 160,000 vehicles sold in the French market. Figure 5.5 shows the evolution of the number of cars produced in France and Germany between 2002 and 2016. The analysis underlines the negative trend in production of French manufacturers, while the German industry observed an increase over the past two decades. The plummeting in the French production is more pronounced after 2009, when the VAT fraud cases were increasingly reported.

As presented in Chapter 2, the VAT fraud on cars is managed by organized groups that moved cars from Germany to other countries in Europe and sold them there at a lower price.

Moreover, German car dealers and rental companies can avoid legally the VAT payment on vehicles, and they can resell them to the French market, VAT-free, once the cars are six months old and have on board over 6,000 kilometres. This scheme circumvents the payment of VAT towards the French government, while Germany profits from exporting cars.

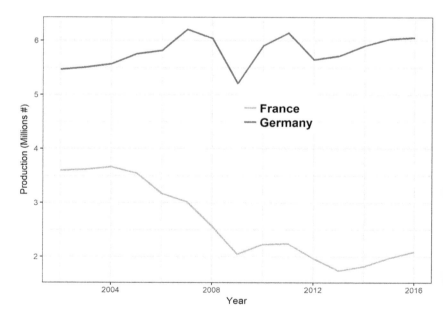

Figure 5.5 Evolution of the number of cars produced in France and Germany between 2002 and 2016.

Source: www.oica.net.

Competitive distortion of the food markets

The agricultural sector in Europe is highly subsidized and regulated by the European Commission. But this does not avoid entirely the potential distortion in completion and efficiency. In 2016[2] the French representative of the pork industry filed a complaint to the European Commission, accusing German farmers of a 250 million euro VAT fraud.

French farmers accused their German peers of a large-scale VAT fraud on pork meat, aiming to distort the competition amongst producers and shut down the French producers.

As in the car industry the number of French pork farms collapsed from 3,500 in 2005 to 2,700 in 2015. Over the same period, Germany's overall production grew by 20% and 40% in the two regions from the eastern part: North Rhine-Westphalia and lower Saxony, respectively.

The French pork producers suspected Germany of deliberately practising large-scale tax avoidance by allowing farmers to use a flat-rate VAT scheme where they pay per animal. In France the flat VAT rate is available for sole traders with a turnover below 76 thousand euros but cannot really be used because French farmers are organized in companies with larger revenues. Therefore, the pork producers have an obvious disadvantage in France, compared to its German counterpart. German producers gain around 0.013 euro per kilogram of meat, which would be the equivalent of 15 euros for one animal weighing 200 kg.

Moreover, the French producers accused the German ones of being organized around VAT collectors, encouraged by local chambers of commerce in the regions concerned, which were helping the producers to avoid VAT payments.

Another similar complaint was signalled in Hungary in 2012.[3] United States commodities firm Bunge Ltd. estimated that tax fraud linked to food products is worth up to 1 billion euros. Beyond the loss for the Hungarian taxpayers, the massive VAT fraud affected the completion of the domestic food markets. The price of products, including meat, grains and cheese, plummeted in certain retail stores. That left the legitimate business with huge stocks of foods that could not be sold because the prices were much higher than those of their rogue competitors.

2 www.euractiv.com/section/euro-finance/news/french-pork-farmers-accuse-germany-of-vat-fraud/.
3 www.reuters.com/article/us-hungary-vat-fraud/exclusive-hungary-losing-1-billion-euros-a-year-from-food-vat-fraud-idUSBRE85614B20120607.

6 How the VAT fraud proceeds are laundered

Why pocketed funds cannot be recovered

> If you follow only the money flows, that might not be enough.
>
> Davide T., Italian police officer

Value Added Tax (VAT) fraud touches most countries that adopted indirect taxation. The most disruptive form, the carousel, developed mainly in the European Union (EU), entails huge losses to the national treasuries. The estimates fluctuate between 50 and 70 billion euros per year. The main problem with the VAT fraud is that the recovery rate of the illegal proceeds is very small. In many cases, law enforcement manages to seize the assets or bank accounts of the gang leaders, but it represents only a fraction of the evaded tax.

The United Kingdom has an incentive system for criminals to return the stolen funds, offering reduced sentences in jail. With massive tax losses occurring in fraud episodes like the *Carbon Connection*, the British courts gave double-digit imprisonment time to incentivize the criminal to consider seriously the refunds. Prior to that, tax evaders would prefer to execute a sentence up to five years and profit afterwards off their illegal gains. It was the case with the French-Israeli group from the *Carbon Connection* (i.e., Zaoui, Sakoun and Astruc), who spent as many as two years in prison but managed to enjoy the tens of millions they pocketed.

There are four main structural reasons the recoveries are low in the VAT fraud cases.

First, the timegap between the moment when the fraud is committed and the moment when the investigation is completed and prosecuted is big. Some cases appear in courts ten years after the fact occurred. Even a one-year timegap is sufficient for a gang to move the money through a few accounts in a few jurisdictions until their track is lost. Therefore, given the way the VAT fraud is addressed today by law enforcements, it is structurally almost impossible to have a good recovery rate.

Second, the capacity of justice to seize assets or accounts is very limited, even when the funds remain in the country where the crime took place. The task becomes more complex when assets are overseas. Even within the EU seizing assets in another country is not a straightforward process and faces many bureaucratic procedures. The creation of Eurofisc facilitates somehow the cross-border assets

DOI: 10.4324/9781315098722-6

freezing and seizing. But when the assets are in offshore locations like the Caribbean islands, Dubai, China or the Russian Federation, recovery is rarely possible.

Third, the lifestyle and spending habits of VAT evaders increase rampantly once they get the funds. The VAT scammers spend a huge amount of money on luxury or high-end products or services. This change in behaviour comes from the fear that one day their money might be seized by law enforcements. By the time the court has seized their assets, part of the funds have been spent, and the products seized can be resold only for a small percentage of their initial value. Therefore, even losses from small-scale VAT frauds cannot be fully recovered.

Last, but not the least, money laundering underwent a paradigm shift, thereby making the traditional asset tracking methods less relevant. VAT fraudsters are not concerned with placing the unpaid tax into the legal system. The pocketed funds come from the legal system. Their goal is to move the funds or assets with equivalent value as far as possible from the reach of the legal system. Money laundering as a process changed structurally over the past decade. Globalization, digital currencies and change in crime trends are only a few factors that drive this change. Modern money laundering aims to cut any links between the proceeds of crime and the criminal groups, while keeping the right of criminals to control their funds.

This could take two avenues. One way is in the legal system and would involve a myriad of companies in various jurisdictions. The other approach involves extracting the funds or the associated value from the reach of the legal system. This would imply converting the funds into physical cash or high-value commodities, or moving them into digital currencies.

Money rinsing: 'Cash is (still) king'

Traditionally money laundering refers to the placement of illegal funds, mainly physical currencies, aka cash, into the banking system. This view of money laundering comes from a reality of the 1980s, when crime was mainly blue collar, and the profits were taken in cash, which need to be introduced into the legal system, aka banks. This view is certainly outdated because economic crime became prevalent, and the illegal gains come as electronic funds. Thus, the placement in the legal system has not the same connotation that it had in the 1980s. As mentioned earlier criminals aim to move their crime profit away from the reach of the law. Physical cash is one traditional avenue that came back under scrutiny in past years. With the improvement of software for transactions monitoring in the banking system, keeping the funds in the banking system has become a very risky bet for tax evaders.

'Dirty money' is not so bad

One of the investigations in the *Carbon Connection* pointed out that the French scammers sent funds to Hong Kong in a local bank. The French group went to Hong Kong to meet the bank's managers. The Hong Kong bank transferred the funds to a bank in China. After a trip in the region the criminals came back with the proceeds in cash. For example Morgan Erulin, Stéphane Villeneuve and Mickaël Kolkowicz, controlling the Power Trade company involved in the VAT fraud with CO_2 emissions, made a few trips to Hong Kong, Shenzen and Wenzhou to get the funds in cash.[1] Another way to repatriate the VAT fraud proceeds in Europe was through the Chinese communities implanted in various sectors of the economy. This is just an example showing that criminals prefer 'dirty cash' in their hand to funds in some forlorn offshore bank.

A report of Europol indicates that in the EU, the use of cash is the main trigger of suspicious transaction reports within the financial system, accounting for more than 30% of all reports.[2] Reports on detection of suspicious physical cash movements represent around one-third of all contributions to Europol in the area of money laundering. The 500 note alone accounts for over 30% of the value of all banknotes in circulation. This raises questions about the purpose for which they are being used and whether this could be linked to criminal activity, which should be further explored.

The 'war on cash'

The term 'war on cash' was introduced in the media[3] to label the offensive of companies like Visa and Mastercard, and of certain governments to eliminate cash completely from economic transactions. The aim of these measures would be to tackle tax evaders, terrorists and organized crime. A cashless society would lead to a system 'in which all financial wealth is electronic and represented digitally in the records of a small number of megabanks and asset managers'.[4]

Pros and cons of the war on cash are mainly presented from an economic perspective. The effect on financial crime and tax evasion is not taken into account in the debate. A counter-intuitive effect of the war on cash might be that it will not hamper money launderers as much as policymakers think. Cash is just a value-carrying vehicle issued by a government. If this vehicle disappears, it is not clear whether it will be replaced by other equivalent vehicles. One could imagine that a crime group will issue its own physical currency, competing with the official digital currencies. Also, the recent development of cryptocurrencies shows that it is much easier today to create a digital currency, and the number of such vehicles is hardly controllable. Therefore, a cashless society might not deter as many tax evaders and money launderers as is thought and might in the long term have uncertain effects.

Alternative banking platforms (Fintechs)

The banking system has increased its level of scrutiny of suspicious transactions, and laundering funds through the regulated financial system is become more complicated, more expensive and more risky. Therefore, tax evaders opted for

1 www.challenges.fr/economie/la-chute-d-un-petit-prince-de-la-fraude-au-co2_19482.
2 www.europol.europa.eu/newsroom/news/cash-still-king-criminals-prefer-cash-for-money-laundering.
3 http://uk.businessinsider.com/the-global-war-on-cash-2017-1?r=US&IR=T.
4 www.zerohedge.com/news/2017-08-16/why-elites-are-winning-war-cash.

using or developing alternative methods that provide the same service as the banking sector without facing the regulatory burdens. These alternative banking solutions are part of the 'Fintech revolution' and provide with global funds transfers solutions which are not submitted to Anti-Money Laundering regulation in the same way banks are. VAT fraudsters used various solutions, including electronic exchanges and alternative banking platforms (ABPs). An ABP is a virtual bank account that operates outside of the regulated global financial sector. The owner of such an account can receive and send funds in other countries to other virtual bank accounts.

Swefin

A first example of such an infrastructure is the Danish internet bank Swefin, which has played a key role in the extensive scam of CO_2 quotas. The bank operated through the website swefin-online.se.[5] The bank's directors were Kashif Ghaus Qadri and Anders Garbro, both Swedish citizens. Qadri moved to Dubai when the scam was exposed by the Danish media. Behind the online bank were two Swedish registered companies: Swefin AB and Skancom Finans AB. Kaschif Qadri owned several accounts in the Danish CO_2 quota registry with the company KUGA DATA SmbA. The Danish register was one of the points of intersection for *Carbon Connection* VAT fraudsters from all over the world.

The company behind Swefin-online has an official address in an apartment in Stockholm, but on the website the online bank indicated an address in Helsingborg. Swefin-online stated on the website to use a bank account in Forstædernes, a reputed Danish bank which was acquired in 2010 by Nykredit bank. Swefin-online was part of a whole network of shadow banks operated by a small number of people. Anders Garbro, chairman of the board of Swefin AB, was registered as director of Interfin Trust & Finance Ltd. in New Zealand. Interfin Trust & Finance Ltd. also served as payment platform. Anders Garbro was registered as director, replacing the Spanish citizen Joaquim de Almeida. Almeida was also the director of another shadow bank from New Zealand, 'Technologies Savings & Loans', which had also largely been used for laundering proceeds of the *Carbon Connection*. The persons involved in Swefin AB were indicted in 2016 by an operation of the Europol called *Vertigo*.[6]

BlueNext

Another example of 'shadow banking' is the electronic exchanges. Electronic exchanges where virtual process can be traded are ideal infrastructure for transferring value. BlueNext was one of the targets of VAT fraudsters in the *Carbon Connection*. The Paris-based platform served for two goals of the VAT criminals:

5 https://ekstrabladet.dk/nyheder/samfund/article4127967.ece.
6 https://nbjour.wordpress.com/2016/02/01/dr-interactive-graphics-see-how-danish-company-did-money-laundering-for-billions-of-dkk-the-billions-stemmed-from-vat-fraud/.

- First, it facilitated the tax evasion due to the fact that VAT was paid on each transaction.
- Second, it helped with money laundering. The transfer of funds between accounts was in fact a transfer of CO_2 quotas, which served as a virtual currency.

The rogue transactions represented more than 80% on the BlueNext spot market. Moreover the spot volumes were comparable to the futures market volumes. Between October 2008 and October 2009 the spot trades accounted for more than 30% of the futures volumes. Usually the spot volumes represent only a small share of the futures trades due to the use of leverage for the latter instrument. The ratio peaked in February–March 2009, when spot trades represented 70% of the futures volumes. This finding not only underlines a disequilibrium between the spot and the derivative market but also emphasizes a massive influx of liquidity on the spot market, given the fact that spot trades cannot use leverage as derivatives do and require the use of liquidity. The preference for the use of liquidities for financial market trades is uncommon in the modern markets, both financial institutions and industrial corporations preferring derivatives (i.e., futures) as they are less cash intensive. The overwhelming preference for cash trades is even more illogical in conditions such as when the credit market was blocked in 2009, after the default of Lehman Brothers and the subsequent financial crisis.

The origin of this huge turnover on BlueNext is explained not only by the VAT fraud but also by the transactions that abused the exchange in order to launder funds (Frunza, 2013). It should be underlined that at the time of the fraud the KYC on BlueNext was very light, thereby allowing many scammers to register as brokers on the exchange.

Nexor One

Another ABP case involved a Swedish citizen, Carl Michael Magnusson,[7] and a Dutch citizen, Remy Swaab. They were arrested for controlling a set of offshore New Zealand finance companies and an online banking platform apparently based in New Zealand but run from Panama. Allegedly, their scheme helped launder more than 100 million dollars.

Magnusson controlled Zealand Financial Group and online banking platform Nexor One, both unregulated financial service providers. He operated the transactions through websites with New Zealand IP addresses, including banking4bankers.com, banclear.com, eurowire.com, startabank.net, swedishtrust.eu, serviceproviders.co.nz and michaelmagnusson.com. New Zealand had a framework where a financial services provider (FSP) could be registered with the New Zealand Companies Office. The FSP could in fact be accounts of alternative banking which would not be entering under the scrutiny of any regulator.

---

7 www.panama-guide.com/article.php/20120802095530830.

The Nexor One website presented the company as based in Auckland and as a 'respected offshore jurisdiction that complies with all payment card industries Compliance Secure Banking Standards'. It claimed also to have hundreds of thousands of customers in 20 countries and in 12 different languages. Nexor One was integrated with Eurowire Finance Ltd., another company registered by Magnusson in New Zealand in 2008, where Swaab was chief information officer. Magnusson charged between 55 and 65,000 USD to set up and manage an FSP with a virtual office and appear to feed into two specific dispute resolution offices that are required as part of setting up an FSP.

At the other end of the laundering chain, for individuals wanting to open accounts from onshore locations Magnusson established the 'Swedish credit unions', a network of global investment vehicles which appeared in places like the United States and Malaysia. The British prosecutors indicated that VAT fraud was laundered with the help of Nexor One.

John Deuss[8]

John Deuss was a controversial multimillionaire oil trader and banker[9] arrested by Dutch police in connection with illegal activities at his First Curaçao International Bank Britain that involved helping criminals to launder funds from carousel fraud scams.

He has been involved in many controversial business deals over time. In the early 1990s it was reported that through his company Transworld Oil, Deuss had been running oil to South Africa in violation of international sanctions against the apartheid regime. He refused to pay 100 million dollars he owed to the Soviet government for oil he was exporting out of Russia. In 2006 all 2,500 companies suspected of running carousel fraud in the United Kingdom opened accounts with First Curaçao. The offshore bank allegedly offered complete anonymity and lightning-fast transfers, allowing fraudsters to create instantaneous false paper trails of trades in goods.

Tax-havens are dead. Long live the no (tax)man's land

The joint efforts of national criminal police organizations, regulatory bodies and tax authorities focussed over the past decades on the so-called tax-havens. The term 'tax-haven' has still a very ambiguous meaning that is associated with several aspects, including:

* preferential tax regimes,
* opacity of the financial system and
* ties with financial crime and money laundering.

---

8 www.theguardian.com/money/2006/oct/23/crime.scamsandfraud.
9 www.dutchcaribbeanlegalportal.com/news/latest-news/360-caribbean-bank-to-yield-p200m-after-unpaid-vat-fraud-probe.

In December 2017, the Council of the EU adopted a detailed list of 17 so-called non-cooperative tax jurisdictions failing to meet agreed-upon tax good govern ance standards.[10] The countries[11] in the following list are those that refused to engage with the EU or to address tax good governance shortcomings (situation on 23 January 2018):

- American Samoa,
- Bahrain,
- Guam,
- Marshall Islands,
- Namibia,
- Palau,
- Saint Lucia,
- Samoa and
- Trinidad and Tobago.

The assessment of the Council of the EU is based upon several hypotheses that restrict the scope:

1   For a given geographical region the banking and taxation systems are cen- tralized and depend on a given jurisdiction.
2   All geographical regions on the globe are covered by a national jurisdiction.
3   The government of a country has the same degree of administrative control over its full territory.
4   The transparency in terms of taxation is applied uniformly over the entire territory of a country.

If at least one of these hypotheses is not respected, the exhaustivity and the ex- actitude of the list published by the Council of the EU are challenged.

The reshape of the geopolitical equilibrium after the fall of the Berlin Wall left many regions disputed by two or more countries. Also there are territories aim- ing at independence or autonomy. Those territories are, in many cases, subject to military conflict or military occupation. A *de jure* region is part of a country, but the de facto authority of that country does not have any control over that region. Thus, taxes cannot be collected, and tax offices cannot control the economic activities in those regions. Nevertheless, these types of territories are far from being dried of economic and financial activities. But the companies registered in those countries are de facto not subjected to any control or tax liability. From a tax perspective they are 'No man's lands' or 'Terra nullius'. These regions are harbours praised by tax evaders and economic criminals, which use them to avoid governmental controls and the surveillance of law enforcement. Table 6.1 synthesizes a list of regions fitting this description.

---

10 The EU list of non-cooperative jurisdictions for tax purposes www.consilium.europa.eu/media/ 31945/st15429en17.pdf.
11 https://ec.europa.eu/taxation_customs/tax-common-eu-list_en.

Table 6.1 List of territories categorized as 'No man's land' from a tax perspective

Territory	Observation
Novorossiya, Donetsk People's Republic	The eastern part of Ukraine, including the cities of Donetsk and Lugansk, is, since 2014, not under the control of the Ukrainian government. It was Ukraine's main industrial region.
Transnistria (aka Perednistrovia)	The eastern part of the Republic of Moldova has been occupied by secessionist groups and the 14th Russian army since 1991 and is not controlled by the Moldavian government. There are more companies registered in Transnistria than in Moldova.
Autonomous Republic of Crimea	Crimea was occupied by Russia in 2014 and is now an Autonomous Republic in the Russian Federation. It benefits from massive investment from the Russian government. It is also a tax-free region.
Srpska Republic	Srpska is a separatist region from Bosnia Herzegovina. It is a region with mainly Serbian ethnics.
South Tajikistan/North Afghanistan	After the civil war that took place in Tajikistan after the fall of the Soviet Union, the region bordering Afghanistan has not really been controlled by Dushanbe, despite not being a separatist region. The territory rich in precious stones and rare metals is controlled by crime lords involved in drug trafficking and terrorism.
Nagorno-Karabakh[1]	Known also as Republic of Artsakh, Nagorno-Karabakh is a region disputed by Azerbaijan and Armenia. Money laundering is supposed to take place through banks incorporated in Karabakh.
Abkhazia	After the Abkhazian war in 1992, the resulting Autonomous Republic is not anymore under Georgian Control but under Russian protections.
South Ossetia	After the 2008 unrest, Georgia lost control over South Ossetia, which entered under Russian 'protectorate'.
Uzbek enclaves on south Kirgizstan	After the 2010 revolution, an ethnic war started in Southern Kirgizstan between Uzbeks and Kirgiz. The numerous enclaves are not controlled by any government.
Kosovo	The southern part of Serbia proclaimed its independence after a violent war in 1999. Despite strong international support Kosovo is controlled in many areas by organized criminal groups.
Syria/Iraq	The rise of Islamic State of Iraq and Syria (ISIS) in 2012 and the Syrian Civil War resulted in big regions in Syria and Iraq not being controlled by any government and being split between various military and terrorist factions.
Northern Cyprus	After the Turkish invasion of Norther Cyprus the region is not recognized internationally. Many fugitives of Turkish or Greek descent hide there from justice.
Jammu and Kashmir	The only state in India with a Muslim majority is disputed between, India, Pakistan and China.
South Mali	Southern region of Mali has been controlled by terrorist organizations since 2014.

(Continued)

Territory	Observation
Libya	After the Arab Spring, Libya is not controlled by its government but by few local warlords.
Western Sahara	A country aiming at independence from Morocco is not yet fully recognized at the international level.
Triple Frontier (Argentina, Paraguay, Brazil)	Placed in a hardly accessible landscape, the region is de facto controlled by drug lords and organized crime.
Amazonian Jungle[2]	Placed in a hardly accessible Amazonian jungle, the region rich in gold is controlled by gangs illegally extracting precious metals and trafficking drugs.

1 https://en.trend.az/scaucasus/armenia/2487379.html.
2 www.theguardian.com/global-development/2016/aug/16/illegal-mines-local-mafia-take-shine-off-latin-american-gold-peru.

7 Perspectives upon the VAT fraud in the Eurasian Economic Union

A Union leveraging the European model...

> The roof protects everybody, but there are many things happening above the roof.
>
> Leonid Mackintosh Bilunov, Russian crime figure

The fall of the Soviet Union represented a real global earthquake from a geopolitical point of view, especially for the countries of the ex-Eastern bloc. Some of the ex-'satellite' countries, like the Czech Republic, Hungary and Slovakia, had real success stories with their integration into the European Union (EU). Moreover, the Baltic ex-Soviet countries (Estonia, Latvia and Lithuania) are now at the core of the European project, and the Soviet era is seemingly just a shady memory.

But for the other countries, including Ukraine, Moldova, Kazakhstan and Byelorussia, the situation was more complicated as their economies were highly integrated with the Russian economy. Thus, the memory of the Tetragrammaton 'CCCP' aka 'USSR' is still alive, and decision makers in the regions are tempted to use this sham dream in order to reinforce their position. The president of the Russian Federation has stated on numerous occasions that the fall of the Soviet Union[1] was the biggest catastrophe of the past century, and he would do anything to reverse time back to the Soviet era, if possible. If the time machine is not yet in production, the reconstruction of an Eurasian Economic Union (EAEU) based on a Single Market and a Customs Union was realized in 2015.

The Eurasian Economic Union (EAEU) began existence on January 2015, based upon the Russia-Belarus-Kazakhstan Customs Union, which had already been established in 2010. Armenia joined the EAEU on January 2015, while Kyrgyzstan did the same during August 2015. The total Gross Domestic Product (GDP) of the Eurasian Union accounts for 1.28 trillion euros (2016

---

1 www.reuters.com/article/us-russia-election-putin/putin-before-vote-says-hed-reverse-soviet-collapse-if-he-could-agencies-idUSKCN1GE2TF.

DOI: 10.4324/9781315098722-7

estimate), thereby representing 8.7% of the EU's GDP. Vietnam, Iran, Egypt and Serbia have already signed Free Trade Agreements with the EAEU which are or will be ongoing. Ukraine, Moldova and Uzbekistan have had the status of observers since 2011.

The tariffs of the Eurasian Customs Union, the quotas, the technical regulations, the licensing and the certification are reviewed and approved by the Eurasian Economic Commission (EEC), which is a supervising body established by the members of the EAEU, similar in many aspects to the European Commission. The Eurasian Customs Union functions in a similar way with its European peers. No customs taxes are charged on goods delivered within the Customs Union. When exporting goods within the Union, a zero-rated, Value Added Tax (VAT) is applied, similar to the VAT Directive in the EU.

EAEU is the result of two visions. On the one hand, it was the vision of the Russian Federation to revive the Soviet Union, and on the other hand, it was the vision of the Kazakh government to revive the Eurasian project fathered by Genghis Khan. Consequently, the EAEU faces numerous challenges due to the heterogeneity of its Members' objectives. One of these challenges is the tax policies of intra-EAEU trades of goods and services. With respect to VAT, the EAEU adopted similar functioning processes to the EU, all intra-Union trades not being submitted to VAT. The countries of the ex-USSR experienced low tax collection rates and big tax gaps during the 1990s. This trend was curbed during the 2000s, but the national government still has a long way to go to improve the tax collection, especially the VAT. VAT rates in the Member states of the EAEU are as follows:

- 18% in Russia,
- 20% in Belarus,
- 12% in Kazakhstan,
- 17% in Armenia and
- 12% in Kyrgyzstan.

...with significant progresses towards a Digital VAT...

The leaders of the Eurasian Union were aware of the issues concerning tax evasion in their countries and of the fact that the EAEU can only amplify the tax fraud. Therefore, the Member states accelerated the implementation of an online platform for tax statements and payments. This platform is part of a bigger project of digital transformation of the Eurasian Union.[2] Moreover, companies trading products within the Eurasian Customs Union are required to fill out through dedicated digital platform information concerning the type

---

2 Digital transformation of the EAEU is the success of specific projects (www.eurasian
commission.org/en/nae/news/Pages/6-02-2018-3.aspx).

of product, the invoice, the deliveries and the tax identifier of the counterparts. The aim of this platform is to control the circulation of products in the Union and to deter any potential Missing Trader Intra-Community (MTIC)-like fraud. It serves also as a way to assess whether the VAT refund claims are accurate or not. The framework is similar to the concept of Digital-VAT described in Chapter 13.

The experience of the EU concerning Missing Trader Extra-Community (MTEC) fraud on services and digital products was also leveraged. From July 2016, the foreign companies and intermediaries providing electronically supplied services are required to register for VAT in the Russian Federation. The online marketplaces are obviously targeted by this law, similar in nature to European directives concerning the Mini One-Stop-Shop (MOSS).

...but far from a fully integrated framework

The consistent VAT reimbursement policy in the Member States of the EU confers financial stability for domestic exporters of goods and providers of services. In the absence of a reliable VAT reimbursement process, European exporters would face massive working capital issues that would affect the price of their products and their competitiveness. This policy is abused massively by the MTIC fraudsters through the mechanism exposed in the Chapter 1.

The core members of the EAEU, Russian Federation and Kazakhstan opted to avoid the risk of any systemic VAT fraud, as in the EU. Thus, Treasury offices of EAEU Member States have a very selective VAT reimbursement policy. Exporters of goods and services from the EAEU undergo a long process before benefitting from any tax credit reimbursement. In practice, companies exporting to other countries of the EAEU do not count on the VAT refund. Therefore, they mitigate this by adding the amount of VAT to their commercial margin when exporting a product or a service. This affects massively the fluidity of the trading goods within the EAEU. In many cases in an EAEU Member state, it is cheaper to import products from outside the EAEU than to buy them from a producer based in another Member state. The policy of restrictive VAT refunding in the Member states of the EAEU might tackle partially the risk of systemic VAT fraud but at the same time hampers the integration of the Union.

VAT fraud in the EAEU

Mechanisms

The particular features of the way the VAT refunding works in the Member states of the EAEU shape the mechanisms of the VAT frauds that adapted over time to that reality. Exporters based in the EAEU face randomness in the reimbursement process, while importers need to pay the VAT up front when the goods pass customs.

With VAT being required up front from importers, the main avenue for defrauding VAT is through fake VAT refunds claims.[3] As mentioned earlier, getting VAT refunds is not a simple process in the Russian Federation or in the other countries of the EAEU. Therefore, the VAT fraud cases mostly involve influential people and officials from the tax offices. The VAT frauds are frequently linked with the corruption of governmental officials, who 'grease' the mechanism of VAT refunds for 'friendly' companies involved in VAT scams. An indirect result of this framework is that, in general, the pocketed funds are very big and often reach tens or even hundreds of millions of euros.

The basic VAT fraud mechanism in the EAEU involves a company that claims rogue exports to another country of the Union and claims a refund. The goods are in reality not exported but sold domestically on the black market.

Since the introduction of the digital VAT platforms in the EAEU, fraudsters changed this modus operandi. The exporter delivers in reality some products but those products do not correspond to what was indicated on the invoice. For example, a company could buy new smartphones with VAT, export them to another country with no VAT and deliver in reality some old cheap mobile phones.

Another VAT fraud mechanism is based upon the misclassification of goods. In the Russian Federation, fraudsters explore the difference in VAT rates for various types of products. For example, in the Russian Federation some goods, like pharmaceuticals, children's products and some food products, are subject to 10% VAT, while some categories, including medical goods and equipment, may be VAT exempted. For example, a company could buy herbal tea with 18% of VAT and resell it as a medicine with 10%. The company would claim reimbursement on the 8% difference.

Examples

The EAEU was enacted recently; therefore proper cases of VAT fraud within the Eurasian Customs Union are scarcely documented. Nevertheless, many VAT frauds were signalled and investigated prior to 2015 in the Russian Federation. The VAT fraud in the Russian Federation kicked off immediately after its introduction in 1992.[4] If during the roaring 1990s the question of the VAT fraud was not a priority for Russian law enforcements, since the 2000s the interest has increased massively, especially after the 2009 crisis. Russia is a federation of various regions and autonomous republics. The VAT collection and reimbursement is dealt with at a regional level. Therefore, a centralized view and control over the enormous territory of the Russian Federation was almost impossible, and VAT fraud flourished not only in Moscow but also in the Far East.

---

3 www.forbes.ru/kompanii/343999-nds-v-zakone-pochemu-eto-samyy-lyubimyy-nalog-rossiyskih-prestupnikov.
4 www.audit-it.ru/news/account/208726.html.

For instance, in February 2010, three officials of the Federal Tax Service (FTS) were indicted in Tuva (a region situated near the Mongolian border) in connection with the attempt to obtain a large bribe for facilitating a VAT refund. The Tuvan officials asked for 6 million roubles (100 thousand euros) in order to help a company with an illegal refund of 350 million roubles (6 million euros). This example fits the mechanism described earlier wherein the VAT fraud is paired with bribery of tax officials.

Another relevant example was investigated in 2010 by a Moscow court in relation to a 230 million rouble (4 million euro) VAT fraud. The scam was organized by T. Stoyakov, a citizen of North Ossetia, who started his scam in 2005. At that time Stoyakov was employed by a legitimate firm, Voyage Ltd., which traded alcoholic beverages. Stoyakov organized fake deliveries and payments between participants in the fictitious transactions. Through this scheme he managed to pocket 15.6 million roubles (250,000 euros). In 2006, he joined an organized VAT fraud group and specialized in the misclassification of goods. The new scheme of fraud involved 40 shell firms and was organized around the company Balcom LLC, registered in a city near Moscow, allegedly producing sour-milk drinks. Obviously, there was no production, but criminals claimed they had the technology to manufacture this product. For example, they provided fictitious contracts to the tax authorities as well as transportation bills and payment orders confirming the supply of such exotic raw materials as 'concentrate of thermophilic milk' or 'extract from mountain herbs'. Between 2006 and 2007, the group pocketed more than 215 million roubles (3.5 million euros) in VAT refunds from the taxpayers. The officials of the local tax office were suspected of bribery in this case.

A typical example of a VAT scam in the Russian Federation[5] is that of ex-senator Alexander Sabadash, who was convicted in 2015 for a VAT fraud of 1.8 billion roubles (30 million euros). As established by the investigation and the court, in 2010 Sabadash (as the actual owner of OJSC Vyborg Cellulose) created an organized criminal group to steal money from the budget by illegally reimbursing VAT. Sabadash and his associates provided false documents to the tax authorities, confirming the construction of a company, Vyborgskaya Cellulose LLC (ОАО «Выборгская целлюлоза»), owned by Sabadash. The construction was supposed to be delivered by a Moscow-based company, Es-Kontrakstroy Ltd. (ООО Эс-Контрактстрой), which subcontracted the project to two other companies: Novostroy LLC and Construction business management-88 Ltd. Es-Kontrakstroy Ltd. submitted fictitious documents claiming that the construction was completed and valued the work for 12.5 billion roubles (210 million euros). Thus, it filed for a VAT refund of 1.8 billion roubles. In reality, the subcontracted works were conducted by other firms and were not completed, the real cost of the work in progress amounting to 5.4 billion roubles (90 million euros).

---

5 www.vedomosti.ru/library/articles/2014/05/22/byvshego-senatora-sabadasha-obvinili-v-pokushenii-na.

Sabadash was already a well-known business figure in Russia. He began as an importer of Absolut Vodka; in 1997 he became the owner of a company, Liviz, one of the oldest Russian vodka plants; and in 1999 he bought Vyborgskaya Cellulose LLC. Liviz entered into the bankruptcy procedure in 2008; the total amount of creditors' claims is 811 million roubles (13.5 million euros).

Another high-profile figure involved in VAT fraud was signalled in 2013 when the Russian justice condemned Fidel Chogin[6] to 4.5 years of prison for trying to get an illegal VAT refund of 32 billion roubles (0.5 billion euros). In 2006, Chogin was already convicted of attempting to pocket 500 billion roubles (10 billion euros) through the same mechanism. Chogin was Ministry of the Interior in Saint Petersburg and the founder and president of a company called ZAO Rosmash. He used his official influence to try to get the VAT refunds. In February 2012, his company submitted a fictitious VAT declaration for the first quarter of 2009 to the tax authorities for a tax refund. The document included false information, and the audit revealed that the company was not located at the indicated address, which was in fact a postal box.

The investigation of the VAT fraud became more complicated in the autonomous republic, where the powers of the federal agencies are more limited. As an example, in 2010 a VAT fraud case was opened in the Trans-Baikal region against a local company that failed to pay a VAT liability of 79 million roubles (1.1 million euros) and claimed unjustified VAT refunds for 118 million roubles (2 million euros).

In another instance, in 2017[7] a court from Nizhny Novgorod in the Russian Federation sentenced Gennady Boykin to eight years of prison for evading VAT in 2009. The Russian businessman filed fake tax returns that contained fictitious information about the purchase of goods worth more than 8 million euros, thereby entailing a loss to the FTS of 1.5 million euros.

Gold,[8] a popular underlying for VAT scammers, was also targeted by Russian criminals. In 1998, Robert Martirosyan, along with Igor Mavlyanov, established JSC 'Trade and Production Company (TPK)' Yashma, a leading jewellery company. The network of retail stores of Yashma were independent legal entities and had no formal association with the 'Yashma' company.

The era of prosperity ended in 2015, when TPK 'Yashma' and a number of affiliated companies accumulated huge debts towards big Russian banks, including Sberbank, Promsvyazbank and VTB, the total amount exceeding 31 billion roubles (0.5 billion euros).

At the end of 2017, a criminal investigation for tax evasion targeted Yashma. During 2011–2012 the company reduced artificially the VAT liability using a chain of loans involving 24 shell companies. The loans were guaranteed with gold ingots. Then the VAT liabilities of 'Yashma' were repaid by the netting

---

6 www.kommersant.ru/doc/2335807.

7 www.kommersant.ru/doc/3488077.

8 https://crimerussia.com/financialcrimes/zolotaya-zhizn-vladeltsev-obankrotivshegosya-kholdinga-yashma/?sphrase_id=235395.

of claims. Then the 24 companies entered in a chain of trades with gold ingots without paying the VAT liabilities. The scam caused a 7.16 billion rouble (110 million euro) loss for the Russian taxpayers.

VAT: A new form of 'roof'?

The term 'roof' or 'krisha' (крыша) designated in Russian slang the protection tax which an entrepreneur was paying to the criminal world in order to be able to conduct business. As already presented, the VAT refund is a big issue in the Russian economy and in the whole EAEU.

Because of the growth in the number of VAT frauds in the 2000s, the Federal Tax Office sees a potential fraudster in almost every entrepreneur. Therefore, in order to get its VAT reimbursed, a business needs to get the case in court. Due to the fear of indictment over corruption and bribery the tax offices transfer responsibility of VAT refunds to the justice system.

By 2010 for more than 80% of all VAT refunds in Russia, entrepreneurs were forced to claim the reimbursement in courts. The rate of success for businesses was between 70 and 80%. But the court system introduced delays of over several months into the VAT refund, and this could have affected the economics of a company.

After 2010, the Russian government put more pressure on the tax office to increase the rate of collection of VAT. The tax office took tough measures to plug holes in the federal budget. The architect of these measures was the head of the FTS, Mikhail Mishustin. He oversaw the digitalization and the centralization of the tax collection across the whole Russian Federation. One of the ways to increase the collections of the budget was to reduce even more the number of VAT refunds. This reform entailed a lot of discontent in the business world and a lot of abuse from the tax officials. Moreover, a new business started to flourish, with dozens of companies providing VAT refund services to exporters for a standard price of 2–5% of the VAT refunded amount or an hourly payment of 100 euros. These 'VAT brokers' would help to intermediate the relationship of a company with the local tax office.

As a result, in 2014, entrepreneurs from Saint Petersburg demanded an investigation on the local tax office in charge of the VAT refunds.[9] Saint Petersburg is the main port of the Russian Federation, and most of the imports and exports of goods in the EAEU go through companies registered in this region.

The scandal erupted between the tax inspectors and representative of the business sector. Entrepreneurs incriminated the tax authorities for inventing ways to block the VAT refund and using illegal methods to discourage the companies from asking for refunds. A common practice of tax officials was to initiate a criminal case of VAT fraud against a company benefitting from a VAT refund in order to delay or block the reimbursements. Some companies received no funds,

---

9 www.dp.ru/a/2014/07/09/Vozvrat_NDS_grozit_srokom/.

even after battling and winning the right for a VAT refund in court. Moreover, the local tax inspections started criminal investigations for alleged tax evasion, thereby postponing the reimbursement of the VAT. By law, the tax inspectors in Russia have six months to come up with an object of investigation, thereby saddling the business with additional burdens.

In this type of situation a company can go bankrupt, unable to withstand litigation, as usually participants in such processes are small companies. Other companies, fearing the investigation, do not even apply for a VAT refund. In any case, the non-reimbursed VAT amounts are credited to budget revenues, improving the reporting of the Federal Tax Office.

There were also reports where the tax service used the police to scare companies asking for VAT refunds. A police officer delivered the message that the company might have problems if it did not reconsider the VAT refunds. There are documented cases in which a company director who applied for a VAT refund was invited to a sit-down with the Agency for Combating Economic Crimes for alleged VAT fraud charges.

The situation is very similar to that in the 1990s, when organized crime charged businesses with a protection tax ('krisha'). If the entrepreneurs were unwilling to pay, the local police or other authorities were sent to shut down their business. The practice seemed to be leveraged by the tax office of the Russian Federation and of member states of the EAEU, including Kazakhstan, for improving their statistics of tax collection.

Sanctions: A new variable for the VAT fraud

After the debut of the Ukrainian crisis in 2014, the EU, the United States and other countries imposed a set of sanctions against the Russian Federation. The scope of the sanctions was relatively wide, going from embargo on European agricultural product to financial services and energy-related technology. Moreover, some sanctions concern the delivery of equipment and services in Crimea, which became an autonomous republic of the Russian Federation after its annexation in 2014.

Nevertheless, the Russian importers found several ways to bypass the sanctions. The amusing examples of the Tunisian oysters or the Byelorussian 'Roquefort' cheese only underline the gravity of the problem. A few big corporations were accused of breaking the sanctions against the Russian Federation. For instance on July 2017, the US Treasury Department fined Exxon Mobil $2 million for violating sanctions.[10]

In 2015, a Dutch freight company was accused of delivering two radar units to Yekaterinburg airport in 2015, a year after the EU brought in sanctions against Russia following its invasion of Ukraine. The parts were sent to an arms

10 www.nytimes.com/2017/07/20/us/politics/exxon-mobil-fined-russia-tillerson-sanctions.html.

manufacturer which makes fighter jets for the Russian army. The parts were for a specific plane, which had been ordered by the Indian army.[11]

A year later, the Dutch prosecutors opened a criminal investigation into seven Dutch companies and their directors for allegedly breaching EU sanctions against Russia by helping Russia build a bridge in Crimea.[12] In 2017, the German giant Siemens, provider of equipment, ended up being caught in the web of the sanction's scandal.[13]

After the sanctions, an entire 'industry' of 'smuggling' goods, technology and services was developed. A way of bypassing the sanctions was to sell a product to intermediaries from the EAEU countries which were not concerned by sanctions (usually Belarus), which afterwards resold it to a Russian counterpart without any tax or duty.

Another way to bypass sanction was to emit fake delivery statements for products which are out of the sanction's scope when in fact the banned products were delivered. Companies based in European countries, mainly in Germany and the Baltic countries, specialized in overseas deliveries and logistics that emitted fake transportation documentation, thereby facilitating the breaking of the sanctions. The merchandise was sold on the black market in the Russian Federation. The development of these bypasses is hurting the collection of VAT in the Russian Federation as both avenues are not liable to VAT.

Estimates of VAT fraud in the EAEU

Estimating the losses entailed by the VAT fraud in the EAEU is a hard task due to the scarce and unreliable data for all the Member states. A first estimate of the VAT fraud came in 2009 from the Department of Economic Security of the Ministry of Internal Affairs of the Russian Federation[14] which indicated that about 21,000 VAT crimes took place in that year, encompassing a 10–30 billion rouble (0.2–0.5 billion euro) loss for the Federal treasury. Another estimate provided by tax experts in 2014 pointed out that the total amount of VAT refund in Saint Petersburg is around 150–200 billion roubles (2.5–3.5 billion euros) a year. The share of illegal return is at least 50 billion roubles (~ 1 billion euros).[15]

If the ratio of the VAT loss to the GDP observed in the EU was applied to the EAEU, the global figure for 2016 would represent around 20 billion euros of losses for the five Member States. The MTIC fraud is obviously less developed than in the EU, but the other forms are more prevalent; thereby the 1.6–1.7% ratio is a conservative estimate. Almost three-quarters of that loss in

---

11 www.dutchnews.nl/news/2017/11/dutch-firm-investigated-for-breaking-eu-russian-sanctions/.

12 www.reuters.com/article/us-russia-netherlands-sanctions/dutch-firms-probed-for-alleged-breaches-of-eu-sanctions-on-russia-idUSKBN1I5201.

13 www.lexology.com/library/detail.aspx?g=5ee57082-3464-4da8-906b-bdfc485d6393.

14 www.audit-it.ru/news/account/208726.html.

15 www.dp.ru/a/2014/07/09/Vozvrat_NDS_grozit_srokom/.

Table 7.1 Estimates of the VAT fraud losses to the national treasuries in the EAEU

Year	Estimate (billion euros)	Source/method
• 2009	• 0.7	• The Ministry of Internal Affairs of the Russian Federation (rescaled to EAEU)
• 2014	• 30	• Estimates of illegal VAT refund in Saint Petersburg (rescaled to EAEU)
• 2016	• 20	• Simple proportional calculation based on the VAT loss to GDP ratio in the EU

VAT is supported by the Russian Federation. Table 7.1 synthesizes the estimates presented earlier. The local estimates are rescaled depending on the GDP of a given region and the GDP of the EAEU economy. The estimation based on the rescaling of the VAT fraud in Saint Petersburg and the size computed with a proportionality rule related to the EU case are close in value.

8 The economy of terror

VAT fraud and terrorism financing

Uber-terrorism and low-cost terrorism as new directions of global terrorism

> We're not in Wonderland anymore, Alice.
>
> Charles Manson, American criminal

Boston, Charlie Hebdo, Bataclan, Sharm ElCheik, San Bernardino, Brussels… Facing an unprecedented wave of Islamist terrorism, modern society is confronted with a new public enemy who is both invisible and ubiquitous. Western society, especially Europe, has experienced since the end of the Second World War several episodes of terrorism. The actions of the Red Brigades in Italy or those of the Irish Republican Army in Great Britain are still living memories in the collective unconscious.

A paradigm shift

Compared to previous terrorist episodes, the recent wave of terrorism exhibits different features and mechanisms. The Irish Republican Army, the Basques and Corsican separatists and Al-Qaeda had solid long-term financing, a defined hierarchy and an effective chain of commands. In addition, they were operating in a defined geographic area where they had a support network. The separatist terrorists had a pool of recruitment in a certain geographical area; their members shared the same religious and ethnic backgrounds. Al-Qaeda was one of the first global terrorist organizations with a multinational structure.

The Islamic State (aka Daech) aimed to claim a territory governed by principles based on a certain interpretation of Quranic laws. Their approach is not only to carry military actions against the governmental forces of Syria and Iraq but also to spread terror in the local population and overseas.

An organization similar to the Islamic State was the 'Emirate of Caucasus', an ephemeral entity born from the ashes of the Second Chechen War. The Chechen militants tried to govern a geographical area in the Caucasus according to Islamic law. And, to achieve this, they deployed terrorist actions all over the Russian Federation.

DOI: 10.4324/9781315098722-8

To fight Al-Qaeda or the Emirate of Caucasus, tackling terrorism financing has become a priority for the intelligence services. The aim was to weaken the power of terrorist groups by dismantling the financing network and cutting financial flows needed for operations, logistics and support.

Clearly, the rapid expansion of the Islamic State represented a paradigm shift in the terrorist phenomenology. Thus Daech differs from its predecessors who sowed terror in the United States and Europe, and operates on a different model. Indeed, the Islamic State 'oversaw' de facto in 2014 an area of about 215,000 km^2 but was and is able to support terrorist actions on several continents.

A low-cost modus operandi

Presumably, the Islamic State has learned valuable lessons from the experience of others. Its vision of terrorism focusses on low-cost actions and strong media impact. Why?

Probably because financing and organizing a global extremist network, managed by a centralized chain of commands, has become a difficult task. Consequently, Daech aimed to a lesser extent for complex actions, such as the attacks of 11 September 2001, that would require lengthy preparations and implicitly substantial financial resources. Rather, it focussed on actions organized by local groups managed in a decentralized manner requiring minimal funding.

The recent attacks in Boston, Paris and San Bernardino marked the emergence of a new era of low-cost terrorism. Under this model, the organization of the attacks should not rely solely on centralized commands or on a clear hierarchy. The manufacturing and acquisition of weapons may be provided near the area where the attacks are planned. The logistics of the attacks may be financed by means that do not involve significant fund transfers, which would be easily detectable by the banking network. Everything can be achieved without having a direct link to Daech.

Financing terrorist activities traditionally relied on massive long-term funding involving overseas money transfers from generous donors. Modern terrorism changed the paradigm and understood that the main resources are not the financial ones but the human ones.

A centralized global extremist network has become almost impossible to manage due to the increased scrutiny and monitoring of financial transactions. Banks and financial institutions have Counter-Terrorism Financing systems that generate alerts when suspicious transfers are detected.

Thus, the uber-terrorism work involves amounts below the thresholds of processes and systems designed to tackle the terrorist financing. Moreover, organizations like Islamic State of Iraq and Syria (ISIS) focussed on actions organized by local groups managed in a decentralized manner and requiring minimal funding. ISIS aims to a lesser extent for complex actions such as the attacks of 11 September 2001 but targets actions with a higher frequency and lower severity. For example, the Bataclan terrorist attacks in Paris were budgeted at 50,000 euros.

The uber-terrorist: a ubiquitous but invisible enemy

A potential terrorist on a radicalization path or even a simple follower can attack a target independently. For example, Daech (ISIS), through its decentralized structure and its 'social network', can provide an extremist with links to other people nearby able to quickly supply them with funds, logistics or skills and thereby rapidly perform an attack.

Thus, organizations like Daech managed to establish the foundations of a 'terrorist social network' that can facilitate the interaction of Islamists and the organization of a terrorist action. The new wave of terrorism is 'uberized'. It is no longer a centralized structure which ensures the financing, organization and preparation of a terrorist group. Daech, for example, seeks to link its followers and transmit technical expertise, thereby strengthening the potential terrorist locally. Apparently, for this reason, Daech opted to develop the uber-terrorism at a global level, thereby becoming a trademark of fear.

The uberization of terrorism makes the task much more complex for the intelligence services because the target is not a clearly defined entity. The fight against the financing of terrorism becomes also difficult as the uber-terrorism does not require structured and long-term funding or significant transfer of funds.

Any 'radicalized' individual may at any time become a threat. Current surveillance systems are too focussed on cyberspace and funding, and risk becoming obsolete in this new era of low-cost uber-terrorism. The enemy would be invisible yet ubiquitous. Therefore, the defeat of ISIS in Syria and Iraq does not signify by any means the end of the terrorist attacks having ISIS's signature.

How is the uber-terrorism financed?

The stringent question of how this way of functioning can be sustained needs to be cautiously discussed. Uber-terrorism brought not only the decentralization of hierarchy but also the centralization of finance and responsibilities. The leader of the Islamic State understood for instance that they cannot rely on donors, and they should insure their own resources through a dedicated economy. The economy of terror goes beyond financing and includes the products from all assets, capital and resources engaged by the terrorist organizations to make profits channelled towards terrorist acts. This economy also includes a sociological dimension as not all elements involved in this economy are related to terror directly. Some of them are part of a lobby or adhere at a high conceptual level or not at all, looking only after financial profit.

ISIS recruits come from almost 80 countries, the top suppliers being Saudi Arabia, Tunisia, the United Kingdom and the Russian Federation. The multinational dimension of the terror economy should be understood in its specific context with its various layers, from the top organizations involved directly in supplying the terror to the smaller organizations and sole traders. Despite an appearance of independence between the various layers, this economy can be apprehended as a unified corpus.

ISIS and its economy have various enterprises depending on geographic area: in Asia they rely on donors from Gulf countries but exert activities in trading precious metals and stones. Drug trafficking also sponsors ISIS in some regions of Central Asia.

In the Middle East, ISIS still depends on donors from Gulf countries and is financed by activities including physical oil trading, trading of local currencies, cryptocurrencies and commerce with precious metals. In ex-USSR countries, drug and weapon traffic, and organized crime are amongst the contributors to terrorism. In the Western world and especially in Europe, drug traffic and human traffic are a few of the sources of financing terror. In recent years additional non-crime related financing sources were signals:

- Business loans: a company takes loans that can be used for financing terror. The company files for bankruptcy, and the loans are not reimbursed.
- Rents paid by sympathizers: people who follow a cause can help by paying flat rents, renting cars, etc.
- Personal loans: application fraud is a loan taken by a person with the intention of never paying it back.
- Social Security fraud: claiming benefits on fraudulent bases.
- Crowdfunding: funds raised from the social network of the terrorists.
- Value Added Tax (VAT) fraud: tax evasion is a thorough and rapid way of providing funds. This aspect will be discussed in the following section.

VAT fraud as a source of financing of terrorism

The link between Missing Trader Intra-Community (MTIC) fraud and terrorism financing is a highly speculative topic. The first signals highlighting a potential link came during the carousel fraud on CO_2 emissions permits. The revival of the 'Dubai Connection' and the massive presence of Asian-Pakistani groups raised the question of whether or not terrorist networks could be linked to this fraud[1] (Frunza, 2015).

The prosecution of Samir Azizi in the United States brought new inputs to the questions. Samir Azizi is a German-Afghan citizen who was extradited from the United States in April 2015 with charges related to VAT fraud. In the extradition order, Judge Howard R. Lloyd[2] mentioned allegations of terrorism financing (Ainsworth, 2015).

The MTIC connection to terrorism has been highlighted with deeper research by Danish journalists from the national Danish television network DR1 since

---

1 Changement climatique et crime organisé: une vision scientifique (Climate change and organised crime) (www.voxfi.fr/changement-climatique-et-crime-organis%C3%A9-une-vision-scientifique/).
2 'The RFE says this was the subject of various press reports in Germany; and, there were also indicators that perpetrators were using the VAT procured through such fraud, not only for personal enrichment, but also to finance terrorism' (Source: www.leagle.com/decision/infdco20150320f94).

2014. A dedicated documentary was pursued in 2016 by Dutch journalists from Zembla agency, with a special focus on VAT fraud in connection with terrorism.[3]

The allegation started to look more plausible in 2017, when the European Union (EU) Commissioner in charge of tax policies, Pierre Moscovici,[4] mentioned that VAT fraud could be a source of concerning terrorism financing. The first question that came up was why VAT fraud and more particularly MTIC would be fit for financing fraud?

Why VAT fraud?

The fight against modern terrorism or uber-terrorism concerns mainly the strengthening of security measures. Whilst in the United States, Facebook's privacy-related policy opens new ground for debate around individual freedoms, in France the emergency state which empowers authorities with very restrictive measures and a thorough monitoring of individuals seems to be the preferred mechanism of defence against the terrorist threat.

Recent events show that in fact the economic and financial aspects of terrorism play a crucial role. Yet governments and the public seem only a little sensitized to the problems related to economic crime which support terrorism worldwide.

Terrorists allegedly linked to ISIS who are involved in bloody attacks represent only a minority of Islamists or the peak of the iceberg. A segment less known but more significant is represented by those adepts who have built across Europe and worldwide an economic and financial backbone supporting the criminal attacks. This category of terrorist is involved in economic crime and has various businesses with doubtful character.

Among the financial crimes, the VAT fraud seems to be the favourite tool for these 'economic terrorists'. This fraud is based on a network of shell companies taking advantage of the laxity in the EU's tax system.

VAT fraud is particularly easy to implement, requires relatively little seed-funding and can be leveraged across markets and countries. The product targets are electronic gadgets; food and agricultural commodities; and intangible goods or services, including CO_2 emissions, electricity, 'cloud memory' or Voice over Internet Protocol (VoIP).

This crime remains barely detectable, and investigations are usually long and winding. In addition, the recovery of the embezzled funds is almost illusory, the money being lost as quickly in the meanders of the tax-havens and 'shadow banking'.

The Islamists engaged in the economic side of terror are generally directors of small- and medium-size enterprises, sole traders or merchants. Their business turnovers do not account for more than a few million dollars, and this makes

---

3 Dutch companies involved in tax fraud, terrorism financing: report (https://nltimes.nl/2016/10/24/dutch-companies-involved-tax-fraud-terrorism-financing-report).

4 'We know that VAT fraud can be a source of financing for criminal acts, including terrorism', Pierre Moscovici(https://uk.reuters.com/article/uk-eu-tax-vat/eu-commission-proposes-measures-to-tackle-sales-tax-fraud-idUKKBN1DU1G9).

them less visible to the banking systems that are focussed on the detection of large financial flows.

Tax evaders with links to terrorism have an Asian or Middle Eastern background or ties with companies from those regions. Asian and Middle Eastern civilizations have a long tradition of overseas trading. Thus, for many citizens coming from these cultures, establishing companies in a few countries and doing global business is a natural pattern in life.

VAT fraudsters' organize training sessions to induce beginners into the VAT fraud ring. 'New blood' is crucial as many veterans of the VAT scams became banned from directorship. VAT fraudsters have significant research 'departments', which analyze markets and countries to find favourable ground for implementing the fraud. VAT fraud boot camps are organized for training and exchanging best practice. Transnational organized crime and terrorist groups do intersect in the VAT fraud arena, and in some cases they work together, even if they are from completely different avenues. Some extremist religious leaders encourage young adepts to engage in VAT fraud schemes as part of an economic warfare against the enemies of their religion.

In some religions like Islam, religious taxes are applied to companies. In the view of some Islamist extremist activists, VAT might not be complaint with their view on religious taxation code. For example, VAT might not be compulsory with Sharia in the views of religious extremists. They will push adepts to divert the official tax to other taxes which are complaint with religious rules. The role of Zakat[5] in terrorism financing was pointed out by Chugani (2008). Therefore, not paying VAT and diverting the funds towards the Zakat is a — realistic scenario.

How does it operate?

Figure 8.1 presents in a synthetic manner the way VAT fraud can support and finance terrorist activities. Company X buys items from other EU countries and resells them domestically without clearing the VAT liability with the national tax office. As in any other MTIC scam, the pocketed VAT is sent to another company which can be based in another country. Finally, the funds arrive to a sole trader or a physical person. The funds can be transferred as part of a service, donation, sponsorship or a religious tax in concerned countries (i.e., Zakat). The final receiver of the funds uses them to support terrorist activities.

Those funds are used to the benefit of various recipients for renting cars or accommodation, buying travel tickets or prepaid cards, purchasing material, etc. The recipients will finally be those in charge of the act of terror. The perpetrators are disconnected from the people who run the MTIC fraud, and in many cases they do not even know the MTICers.

---

5 Zakat is an obligation upon Muslims to pay two and a half percent of their wealth if and when it exceeds a minimum level or nisab.

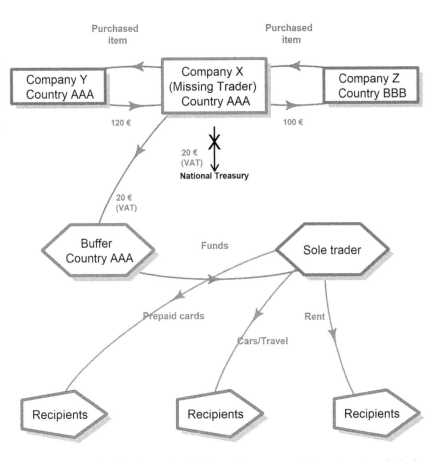

Figure 8.1 MTIC fraud and terrorism funding. The amount of the pocketed tax fuels the terrorist backbone through various recipients and avenues.

The 'economy of terror' unveils a universe underlying the jihadist networks, less violent and yet very powerful, with ramifications in all levels of society. We are also witnessing the development of a true transnational criminal infrastructure designed to take advantage of those countries where the economic system is based on trust and individual responsibility.

The European Commission created in the beginning of this year a special unit engaged in countering terrorism financing. Indeed, the European approach that brings together the efforts of all countries is surely the right one. Nevertheless, the means and the powers which this unit will have are the key points of its viability. In this aspect, the EU has many lessons to learn from the United States for countering the threats at federal level. European countries will be forced by circumstances to adopt a model similar to that of the Federal Bureau of Investigation (FBI), which showed from its inception its utility in tackling serious organized crime. The development of a European FBI should hence be only a question of time.

Case studies

The fraudsters involved in MTIC scams with alleged ties to terrorism have a slightly different profile from their peers involved in VAT scams. First, they are less flamboyant and avoid media when compared, for instance, to their comrades from the French-Israeli Connection. Second, they seem to be careful about hiding facts. Without any doubt the discovery of invoices for an Italian brokerage firm in a stronghold of the Taliban on the border between Pakistan and Afghanistan remains the most famous case. It proves that the VAT fraudsters initially aimed to conceal the proofs from an eventual investigation. Therefore, they physically moved all invoices to a remote location. Last but not the least, these networks operate at a multinational level and have connections with other groups. Moreover, some of the fraudsters have multiple identities and can easily move to locations like Iraq, Syria or Afghanistan and come back to Europe without being detected by intelligence and law enforcement. Table 8.1 presents a synthesis of the main cases where MTIC fraudsters were allegedly linked to terrorist organizations.

Table 8.1 Snapshot of VAT fraud cases with alleged links to the terrorist financing

Year	Facts	Countries of the VAT fraud	Countries of terrorist operation
2014	A patrol of the United States army found in a Taliban camp located on the border between Afghanistan and Pakistan the invoices of an Italian company involved in a carousel of VAT on the market of the emissions of CO_2.[1]	Italy	Pakistan
2014	Abdessamad Fateh of Danish nationality has been introduced by the American authorities onto the list of terrorist persons. He was the director of a company involved in the VAT fraud on the trade of electronic gadgets and food products.[2]	Denmark	Syria/Iraq
2015	Zakaria Said Mohamed is currently being searched by the Spanish police on the charge of terrorism. He was in the process of recruiting activists to join ISIS in Syria and Mali. He had a trading business for non-alcoholic beverages in Denmark, where he was investigated for fraud.[3]	Denmark/ Spain	Syria/Iraq/ Mali
2015	An American court approves the extradition procedure for Samir Azizi, Afghan and German citizen. Azizi is wanted in Germany for having orchestrated a VAT fraud. The American judge indicates that the pocketed funds have served in the financing of terrorism.[4]	Germany / United States	?

1 VAT fraud in Italy in the carbon market (http://cphpost.dk/news14/international-news14/danish-co2-quotas-part-of-colossal-italian-fraud-case.html).
2 www.thelocal.dk/20140926/dane-added-to-us-terror-list.
3 www.nytimes.com/2014/06/17/world/europe/spanish-police-target-cells-recruiting-war-volunteers-for-insurgencies-from-western-africa-syria-iraq.html?_r=0.
4 www.usmarshals.gov/news/chron/2014/040714.htm.

SF Energy Trading

The first case that came up in the media about VAT fraud and terrorism concerned the Italian company 'SF Energy Trading'. In 2014 the Italian journal 'Corriere della Sera' disclosed that in 2010 after a SEAL[6] raid in a Taliban stronghold, British and American intelligence agencies found a pile of invoices concerning that company. The place where the documents were found was a cave near the Afghanistan-Pakistan border – not far from the town where Osama bin Laden was killed by the United States special forces in 2011. Those invoices concerned CO_2 emissions trades with other European companies.

In 2012 the name of the company, SF Energy Trading, appeared in an investigation of the Italian financial police ('Guardia di Finanzia') concerning the Italian energy firm Axpo Italia. Axpo Italia was investigated concerning involvement in MTIC fraud in the CO_2 emissions market. Jean Stephane Richet and Yakub Imran Ahmed, director of the Milan-based SF Energy Trading, were also indicted as part of that investigation.[7]

In 2014, the Italian police put no less than 38 people under investigation concerning the company SF Energy Trading with respect to VAT fraud on CO_2 emissions. Amongst the investigated, there was again British-Pakistani citizen Yakub Imran Ahmed. The total VAT pocketed in the carbon Italian Connection was estimated to be 1.15 billion euros.[8] Part of the proceeds were invested in precious stones and in real estate in Dubai.

The Italian company SF Energy Trading traded with a series of companies in Denmark, Germany, the Netherlands and the United Kingdom. A company with a similar name was also incorporated in France and headed by Jean Stephane Richet, who appeared also in the Italian indictment. The funds were transferred through various banks in Cyprus, Hong Kong and Dubai. The scammers used fake identities, fake addresses and links to companies based in China. This enabled the fraudsters to continue the scheme elsewhere (Normark, 2015).

Figure 8.2 shows a snapshot of the main companies that have direct or indirect links with SF Energy trading. Table 8.2 provides additional information concerning those companies. The crime had a multilayer structure, including the fraudsters, the buffers and the big financial institutions.

SF Energy traded mainly with a company based in Dubai (World Base). Imran Ahmed was also an account manager for that company. The companies involved directly in trades with SF Energy trading had their account for CO_2 emissions on the Danish registry. The Danish registry was, before 2011, one of the main harbours of assets for companies involved in VAT fraud on CO_2 emissions all across the world.

6 United States Navy Sea, Air, and Land Teams.
7 Maxi raggiro nel settore del gas Gdf sequestra 80 mln a società energetica (Maxi scam in the gas sector Gdf sequestrates 80 mln to energy company) (www.repubblica.it/economia/finanza/2012/11/16/news/gdf_milano_sequestra_80_milioni_a_societ_energetica-46775636/).
8 Briton wanted for £1 billion fraud used to 'finance terror' by ripping off Italian government through scheme designed to combat global warming (www.dailymail.co.uk/news/article-2768348/Briton-wanted-1-billion-fraud-used-finance-terror-ripping-Italian-government-scheme-designed-combat-global-warming.html).

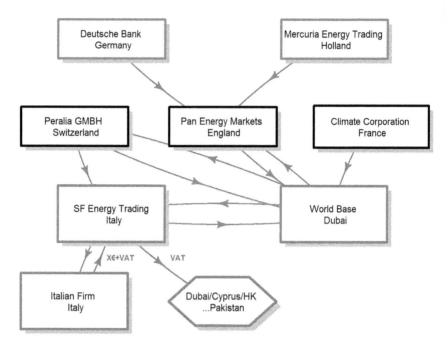

Figure 8.2 VAT fraud involving SF Energy Trading. Snapshot of various firms involved in the scam.

Table 8.2 Companies that had direct and indirect trades with SF Energy Trading between 2008 and 2010. The country of the carbon account is the country where those companies had an electronic account for CO_2 emissions

Company	Country	Carbon account	Observations
SF Energy Trading	Italy	Denmark/Italy	Traders: Stephane Richet, Nicholas Plant
World Base	Dubai	Denmark	Traders: Imran Ahmed, Mathew Joseph
Peralia GMBH	Switzerland	Denmark	Traders: Beat Walker, Shafqat Adnan
Pan Energy Markets	United Kingdom	Denmark/United Kingdom	Traders: Sezer Yurtseven, Ozer Yurtseven
Climate Corporation	France	France	
Mercuria	The Netherlands	The Netherlands	
Deutsche Bank	Germany/United Kingdom	Germany	Bank was the subject of Federal investigation in Germany for VAT fraud

Dutch investigation journalists from Zembla indicated that the Dutch company EcoDutch Carbon is linked to SF Energy Trading. Another Dutch company, VDL Duty Free Wholesale from Numansdorp, which appears in a VAT scam on CO_2 emissions, would be allegedly linked to terrorist financing.[9]

Q-Transport case

In 2016 Danish journalists from the national television network put together evidence that VAT fraudsters from Denmark and Sweden were linked to the terrorist group in Syria. The tale started in 2014 when the Spanish police arrested six persons as part of a terrorist group in the Spanish enclave Melilla in Northern Africa.[10] In March 2013, in the same location, the Spanish police arrested few Spanish and French citizens accused of terrorism. The Spanish police indicated that at least 28 fighters (26 Moroccan citizens and 2 Spaniards) were trained and sent to the conflict zone by that group.[11] The alleged leader of the group was Benaissa Laghmouchi Baghdadi, who spent about eight months in Syria and had returned to Spain, through Mali, before the arrest. He was one of the first Spaniards to be detected working with terrorist groups in the Sahel region of North Africa. The other five suspects arrested were identified as Mustafa Al Lal Mohamed, Kamal Mohamed Dris, Rachid Abdel Nahet Hamed, Mohamed Mohamed Benali and Mustafa Zizaoui Mohand.

One of the suspects, a Danish citizen living in Malmo, Sweden, was never arrested. Information from the Spanish police investigation leaked to the media. Intercepted phone and email conversations revealed that the Danish citizen was in charge of jihadist recruitment.[12] The Danish 'Connection' of this group pointed towards a few names that had appeared previously in CO_2 emissions VAT fraud, including Niaz Ahmed, Hasnat Siddique Ahmed and Tariq Yasin. The list of Spanish citizens linked to that group included a few names that had appeared as belonging to the directors of some Danish companies:[13]

- Zakaria Said Mohamed was in 2014 a fugitive, wanted by Spanish police. He served as director, most likely as frontman, in a few Danish companies, including King Bev ApS, a soft drink trading business.
- Mustafa Zizaoui Mohand was in the group of those arrested in Melilla. He appeared as a director of the Danish companies IFT Food ApS and Sky ApS, specialized in soft drink trading.

9 Dutch companies involved in tax fraud, terrorism financing: report (https://nltimes. nl/2016/10/24/dutch-companies-involved-tax-fraud-terrorism-financing-report).

10 Seis detenidos en España acusados de terrorismo http://cnnespanol.cnn.com/2014/05/31/ seis-detenidos-en-espana-acusados-de-terrorismo/.

11 Tax scam money linked to terrorist cell in Spain http://sverigesradio.se/sida/artikel. aspx?programid=2054&artikel=6707565.

12 Massive Tax Fraud in Sweden, Denmark Stirs Suspicions of Support for Terrorism https://sputnik news.com/europe/201705301054116805-sweden-denmark-tax-fraud-terrorism/.

13 Six arrested in Spain accused of terrorism (http://cnnespanol.cnn.com/2014/05/31/ seis-detenidos-en-espana-acusados-de-terrorismo/).

- Rachid Abdel Nahet Hamed was also part of the group arrested in Melilla He served in Denmark as director of GM Enterprise. He left Denmark in May 2013.

The network of people and companies linked to the 2014 Melilla arrest provides evidence of the existence of a Danish group of terrorists, including:

- Danny Bak aka Zakaria Abbas el Hajj, a Danish citizen who was listed at that time as director of multiple Danish companies involved in the car business and importing foods and beverages.
- Osman Sesay, a Danish citizen killed in December 2015 in a United States drone attack near Raqqa, Syria. In the same drone attack Rawand Dilsher Taher,[14] also a Danish citizen and a leader of Danish terrorists, was killed. Osman Sesay was a director of several companies involved in food and beverages trading.

Additionally, the Danish journalists found links of these groups to a company specializing in the recruitment and supply of temporary workers.

The main investigation leads were pointing to Abdessamad Fateh, also known as Abu Hamzah, and to the VAT-fraud enterprises that he pursued in Denmark. Abdessamad Fateh was officially on the United States' list of foreign terrorist fighters and a member of a Scandinavia-based network of extremists with alleged ties to Al-Qaeda. Intelligence reported that he travelled back and forth to Syria. Abdessamad Fateh, aka Abu Hamza, was already known to law enforcement in Denmark. In 2008 he was arrested and charged as a suspect in a murder attempt against Kurt Westergaard, a Danish cartoonist who created the controversial cartoon of the Islamic prophet Muhammad wearing a bomb in his turban (Normark, 2017).[15]

Abdessamad Fateh acted during a brief period of time as the director of Q-Transport, a Danish import-export company. The Q-Transport company, incorporated in Denmark since 2005, was registered to conduct economic activities in road freight. The company imported in a short time very large amounts of chicken meat, mobile phones and Gouda cheese from other countries of the EU and resold them domestically. Between 2013 and 2014, the company changed directors four times in less than six months. For that period the directorship timeline was as follows:

- 17/01/2005–26/06/2013: Inam Ashraf
- 26/06/2013–01/10/2013: Niaz Ahmed
- 01/10/2013–01/11/2013: Abdessamad Fateh
- 01/11/2013–08/08/2014: Najim El Bachiri Agharbi

The company closed its account with the Danish retail bank BRFkredit in January 2014. The company filed for bankruptcy in August 2014. When Abdessamad

14 Sådan endte en student fra Frederiksberg i toppen af Islamisk Stat (This ended a student from Frederiksberg at the top of the Islamic State) (https://politiken.dk/indland/art5648737/S%C3%A5dan-endte-en-student-fra-Frederiksberg-i-toppen-af-Islamisk-Stat).

15 https://ctc.usma.edu/microfinancing-the-caliphate-how-the-islamic-state-is-unlocking-the-assets-of-european-recruits/.

Fateh, who served as director in October 2013, was wanted for terrorist activities, Niaz Ahmed, the prior director, denied any link to Fateh's activities. Intelligence showed also that Ahmed made a few trips to Pakistan during that time.

The company was incorporated in 2006 but started trading in November 2013, thereby being submitted to VAT and to the Danish tax agency (SKAT). SKAT received from Q-Transport no VAT returns nor payments made from November 2013 to January 2014. The mechanics of the MTIC fraud are depicted in Figure 8.3. Mobile phones were bought mainly from German companies,

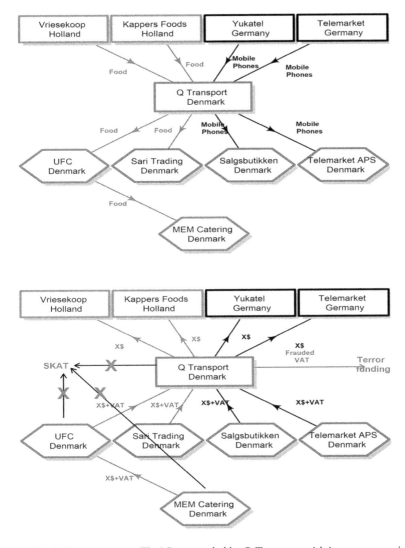

Figure 8.3 Q-Transport case. (Top) Items traded by Q-Transport with its counterparties. (Bottom) Financial flows with companies involved in trades with Q-Transport. In the aftermath, Q-Transport, UFC Denmark Aps and MEM Catering (red boxes) all failed to pay their VAT liability.

including Telepart Distribution, Yukatel and Telemarket. Food was purchased from Dutch companies, including Kappers Foods BV and Vriesekoop BV.

Mobile phones were sold in Denmark to domestic companies like Salgsbutikken A/S and Telemarket APS. Food products were sold locally to companies like Sari Trading Consult Aps and UFC Denmark Aps. UFC Denmark Aps, one of the Q-Transport buyers, resold the products to MEM Catering. In the aftermath, Q-Transport, UFC Denmark Aps and MEM Catering have all failed to pay their VAT liability. The pocketed VAT funds were diverted through a series of shell companies, including a travel agency, which were created and dissolved (Normark, 2017).

A summary of the three companies implicated directly in the VAT fraud is presented in Table 8.3. The last director of MEM catering, Zakaria Said Mohamed, aka Abu Nur al-Andalusi, died in February 2016, killed by French forces in Mali. He was part of an Al-Qaeda chapter in *Magreb*.[16]

The bankruptcy statement of Q-Transport provides detailed documentation of the financial status of the company between November 2013 and January 2014, including the bank account statements (Figure 8.4).

Figure 8.5 shows the evolution of Q-Transport's bank account balance with BRFkredit. The balance exhibits big swings and becomes nil towards the end of January 2014. Figure 8.6 depicts the transfers in and out of Q-Transport's bank account. It underlines the fact that big inflows of funds are followed immediately by similar size outflows, a fact which is specific to VAT fraud. One of these big swings was observed in mid-January 2015, just before the company was declared bankrupt. Between November and December 2013 the company had outflows corresponding to the purchase of food. In January 2014 all food stocks (if any) were sold, and funds entered Q-Transport's account.

Table 8.3 Summary of companies that defrauded the Danish tax office in the Q-Transport case

Company	VAT pocketed	Observations
Q-Transport	~300,000 euros	1.2 million euros were owed to all creditors
UFC Denmark	UFC declared bankruptcy with a debt of at least 1 million euros to creditors and tax authorities.	UFC is owned by Niaz Ahmed, the Q-Transport director. UFC and MEM Catering had the same address.
MEM Catering		Before the bankruptcy, a new director comes, a Spanish 'non EU-resident' residing in the enclave of Melilla in Morocco.

16 The jihadists dedicate a video to the Melilla terrorist Zakaria Said (www.melillahoy.es/noticia/84428/sucesos/los-yihadistas-dedican-un-video-al-terrorista-melillense-zakaria-said-.html).

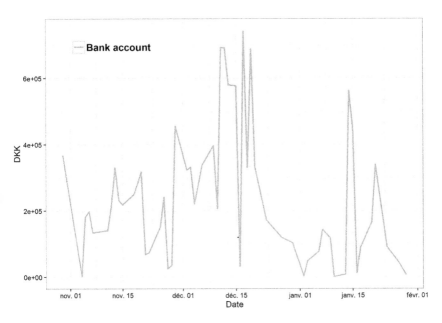

Figure 8.4 Q-Transport account with BRFKredit. Evolution of the bank account balance in the period of the VAT fraud. Numbers are expressed in Danish kroner (1 EUR =7.34 DKK in 2018).

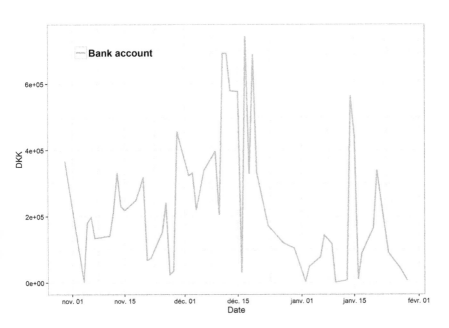

Figure 8.5 The evolution of Q-Transport bank's account balance with BRFkredit.

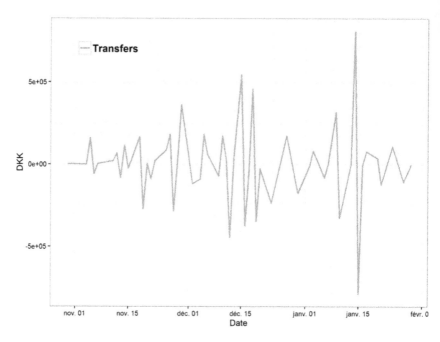

Figure 8.6 Q-Transport account with BRFKredit. Evolution of the bank transfers in the period of the VAT fraud.

Similar cases were reported in Sweden, where a 30-year-old Salafist preacher was charged with MTIC fraud. He purchased mobile phones and tablets from the United Kingdom, which were shipped via one of the indicted companies in Finland and resold to a Swedish company in Bergsjön managed by a 23-year-old Swedish resident. The total purchased merchandise accounted for almost 3 million euros over a period of four months in 2013. The pocketed VAT represented approximately 600,000 euros, out of which 500,000 euros were allegedly diverted to support terror acts in the Middle East or North Africa (Gustafsson, 2017).[17]

17 www.fi.se/contentassets/1944bde9037c4fba89d1f48f9bba6dd7/understanding_terrorist_finance_160315.pdf.

9 Technology

A real leverage for the VAT fraudsters

The mechanisms of Value Added Tax (VAT) fraud have remained unchanged since the inception of the European Union's (EU's) Intra-Community system. Nevertheless, the way the VAT fraud operates was massively reshaped by technology. Traditionally, VAT fraud was very lucrative for items with a small physical volume and high price or market value. Thus, the costs of freight and storage are negligible compared to the amount of pocketed VAT. The development of virtual products and services traded through electronic platforms increased the frequency and the severity of the fraud.

The cargo aircrafts filled with products flying many times across the continent were replaced by electronic trading platforms, thereby increasing the severity of VAT fraud effects (Frunza, 2015). Therefore, the following innovation tendencies need to be discussed in relation to the way VAT fraud functions or can be enhanced by innovative technologies. This chapter explores the following topics:

* e-commerce and trading infrastructure,
* social engineering,
* blockchain and cryptocurrencies, and
* Fintech.

E-commerce and trading infrastructures

The commerce of goods and services changed dramatically at the dawn of the new millennium. In the pre-technology era, the commerce was based mostly on direct physical interaction between a buyer and a seller. From product pitching and price negotiation to contractual paperwork, all steps of the trading process required human intervention and interaction. Establishing a commercial relationship was a relatively long process and relied on the affinity between the buyer and the seller. The international trade was reserved for bigger multinational entities, while most sellers of goods and services had a local coverage.

Technology and the development of the World Wide Web reshaped the commerce in three main aspects. First, it reduced and even eliminated the direct human interaction at all stages of the sale process. A product can be sold today without any formal contact between the buyer and the seller, and no physical signature of

DOI: 10.4324/9781315098722-9

an agreement. Thus, the sale cycle of a product is much shorter, thereby increasing the potential sales volume Second, technology moved the commerce from local to global. Today, trading internationally is accessible to a broader range of commercial agents than it was 30 years ago. Last, with the development of online trading platforms commerce has become decentralized. A buyer and a seller from two different parts of the world can enter into a commercial agreement without knowing each other, the transaction being intermediated by dedicated internet platforms. Nevertheless, the platform is neither the buyer nor the seller in this context. In most of cases the identity of the buyer is not known by the seller, and vice versa.

The mechanisms of VAT fraud followed the same pattern. All three of the aspects discussed fuelled the skyrocketing of losses due to VAT fraudulent schemes. Two technologies used by missing traders are discussed here: the electronic exchanges and the online marketplaces. Furthermore, the potential role of peer-to-peer delivery services in VAT fraud is highlighted.

Electronic exchanges

Electronic exchanges or electronic trading platforms are infrastructures where the price is negotiated over a computer terminal. All trading takes place over an internet-based system; the buyer and the seller do not have any physical interaction. Electronic trading exchanges took over the traditional pit trading in the 1990s. The pit trading involved a negotiation of price and quantity over the phone between two parties.

More evolved electronic exchanges do automatic execution by matching the bid and the ask, thereby implying no human intervention besides programming the execution algorithm.

Electronic exchanges are linked mainly with the trading of financial instruments, but they are also used for trading spot commodities, including oil, oil distillates, gas, power, grains, orange juice, etc.

The spot commodities, like any other good, carry VAT; therefore trading them through electronic exchanges bears a risk of tax fraud. Most of the trading for physical commodities would require physical delivery, thereby reducing the risk of a systemic VAT fraud. Putting in place a VAT carousel with oil or oil distillates would require a complex infrastructure with potentially big logistics costs. Amongst the commodities cleared on exchanges at least three make the perfect candidate for VAT fraud: CO_2 emissions, electricity and gas. Case studies related to these markets are presented in Chapter 10. Therefore, this section addresses only the role of an exchange in a VAT scam.

The markets mentioned earlier as targets for VAT scammers have the particularity that the traded contracts have no physical counterparts:

- CO_2 emissions permits are pollution rights held in an electronic account, thereby implying no delivery cost.
- Gas and electricity do not involve the physical exchange. What is sold is 'capacity' utilization from the power grid or from the gas pipeline (gas).

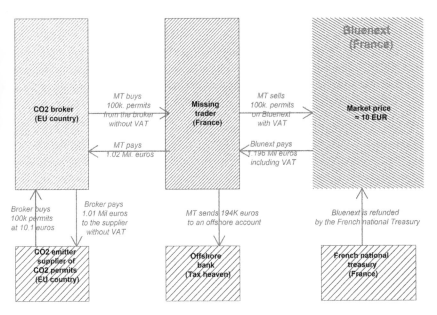

Figure 9.1 VAT fraud on CO₂ emissions exchange. The Missing trader based in France buys permits without VAT from a broker based in a different EU country. The broker gets the permits from an industrial company based in a different EU country without VAT. The Missing trader sells the allowances in France on BlueNext, which pays the market price plus VAT. The Missing trader sends the VAT proceeds to an offshore account and leaves the company in insolvency.

A simple example of how VAT fraudsters used an electronic exchange to pocket in record time is the case of the CO₂ emissions exchange *BlueNext* (Frunza, 2013). *BlueNext*, a Paris-based company, was between 2005 and 2011 Europe's biggest spot exchange for CO₂ emissions permits (EU Allowances – EUAs[1]). Between 2008 and 2009 the exchange was hit by a massive VAT fraud, accounting for 1.9 billion euros of losses for the French taxpayers. The Missing Trader Intra-Community (MTIC) fraud involving CO₂ emissions permits (allowances) or carbon credits is summarized in Figure 9.1.

The missing traders involved in the scheme allegedly imported large volumes of carbon credits VAT-free from other countries and then sold the credits on BlueNext, having already marked up the price with VAT. The scheme has the following steps:

- A carbon broker tied to the missing traders buys CO₂ permits from an industrial company at 10.1 euros when the market price for a CO₂ permit is 10 euros. No VAT is charged, the transaction being deemed an intra-Community trade.

---

1 The trading of the CO₂ emissions permits in the EU Emissions Trading Scheme (EU ETS) was a consequence of the Kyoto regulation concerning global warming. One allowance (EUA) allowed its owner to emit one tonne of CO₂.

- The missing trader based in France buys permits without VAT from a broker based in a different EU country. The price is 10.2 euros per allowance.
- The missing trader sells the allowances in France on *BlueNext*, which pays the market price plus VAT, representing 11.96 euros per permit.
- The missing trader has a total bank balance of 176,000 euros after transacting 100,000 permits. The missing trader sends the VAT proceeds to an offshore account and leaves the company in insolvency.

This process took between 15 minutes and 4 hours, and the speed of the electronic exchange facilitated the propagation and amplification of this fraud. It is crucial to underline that both the broker and the missing trader were overpaying the CO_2 permits. It was reported in many cases that industrial companies that have allowances to sell were offered prices higher than the *BlueNext* price. The scammers needed the permits to pocket the VAT from *BlueNext*; therefore they needed to incentivize the industrial companies to sell their allowances.

At its top, the exchange had a record turnover of 19.8 million CO_2 emissions permits on 2 June 2009. BlueNext's transaction fees were around 2 cents per permit at the moment when the fraud took place. The revenue of the exchange was directly dependent on the volume of allowance exchanged over the infrastructure. Thus, *BlueNext* had an incentive to attract and maintain high trading volume from its members. In order to keep the growth of the market, the exchange took two measures that played, in the end, in fraudsters' favour:

- The exchange decided to pay and charge VAT on all transactions. VAT scammers leveraged this aspect and sold massively on BlueNext in order to get the VAT funds.
- The exchange was confronted very soon with more VAT payments to its seller client than VAT receipt from buyers' receipts. The exchange reached an agreement with the French national treasury for monthly VAT refunds, even when the amounts reached astronomical figures.

Electronic exchanges are mainly related to financial markets, where the traded instruments are overseen by a regulator and do not have VAT. The CO_2 emissions market and potentially the gas and power markets are currently the only relevant cases.

Unregulated exchanges are also used in the telecommunication sectors. Voice over Internet Protocol (VoIP) exchanges experienced a strong growth with the increase of online communication replacing the traditional landlines and GSM[2] mobiles. VoIP exchanges refer to an online platform where VoIP minutes are bought and sold by telephone service providers, wholesalers, retailer and carriers. For example a French telecom operator can sell voice traffic for the United States to an American operator, and it receives back traffic to the United States.[3] The aim of a VoIP exchange is to

---

2 Global System for Mobile Communication.
3 Source: http://telecomsxchange.com/blog/what-is-a-voip-exchange/.

provide liquidity at relatively transparent prices and good geographical coverage for VoIP solution providers.[4] For example, if a multinational company needs to organize videoconferences with teams from various countries and continents, in order to hedge this demand the VoIP provider of the multinational corporation will hedge this future exposure on a VoIP exchange depending on the countries of interest.

TelecomsXChange is an example of such an exchange. The average profit margin for wholesale VoIP providers trading on exchanges is around 3.2%. Other examples of VoIP exchanges are VoIP Business Forum,[5] RouteCall[6] and VoIPexchange.[7]

VoIP market and VoIP exchanges are attracting VAT fraudsters due to the fact that they exchange services and are unregulated (Ainsworth, 2010). Moreover, on these exchanges a broker can trade VoIP minutes for very exotic countries like Tuvalu or the British Virgin Islands. This would be a perfect cover for a VAT fraudster who would need to move their scammed funds to an offshore country.

Online marketplaces

VAT fraud is profitable when the traded items have a small physical volume and a high price, like electronic devices, gold and diamonds. Thus, the costs of freight and storage are negligible compared to the amount of pocketed VAT. The development of e-commerce and online marketplaces created new opportunities for VAT scammers.

- VAT fraud became lucrative, even for small-value goods sold in high volumes.
- Online marketplaces make the connections between goods traders from different regions.

The development of the trading through electronic platform changed the pace and the size of the fraud. The cargo aircrafts filled with products flying many times across the continent were replaced by electronic trading platforms, thereby increasing the severity of VAT fraud effects.

Online marketplaces are a segment of the online retail sector. Many online retailers are operating online marketplaces (Table 9.1).

In 2017, it is estimated that more than 1.66 billion customers worldwide bought products online. During the same year, global online retailers sold goods and services accounting for 2.3 trillion USD[8] with a foreseeable annual growth of over 12%. Online marketplaces represent more than 60% of the total revenues of the online retailers. In 2017, the top 75 marketplaces in the world cumulated over 1.47 trillion USD in turnover.[9]

---

4 VoIP Unlimited launches VoIP exchange (https://commsbusiness.co.uk/news/voip-unlimited-launches-voip-exchange/).
5 www.voipbusinessforum.com/.
6 www.routecall.com/.
7 www.voipexchange.eu.
8 Source: Statista.com.
9 Source: www.digitalcommerce360.com.

Table 9.1 Top online retailers in 2017

Online retailer	2017 Revenue (billion USD)[a]	Focus on online marketplaces
Amazon (US)	136	Amazon.com is the biggest B2C online marketplace outside China.
Alibaba (China)	15.6	Alibaba operates few online marketplaces:
		• Alibaba.com is the primary marketplace dedicated to wholesale trades (business to business).
		• Taobao is the world's biggest online marketplace. It is a consumer-to-consumer ('C2C') marketplace, very similar to eBay.
		• Tmall is the world's second biggest online B2C marketplace, similar to Amazon.com.
		• Alipay is an online payment system for the marketplaces.
Walmart (US)	13	Walmart.com was founded in 2000. Walmart's focus on online marketplaces has increased over the past five years.
Otto (Germany)	12.1	Otto.de was created in 1995. It is Germany's biggest online retailer, specializing in fashion and lifestyle products.
Jingdong Mall (China)	11.6	JD.com went online in January 2004. It is currently the second Chinese online marketplace.
eBay (US)	8.9	eBay.com is an online marketplace where sellers list their products for auctions, and buyers put bids on the products of their choice. The auction process is automated, very similar in nature to an electronic exchange, the only difference being that the products are not standardized.

Source: https://www.mbaskool.com.

a The figures correspond to total company revenues.

The top five online marketplaces are run by United States- and Chinese-based companies:[10]

1   Taobao.com (Chinese platform operated by Alibaba),
2   Tmall.com (Chinese platform operated by Alibaba),
3   Amazon.com (United States business-to-client (B2C) platform operated by Amazon),
4   eBay.com (United States auction platform operated by eBay),
5   JD.com (Chinese B2C platform operated by Jingdong Mall).

In the EU, the figures of e-commerce increased rapidly from 424 billion euros in 2014 to 602 billion in 2017, with a 14% annual growth.[11] Thirty per cent of the

10 Source: www.digitalcommerce360.com.
11 http://ec.europa.eu/eurostat/statistics-explained/index.php/E-commerce_statistics.

transactions concerned purchases from sellers based in countries other than the seller's. The data of the European e-commerce is detailed on the Eurostat database, thereby being part of the national trade gap figures. This point is critical with respect to the exhaustivity of the VAT loss model presented in Chapter 3, which uses the figures of imports and exports as model inputs. Therefore, the scope of the model results presented in Table 9.2 encompasses the European e-commerce which is part of the import and export figures for each of the EU countries.

With the large volume of global transactions, suspicions of tax evasion or avoidance surfaced in 2015. An investigation article from the British newspaper *The Guardian* indicated that Amazon and eBay might have taken profit from on-line VAT fraud.[12] The facts showed that during Christmas, Europe's warehouses and delivery services were overwhelmed by a large number of parcels from overseas ordered through online marketplaces.

Many Chinese sellers were declaring goods shipped to the United Kingdom and the EU low-value packages so they could avoid VAT charges.

Indeed, the European legislation does not require VAT for the importation from outside of the EU of low-value items (below a threshold of 10–22 euros, depending on the country). Additionally, shipments with goods of a total intrinsic value higher than 150 euros are subject to import duty. The legislation dealing with the treatment of imported items of small value is called the Low Value Consignment Relief (LVCR) and is part of Council Directive 2009/132/EC.[13] This directive was designed in 1983 as a simplification measure to optimize the workload of customs administrations and economic operators in the customs clearance of low-value goods.

The EU's regulatory bodies became aware of the LVCR issue in early 2010 with respect to the Chanel Islands' situation. Guernsey and Jersey were the main locations for channelling goods without VAT from outside the EU into the United Kingdom by mail order. These aspects are discussed further in the chapter dedicated to Brexit.

Figure 9.2 describes the way the VAT payment is avoided in this scheme. On-line sellers from outside the EU sell goods in the United Kingdom to final clients or local retailers. The goods are delivered directly to the final client or, in the case of high-volume orders, the items arrive to warehouses operated by the

---

12 Amazon and eBay face crackdown over VAT fraud by overseas sellers (www.theguardian.com/politics/2015/dec/22/tax-officials-investigate-amazon-ebay-vat-fraud-overseas-sellers).

13 *Article 23*: Goods of a total value not exceeding EUR 10 shall be exempt on admission. Member States may grant exemption for imported goods of a total value of more than EUR 10, but not exceeding EUR 22. However, Member States may exclude goods, which have been imported on mail order from the exemption provided for in the first sentence of the first subparagraph.

Article 24: Exemption shall not apply to the following:

a) alcoholic *products;*
b) perfumes *and toilet waters;*
c) tobacco *or tobacco products.*

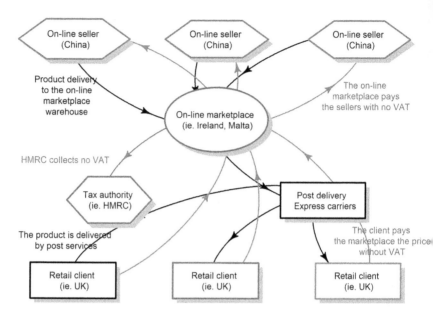

Figure 9.2 VAT evasion through online marketplace. Online sellers from outside the EU sell goods in the United Kingdom to final clients or local retailers. The goods are delivered directly to the final client, or in the case of a high-volume order the items arrive to warehouses operated by the online marketplace. From there the items are redirected using the local postal services to the final customers. The final retail customers pay the agreed-upon price to the marketplace without VAT. The amount is transferred to the seller by the online store. The taxman is completely bypassed in the process.

online marketplace. From there the items are redirected using the local postal services to the final customers. The final retail customers pay the agreed-upon price from the marketplace without VAT. The amount is transferred to the seller by the online store. The taxman is completely bypassed in the process.

The avenues used by the online sellers for VAT evasion include:

- Declaring item values below their real value. For instance a seller can declare a value below 15 euros when delivering a smartphone in the EU.
- Providing a false VAT number in the receipt delivered to the customer. A seller can claim that VAT will be paid and provide a fake VAT number.
- Providing the VAT number of another business. This was the case for a few eBay sellers.
- Registering on an online marketplace as a non-domestic seller while selling to domestic clients. For example a United Kingdom-based seller can register as based in a non-EU state and sell the products to United Kingdom clients.

- Dispatching a big order into small packages, each being below the VAT threshold. This is similar to smurfing in the area of money laundering. For example an exporter that needed to send a few thousand clothing articles to a European country could send a few hundred packages with small value, thereby avoiding the VAT on the whole transaction.

The way VAT is lost due to practices from online marketplaces is similar to the Missing Trader Extra-Community (MTEC) fraud. In the first case, concerning online marketplaces the VAT is not pocketed in the same way as in a classic missing trader case. The tax loss occurs in two instances:

- By misusing LVCR, overseas sellers can sell high-value items at a lower price due to the fact that VAT is neither charged nor paid. This scheme generates a non-recognized VAT liability to the national government. This will affect the sellers that are charging VAT and consequently sell the same items at a higher price. The competition is distorted in favour of the overseas sellers.
- Other sellers are selling products at the same price as domestic retailers, thereby pocketing the VAT charges. This fraud is nothing else but an MTEC scam if the seller is outside the EU and an MTIC scam if the seller is from a different country of the EU.

The key point is to establish the role and the responsibilities with respect to collecting VAT in the mechanism presented in Figure 9.2. Many companies operating the online marketplaces underlined that they have no responsibility for checking the compliance of their sellers with respect to VAT payment. For example in the case investigated in the United Kingdom, eBay and Amazon[14] underlined that their role is to match supply and demand, and that they have no responsibility to insure VAT compliance by sellers using their sites and no liability in cases in which sellers registered on their platform do not comply with the VAT regulation.[15]

One of the main problems in this VAT evasion is related to the 3,000 warehouses based in the United Kingdom that were serving as storage for the imported parcels from overseas. Major companies operating online marketplaces

---

14 Amazon stated, concerning the LVCR VAT evasion,

> Marketplace sellers are independent businesses responsible for complying with their own VAT obligations. We do offer tools and information to assist sellers with their compliance, but we don't have the authority to review their tax affairs. Naturally, we cooperate with HMRC as we are required to by law.

eBay stated, concerning the LVCR VAT evasion, 'We are committed to working with HMRC to ensure our sellers are complying with their legal obligations' (Source: www.theguardian.com/business/2015/nov/01/uk-losing-millions-vat-non-eu-sellers-amazon-ebay).

15 UK losing millions in VAT from non-EU sellers on Amazon and eBay (www.theguardian.com/business/2015/nov/01/uk-losing-millions-vat-non-eu-sellers-amazon-ebay).

like Amazon and eBay operated such warehouses. Even the big Chinese online retailers operate warehouses in the United Kingdom.

After *The Guardian*'s article from 2015, Her Majesty's Revenue and Customs (HMRC) published a report[16] estimating that non-EU traders selling online to United Kingdom customers evaded 1–1.5 billion pounds (1.15–1.67 billion euros) of VAT in 2016. The report incriminates the overseas sellers for 'unfairly undercutting all businesses trading in the UK, abusing the trust of UK consumers and depriving the government of significant revenue' (HMRC, 2016). HMRC proposes as a foreseeable solution the registration and regulation of warehouses, called in HMRC's report 'fulfilment houses'.[17]

After HMRC's assessment a British Parliament's report criticized the estimate of the VAT loss as too cautious. The report incriminated directly online marketplaces for profiting from fraud by sellers who avoid paying the VAT liability and for taking very little action against those sellers.

The European Commission assessed for the first time the size of the potential VAT loss due to LVCR (EY, 2015). The report estimated that the number of small packages shipped into the EU increased from 26 million units in 2000 to 115 million units in 2013. The analysis showed further that VAT loss due to the wrong application of LVCR was somewhere between 309 million and 628 million euros in 2013.

A second evaluation of the European Commission from 2015[18] indicated that 144 million parcels entered under the low-value exemption. The estimate of the VAT foregone increased to almost 1 billion in 2015. In 2016 the European Commission indicated that 150 million packages were coming from non-EU countries and benefit from the LVCR, the potential VAT loss being estimated at 5 billion euros.[19]

Another key point in the analysis of the VAT fraud developed around the LVCR is the role of postal services and express carriers. Until further regulatory evolution that will attach some liability to online marketplaces the responsibility

Table 9.2 Percentage of parcels where VAT and customs tax are collected. Breakdown by delivery type between postal services and express carriers

Tax type	Collection rate for express carriers	Collection rate for National postal services	Total collection rate
VAT	98%	35%	70%
Import duty collection	99%	47%	79%

Source: (Basalisco, Wahl, & Okholm, 2016) and Copenhagen economics.

16 www.theguardian.com/politics/2017/oct/18/amazon-ebay-profiting-online-vat-hmrc-watchdog.
17 A fulfilment house is a business that provides services of storage, breaking bulk, unpacking, repacking and making (or arranging) subsequent deliveries to its clients' customers of goods imported from outside the EU which have been cleared for customs purposes.
18 https://eur-lex.europa.eu/legal-content/EN/ALL/?uri=CELEX%3A52016SC0379.
19 Brussels to crack down on VAT fraud by firms shipping goods to EU (www.theguardian.com/business/2016/nov/30/brussels-to-crack-down-on-vat-by-firms-shipping-goods-to-eu).

of collecting VAT comes to postal services and express couriers. A study mandated by the American postal services company United Parcel Service (UPS) provides a deep-dive analysis of the couriers' liability in collecting both VAT and customs taxes (Basalisco, Wahl, & Okholm, 2016).

The report estimated through an experimental study on 400 online purchases the percentage of items with a lock of VAT payment. The main findings of the UPS report are that for 65% of items delivered through national postal operators the VAT is not collected, whereas for express couriers in only 1% of the cases the VAT is not collected (Table 9.2). Moreover, import duty is collected on only 47% of items imported by postal operators, whereas express carriers score better at 99%. The VAT loss due is estimated to be around 1.05 billion euros. This estimate takes into account only the frequency of collecting VAT on a given item. It does not assess, to a full extent, the likelihood of the value of that item being under-declared by the seller in order to benefit from the LVCR.

A straightforward macro-approach to the VAT loss due to imported parcels from overseas starts with the total value of the products purchased online in the EU. The formula will have the following form:

VAT defrauded = Total number of parcels from overseas
× The average value of a parcel
× Percentage of items where VAT is not collected
× VAT rate

The total number of parcels in 2016 which benefitted from the LVCR was 150 million, the average purchase online was around 90 euros (177 euros is the average above the VAT threshold), the VAT is not collected for 70% of items and the VAT rate is considered 20%. The resulting estimate is 3.7 billion euros, which represents an inferior boundary for the potential VAT loss. This figure would be encompassed by the MTEC fraud estimate provided in Chapter 3.

Table 9.3 synthesizes the main estimates of the VAT loss due to online marketplaces. The 2016 European Commission estimate and the result of the macro-approach are more conservative. The bottom line is that more than half of the loss at the European level occurs in the United Kingdom.

Table 9.3 Estimates of the VAT loss due to non-compliant sellers trading through online marketplaces

Study	VAT loss estimate (billion euros)	Scope
UPS (2015)	1.05	EU
European Commission – EY (2013)	0.5	EU
HMRC (2016)	1.65	UK only
European Commission (2015)	1.00	EU
European Commission (2016)	5	EU
Estimate macro-approach (2016)	3.7	EU

Peer-to-peer delivery services

The progress of the sharing economy started by Uber and Airbnb touched recently the delivery and shipping sectors. The aim of peer-to-peer delivery services is to compete with traditional delivery services like the national postal services and express couriers. Peer-to-peer delivery services are online platforms that bring together senders and bringers. A person who needs to send an item from one point to another will find ad hoc purveyors that make the journey between the desired points as part of their commutes. The delivery person will charge a fee to the sender, which will be lower than the cost of a postal services or an express courier.

The pioneer of peer-to-peer services is the Norwegian company Nimber.[20] Nimber's fee, paid by the sender, is computed with a pricing algorithm[21] that estimates a fair price depending on the conditions of the delivery. Grabr, Roadie and GoShare are a few examples of start-ups seeking growth in this niche.

Peer-to-peer delivery services could potentially reshape e-commerce. If currently deliveries are done through professional services, in the future deliveries from Amazon or Alibaba could be operated by peer-to-peer services. For instance if a buyer from London purchased an item from a Hong Kongese seller over the internet, the delivery could be done by a bringer that had a trip from Hong Kong to London. Thus, this trade would pass below every radar of the customs or tax office. No authority would be able to collect VAT or customs taxes on such schemes.

Multilevel marketing

Multilevel marketing (MLM) is a commercial technique used by some sales and distribution companies to incentivize their current sales force to recruit new sales agents and distributors. Each sales agent involved in such a scheme has two streams of revenue:

- a first stream from the direct sales of the product,
- a second stream consisting of fees from the sales force that (s)he recruited.

MLM appeared in the mid-1960s and spread since in almost all developed and emerging countries (Ella, 1973). A simplified structure of an MLM pyramidal scheme is presented in Figure 9.3. The pyramid is organized in levels. Each agent in a given level k is in charge of selling the product of the company and of the recruitment of new agents. The new agents in the level $k + 1$ will pay fees (sometimes called referral fees) to agents in the upper level. The fees are in many cases fixed and in some cases include a variable part, depending on agents' turnover.

---

20 'Shipping anything, anytime, anywhere' is the motto of the Norwegian pioneer of the peer-to-peer delivery.
21 Peer-to-peer delivery service arrives in UK (www.edie.net/news/5/Nimber-peer-to-peer-social-delivery-service-arrives-in-UK/).

Multi-level Marketing: Pyramidal structure

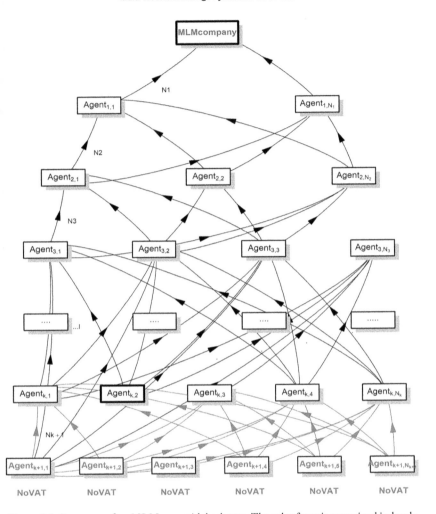

Figure 9.3 Structure of an MLM pyramidal scheme. The sales force is organized in levels. Each agent in a given level *k* is in charge of the recruitment and the collection of referral fees from the agents in the next level *k+1*. The agents in the newer (lower) levels are in most cases sole traders and not registered for VAT.

Pyramidal marketing companies have been exposed to frauds and scams since the 1970s, a fact largely covered by the specialized literature (Vander Nat, 2002; Muncy, 2004). Big MLM companies raised suspicions around their practices, including Herbalife, an American-based company listed on the stock exchange.[22] Herbalife revenue in 2015 was around 4.5 billion USD.

22 www.newsweek.com/john-oliver-last-week-tonight-herbalife-pyramid-scheme-517881.

In 2014, the Federal Trade Commission (FTC) opened an investigation into Herbalife.[23] The company was accused for its deceptive earnings claims, many agents being misled by Herbalife with promises of quick financial gains. In July 2016,[24] Herbalife settled with the FTC and agreed to pay 200 million USD and fundamentally restructure its business. Nearly 350,000 people who lost money running Herbalife businesses were reimbursed as part of the FTC settlement deal. One avenue in the crime spectrum that has not yet been explored or investigated is the tax evasion and in particular the VAT fraud.[25]

There is currently no material evidence or case around the involvement of MLM businesses in VAT fraud. Nevertheless, MLM is the perfect candidate for front-running a VAT scam for various reasons:

- MLM structures are semi-centralized. The biggest part of sales agents are not employed with the MLM company and have, in many cases, no direct link with it. Agents in the lower levels do not report to the MLM company's management and are not invoiced or do not pay the fees directly to the company. In the simplified structure depicted in Figure 9.3 only the upper-level agents (level 1, 2 or 3) may be in direct contact with the MLM company, while the agents in level $k+1$ will report to the level k. Thus, any potential tax or accounting-related issue *does* not concern the MLM company.

- MLM companies sell mainly low- and medium-value products tailored for high volume. The range of products marketed through MLM (or direct sales[26]) includes health, wellness and alternative-medicine products. Over the past years, the MLM product range became wider based on online sales capacity, thereby including non-physical products like training packages, retail trading kits and self-help methods. The non-physical products do not have a clear status with respect to VAT regime. Training or self-improvement packs are in theory services that should change VAT. In the context of an MLM pyramid, an agent can pay the value of the product as part of the referral fees or upfront subscription for joining the pyramid.[27]

- MLM's organization includes both incorporated companies and sole traders. In fact, the MLM companies are recruiting people that look for sources of additional income or to be able to work from home. Thus, they will be generally below the threshold of VAT registration, and revenue from selling the products or from other agents' fees is not liable for VAT.

---

23 www.businessinsider.com/herbalife-halted-2014-3.

24 www.ftc.gov/news-events/press-releases/2017/01/ftc-sends-checks-nearly-350000-victims-herbalifes-multi-level.

25 www.forssen.com/Momsp%C3%A4rm2007eng.pdf.

26 The terms multilevel marketing and direct sales are related but not similar.

27 There were cases of MLM companies selling training packages on how to become an MLM agent. In this particular case, it is not clear whether the agent pays for the pyramid fee or is a client of the pyramid and pays for the product.

- MLM structures are transnational and have big networks of agents in different countries, with different VAT regimes, thereby making them almost impossible to fully audit.
- The turnover of the commercial sales force including all agents is high. Therefore, the traceability of the various revenue streams requires complex processes.
- Due to its complex structure, governance policies and internal controls and audits are very difficult to implement in an MLM company.

In a simplified MLM structure (Figure 9.3) the number of sales agents $\left(n_1,n_2,n_3,\ldots,n_K,n_{K+1}\right)$ should increase exponentlially with each level k in order to keep the pyramid running. For increasing the number of agents, the recruiting agents use high-pressure sales techniques. Successful MLM companies have not only a big number of agents but a quickly increasing pool of agents.

If the sales revenues of an agent are small, the total turnover of an MLM company can reach billions of euros. The revenue generated by an agent may not be liable for VAT, but when consolidated into the full pyramid with all its levels, the VAT liability is very big. Therefore, MLM structures would be ideal for defrauding VAT and going below the radar of the taxman.

No VAT liability is paid by the lower-level agents after a product is sold, even if the product is sold locally at a price including the equivalent VAT mark-up equal. The products are provided by the MLM company from overseas at a price that does not carry VAT. Online commerce trading and delivery platforms like Amazon, Alibaba, eBay and many others facilitate the delivery of small-volume products overseas and can be easily used in the MLM structure as part of the supply chain. Similarly to a basic MTIC (or MTEC) fraud, goods or services are purchased from another country without VAT and sold locally at a price that includes a VAT equivalent.

The MLM structure will afterwards centralize the equivalent amounts of VAT not declared in the countries of its agents. The transfers would be under the form of pyramids fees or other various labels like subscription, referral or royalty fees.

Without any link between the top of the pyramid and the lower strata, it is almost impossible to trace a potential fraud. When a pyramid stops or the MLM company decides to stop it, the lower layers are exposed to any potential tax liability. In a typical MLM company agents are generally located in the EU as well as outside of the EU. Thus, any VAT fraud would be a mix of MTIC and MTEC.

An MLM pyramidal structure could serve for the more sophisticated version of the VAT fraud: the carousel. The carousel can be established with the participation of agents from a few levels of the pyramid. Some agents would be required in this case to register for VAT in their countries.

The scenario described earlier is one of those cases where the line between the tax evasion and the tax avoidance is very murky, thereby making any investigation with respect to VAT fraud long and complex.

A recent investigation of a 250 million euro carousel scam, dismantled by the Spanish authorities as part of Operation *Dreams*,[28] revealed that part of the system used to transfer and launder the funds of the VAT fraud was based on an MLM structure.

Social engineering

Introduced in the popular culture by Kevin Mitnick[29] (Mitnick, 2002), the term 'social engineering' denotes manipulation of people resulting in the disclosing of confidential information. The definition provided by Mitnick (2002) states that

> social engineering uses influence and persuasion to deceive people by convincing them that the social engineer is someone he is not, or by manipulation. As a result, the social engineer is able to take advantage of people to obtain information with or without the use of technology.

The initial meaning of social engineering referred to tactics used by fraudsters to obtain the credentials of credit cards or online banking access. Usually, the victim received a letter or a phone call from a social engineer, who pretended to be working for a bank or for another institution. The victim was required to share confidential information or even to send money to a given account. The development of the internet was a catalyst for social engineers. The term phishing was introduced for all the techniques leveraged by technology for obtaining sensitive information. In the early 2000s, email spoofing was the preferred technology, many banks being touched by this fraud.

The range of tools and techniques labelled as social engineering has widened over the past decade, bolstered by social media and the technology for smartphones. The use of social engineering is not limited anymore to extracting confidential information. Creating or stealing identities is one of the most recent social engineering tools used by criminals in the sphere of financial crime. Erasing trails or creating misleading information for investigators after a crime is committed is another silo of social engineering. With the quick development of private intelligence agencies, fraudsters are able to hire trained resources to better dissimulate and hide their crimes.

A resurgence in crimes related to the 'social engineering' concept was revealed by the Israeli police.[30] The 'social engineers' moved from skimming credit card

28 www.laverdad.es/murcia/detenidos-operacion-internacional-20180504114641-nt.html.
29 In the 1990s Kevin Mitnick was on the Federal Bureau of Investigation (FBI)'s most wanted list. He was one of the most dangerous hackers, breaking into the networks of major companies (i.e., IBM, Nokia and Motorola). After serving a sentence in prison for few years he became a researcher and consultant in cyber-security.
30 As Israel-based financial fraud soars, police swoop on 20 suspects as part of global, FBI-led sting (www.timesofisrael.com/as-israel-based-financial-fraud-soars-police-swoop-on-20-suspects-as-part-of-global-fbi-led-sting/).

information towards more profitable frauds against corporations. In 2017, a joint investigation between the Federal Bureau of Investigation (FBI) and Israeli law enforcement identified a criminal group which allegedly approached companies, including insurance companies, banks and pension funds abroad. They deployed a very complex and evolved social engineering crime type under the form of the so-called CEO fraud (described later in this section). The criminals claimed to be senior managers of the targeted companies and approached regular employees of the companies. They used their persuasion techniques to engage the legitimate employees in financial transactions and entrusted them with transferring large amounts of money to other accounts for various fictitious reasons. The transferred money moved through a few bank accounts, mainly located in China and other jurisdictions, and finally reached the criminals. Israeli police revealed that the targeted companies were based in Poland, Finland, India, France and the United States.

The Israeli investigators revealed also that the 'social engineers' had ties with the Israeli-Arab Hariri crime organization, one of Israel's most powerful and dangerous organized crime groups. This pattern was also observed in the *Carbon Connection* era, when criminals from France fled to Israel and then got acquainted with the local organized crime. These alliances were necessary as both groups needed protection from other criminal gangs, services which are obviously offered in exchange for a percentage of the proceeds.

Currently, Israel seems to be the main hub of the social engineering crimes. Two factors contribute to this phenomenon:

a   Israel has a policy of compulsory military service. The young population is trained with respect to military techniques, and many see real action in the conflict zones. This constitutes an excellent recruiting pool for organized crime.

b   Israel has a strong education system in technology fields, being the world's top country in terms of technology start-ups. Israeli firms are the main players in the security software market. Thus, crime has also a pool of highly competent people for recruitment.

These two features create a unique environment for the development of social engineering crimes. The European investigators became aware of a new trend in the underworld originating from the social engineering universe and resulting in new type of scams like the CEO fraud.[31]

Many of the VAT fraudsters involved in the '*Carbon Connection*' have allegedly followed a professional reconversion in social engineering. Therefore, it is expected that the new wave of the VAT frauds will be empowered by the techniques of social engineering.

---

31 EU and Israeli police join forces against social engineering (www.europol.europa.eu/newsroom/news/eu-and-israeli-police-join-forces-against-social-engineering).

This section presents the following aspects relevant for the VAT fraud with respect to social engineering:

- psychological manipulation and
- identity engineering.

Psychological manipulation

Psychological manipulation occurs in many walks of life, encompassing both legal and illegal activities. It stems from the human need to enhance or reinforce one's position in a group by misleading other individuals of that group. Technology can enhance or accelerate this manipulation. The techniques of psychological manipulating are not recent and encompass an area extensively studied in psychology (Buss, 1987).

In the criminal world and especially in the financial crime, psychological manipulation is the key tool for developing any scam. Psychological subversion and verbal manipulation are terms used to describe the process in which a criminal exploits irrational components in civilians' behaviour.

The association of criminal behaviour with psychological manipulation was explored by psychologists Hofer (1989) and showed that manipulation is a psychological defence mechanism which plays a key role in shaping antisocial personalities. Hofer (1989) shows that the defence mechanism is associated with two types of antisocial personality: 'primitive' borderline and 'narcissistic', which manifest a different pattern of manipulative.

The research concerning the link between psychological manipulation and financial crime is very scarce. Wood (2016) addressed cognitive factors that result in susceptibility to financial crimes, including financial literacy, numeracy and deliberative reasoning.

This research showed that financial scammers tend to use manipulative techniques to engage with the victim on an emotional level and to put them in a position to make impulsive decisions. The factors that increase the likelihood of impulsive decision-making versus rational decision-making are linked to the victim's preconditioning and to their low financial literacy.

The VAT scammers and especially the carousel fraudsters exceed in this area. Engineering, a big-scale fraud, involves contacts with various institutions, including business registries, banks, legitimate clients, customs officers and tax authorities. A basic carousel scheme, such as that presented in Figure 9.4, is seemingly simple, but in reality, each step involves many likelihoods of failure for the fraudsters. A few of the reasons are:

- The VAT fraudsters raid a market where they have no expertise. The scammer needs, in a very short term, to be able to present himself to the main players of that market as an expert with extensive experience and knowledge in order to be able to establish trading relationships.
- VAT evasion is using the banking systems. At a given time the fraudsters need to transfer huge amounts of money (in some cases hundreds of

millions) to accounts from other countries. Even basic Know Your Customer (KYC) filters in a bank are alerted by this type of transactions. The criminal needs to inspire confidence to the banker in order to execute big transfers.

- Companies involved in VAT frauds are often audited by legitimate accountants. The manager of the company involved in a carousel scheme needs to influence the accountant in such a way that will distract its attention from the VAT liability.
- Authorities have in some cases investigated companies involved in VAT fraud while they were operating. The results were limited, and the fraud was neither stopped nor reduced following those investigations.
- In many cases VAT fraudsters were known by the police for being part of criminal networks. In spite of those evidences, they were able to pocket VAT from taxpayers.
- Public opinion was advertised in most VAT cases by journalists in the media. Nevertheless, the reaction was very limited, and the level of awareness remained unchanged.

The aspects mentioned here are the results of a criminal's ability to manipulate people from various walks of life. The manipulated people were different in behaviour, training and social position. Their common trait is the fact that each one has an irrational and inconstant pattern in decision-making. This irrational judgement was targeted and exploited by criminal psychological manipulation. Thus, VAT fraudsters were able to gain the confidence and misuse the trust of legitimate and honest citizens.

The trait of individuals towards a systematic pattern of departure from standards of logic and accuracy in the decision-making process is labelled as a cognitive bias (Haselton, 2005).

The psychological manipulation targets the cognitive biases of the various third parties that enter into contact with a criminal. As pointed out by Hofer (1989), in this case the manipulation is nothing more than a defence mechanism. The criminal needs to protect his/her fraudulent enterprise from external factors and has to mislead third parties into thinking he/she is legitimate.

A few examples of cognitive biases used in relation to the VAT frauds are discussed hereafter and include stereotyping, expectation, confirmation biases, etc.

Stereotyping

Stereotyping is a common form of cognitive bias which refers to the expectation that a person has certain attributes or qualities based on the characteristics of a group they belong to, without having real information about that individual.

Stereotyping leads people to expect certain actions from members of social groups.

For example, a person dressed in a navy-blue suit would be, in many cases, associated with a banking or law professional, while a person dressed in a flamboyant-coloured suit might raise questions to an unadvised person.

Stereotyping is a common bias in all walks of life. The bias is reverse-engineered by criminals in order to access information or to manipulate the various people they are interacting with. Most people have very strong stereotypes, with respect to organized crime and towards criminals.

The role of media in reinforcing stereotyping was underlined by previous researches. Kidd-Hewitt (2002) analyzed the way the media presents crime stories. The study concluded that the media distorts and manipulates public perceptions about criminals, thereby reinforcing stereotyping and prejudice.

In everyday life, people would expect that a criminal would look and behave like a character portrayed in a Hollywood production or a tabloid report. These stereotypes apply also for white-collar criminals. In real life, criminal and especially white-collar criminals do not fit at all the classic stereotypes. Most are very well educated, well brought up, fluent in a few languages and interested in charity work. A bank manager or a compliance officer in a financial institution would not have any doubt that such a person was an honest professional. Criminals are aware of this bias and use it in their favour.

An example is that of the American banker Eugene Gourevitch,[32] allegedly involved in laundering VAT fraud proceeds in the *Phuncards-Broker* case. Gourevitch had all the features of an honest professional. Groomed in the Berkeley University, he was fluent in four languages and was frequenting influent political personalities. Before the VAT scam episode he was president of a United States-based management consultancy between 2001 and 2007 (Virage Consulting Ltd.) and a director of a commercial bank based in the Kyrgyz Republic (Asian Universal Bank). He was also involved as an executive in a New York-based hedge fund (Gamma Square Partners). Despite an impressive resume, Gourevitch was accused in Operation *Phuncards-Broker* of laundering huge amounts of pocketed VAT for various crime gangs in connection with the Calabrian syndicate 'Ndrangheta. In a first instance, he managed to avoid the Italian justice system, but a few years later the American justice system condemned him for wire fraud.[33] His character would never be suspicioned at the first sight of ties with criminals or of criminal behaviour. This is for the simple reason that he would not fit the stereotypes. Thus, a person like Gourevitch would have an easy time navigating high social strata. He was able to gain trust from other bankers or honest business partners in establishing his alleged schemes.

This is just one example of how stereotyping bias can limit the assessment of an individual. The modern-type criminal is very far away from the mainstream stereotype, thereby being difficult to spot, even by a professional investigator.

---

32 US citizen was a key player in alleged Italian telecom fraud (www.reuters.com/article/urnidgns 002570f3005978d8852576df0080ec42/us-citizen-a-key-player-in-alleged-italian-telecom-fraud-idUS362983270120100308).

33 www.bloomberg.com/news/articles/2016-07-10/banker-sitting-in-u-s-prison-has-a-most-incredible-tale-to-tell.

Another avenue where stereotyping works in favour of the criminal is related to the way in which a corporation or an organization is perceived. Generally, decision makers tend to trust more and accept more easily transactions with a big, well-reputed corporation than with a smaller company. Stereotyping with respect to the corporate world refers to the fact that a decision maker will always be more suspicious when doing business with a small company. Moreover when dealing with a major firm of a given market, a decision maker may even tend to bend the rules of a transaction just to secure a deal.

The case of the VAT fraud on the VoIP market in Italy provides again a sound example. The key company in this VAT scam was Italy's biggest telecommunication operator, Telecom Italia (Richard, 2013). Many individuals that were caught in the web of this huge fraud did not have even the smallest doubt about this company.

One of Telecom Italia's[34] subsidiaries specializing in wholesale voice and broadband unit, Telecom Italia Sparkle, was intermediating VoIP transactions between 2003 and 2006, serving for a VAT scam. The involvement of the firm in Operation *Phuncards-Broker* was unexpected. The banks serving the firm, the Italian tax authorities and the business partners did not suspect such a reputed firm to have ties with organized crime. This did not fit the stereotypes. The criminals used Telecom Italia's reputation in order to get VAT reimbursements from the Italian tax authorities. Indeed, a bigger, well-reputed company would raise less suspicion, when it asks for a big VAT refund, than a small company. This byproduct of stereotyping is often used by MTICers, who try to hook up with big companies in order to be able to claim VAT reimbursement.

Expectation and confirmation biases

The expectation bias represents the propensity of an individual to trust and share information that agrees with the results and outcomes of his/her analysis. A relatively similar cognitive bias is the confirmation bias, which refers to the tendency of an individual to give more weight and attach more importance to information that confirms a priori ideas or hypotheses about a given subject.

In the context of the VAT fraud in CO_2 emissions markets a question arises naturally: why did trading desks from major investment banks involved in the market-making on carbon markets not peak any signal related to the massive inflow of fraud-related transactions?

Investment banks have sophisticated tools and methods to drill down to very detailed aspects of market behaviours. Yet between 2008 and 2009, these approaches have completely ignored the criminal phenomenon.

In the financial sector both expectation and confirmation biases are frequent amongst professional inverts and advisors.[35] The bias also exists on the trading

---

34 Fresh scandal embarrasses Telecom Italia (www.ft.com/content/09d43776-2244-11df-9a 72-00144feab49a).

35 How to ignore the yes-man in your head (www.wsj.com/articles/SB10001424052748703811604574533680037778184).

floors of major financial institutions, a fact that leads in many cases to irrational market behaviour. A study on stock message boards using data from one of the largest message board operators in South Korea revealed that investors exhibit confirmation biases (Park, 2013). The traders analyzed in that research exhibited a strong propensity and interest towards messages that support their prior beliefs. The study showed that this flaw is more pronounced for traders with higher perceived knowledge about the market and higher strength of belief toward a particular stock.

Recent research concerning the European CO_2 market showed that policy issues could lead to expectation bias (Yang, 2018). The research showed breaches in the weak efficient-market hypothesis (EMH) for the CO_2 prices. This finding is explained in the fact, by the strong role of policies on the carbon market. The changes and arrangements in policy can affect massively the price signal.

These two cognitive flaws could partially answer the question:

- *Confirmation bias*: In March 2009 the CO_2 emissions permits traded on BlueNext exchange (spot) and on the London exchange Intercontinental Exchange (ICE) (futures) dipped sharply to a level below 9 euros, representing at the time an absolute minima. The investment banks justified this drop in prices at the time using the economic downturn and the fact that the market was massively selling. Markets touched by MTIC fraud experienced contraction in prices. This fact was ignored, and the major institution gave more weight to outcomes that confirmed their analysis. Thus, low prices of CO_2 emissions permits were considered to be related to economic downturn and not to VAT fraud.
- *Expectation bias*: The a priori belief was that the market is driven by industrial companies that hedged their exposure to the emission market. The information concerning the likelihood of massive fraudulent trades was ignored. Traders and analysts in major investing banks treated preferentially the information linked to their a priori beliefs regarding the supply-demand equilibrium in carbon markets. Furthermore, policy changes operated by the European decision makers between 2008 and 2009 often led potentially to expectation bias, as shown by Yang (2018). This bias accentuated the fraud as major banks brought liquidity to the CO_2 market; this liquidity worked in favour of VAT fraudsters.

Status quo bias

Status quo bias refers to the propensity for the current state of things and to adversity towards any change that would be perceived as risky. Status quo bias is mentioned in studies analyzing governments that often fail to adopt policies which economists consider to be efficiency enhancing (Fernandez, 1991). Governments are reluctant to change whenever the individual which would profit or lose from a policy reform is not clearly identified.

A similar phenomenon occurred over the past decade in the case of the reforms and measures for tackling VAT fraud. A reform of the VAT system like that started by the European Commission in 2017 could have a complex impact and consequences on the EU's economy.

European governments' representatives were very reluctant to accept that the endemic VAT fraud has a massive impact on the EU's economy. The various waves of tax fraud that raided different markets starting with electronics devices in the early 2000s did not make aware the European decision makers.

The attitude changed since 2010, with journalists exposing the size of the fraud. Nevertheless, the inertia of leaving the VAT policies unchanged and avoiding being accountable for a potential change have still persisted. The European decision makers choose quick fixes, including the Reverse Charge in order to tackle the spread of the MTIC on a given market.

Mental accounting bias

Mental accounting is a concept that refers to the tendency of individuals to classify their financial flows depending on subjective criteria (Thaler, 1999). These criteria encompass the source of the financial resource, the way the money is gained and the purpose of their spending. Mental accounting leads to financial decisions deviating from optimal spending and investing.

Mental accounting is responsible for bad decision-making in most personal finance issues: debt, overspending, etc. While this aspect is widely studied, the role of mental accounting in decision-making within organizations is less covered by specialists. Nevertheless, some research underlines the presence of mental accounting amongst professional investors (Lim, 2006) and traders (Haigh, 2005).

Some interesting events that occurred in 2009 on the Paris-based CO_2 emissions exchange BlueNext could have been the result of mental accounting. At that time, BlueNext was the world's biggest environmental exchange, focussed mainly on CO_2 emissions. The exchange was targeted by VAT fraudsters due to the fact that the exchange was paying to its French customers the price with VAT upon sale.

A relatively obscure French company called 'Crepuscule'[36] was in the top five of BlueNext's clients in terms of transactions, next to big names like Barclays and Societe Generale. The company was managed by a group of individuals with no background or training in the financial market. 'Crepuscule' traded between 2008 and 2009 CO_2 emissions permits for a value of 827 million euros, which represents the sale of 65 million tonnes, accounting for half of the allowances allocated to French emitters. The proceeds of crime were transferred to Hong Kong, Cyprus, Montenegro and Latvia (Frunza, 2015).

A simple question comes up: how a company with no track record managed to trade such big volumes on the world's biggest CO_2 exchange and why BlueNext's depositary bank[37] sent hundreds of millions of euros towards tax-havens. This

36 Crepuscule means twilight in French.
37 BlueNext's bank was 'Caisse de Depots et Consignation', an institution owned by the French government.

question was also raised by Crepuscule's attorneys when the case[38] was judged in a French court.

BlueNext's management most likely separated the financial flows related to market operations from those related to VAT collection and reimbursement. Thus, a client like Crepuscule with a big turnover was perceived as profitable in light of its market transactions because the VAT concerning the VAT reimbursement was allocated to a different silo. This is in fact a depiction of mental accounting, where financial flows are accounted for separately, even if in reality they were supposed to be part of the same picture. This resulted in BlueNext having a huge balance of reimbursements from the French treasury with respect to VAT. The separation between market transactions and VAT flows was corrected when the gap reached astronomical numbers. By the time the bias was wiped out, the VAT fraud had already disrupted the market.

In the case of the VAT fraud, the parties involved in a transaction dissociate the funds due as VAT liability and the profit of the company.

Weber's law

Weber's law is a common cognitive bias linked to the perception of an external stimulus. The difference in the perception of stimulus decreases with the increase in the intensity of the stimulus.[39] The formal definition of Weber's law provided by size (Fechner, Howes, & Boring, 1860) states that the 'Simple differential sensitivity is inversely proportional to the size of the components of the difference; relative differential sensitivity remains the same regardless of size'.

Mourao (2012) studied Weber's law in relation to the public expenditure and the increased level of debt in the developed country. The research showed that an expanded public sector leads politicians to make more significant, opportunistic distortions of public expenditures than the distortions observed when the public sector is diminished.

This observation can easily be extended to governments' decision-making processes with regards to VAT fraud. When an economy has already suffered huge economic losses, the political decision maker will be less sensitive to a big loss due to a fraud. This was the case during the 2009 economic crisis when the CO_2 emissions VAT fraud took place. European economies had already suffered huge losses and an increase in the public debt. The Eurozone required a budget of hundreds of billions of euros to bail out major banks. The additional 10 billion euros of pocketed VAT evasion on the CO_2 emissions markets were lost like tears in rain. This could explain why in 2009 the European governments reacted apathetically to the spread of the fraud into CO_2 emissions markets.

---

38 www.liberation.fr/france/2017/05/28/arnaque-a-la-tva-itineraire-d-un-cerveau-carbonise_1572927.

39 A simple example would be the difference in perception of a heat source placed near the skin of a human. The human will have a better differential sensitivity when the temperature of the heat source increases from 40°C to 50°C compared to the case when it increases from 400°C to 410°C.

The law applies also to the way the public opinion reacts to the size of various crimes. In plain words Weber's law can be summarized as the fact that the public opinion will be more sensitive to a pickpocket stealing a hundred euros than to a VAT scheme defrauding billions of euros.

This cognitive bias is leveraged by criminals knowing that it is easier from a given angle to operate a scam defrauding billions than to commit a small theft.

Identity engineering

The term identity engineering encompasses a set of techniques used to dissimulate the information concerning a person. Identity engineering aims to dissociate the criminal identity from its real identity and to make a foreseeable crime investigation more difficult to investigate.

Multiple identities

The fall of the Soviet Union was one of the turning points in the modern history that influenced global migration. The accelerated expansion of the EU as well as the fast-paced globalization of the economy led to mass migration between different regions of the planet. The migration led to people being able to obtain multiple residences and multiple passports. The issue of multiple identities is a direct consequence of globalization (Lane, 2017) and is one of the critical points in tackling transnational crime.

Assessing a person's background becomes more complicated when that person has multiple passports from countries using different alphabets.

When an individual holds a few passports from various countries with different languages, and a name needs to be translated from one language to another, a few versions are available, depending on the transliteration method. As a result, one individual would be able to have multiple identities in a relatively easy way. Chapter 12 discusses the way transliteration works and what methods can be used to address this issue. For example a citizen born in Ukraine during the Soviet Union and emigrating to Israel and after to France would have at least four passports in four different languages, and the names would have different versions when transposed in the Latin alphabet. Politically exposed persons[40] are a special category with respect to the issue of multiple identities. Background checking for persons with multiple names in different identity documents (Olson, 2012) is a real challenge for investigators.

The VAT carousel fraud requires the registration of multiple companies in multiple jurisdictions as well as opening bank accounts in different countries. Most of the big VAT carousel cases involved citizens holding at least two passports, depending on the gang they were involved with. Binationals can open

---

40 An example is the Moldovan entrepreneur Vladimir Plahotniuc, who owns also a Romanian passport under the name Vlad Ulinici (www.intellinews.com/the-talented-mr-plahotniuc-500015455/?archive=bne).

banking accounts in different banks based in different countries with different passports. The name associated with the account would not necessarily be similar. Thus, in the case of an Enhanced Due Diligence about this type of client, a bank would face real difficulties in establishing all the links of the criminal network. This can explain why stolen VAT funds are in most cases not recovered.

Synthetic identities

The increasing role of social media and online content in the life of individuals brought deep societal changes. Moreover, online profiles play an increasing role in establishing the virtual footprint of an individual. A person can be profiled through his/her online activity including social networks or other virtual data sources.

Identity fraud is an increasing trend in the criminal activities, netting over 1.3 million victims, 16.8 billion USD stolen, in 2017.[41] Criminals would always prefer to use identities different from their own for multiple reasons:

- to avoid and mislead the direct surveillances of the authorities,
- to protect themselves from enemy groups and
- to avoid divulging their identity to agents infiltrating the criminal world.

Identity fraud is a classic avenue used by criminals to operate transactions or open accounts with a different identity. Yet identity fraud is increasingly difficult to operate due to more effective security tools.

Synthetic identity fraud is a recent trend which does not involve taking information from a different person but creating a synthetic fake identity. The creating of the synthetic identity can be done by using various data from a few persons and adding them into an identity: for example a driver ID from one person, a name from another, a proof of address from a third person and a social security number or tax identifier from a fourth person. Thus, a synthetic identity is engineered using both real and fake data. The person behind this synthetic identity is fictitious and does not exist in reality. Because part of the info behind a synthetic identity is real, screening systems have a hard time detecting them. This is also explained by the fact that information concerning individuals in a given jurisdiction is harboured in siloed, unlinked databases. For instance, information concerning the tax identifiers, social security numbers, ID numbers and phone numbers are in most countries managed by different administrative entities, with different operating models and different data-warehouses which do not talk to one another. With this information a criminal obtains other documents, like IDs or passports, opens bank accounts or registers for a business.

Online platforms and the dematerialization of the governmental services facilitate the creation of fake synthetic identities. The increasing trend in the digitalization of public administrative processes leads to the risk that an individual can apply for an ID, a passport or a taxpayer number without having any physical

41 Source: Javelin Strategy & Research's 2018 Identity Fraud Survey (https://kyc360.com/news/2018-identity-fraud-survey-17-billion-lost-crooks/).

contact with a representative of an administration. Once created this synthetic identity is brought to life by a series of actions which would not require an ID:

- registering at conferences or events,
- booking hotels in various locations around the world,
- purchasing travelling tickets for trains and buses,
- creating content on social networks and social media – for example using Facebook to indicate the place they are at and the activity they are doing at a given time (the 'check-in' feature),
- building websites related to a business or a professional activity and
- creating CVs on professional platforms like LinkedIn.

Private intelligence services providers propose services consisting of creating and managing synthetic identities in order to mislead the possible investigators or asset-recovery companies.

Synthetic identities are used to open a new financial account with the primary intent of committing fraud (also called the new account fraud). This fraud accounted for 5 billion USD in losses in 2014, with an annual cumulated annual growth of 44%, reaching 8 billion USD in 2018.[42] Also, it is estimated that synthetic ID fraud accounts for 80% of all credit card fraud losses and nearly one-fifth of credit card charge-offs.[43]

The synthetic identity will constitute a growing issue not only for credit cards frauds but also for tax fraudsters. The electronic residence is a new service proposed by a few countries. As an example Estonia[44] had proposed since 1 December 2014 a virtual e-residence for the cost of only 100 euros. The virtual residence allows its owner to open and operate a business in an Estonian territory without physically being there. The Estonian authorities prescreen the applicant before approving a e-residence application. The number of applications for the Estonian virtual residence peaked with the Panama Papers scandal and Brexit. Since 2017, a Finish online banking company, Holvi,[45] has proposed banking services for business registered virtually in Estonia. Therefore, an applicant can obtain an e-residence register a business and open a business account in a country without being there.

CEO fraud is an example of how the newest crimes are using the principle of synthetic identity fraud. CEO fraud, known as Business Email Compromise (BEC), refers to a crime where a criminal creates a synthetic identity of a company's CEO or a senior executive in a company. By pretending to have a high position in a firm the criminal aims to extract funds from a victim or to obtain information that could potentially result in illegal financial gains. To build this image the criminal uses social networks like LinkedIn or Facebook, posting references to their professional activity. The online content and social networks

---

42 Source: Javelin Strategy & Research (www.trulioo.com/blog/synthetic-identity-fraud/).
43 Source: Equifax (www.equifax.com/assets/IFS/syntheticID-fraud_wp.pdf).
44 www.theguardian.com/world/2016/sep/15/estonia-e-residency-european-union-brexit-eu-referendum.
45 https://about.holvi.com/.

also provide them with leads about the potential victims and the organization to which they belong. The CEO fraud has the following steps:

a   Criminals create a synthetic profile of a CEO, senior executive or attorney. They generally have fake online profiles, fake websites and fake corporate email addresses. For the sake of argument if a criminal wants to appear as an executive in a big corporation, an email similar to the official email of that corporation will be used. (i.e., @jpmorganoffice.com instead of @jpmorgan. com). Criminals also pretend to be senior managers in tax authorities, and they use email version that would sound like the real one. For instance, if they are claiming to be from the British customs and revenues office they may use emails like @hmrc-online.co.uk instead of @hmrc.co.uk.

b   Criminals carefully choose their victims. They target both individuals and corporations. In the corporate world criminals can target legal, accounting or human resources in a company in order to get information or claim a refund.

c   Criminals start a campaign of phishing and cold calls, and solicit the victims for wire transfers or for confidential information. The money transfer is not always the main goal. Extracting confidential information from the victims can help criminals to pursue and develop other frauds. For example obtaining an ID number and passport code can be useful for the synthetic identity fraud. Also, tax-related information can be useful for tax evasion, especially in the VAT fraud area.

d   Once the criminal reaches his goal (s)he erases all information related to his synthetic identity of CEO.

Currently there are no investigations concerning the use of synthetic identities in VAT scams. Missing traders are comfortable with exploring many flaws of the VAT system. The foreseeable digitalization of the VAT system will close the gate for VAT evasion in its current state. The scammers will need to explore new paths, and creating synthetic identities is an option that criminals will seriously consider.

An example of a VAT fraudster who used multiple synthetic identities is Alison Reynolds.[46] The scammer was sentenced in 2011 by a British court for a total of seven years for illegally reclaiming 118,000 pounds in VAT and committing forgery. Alison Reynolds, a British citizen, had used at least 15 different names and identities in recent years. HMRC officers discovered that Reynolds had forged purchase invoices and Companies House documents, and used various bank accounts and identity documents, including passports and driving licences with a number of names, false identities and a string of mailbox addresses, to evade VAT. The fraud was engineered over more than five years between July 2003 and January 2008.

Alison Reynolds was born on 17 June 1962 in Buckinghamshire under the name Virginia Ruth Povall. The set of names used by the fraudster includes

---

46 Her Majesty's Revenue & Customs (National): Multi-identity tax fraudster jailed for seven years   www.mynewsdesk.com/uk/pressreleases/hm-revenue-customs-national-multi-identity-tax-fraudster-jailed-for-seven-years-628861.

Claire Thomas, Rebecca Perry, Catherine Lewis, Jane Ditchfield, Jessica Maynard, Katerina (or Katrina) Mallory, Gina Andersen, Denise Bryan, Verity Connor, Claire Eliot, Chess Eliot, Vanessa Justine Galbraith, Alison Kennedy, William Povall and Caitlin Thomas. These names were either fake or were names of real people known to Reynolds. In order to be able to use all of these identities Reynolds practised extensively signature forging and adopted different appearances. Also, one of the aliases seemed to be missing in the 2004 tsunami. Reynolds had even worked as a personal assistant at a firm of solicitors called Warner & Richardson under the identity of Jessica Maynard and stolen an official stamp and headed paper in order to forge documents for HMRC.

Reynolds incorporated five companies in the United Kingdom, all claiming VAT refunds:

1   Belle Gray, a women's clothes shop in Hampshire, ran under the identity of Jane Ditchfield;
2   Dreamweavers Theatre Company, registered in Sheffield with the fake identity of Rebecca Perry;
3   Theatre Productions, a theatre registered in Bristol under the name of Claire Thomas;
4   Myths and Mirrors Theatre Company, registered in Manchester under the fake identity of Catherine Lewis;
5   Gossamer Web, registered in Hampshire under the false name of Jessica Maynard.

In the aftermath, the prosecutors discovered that Reynolds had previous convictions for dishonesty dating back to 1987. Over the three decades of her criminal career she had used 32 different names and 13 different dates of birth.[47]

The amount of the pocketed funds is small compared to other large-scale carousel operations. It is the ingenuity of the criminal and the capacity to create synthetic identities and to use them in all walks of life that makes this case unique. Reynolds managed not only to forge identities but also to open bank accounts with major institutions under various names. This case underlines the easiness of forging, creating synthetic identities and using them over a long period. This criminal created identities in only one jurisdiction, but what if a fraudster created synthetic identities in many jurisdictions? That would be a much more complicated case to investigate and prosecute.

Vanishing identities

Creating virtual or synthetic identities is necessary for engineering frauds that are able to bypass the increasingly sophisticated screening systems of financial institutions, governments and criminal police. When it comes to making somebody 'disappear' the justification has more nuances. The power of the criminal justice

47   www.mirror.co.uk/news/uk-news/fantasist-alison-reynolds-who-used-179573.

system with respect to financial crimes has become stronger and more consistent, and can impact criminals decades after a crime was committed. Bilateral extradition agreements are becoming current practice across many jurisdictions that traditionally did not cooperate. Moreover, freezing and seizing assets are practices more frequent today than they were a few decades ago. Investigators and intelligence providers have developed over the years sophisticated tools for finding individuals or tracking and recovering assets. Thus, a criminal will look to erase all traces following a criminal action; also it becomes frequent that a criminal will seek a new 'life', by ending his previous life, in order to avoid any likelihood that the justice system could track him and take over the criminal proceeds. This can also be useful, in the case when a person or an organization is facing legal or financial liabilities.

In the criminal jargon, the term 'cleaner' refers to a person who can clean up and remove traces after crimes are produced. Cleaning services[48] evolved over time, and the term also encompasses erasing the traces of financial crime. It involves destroying evidence, creating fake investigation lead and even making a person 'disappear'. Making a person disappear is not only about the physical side but encompasses the transition of person, his assets and maybe his family into a new life. It would be an equivalent of the FBI's famous Witness Protection Program.

Confronted with the real demand of protecting individuals, various security and intelligence service providers offer this type of protection to their clients. These sets of services aim to cut the links between an individual or an organization and his/her connections, and to facilitate migration towards a new identity that has nothing in common with the previous life. Deleting identities and creating new synthetic identities are two sides of the same coin.

The justice system's capacity to recover the assets of VAT fraudsters is currently weak. VAT scammers do not employ these approaches yet, but further reforms of the VAT system will encourage scammers to use more sophisticated tools in avoiding justice.

Blockchain and cryptocurrencies

'Crypto-mania' or 'Bitcoin-mania' is a natural consequence of a paradigm shift, which parts of society reclaimed after the past financial crisis. Taxpayers from countries touched heavily by the financial crisis asked a few legitimate questions:

- Why should taxpayer money bail out an industry which is the very same industry that has the monopoly over financial transactions?
- Why should taxpayers pay additional taxes when the government cannot reduce the loss due to VAT evasion?
- Can a currency backed by an overleveraged government be trusted?

Before cryptocurrency, the only instrument able to transfer value between individuals and companies were fiat currencies issued by central banks on behalf of

---

48 Mike Ehrmantraut's character from the cult American series *Breaking Bad* was presented in the show as a cleaner.

governments. Moreover, all transactions involving fiat currencies are channelled through the banking system. With many countries intending to move away from cash, the banking system will surely have a monopoly on the value transactions involving fiat currency. Once cleared by the banking system a transaction is eligible for taxation by a government. All value transfers in the current economy are held in the claw of the vicious circle: fiat currency – banking – taxation.

Therefore, the mésalliance between governments, central banks and financial institutions created a lot of discontent, especially in the libertarian milieu. The aim of most cryptocurrencies, especially Bitcoin's, is to break the monopoly of this tricephalic system as follows:

- avoid the government's direct and indirect taxation on exchanges of good, services and capital;
- break the monopoly of central banks for emitting currencies; and
- bypass the banking system for financial transactions between individuals and banks.

Cryptocurrencies not only are helping individuals and corporations to avoid taxation but also represent services which are not currently taxed. Governments are processing and analyzing ways of establishing taxation policies around cryptocurrencies. But the implementation of those policies will be a long and complex process.

In order to pursue a proper assessment of the potential taxation issues that could appear in the cryptocurrencies economy, a detailed and in-depth understanding of the crypto-universe is required. What is the nature of cryptocurrencies? Are they financial assets or maybe financial instruments? Where do accounting standards stand with respect to cryptocurrencies? What is the nature of the services specific to cryptocurrencies, like mining, for example? All these questions need to be cautiously addressed in order to assess the role of indirect taxes, and especially of the VAT with respect to cryptocurrencies.

Cryptocurrencies are a nascent asset class...

The crypto-universe currently proposes more than 1,500 currencies (tokens). Moreover, the recent series of capital raised through Initial Crypto Offerings (ICO) increased the dimensionality of the crypto-universe. Nevertheless, the pioneer of this universe and currently the most praised cryptocurrency remains Bitcoin. Despite a negative and reluctant reception from part of the public opinion, cryptocurrencies are without any doubt the main financial innovation since the credit derivatives.

Many libertarian economists see this new 'virtual' currency as the new Holy Grail of a 21st-century global economy trapped in a long-term recovery post-crisis scenario. Its advocates pledge for its advantages as a source of progress in the electronic economy and for democratizing the global trade and the access to currencies. Whether a cryptocurrency can or cannot replace a classic one is still an open debate (Frunza, 2015).

Bitcoin, by far the most popular cryptocurrency, surfaced in 2013 (Figure 9.4), when its exchange rate with the US dollar rallied from almost nothing to 1,000 USD for one Bitcoin, thereby making it most likely the first virtual financial bubble.

Going back into recent history it appears that alternative payment methods are not new, and many solutions, like PayPal, Apple Pay and Google Wallet, which are still based on fiat currency, represent viable solutions mainly for the e-commerce. Beyond these digital ways of using fiat money, new digital currencies have risen over the past two decades, cryptocurrencies being only a subcategory of digital currencies (Lee, 2015).

Attempts to create a distributed digital currency date back to 1990, with DigiCash, Inc. founded by David Chaum (Chaum, 1990). DigiCash introduced eCash as probably the first cryptocurrency. Despite some initial popularity eCash did not survive to the 2000s internet bubble.

When in 1971 the Nixon administration liberated the US dollar from the Breton Woods' covenant, which implied a monetary mass backed by gold, many economists predicted the beginning of the country's economic decline. Nixon's idea that the dollar is backed by confidence remained one of America's fundamental doctrines. Yet investors had an appetite for a currency backed by gold, and the opportunity came with the internet era in the early 2000s, when digital gold currencies started to become popular amongst alternative investors.

Most of those second-generation digital currencies, like iGolder, gbullion and e-gold, were in fact electronic money backed by one ounce of gold, which was stored for a fee. Their legacy was short-lived as the companies that ran those currencies were either shut down by the American federal government for various offences or faded away due to heavy regulatory burdens (Frunza, 2015).

And yet the concept of cryptocurrency is linked to the birth of Bitcoin in 2008 and its enigmatic founder, known under the alias Satoshi Nakamoto, who published a working paper presenting a peer-to-peer electronic cash system. Bitcoin spread very quickly and started to be accepted as a means of payment by major online retailers, tour operators, restaurants and even real estate agencies.

... with a foggy accounting treatment

Bitcoin is the most significant cryptocurrency, but a myriad of alternative currencies (Altcoins) have risen since 2014. Ether, Bitcoin Cash, Litecoin, Monero, Ripple and Neo are only few examples (Figure 9.4).

With cryptocurrencies being more involved in the modern economy, the question regarding the accounting treatment of Bitcoin and Altcoins is crucial.

The first avenue to be explored is whether cryptocurrencies can be classified as financial assets from an accounting point of view. The International Accounting Standards (IAS) define specifically a financial asset[49] as any asset that is

a   cash;
b   an equity instrument of another entity;

49 IAS 32 Financila instruments (www.iasplus.com/en/standards/ias/ias32).

c   a contractual right to receive cash or another financial asset from another entity, or to exchange financial assets or financial liabilities with another entity under conditions that are potentially favourable to the entity; or

d   a contract that will or may be settled in the entity's own equity instruments and is:

- a non-derivative for which the entity is or may be obliged to receive a variable number of the entity's own equity instruments;
- a derivative that will or may be settled other than by the exchange of a fixed amount of cash or another financial asset for a fixed number of the entity's own equity instruments; and
- puttable instruments classified as equity or certain liabilities arising on liquidation classified by IAS 32 as equity instruments.

Bitcoin and Altcoins are neither cash nor equity instruments, nor contracts nor contractual right. Bitcoin could potentially be a cash equivalent, but its massive fluctuation with respect to other fiat currencies does not make it eligible. If a company has cryptocurrencies on its balance sheet, it could classify them as either inventory or intangible assets.[50]

Inventory is an asset that is intended to be sold in the near future. Inventories are expected to be physical in the form of raw materials, works in progress and finished goods. But inventories can encompass non-physical goods if the item is part of a company's ordinary course of business.

Intangible assets are long-term, identifiable non-monetary resources that have no physical existence. Cryptocurrencies are separable as they can be traded, even in very small measurable quantities. They are immaterial as they do not have a physical form, and they exist only as cryptographic instruments. Cryptocurrencies can be considered non-cash assets for the reasons explained in the previous paragraph.

Cryptocurrencies (Figure 9.4) can be classified as both inventories and intangible assets. In both cases, cryptocurrencies would be measured at cost value, thereby misrepresenting the economic reality of the company. The company might acknowledge in both cases the fair value of the cryptocurrencies, but this would not solve the issue entirely.

CO_2 emissions permits faced the same dilemma, and they were in the beginning considered as inventory. With the VAT fraud developing, the regulators imposed that CO_2 emissions permits are financial instruments. From a purely technical point of view with regards to IAS, cryptocurrency would be difficult to classify as a financial instrument. IAS 32 specifies that a financial instrument is 'a contract that gives rise to a financial asset of one entity and a financial liability or equity instrument of another entity'.

Before assessing the role of the crypto-universe in the VAT fraud, it is crucial to question whether cryptocurrencies are in fact currencies. Scholars seem to find consensus (Selgin, 2015) in considering Bitcoin and virtual currencies in general

---

50 Accounting for crypto-currency (http://pwc.blogs.com/ifrs/2017/11/accounting-for-cryptocurrency.html).

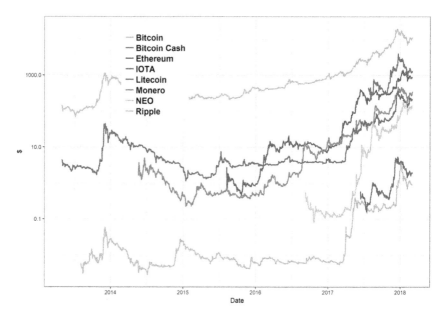

Figure 9.4 Evolution of the most popular cryptocurrency prices over the past four years.

as 'synthetic' commodities because they share features with both commodities and fiat money. Bitcoin offers to its owner an alternative that carries value in the same way stamps or art objects do. Thus, most of the cryptocurrencies could be more like a digital commodity that has a circumstantial intrinsic value related to investor propensity towards it. The only difference with classic commodities is that cryptocurrencies do not carry physical/real value (besides the value of the hardware used for mining). Bitcoins and Altcoins could be perceived as virtual goods or services used for transactions as simply as electricity or gas is used for making functioning houses and industries. This argument puts Bitcoin closer to a commodity than a currency.

How cryptocurrencies enhance the VAT fraud

The crypto-universe and especially Bitcoin generated a revolution in the way financial criminals operate. As pointed out in the previous section, most transactions in the cryptocurrencies universe go under the radar of authorities. Bitcoin and Altcoin are mediatized for conferring anonymized transactions. But this image is far from real; in fact the complete opposite is the sheer truth. In fact, all the details of the transactions are encrypted in the blockchain and the ledger, including the full history of the transactions, which is public. The blockchain records the wallet identifiers and the transaction between the different wallets.

Despite the fact that Bitcoin transactions are public, they are considered anonymous because nothing ties individuals or organizations to the accounts that are identified in the transactions. However, individuals sometimes post account numbers online in ways that can be connected to their online identities. As pointed out by Grinberg (2012) it can be possible, using statistical techniques and some identified accounts, to undo the anonymity of the system.

Moreover, most investors (e.g., Coinbase, binance, Bitstamp and Gdax) buy and sell cryptocurrencies over crypto-exchanges. With the explosion of the Bitcoin price in 2017, most of these exchanges are scrutinized by authorities, and each account holder is required to provide an identification document and a proof of address. Indeed, these measures can only increase the transparency of the cryptocurrencies. Nevertheless, a big silo of the crypto-transactions will still remain opaque to some extent.

Cryptocurrencies as payment services which are difficult to trace are a serious enabler for tax evasion, encompassing VAT fraud. MTIC and MTEC frauds involve the transfer of significant amounts from one jurisdiction to another. Traditionally criminals relied on the banking system. With the increased performance of the Suspicious Activity Reports (SAR), fraudsters put their enterprises at risk when relying entirely on financial institutions. Over the past decade VAT fraudsters used alternate banking platforms in order to avoid the systems of transaction monitoring deployed in banks. Many investigations in the MTIC arena start from SAR launched by financial institutions. Thus, Bitcoin and a few Altcoins appear as a viable alternative that could enable the VAT frauds.

Money laundering

Cryptocurrencies can move 'anonymously' (or almost anonymously) from one wallet to another and from one jurisdiction to another. Therefore, the layering step of money laundering is the main use of cryptocurrencies in laundering funds.

Some countries explored the possibility of considering cryptocurrencies as a legal currency or at least as a legal alternative payment tool. If this happens, the integration phase of money laundering can also be realized throughout cryptocurrency.

Criminals and especially VAT fraudsters need a payment system that is private, anonymous and not monitored by the taxman or the law enforcements. With the deployment of KYC processed in the cryptocurrency exchanges the anonymity of the transaction is partially or entirely lost.

After the first crypto-exchanges introduced identity screening for their traders, the crypto-community was divided into two parties:

- A first party supported the increase in transparency and regulation of cryptocurrencies. This party saw in regulation and transparency an avenue for the cryptocurrency to become a regular asset class, thereby attracting a huge inflow of funds from Wall Street.
- A second party that saw in this trend a real threat of losing the privacy and the anonymity of the crypto-universe. And in their view, the anonymity based on cryptocurrency transactions like Bitcoin preserves the 'democracy' in the crypto-universe, the final goal of cryptocurrencies being that of bypassing Wall Street, central banks and governments.

The innovation in the crypto-universe, especially in the Bitcoin universe, is driven by the second party. The anonymity of Bitcoin was the initial 'credo' of its founder Satoshi. In order to insure the anonymity a few solutions are provided:

- cryptocurrencies mixers/tumblers,
- decentralized exchanges and
- crypto-flipping.

The role of the 'mixers/tumblers'

One of the first solutions to the privacy quest in the crypto-universe was the mixers or tumblers.

Crypto-mixing or crypto-tumbling (known as Bitcoin mixing or Bitcoin tumbling in the case of Bitcoin) is a method that employs a third party called a mixer to break the connection between the sender of cryptocurrencies and the receiver of cryptocurrencies. This is achieved by interposing layers between the sending address and the receiving address of cryptocurrency. Crypto-mixing is very similar in nature to the layering step in classic money laundering schemes, thereby being named in some instances crypto-laundering.

The mechanism of crypto-mixing is presented in Figure 9.5. Users A, B and C send tainted cryptocurrencies (Bitcoins) which can be traced by the exchange. Senders (Users A to C) are identifiable. The mixer cuts all links between the receivers (Users D to I) and the senders (Users A to C). A simple parallel would be that with hallmarked physical gold coins. The mixer takes those hallmarked coins, melts them and issues new unmarked coins.

Mixing is a crucial service for those who use cryptocurrencies for illegal trades, especially on dark-net markets. Tax evaders would also need these services in order to keep their profile anonymous. The main providers of mixing services for Bitcoin transactions are Coinmixer.se, Helix, Bitcoin Blender and BitMixer.io. The fees charged by mixer providers range between 0.5% and 3% of the transferred amount,[51] the lowest fees being offered by Blockchain.info, which charges only 0.5%. The processing time varies from a few minutes to 24 hours.

The main issue with mixing/tumbling is that the process depends on a third party. And other risks can rise from this fact, including the likelihood of theft, hacking or snitching to law enforcements.

An alternative to mixing for Bitcoin transactions is Zerocoin, a solution proposed by researchers from Johns Hopkins University. Zerocoin is a cryptographic extension to Bitcoin that augments the protocol to allow for fully anonymous currency transactions. The advantage of Zerocoin over mixers/tumblers is that it uses standard cryptographic assumptions and does not introduce new trusted parties or otherwise change the security model of Bitcoin (Miers, 2013) whereby the trusted intermediary for mixing can be eliminated.

---

51 https://darknetmarkets.co/category/btc-mixer-tumber/.

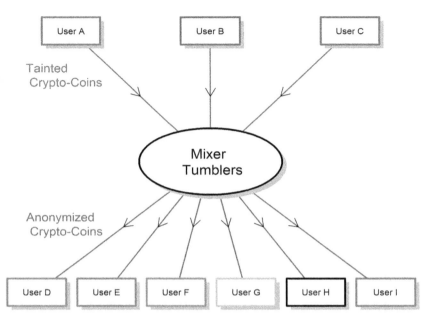

Figure 9.5 Mechanism of a mixer/tumbler. The user sends cryptocurrencies (Bitcoins) which can be traced by the exchange. The senders (Users A to C) are identifiable. The mixer cuts all links between the receivers (Users D to I) and the senders (Users A to C).

Preserving the privacy and anonymity in the cryptocurrency universe is a priority. Not all cryptocurrencies are concerned. The main beneficiary of mixing solutions is Bitcoin, which is also the biggest market in terms of transactions. Ripple, for example, is not concerned by the privacy side. From its creation Ripple was aimed to be transparent, and many serious financial institutions are exploring Ripple as a cheaper alternative to the traditional SWIFT[52] system. Monero, an emerging Altcoin, is set to preserve privacy, and thereby Monero transactions are currently more opaque than Bitcoin transactions.

Decentralized exchanges

Mixing/tumbling is a service aimed at erasing the traces of Bitcoin/Altcoin transactions handled over crypto-exchanges. An exchange is in fact a third party between the various traders of cryptocurrencies. Exchanges not only break the anonymity of the transactions but also expose the clients to operational and counterparty risks. The fall of Mt. Gox in 2014 is a relevant case of the risk bore by every user of a crypto-exchange.

---

52 Society for Worldwide Interbank Financial Telecommunication.

An efficient alternative came with the so-called decentralized exchanges, where transactions do not rely on a third party like they do in the case of centralized exchanges. Transactions take place directly between the users using a peer-to-peer automatized process. The main advantage of the decentralized over the centralized exchanges resides in the fact that the user does not need to deposit funds with exchange's custodian. A direct consequence of the fact that these exchanges are based on a peer-to-peer approach is an increased level of privacy and anonymity of the transaction. Examples of decentralized exchanges are Bitsquare, Waves Dex, Openledger Dex, etc. Decentralized exchanges are still at the beginning of the journey, and more developments are expected in this field. Low liquidity is currently one of the big drawbacks of decentralized exchanges.

Crypto-flipping

Concealing the path of Bitcoin transactions can be achieved thoroughly by swapping Bitcoin with other cryptocurrencies, the most used being Monero. The transfer of Bitcoins between a sender and a receiver includes a step in which the Bitcoin is exchanged in Monero, and afterwards Monero is exchanged back into Bitcoin before arriving to the receiver.

The level of complexity of crypto-flipping can be increased when the intermediary step involves few cryptocurrencies other than Monero.

VAT treatment of the crypto-economy

Cryptocurrencies opened the gate to a whole new economy that is currently not considered part of the formal economy. A simple way to apprehend cryptocurrencies would be as a service to hold and transfer value. Most cryptocurrencies are values with respect to the main fiat currencies; therefore they can be seen as an avenue to hold and transfer monetary value, bypassing the traditional banking services. Analyzing the situation from this point of view, a Bitcoin wallet and a Bitcoin transfer could be similar to a services proposed by a bank. Therefore, a first proxy for a potential legal framework for the VAT treatment would be the current VAT legislation applied to financial services.

In the EU financial and insurance services are exempted from VAT according to Article 135 of the Council Directive 2006/112/EC.[53] Thus, banking services, including holding accounts and deposits, transfers, currency exchanges and credit services, are exempted from VAT with no right of input tax deduction for services supplied.

---

53 Member States shall exempt the following transactions:

a) insurance and reinsurance transactions, including related services performed by insurance brokers and insurance agents;
b) the granting and the negotiation of credit and the management of credit by the person granting it;
c) the negotiation of or any dealings in credit guarantees or any other security for money and the management of credit guarantees by the person who is granting the credit;
d) transactions, including negotiation, concerning deposit and current accounts, payments, transfers, debts, cheques and other negotiable instruments, but excluding debt collection.

The Gulf countries (the United Arab Emirates (UAE) and Saudi Arabia) introduced VAT in January 2018. Similarly to the EU's framework, Gulf countries are exempt from VAT, financial services provided by banks and financial institutions which are regulated. Contrary to the EU financial institutions regulated by the UAE authorities may deduct VAT for acquired services. Another difference with the EU's framework is that the UAE and Saudi Arabia restrict VAT exemption to charges made on the basis of an implicit margin. Thus, VAT exemption will not apply to any services for which an explicit fee is charged.

Making a parallel of cryptocurrencies with banking services the exemption of VAT seems a straightforward approach. Indeed, many countries enacted the exemption of VAT.

Table 9.4 presents a global picture of the international tax policies with respect to cryptocurrencies. The taxation avenues taken by a few of the world's most powerful countries in the cryptocurrencies arena are discussed in the following, with a close focus on VAT.

Table 9.4 Legal status of Bitcoin and Altcoin in different jurisdictions, with a focus on the VAT treatment

Country	Legal status of Cryptocurrencies	VAT treatment
Belgium	Unregulated	Altcoin transactions via an exchange are exempted from VAT.
China	Not fully legal	No clear guidance on VAT treatment.
Germany	Regulated	Altcoin is 'private money' and a 'unit of account' for the purposes of tax and trading. It can be used for a 'multilateral clearing circle' and is regulated the same as domestically held fiat currency. VAT applies.
Israel	Regulated	Israel recognizes Altcoins not as currency or a commodity but as a taxable asset. Miners and traders must pay corporate income tax in addition to a 17% VAT, with sold Altcoins asserting a capital gains tax of 25%.
Croatia	Regulated	No VAT is charged.
Malta	Unregulated	No regulation concerning VAT.
Cyprus	Unregulated	No regulation concerning VAT.
Italy	Unregulated	No regulation concerning VAT.
Norway	Regulated	Norway sees Altcoins as assets subject to the wealth and sales taxes but not the VAT.
Sweden	Regulated	Sweden recognizes Altcoins as currency exempted from the VAT but requires Altcoin businesses that handle fiat currency to apply for a licence.
United Kingdom	Regulated	VAT is waived for exchange purchases but will be collected for other cryptocurrency transactions. Cryptos are subject to capital gains.
Canada	Regulated	Bitcoins and Altcoins are recognized as an intangible under the Personal Property Security Act.
United States	Regulated	In the United States there is no VAT, but capital gains tax are applied.

Source: https://www.bitcoinmarketjournal.com/bitcoin-regulation-by-country/.

The European Union

The EU opted from treatment of cryptocurrencies transaction similar to those of bank services, thereby seeing them as another payment tool. Thus, among the EU's countries, cryptocurrency transactions are exempted from VAT. The question of the VAT treatment came in June 2014 when the Skatterverket – Sweden's tax office – challenged a court decision that ruled that Bitcoin transactions in the country should be exempted from VAT, following a dispute with Bitcoin forum operator Daniel Hedqvist.

Because of Sweden's tax office case, in October 2015 the European Court of Justice (ECJ) ruled that Bitcoin and virtual currencies transactions are to be exempted from VAT.[54] The VAT exemption is justified by the interpretation of Article 135(1) of the VAT Directive concerning transactions relating to currency, bank notes and coins used as legal tender. Therefore the cryptocurrency transaction would benefit from the VAT exemptions as the financial services.[55] Furthermore, ECJ's decisions stipulated that Bitcoin and critical currencies are means of payment.[56]

As a consequence of ECJ's decisions,[57] the following aspects of the Bitcoin (cryptocurrencies) transactions are exempted from VAT:

- Cryptocurrency transactions, encompassing exchanging cryptocurrencies for fiat or other cryptocurrencies.
- Mining services, encompassing the distributed validation of Bitcoin (cryptocurrencies) transactions. In the case of mining the same treatment is applied to solo miners and mining pools.

---

54 www.coindesk.com/bitcoin-is-exempt-from-vat-says-european-court-of-justice/.
55 *According to the Revenue Law Commission, the 'bitcoin' virtual currency is a means of payment used in a similar way to legal means of payment. Furthermore, the term 'legal tender' referred to in Article 135(1)(e) of the VAT Directive is used in order to restrict the scope of the exemption as regards bank notes and coins* (Source: Case C264/14 par 52 http://curia.europa.eu/juris/document/document.jsf?docid=170305&doclang=EN).
56 'In the case in the main proceedings, it is common ground that the 'bitcoin' virtual currency has no other purpose than to be a means of payment and that it is accepted for that purpose by certain operators' (Source: Case C264/14 par 52 http://curia.europa.eu/juris/document/document.jsf?docid=170305&doclang=EN).
57 On those grounds, the Court (Fifth Chamber) hereby rules:

   1 Article 2(1)(c) of Council Directive 2006/112/EC of 28 November 2006 on the common system of value added tax must be interpreted as meaning that transactions such as those at issue in the main proceedings, which consist of the exchange of traditional currency for units of the 'bitcoin' virtual currency and vice versa, in return for payment of a sum equal to the difference between, on the one hand, the price paid by the operator to purchase the currency and, on the other hand, the price at which he sells that currency to his clients, constitute the supply of services for consideration within the meaning of that article.
   2 Article 135(1)(e) of Directive 2006/112 must be interpreted as meaning that the supply of services such as those at issue in the main proceedings, which consist of the exchange of traditional currencies for units of the 'bitcoin' virtual currency and vice versa, performed in return for payment of a sum equal to the difference between, on the one hand, the price paid by the operator to purchase the currency and, on the other hand, the price at which he sells that currency to his clients, are transactions exempt from VAT, within the meaning of that provision.

- Cryptocurrencies received as a result of mining. The ECJ justifies that the proof-of-work reward, consisting of Bitcoins received when the cryptographic puzzle is solved, is not a payment to the miner for a delivered service. Indeed, mining being a distributed validation process, there is no contract between the miner and another party; therefore no formal services supply is agreed upon.
- Transaction fees encompassing the fees charged by exchanges.

If the VAT treatment across the EU's Member States seems to have consensus, the nature of cryptos is not making unanimity. Member states are split between those considering cryptocurrencies as money, those considering it an asset and those considering it a service. This heterogeneous treatment is observed for non-Member countries.

For example, Germany considers cryptocurrency transactions for purchasing goods or services to be a means of payment. VAT is not charged on the cryptocurrency transactions, but no capital gains tax is applied. The German Ministry of Finance considers that:

- fees for the provision of a wallet, for example, are generally subject to VAT,
- that the operator of a digital trading platform for cryptocurrencies also provides a service that is basically subject to taxation and
- goods and services purchased with cryptocurrencies are still liable to VAT.[58]

The German federal financial supervisory authority BaFin (Bundesanstalt für Finanzdienstleistungsaufsicht) considers cryptocurrencies neither electronic money nor foreign currency. BaFin rather considers Bitcoins and Altcoins as 'financial instruments', thereby forcing the exchange and other cryptocurrencies companies to comply with the standard financial service companies. Thus, these organizations will be directly regulated by BaFin.[59]

This treatment as a financial instrument is unique to Germany's case, Austria not considering cryptocurrencies as financial instrument. The United Kingdom and the Netherlands don't consider cryptos as a currency due to the fact that they are decentralized, while Estonia, Finland and Norway do consider them as assets.

United Kingdom

The British tax office (HMRC) repealed the VAT for Bitcoin transactions as early as 2014.

HMRC apprehends Bitcoin as operating 'via a peer to peer network, independent of any central authority or bank', thereby not qualifying for the status of a currency. Thus, the HMRC treats cryptocurrencies as intangible assets. When a company or an investor that is tax liable to the Exchequer trades cryptocurrencies, the following taxes can apply: Corporate Tax, Income Tax and Capital

58 https://medium.com/@info_53583/cryptocurrency-regulation-part-2-europe-7cfeccfeb930.
59 https://payment21.com/blog/how-vat-value-added-tax-bitcoin-handled-different-countries.

Gains Tax. Both inverts and companies are exempted from VAT. The exemption includes mining activities.[60]

HMRCs tax treatment applies to all parties that make or receive payments from activities related to cryptocurrencies, including miners, investors, crypto-currency exchanges, payment platforms, etc. Individuals are liable to income tax on any profits and losses stemming from the cryptocurrency transactions.

Businesses dealing with cryptocurrencies, including mining activities, are liable to corporate tax. Moreover, unrealized gains from appreciation of cryptocurrency portfolios are liable to capital gains taxes.[61]

60 'For VAT purposes Bitcoin and similar cryptocurrencies will be treated as follows; this in no way reflects on how they are treated for regulatory or other purposes:

- income received from Bitcoin mining activities will generally be outside the scope of VAT on the basis that the activity does not constitute an economic activity for VAT purposes because there is an insufficient link between any services provided and any consideration received
- income received by miners for other activities, such as for the provision of services in connection with the verification of specific transactions for which specific charges are made, will be exempt from VAT under Article 135(1)(d) of the EU VAT Directive as falling within the definition of 'transactions, including negotiation, concerning deposit and current accounts, payments, transfers, debts, cheques and other negotiable instruments'
- when Bitcoin is exchanged for Sterling or for foreign currencies, such as Euros or Dollars, no VAT will be due on the value of the Bitcoins themselves
- charges (in whatever form) made over and above the value of the Bitcoin for arranging or carrying out any transactions in Bitcoin will be exempt from VAT under Article 135(1)(d) as outlined at 2 above However, in all instances, VAT will be due in the normal way from suppliers of any goods or services sold in exchange for Bitcoin or other similar cryptocurrency. The value of the supply of goods or services on which VAT is due will be the sterling value of the cryptocurrency at the point the transaction takes place'. (Source: HMRC www.gov.uk/government/publications/revenue-and-customs-brief-9-2014-bitcoin-and-other-cryptocurrencies/revenue-and-customs-brief-9-2014-bitcoin-and-other-cryptocurrencies)

61 'For businesses which accept payment for goods or services in Bitcoin there is no change to when revenue is recognised or how taxable profits are calculated.

- Corporate Tax – the profits or losses on exchange movements between currencies are taxable. For the tax treatment of virtual currencies, the general rules on foreign exchange and loan relationships apply. For companies, exchange movements are determined between the company's functional currency (usually the currency in which the accounts are prepared) and the other currency in question. If there is an exchange rate between Bitcoin and the functional currency then this analysis applies. Therefore no special tax rules for Bitcoin transactions are required. The profits and losses of a company entering into transactions involving Bitcoin would be reflected in accounts and taxable under normal Corporate Tax rules
- Income Tax – the profits and losses of a non-incorporated business on Bitcoin transactions must be reflected in their accounts and will be taxable on normal Income Tax rules
- Gains and losses incurred on Bitcoin or other cryptocurrencies are chargeable or allowable for Capital Gain Tax if they accrue to an individual or, for Corporate Tax on chargeable gains if they accrue to a company'. (Source: HMRC: www.gov.uk/government/publications/revenue-and-customs-brief-9-2014-bitcoin-and-other-cryptocurrencies/revenue-and-customs-brief-9-2014-bitcoin-and-other-cryptocurrencies)

United States

The United States does not have VAT, but sales taxes do exist at the state level. In the United States many governmental agencies looked to take actions for a regulatory and tax framework around cryptocurrencies.

As early as 2014, the Financial Crimes Enforcement Network (FinCEN) defined the circumstances under which virtual currency users could be categorized as money services businesses.

Also in 2014, the Internal Revenue Service (IRS) indicated that Bitcoin and virtual currencies are not currencies but property.[62] Therefore, cryptocurrency investments are liable to capital gains taxes. In the United States the capital gains rate depends on the holding horizon of the investments. A short-term rate or a long-term rate applies depending on whether the investment horizon is below or above one year, respectively.

This treatment could be changed as the United States Congress published in late 2017 a project for a 'Cryptocurrency Fairness in Taxation Act' (CFTA).[63] This act would exempt from capital gains tax all cryptocurrency transactions under a threshold of 600 USD.

62 'The notice provides that virtual currency is treated as property for U.S. federal tax purposes. General tax principles that apply to property transactions apply to transactions using virtual currency. Among other things, this means that:

- Wages paid to employees using virtual currency are taxable to the employee, must be reported by an employer on a Form W-2, and are subject to federal income tax withholding and payroll taxes.
- Payments using virtual currency made to independent contractors and other service providers are taxable and self-employment tax rules generally apply. Normally, payers must issue Form 1099.
- The character of gain or loss from the sale or exchange of virtual currency depends on whether the virtual currency is a capital asset in the hands of the taxpayer.
- A payment made using virtual currency is subject to information reporting to the same extent as any other payment made in property'. (Source: IRS www.irs.gov/newsroom/irs-virtual-currency-guidance)

63 *139G.Gains from sale or exchange of virtual currency*

a) In general: Gross income shall not include gain from the sale or exchange of virtual currency for other than cash or cash equivalents.
b) Limitation
   a. In general The amount of gain excluded from gross income under subsection (a) with respect to a sale or exchange shall not exceed $600.
   b. Aggregation rule For purposes of this subsection, all sales or exchanges which are part of the same transaction (or a series of related transactions) shall be treated as one sale or exchange.
c) Virtual currency: For purposes of this section, the term virtual currency means a digital representation of value that is used as a medium of exchange and is not otherwise currency under section 988.
Any increase determined under the preceding sentence shall be rounded to the nearest multiple of $50. (Source: US Congress www.govtrack.us/congress/bills/115/hr3708/text)

Russian Federation

Russia is the only country to have a dedicated legal framework recognizing cryptocurrency activities as a sector of the economy. In January 2018, the Russian Duma issued a law entitled 'On Digital Financial Assets'.[64] The cryptocurrency exchanges should comply 'with the legislation of the Russian Federation and carry out the types of activities specified in Articles 3 to 5 of Federal Law No. 39-FZ of April 22, 1996 "On the Securities Market"'. They can also be 'legal entities that are the organizers of trade in accordance with the Federal Law of November 21, 2011 No. 325-FZ "On Organized Trading"'. Under this framework, the cryptocurrencies are not liable for VAT.

Israel

In February 2018 the Israel Tax Authority issued guidelines concerning the tax treatment of cryptocurrencies.[65] The position was that Bitcoin and general cryptocurrencies are not recognized as currencies and are in fact assets. Therefore they are liable to capital gains taxes.

With respect to indirect taxation the guideline indicates that investment in cryptocurrencies is not liable for VAT ('a distributed means of payment is an intangible asset, and therefore anyone whose activity in the field is for investment purposes only, which does not reach a business, is not liable for VAT'[66]).

The main difference with the European legislation concerns the treatment of mining. The mined Bitcoins are submitted to capital gains tax (25%) and to VAT (17%) due to the fact that cryptocurrency is considered property, thereby accounting for a total tax of 42%.[67] The application of VAT to mining services is discussed in the next section.

Switzerland

In June 2015 the Swiss Federal Tax Administration on VAT provided rules concerning the application of tax policy to Bitcoin in Switzerland. In the eyes of the Swiss taxman cryptocurrencies are just a payment tool. Therefore, the transactions involving Bitcoin are not considered the delivery of goods or services, and

---

64 Russia finalizes Federal law on crypto-currency regulation (https://news.bitcoin.com/russia-finalizes-federal-law-cryptocurrency-regulation/).
65 Israel Tax Authority: Bitcoin is property, not currency (https://news.bitcoin.com/israel-tax-authority-bitcoin-is-property-not-currency/).
66 https://taxes.gov.il/incometax/documents/hozrim/hor_acc%2015.2.18.pdf.
67 'A dealer whose receipts are accepted by means of a distributed payment method will be paid VAT according to his business activity' [...] and

> regardless of the manner of receipt, so that as a rule, VAT will not be paid; A person whose activity in a distributed means of payment reaches a business (from such trade) shall be classified as a financial institution; And those whose activities are mining, will be classified as a dealer for VAT purposes.
> (Source: https://taxes.gov.il/incometax/documents/hozrim/hor_acc%2015.2.18.pdf)

are not liable to VAT as referred to in Article 21 of the Swiss VAT Act.[68] More-over, the transaction fees charged by exchanges or other transaction platforms are exempted from VAT.

Should cryptocurrencies be liable to VAT?

Policymakers tend to exclude the cryptocurrency transactions from the base of indirect taxes encompassing the VAT. If, for some circumstances, this approach can be fully justified, in many other instances on could raise the question of whether the economy having cryptocurrencies as underlying should or should not be liable to VAT.

The trades of cryptocurrencies paid in fiat currencies or in other cryptocur-rencies are similar in many ways to a financial service of funds transfer. There-fore, the current avenue of VAT exemption can be justified. Nevertheless, this treatment would push regulators to treat cryptocurrencies as financial assets or financial instruments. As explained in the introductory part of this section con-sidering cryptocurrencies as a financial instrument under the current IAS would lead to serious conceptual soundness issues.

If the cryptocurrencies are considered a non-financial intangible asset, which seems to be the case in many countries, that opens the void to a VAT exemption for many similar intangible assets. Therefore, policymakers need to be cautious in categorizing cryptocurrencies.

In the case where cryptocurrencies are seen as a non-financial service, which is the closest interpretation with respect to the intimate nature of cryptocurrencies, then VAT needs to be applied. This is currently the case in other walks of life. For example, if a company wires money to another company, the transaction is not VAT liable. If the same company purchases VoIP capacity and delivers it to a counterparty, then that transaction is VAT liable. Similarly, if cryptocurrencies are perceived as a commodity, VAT needs to be applied.

Besides the financial nature of cryptocurrencies, which most likely will be subject to long debates in the coming years, the following short-term aspects of the crypto-economy need to be discussed:

- the purchase of goods paid in cryptocurrencies,
- the purchases of services outside the crypto-universe paid in cryptocurren-cies and
- the treatment of services within the crypto-universe (i.e., mining).

Purchase of goods

The supply of goods paid with cryptocurrencies should at least theoretically be subject to VAT. In some countries, these purchases are treated as barter trades, thereby being submitted to VAT. But generally speaking the current framework

---

68 www.admin.ch/opc/en/classified-compilation/20081110/index.html#fn-#a21-12.

does not clearly indicate the instances requiring the application of VAT. Even when the VAT application is required, evading the payment is not a complex process. In fact, the tax offices have no levy in controlling the exchange of goods paid with cryptocurrencies, especially when the goods are of small volume and big value.

The cryptocurrency transactions can be very easily anonymized, as explained in the previous section. The acceptance of cryptocurrencies in the formal economy is still a niche phenomenon, but its expansion is very fast.

One marketplace dominated by cryptocurrencies is the mining equipment, mainly for Bitcoin, Ether and Litecoin. The process of verification of cryptocurrency transactions requires a lot of computational capacity. In the early years of Bitcoin the first miners used personal computers, but with the increase in mining difficulty the central processing unit became obsolete. Suppliers like Bitmain are proposing tools for solo-miners and for mining pools. These tools are sold as turnkey solutions ready for mining and generating new cryptocurrencies. The mining machines for Bitcoin and Litecoin are in fact integrated circuits packaged as an application-specific integrated circuit (ASIC) or a field-programmable gate array (FPGA). Mining Ether requires video cards similar to graphical processing units.

The price of a performant of a Bitcoin miner machine starts at 1,500 USD. The main supplier is a Chinese firm called Bitmain[69] that has a 75% market share. The global revenues from mining equipment accounted for 4 billion USD in 2017. The wholesalers of these machines accept payment in cryptocurrencies. They are delivered outside China with express delivery services such as FedEx, DHL or UPS. The customs tax as well as VAT is rarely collected. This issue touches also on the problem MTEC fraud, which is addressed in a different chapter.

Purchase of services

The tax offices have the possibility to scrutinize the purchase of physical goods paid in cryptocurrencies by tracing the logistics and deliveries. The purchase of services paid in cryptocurrencies can pass almost undetected.

Currently, many technology freelancers accept payments in cryptocurrencies. There are also platforms dedicated to linking clients and freelancers, the payment being made in Bitcoin. These platforms are based in countries like Malta, where cryptocurrencies are unregulated, and therefore the tax offices have no levy for following what is going on. The purchase of services paid in cryptocurrencies becomes more popular, especially with freelancers based in offshore countries. This is part of a new social trends called 'digital nomads'.[70]

---

69 https://btcmanager.com/bitmain-recorded-2-3-billion-turnover-following-cryptocurrency-boom-2017/.
70 Digital services providers that travel and work for clients based onshore. They are generally not registered businesses and do not pay taxes in any country.

One of the biggest platforms for exchanging services in the crypto-universe is Ethereum. Ethereum is a 'distributed application platform'[71] that has its own cryptocurrency called Ether and stands in the top three capitalizations amongst all crypto-coins. Ether is similar to Bitcoin, both being mined coins. The Ethereum platform uses an *ethash* encryption process, while Bitcoin uses SHA[72]-256.

Ether-based transaction costs are massively inferior to those charged by Bitcoin. Also the speed of the transaction is higher. The cost of a Bitcoin transaction in 2017 was around 28 USD, and the time of processing was between one hour and one day. Thus, Ether is used by many traders to bypass the high fees and low speed of Bitcoin. Traders use a crypto-flipping process; they convert Bitcoin to Ether, they transfer Ether and then they convert it back to Bitcoin.

Ethereum is a distribution platform for exchanging services. It has its own programming language. An application creator can join the platform to create a new application that can be accessed for an amount of Ether. This application and services platform therefore bypasses any taxation instances, including VAT.

Moreover, the participants in the Ethereum can raise capital to develop their applications by issuing their coins (token) as part of the Ethereum protocol. This process is called Initial Coin Offering (ICO) and represents the initial offering of a digital cryptographically secure piece of data created on a blockchain as part of a decentralized software protocol. ICO can be understood as a service for crowd funding through cryptocurrencies. The investors in the ICO are compensated with access to the application when the development is completed. This type of services avoids all taxation. The role of VAT in this innovative environment is not even discussed by policymakers.

Deregulated commercial contracts

The question regarding whether the cryptocurrencies will or will not be a currency or a financial asset will surely not be closed in the short run. Thus, the roots of cryptocurrencies in the current formal economy are not strong enough, and their future is very volatile.

Despite this murky frame, the outcome of the crypto-dialectic is that blockchain technology is reshaping the formal economy. One of the avenues on which already blockchain leaves its mark is the smart contract. A smart contract is a blockchain-based computer protocol aimed at facilitating transaction by eliminating the need of a third party. Currently, most contractual agreements between individuals, organizations and governments require third parties to clear the duties of the parties. Relevant examples include insurance contracts, merchandise delivery, property purchase, financial products and copyright and intellectual property. The execution of a smart contract would be automatic without requiring a third party and would avoid post-agreement litigation.

---

71 Source: www.ethereum.org.
72 Secure Hash Algorithm.

Smart contracts will affect markets currently submitted to VAT, including music, movies and entertainment supports. The piracy of virtual products encompassing software licences, music, movies and entertainment contents is a stringent issue, and smart contracts could be an efficient solution. The specification for the smart contract would be embedded in a blockchain that also includes the product. Each time the blockchain emits a unit of consumption an amount of currency (fiat or crypto) is debited. This would bypass the intermediaries that sell the products and the potential litigation for the misuse of the products.

The problem posed by smart contracts with respect to VAT is that those contracts would need to include three parties: the buyer, the seller and the tax office. Otherwise, the trade would evade VAT, and the taxman would observe a loss.

Smart contracts can be both friend and foe for VAT collectors. Governments will not be able to regulate all smart contracts. Therefore, VAT fraud will develop when blockchains change heavily in the contractual paperwork. Nevertheless, tax offices could use smart contracts to bend the current epidemic of missing trader fraud. New solutions related to blockchains are discussed in Chapter 13.

Mining: a service in the crypto-universe

Bitcoin and few cryptocurrencies rely on a service consisting of the distributed validation of transactions. This service is known as mining and is provided by all parties connected to the Bitcoin (crypto) protocol. The mining service is remunerated with an amount of cryptocurrencies. Miners can operate on a stand-alone basis or in mining pools, the latter being the most popular solution. Solo-miners can connect online to mining pools and share their computational power in order to accelerate the resolution of the crypto-graphic problem. Thus, by joining a pool a solo-miner can increase the profitability of his/her enterprise. Mining pools for Bitcoin are generally located in countries with low prices of electricity, including China, India, Kazakhstan, Kirgizstan, Russia, Ukraine, etc. The mining enterprises in some cases are registered as businesses and in other cases operate through sole traders.

In most countries, when they operate in a company mining revenues are submitted to corporate tax. Nevertheless mining is not liable to VAT, the only exception being in Israel. But the righteousness of exempting mining from VAT is still open to debate. This was underlined by a working paper of the European Commission after ECJ's decision concerning the VAT treatment of cryptocurrencies.[73]

The first question with regards to the VAT treatment of mining services is related to the status of the miners. Currently, registering mining activities is not compulsory in most countries. One exception is the Russian Federation, where

---

73 'Issues arising from recent judgments of the court of justice of the European Union' (https://circabc.europa.eu/sd/a/add54a49-9991-45ae-aac5-1e260b136c9e/892%20-%20CJEU%20Case%20C-264-14%20Hedqvist%20-%20Bitcoin.pdf).

mining activities have been recognized since 2018 as economic activities. In the case of the EU, mining activities are not considered economic activities.

Pursuant to Article 9(1) of the VAT Directive a taxable person is an individual who carries out in any place any economic activity, whatever the purpose or results of that activity. Therefore, if mining becomes compulsorily an economic activity, miners will be submitted to tax.

The second question concerns the current exemption of mining revenues from VAT. The European framework seems to consider mining a voluntary activity and the Bitcoin (or the mined cryptocurrency) as a sort of incentive for the miner.

If no formal fee is received for supplying a mining service automatically no VAT is applicable.

If the services of verifications are considered to be carried out for the miner's private use pursuant to Article 26(1)(b) of the European VAT Directive, then the miner is liable for VAT.

If the Bitcoin or cryptocurrencies received by the miner are not considered a fee, then a leeway exists for avoiding VAT pursuant to Article 2(1)(c) of the VAT Directive, which states that VAT should not be perceived for voluntary activities.

In fact mining is not a voluntary service, and miners' main objective is to maximize their personal profit. The cost of mining a Bitcoin ranges, for example, from a few hundred dollars in 2011 to almost 7,000 USD in 2017. The high cost and large required investment of mining exclude the voluntary nature of mining. Miners exert their mining activity only when they believe that they can achieve an individual sustainable return.

In fact, a miner provides with nothing else then cloud computing capacity for the Bitcoin verification protocol. The protocol charges a fee for each transaction. Cloud computing services are liable for VAT.

In 2015, HMRC[74] decided that cloud services are eligible for the VAT reclaim. The rules of the British tax office stated that the following services relevant to the mining activity should be included in the VAT refund: hosting computing services, archiving communication services, data communications services and cloud computing.

All these points lead to the conclusion that mining would need to be recognized as an economic activity and submitted to VAT. The current policy for mining services will probably evolve in the near future and probably constitute the basis for the tax treatment of smart contracts.

74 http://vathub.com/hmrc-u-turns-on-vat-rules-for-cloud/.

10 Who is who in the VAT milieu?

VAT milieu: real criminal enterprise or glorified crew?

> I start living from 50 thousands euros per month.
>
> Carbon Connection crime figure

Value Added Tax (VAT) fraud has been documented since the late 1970s. Since its inception, VAT scams attracted criminal gangs that saw an opportunity to make quickly considerable amounts of money without bearing the penal risks of violent crimes, which were much more severely punished at the time.

The VAT fraud went to the next level of complexity in 1993, when the European Single Market was launched and guaranteed the free movement of goods, services, capital and labour across the Member countries. From a local fraud, the VAT scam became a transnational crime and involved more sophisticated structures. In the early 1990s VAT fraud had still a 'blue-collar' crime feature due to the fact that it was relying on moving or smuggling merchandise across borders.

The European Single Market extended gradually to new Members in the European Union (EU) and to non-Members, like Norway, Iceland and Lichtenstein. The expansion of the Single Market took place in the 2000s, which coincided with the development of the digital and services markets. Thus, the VAT fraud not only expanded geographically but also encompassed services. With this shift in trends, VAT fraud changed gradually from a 'blue-collar' crime to a 'white-collar' crime. This change in the nature of the fraud reshaped the profile of the gangs involved in VAT fraud. As in other walks of life, many of the initial gangs that started in the VAT fraud during the 1990s did not survive to the shifts of the economic realities. VAT fraud is no different from any other crime. When a group exits the picture a new one takes its place and leverages the experience of the defunct group.

Despite all these changes there are a few criminal patterns that crystallized over the past three decades with respect to the Missing Trader Intra-Community (MTIC) frauds. These patterns can be resumed in one phrase: in the VAT fraud arena faces might change, but memories remain the same. Therefore, the VAT fraud occurs in waves, and in each wave there is some information from the previous waves. A good example is the 'Dubai Connection' that saw light in the early 2000s

DOI: 10.4324/9781315098722-10

with the VAT evasion on technology goods. In the late 2000s the same connection was used for the VAT fraud on CO_2 emissions. This connection will most likely go to the next level with the recent introduction of VAT into Gulf countries.

The VAT fraudsters are part of various gangs that intersect at some moment. An investigation could potentially show that criminals involved in one fraud can have ties with VAT fraudsters that operated a few years prior. Therefore, analyzing past and present VAT fraud cases is useful not only for understanding the crime but also for apprehending the shape of the future avenues the VAT fraud and fraudster might take.

The 'golden' age (1979–1992)

The VAT fraud on gold started in 1979 when the Thatcher government (Lashmar, 2017) exempted from VAT gold coins, like the South African Krugerrand.[1] The measure aimed to allow individuals to trade gold at reasonable prices. At the same time, the Tory government kept VAT on gold scrap. Moreover, the VAT rate was raised from 8% to 15%. London's underworld figured quickly that an opportunity came from nowhere. Gold coins were bought tax free, melted and transformed into bars or other object, and resold with VAT. Gangsters converted to traders were pocketing the VAT funds and appeared to be missing when Her Majesty's Revenue and Customs (HMRC) officers came to control their enterprise; hence the expression 'missing trader'.

As early as 1982 the British government became aware of the severity of this fraud and reintroduced VAT on gold coins (VAT (Finance) Order 1982 (S.I., 1982, No. 476)).[2] In the hearing that took place in the House of Commons, it was mentioned that the law enforcements indicted 19 persons in five cases of fraud, accounting for 23.5 million pounds of losses in VAT.

In the same parliamentary session an interesting case is mentioned about VAT fraud on imported gold. The case caused a loss of almost 17 million pounds.[3]

---

1 South African gold coin weighing 33.39 grams with a purity of 22 karats.

2

> This order, which came into effect on 1 April, removes the exemption from value added tax for gold coins which are legal tender in their country of issue when supplied as collectors' pieces or as investment articles. The order is intended to counter a particular type of fraud and it may be sensible to begin by explaining how the fraud worked.
> (Source: https://api.parliament.uk/historic-hansard/commons/1982/apr/28/value-added-tax-gold-coins)

3

> The fraud was to import gold bullion which was, of course, liable to VAT. Then, making use of the postponed accounting system which allows a registered trader to postpone the VAT due on importation until his next quarterly return is due, the traders did not pay the VAT at the time of importation. On selling the gold bullion they were able to abscond without paying over the VAT.
> (Source: https://api.parliament.uk/historic-hansard/commons/1982/apr/28/value-added-tax-gold-coins)

Seemingly that case was the ancestor of the MTIC fraud that started to gain momentum in 1993 with the birth of the European Single Market.

The first episode of VAT fraud occurred more than one year after the decline of the old-school London gangsters: the infamous Kray twins and the notorious Richardson family. The tax evasion on gold bullion was situated in London's main marketplace for precious metal and diamond, known as Hatton Garden or the 'Garden'.

Hatton Garden

James 'Bug Eye' Marsden, a Hatton Garden jeweller with alleged ties to London's criminal world, is credited as the mastermind behind the VAT fraud on gold coins (Lashmar, 2017). The scam consisted of buying gold coins which came from South Africa, Canada or Great Britain. They were purchased without VAT by sole traders or individuals pursuant to the 1979 VAT exemption on that kind of trades. The coins were sold through intermediaries to trading companies that transformed the coins into bullion. The bullion was finally sold with VAT to end customers. The traders at the end of that chain then disappeared without paying the VAT liability. Hatton Garden was at the time the playground of one of the finest crews in the British criminal world: the Wembley Mob.

Marsden brought into the VAT scam a few notorious figures of the Wembley Mob who specialized in bank robberies: Ronnie Dark, aka Dark Ronnie, and Mickey Green. The gang managed to scam the Exchequer of 6 million pounds in only few months.[4] With Operation *Finger* HMRC put an end to the Marsden gang on 14 October 1981. Most of its members fled Great Britain for Marbella.

By 1982 a number of groups specializing in the VAT fraud flourished around Hatton Garden. One particular group included figures of the Great Train Robbery,[5] Charlie Wilson and Roy James.[6] Roy James had previously had a successful career in car racing. In one of his early convictions he learned the silversmith trade. After his sport career came to an end he came back to his silversmith trade and, with other felons, engineered a VAT fraud with silver. The gang pocketed almost 2.5 million pounds of VAT (Lashmar, 2017).

In 1982 the British government put an end to VAT exemption on gold coins. The various gangs started to look overseas to countries where gold could be bought without VAT. The gangsters travelled to places like Jersey, Guernsey, Liechtenstein and Switzerland; bought the gold; smuggled it into the United Kingdom; and sold it with VAT. The tax bill was obviously never paid afterwards. It is estimated

---

4 Old-style villain is revealed as UK's most wanted man (www.independent.co.uk/news/old-style-villain-is-revealed-as-uks-most-wanted-man-1106880.html).

5 The Great Train Robbert took place in 1963. A gang of 15 criminals robbed 2.6 million pounds from a Royal Mail train heading from Glasgow to London.

6 Wanted: Racing Driver (www.motorsportmagazine.com/archive/article/december-1998/68/wanted-racing-driver).

that the size of this type of VAT fraud was much higher than what was pulled from the 'Garden', reaching tens of millions of pounds (Lashmar, 2017).

The 'golden' age of the VAT fraud underlined a recurrent behavioural pattern amongst the VAT fraudsters. This pattern consists in the reconversion of criminals towards more sophisticated areas of crimes. In the case of Hatton Garden many fraudsters previously specialized in 'blue-collar' violent crimes. Between 1981 and 1982 HMRC busted 12 cases of VAT fraudsters on gold bullion, and 7 involved criminals specializing in armed robbery (Lashmar, 2017). This pattern will be found in other VAT scams, like that on CO_2 emissions, where criminals previously specializing in small-scale cheats entered successfully into the hyper-sophisticated world of financial markets.

Darius Guppy

A major case of VAT evasion on gold trades was signalled in the late 1980s. In 1993 Darius Guppy and Benedict Mash were condemned to five years for falsely claiming the repayment of VAT for bogus gold bullion exports.[7] The illegal VAT claims were made between October 1989 and July 1990. The gold was bought in Great Britain with VAT, but Guppy applied for a VAT refund as he claimed that the bullions were sold to Swiss dealers with zero VAT. In reality, the gold was smuggled to dealers in India in false-bottomed packing cases.[8] In order to justify their demand for a tax refund, they forged airfreight documents and invoices, falsified signatures and made up a bogus Customs stamps.

Curiously, Guppy was an Eton graduate and had acquaintances among members of the British aristocracy. The pattern of educated people drifting into the world of white-collar crime would repeat one decade later when VAT fraud extended to services.

The age of 'Cancer': Benelux Connection and the birth of MTIC (1993–1997)

The European Single Market was launched on 1 January 1993, and in the same year the first case of MTIC fraud was signalled. The cases concerned British gangs that imported or smuggled gold from Belgium and Luxembourg to the United Kingdom. Those groups leveraged the experience of their predecessors from the Hatton Garden era.

The Benelux Connection marked the debut of a systemic loss for the EU due to VAT evasion. The losses amplified over time, and only in recent years did the European Commission understand the real dangers of this fraud.

---

7 Two jailed over gems firm fraud: Guppy and partner sentenced to five years (www.independent.co.uk/news/uk/two-jailed-over-gems-firm-fraud-guppy-and-partner-sentenced-to-five-years-1499879.html).
8 Guppy spun 'web of deceit' in bullion fraud (www.heraldscotland.com/news/12616608.Guppy_spun__apos_web_of_deceit_apos__in_bullion_fraud/).

One aspect of the Benelux Connection that remained unchanged over the years concerns the responsibilities of law enforcements with respect to MTIC fraud. As will be presented later, the MTIC cases were investigated by national law enforcements under the domestic laws of tax evasion. Nevertheless, MTIC fraud was a consequence of the European Single Mechanism.

The first cases

A first case was reported in March 1993 when British Customs[9] officers dismantled a VAT fraud gang specializing in gold smuggling after a nine-month investigation. The fraud involved ten tons of gold bullions valued at that time at over 60 million pounds. The VAT loss accounted for over 10 million pounds. HMRC's offices arrested 25 people and seized 36 kg of gold in Dover. The fraudsters used a complex series of 'front' companies, the funds being laundered through other bogus businesses.

The gold was being brought into Britain from Belgium, where it had been bought legally at the local rate of VAT of 1%. After being brought into the United Kingdom the gold was melted and sold to local jewellers or gold dealers at a price that included the 17.5% VAT.

The unique feature of this case is the fact that it took place over a period of time that included the opening of the Single Market. Prior to 1993, gold importation in the United Kingdom and in any other country of the EU was submitted to checks by Customs when crossing the border. Thus, the fraudsters were obliged to smuggle the bullion into Britain. After January 1993, smuggling from another Member country was not necessary as goods could circulate freely within the EU. That was an incentive and a facilitator for fraudsters which seized the opportunity to massively size up their operations (Frunza, 2015).

Lucie and Michael Gilmore

The most mediatized case of the Benelux Connection was without any doubt that of Lucie and Michael Gilmore. Lucie Gilmore[10] was a police officer in her early 20s at that time. She acted as a courier in a VAT fraud gang which included her father Michael Gilmore, who persuaded her to join the criminal enterprise.

Michael Gilmore had an insurance brokerage which, by 1991, became insolvent. He decided then to turn towards gold bullion smuggling and VAT fraud. The gold was bought in Belgium and collected in Luxembourg with no VAT. The Gilmores transported over three tonnes of gold valued at around 20 million pounds. They did over thirty trips across the Channel, collecting

---

9 'Biggest VAT ring' cracked by Customs: Treasury estimated to have lost 10 million pounds (www.independent.co.uk/news/uk/biggest-vat-ring-cracked-by-customs-treasury-estimated-to-have-lost-pounds-10m-1500075.html).

10 PC convicted of gold smuggling (www.independent.co.uk/news/pc-convicted-of-gold-smuggling-1316659.html).

over 2,500 bars, which were introduced in Britain through various ports. The tax loss to HMRC was estimated to be 3.4 million pounds. The gold was sold over a period of 18 months to traders from the Asian community in Handsworth, Birmingham. One particular shop in Birmingham owned by the brothers Surinder Kumar and Jeevan Kanda was used for fronting the business and collecting the VAT from gold sales. The gang was dismantled in 1994, all members being arrested and sentenced, with the exception of Kanda, who fled the country for Dubai.

Geoffrey Mann

A case of VAT fraud involving a Hatton Garden jeweller was reported in 1998. Geoffrey Mann[11] was charged with VAT fraud on gold, the amount of pocketed funds being estimated to be 3 million pounds. The fraud took place between 1994 and 1996, well after the Single Market was launched. Therefore Mann's case was probably one of the first documented pure-MTIC frauds. He was also charged in 1988 with VAT fraud, the gold being most likely smuggled at that time. Interestingly, while involved in the VAT scam Mann helped the British Royal family in 1994 to recover some valuable pieces of jewellery that had been stolen.

Mann was involved in various episodes of VAT fraud and most likely played the role of the front company in charge of collecting the VAT from the end sales. By the 1990s, various reports[12] showed that organized crime had taken control over the VAT action in Hatton Garden (Lashmar, 2017), and at that time the London underworld was controlled by the notorious Adams family.

Shabir Karim[13]

The Benelux Connection used mainly gold bullion as defrauding means. Nevertheless versions of the fraud existed with other precious metals, including platinum. This is the case with the MTIC involving Shabir Karim and his Blackburn-based gang. They imported platinum ingots from Italy and resold them in Great Britain. In a period of over two years between 2005 and 2007 the gang managed to steal 4.5 million pounds in unpaid tax.[14] The court case was judged in 2012 and indicated the following roles and responsibilities for the four condemned:

---

11 Jeweller jailed for VAT fraud (www.heraldscotland.com/news/12281010.Jeweller_jailed_for_VAT_fraud/).
12 Jewellery and junk (www.independent.co.uk/arts-entertainment/jewellery-and-junk-1170890.html).
13 www.mynewsdesk.com/uk/hm-revenue-customs-hmrc/pressreleases/blackburn-men-jailed-for-pocketing-the-vat-783710.
14 Blackburn's platinum trio gets 17 years of prison for £4.5 Million VAT fraud (www.lancashiretelegraph.co.uk/news/9865704.Blackburn_s_platinum_trio_gets_17_years_for___4_5m_VAT_fraud/).

- Shabir Karim was the mastermind of the crime and the director of Bullion Traders. He comes from a family of jewellers established in Blackburn.
- Kamran and Imran Bhatti, two brothers from Blackburn, controlled the companies KB Jewellers and Regal Metals, and acted as front men. They deliberately destroyed all documents related to the fraud.
- Raymond Bowden was the director of RBA Trading, a company linked to the three others involved in the fraud. He acted as courier for the platinum shipments, collecting the packages at various airports in Great Britain.

The case of the Blackburn gang is a clear example that the MTIC fraud techniques spread quickly outside Hatton Garden and outside London's milieu. Also the MTIC pattern tested on the Benelux Connection was leveraged to other European countries. Moreover, MTIC started to become 'popular' in the late 1990s with the Asian community in Britain, a fact that remained true until present days.

Benelux Connection reloaded

A VAT fraud case similar to those of the Benelux Connection was reported in 2014 by Finish law enforcements.[15] Between 2011 and 2013 the Helsinki-based company purchased 10 million euros of gold from Belgium. Two hundred and fifty-five kilograms of gold was airfreighted into Finland in 22 shipments. The gold was shipped afterwards to Sweden and finally to Norway, where the VAT rate is 25%. The estimated tax loss was around 2 million euros. The investigation was the result of an undercover joint intelligence operation involving Finnish police and customs. The gold smuggling operation was uncovered in 2012, when customs officers at the Helsinki-Vantaa airport discovered a strange gold shipment. Moreover, the company engaged in that scam forged invoices and customs' documents.

This case has two remarkable features. One aspect is related to the fact that the fraudsters used a very old scam with an old-fashioned method, consisting of the physical transportation of high-value goods. The second aspect is related to the fact that the final target of the fraud was not a country from the EU but a country from the European Economic Space (Norway), which included other countries besides the 28 Member States. Gold was smuggled out of the EU into a non-member country, which was part of the Single Market.

The age of 'Gemini': technology gadgets era (1998–2005)

The late 1990s brought new opportunities for VAT fraudsters in the technology area. The market of technological gadgets, including mobile phones, computers laptops, memory disks and central processing units, experienced a strong growth. The source of this growth was the fact that these products became accessible to the

15 Gold smugglers face millions of euros in tax fraud charges (https://yle.fi/uutiset/osasto/news/ gold_smugglers_face_millions_of_euros_in_tax_fraud_charges/7166562).

retail market. In 1998 the global market for personal computers represented 159 billion USD (Kozmetsky, 2005), European customers accounting for almost a third of the global sales. Between 1996 and 2001 the market had a double-digit growth, with a 22% peak in 1999. The crash of the internet bubble in 2000 entailed a 5% contraction of the market in 2001. Because of the crisis, many retailers saw their profit shrinking, and some opted to walk the path of VAT fraud. Indeed, computers; mobile phones; and, later, smartphones entered into the category of low-volume, high-value items, thereby constituting good opportunities for MTIC fraudsters.

Technology gadgets dominated the MTIC arena from the late 1990s until the mid-2000s, when services became a better prospect for fraudsters. But the period of computers and mobile phones consolidated and crystalized the main groups and the main pattern in the world of MTIC.

The Stoke-on-Trent connection

One of the main patterns of the MTIC fraud is the clustering effect in different regions and around various crime groups. The Hatton Garden circle was the first cluster, specializing in precious metals. Another cluster, specializing in mobile phones and computer components, was formed in the late 1990s around Stoke-on-Trent. Table 10.1[16] synthesizes the main investigations against the gangs from Stoke-on-Trent. The operations started as early as 2002, and a few of the people charged were even on the most-wanted list in 2018.

Stuart Baillie

One of the first raids against the Stoke-on-Trent 'brigade' took place as early as 2002[17] and targeted Stuart Baillie, a reputed businessman from Staffordshire. He controlled Baillies Ltd., a company incorporated in 1999, where he served as a sales representative. The gross revenue of the Stoke-based firm was around 387 million

Table 10.1 Snapshot of the three major operations targeting the Stoke-on-Trent gangs

Operation name	Leader of the group	Number of people involved	Year	VAT loss GBP million	Total prison years
Shepherd	Clive Saunders	7	2002	68	39
Emersed	Craig Johnson	12	2002	20	75
Shoot	Stephen Hancock	4	2002	50	19
Vaulter	Geoffrey Johnson	18	2007	20	150
Euripus	Shehwad Ashraf/ Nasir Khan	42	2003	250	130

16 Organized crime gangs receive 133 years in prison – Overview of Operations *Shepherd–Emersed–Shoot* (www.wired-gov.net/wg/wg-news-1.nsf/0/188055222BB3BC08802574D000600C14?OpenDocument).
17 Mobile phone scam costs VAT billions (www.theguardian.com/uk/2002/aug/17/mobilephones).

pounds in 2001, with a net profit of over 5 million pounds.[18] Baillie was released shortly after the 2002 indictment. His firm entered in liquidation by court decision in 2004. A freezing injunction over Baillie's assets was ordered by the court in 2010.

Clive Saunders

The MTIC fraud attracted also figures from Stoke-on-Trent's crime underworld. In 2006, Clive Saunders, the head of a local gang, was arrested and charged as part of Operation *Shepherd*, carried out by the British law enforcements.[19] Operation *Shepherd* started in 2002 in parallel with two other operations, *Emersed* and *Shout*. Saunders was imprisoned during all those years for a previous offence but managed to control the VAT scam from the yard. His gang of at least seven key persons defrauded the HMRC for a total of 68 million pounds. The prosecutors indicate that the first trades of mobile phones of the gang were through Crownlink Networks Ltd., a company managed by Charles Hackney and Michael West. That company reported a sales figure for mobile phones of 27 million pounds in only a few months. Operation *Shepherd* prosecuted and condemned to prison seven persons, including Craig Saunders, as following:

- Craig Johnson acted as a money launderer for the group. He had also his own carousel fraud, discussed in the following paragraph. He was the brother of another VAT gang leader, Geoffrey Johnson.
- David G. Routledge[20] was the accountant of the gang. He used his knowledge and experience on VAT matters and company registration to help set up the carousel.
- Craig Michael Jones was an ex-soldier and one of Saunders's henchmen. He controlled the companies and fund transfers through the bank accounts.
- Phillip George Hague was the director of Gyraland UK Ltd., a company part of the scheme, which had a 7 million pound turnover in the year prior to the conviction.
- Michael West and Charles Hackney served as company directors and frontmen in the fraud.

Subsequent to this operation, part of Saunders's assets were frozen by British authorities.

Craig Johnson

Craig Johnson, one of those concerned by Operation *Shepherd*, was also charged in another case resulting from investigations in Operation *Emersed*. The operation led to the sentencing of 12 individuals from Staffordshire, Manchester, Leicestershire

---

18 https://beta.companieshouse.gov.uk/company/03824766/filing-history.
19 www.theguardian.com/business/2006/jul/20/crime.money.
20 www.accountancyage.com/aa/news/1781192/bookkeeper-soldier-jailed-vat-fraud.

and Essex. The carousel scam resulted in a 20 million pound loss. Like Saunders, Craig Johnson was a notorious figure of organized crime in Staffordshire. He was living in a 17th-century palace, which was seized and auctioned by authorities.[21]

Johnson's gang owned a freight company as part of the scam in order to legitimize the mobile phone trades providing false paperwork on logistics. The proceeds of the crime were laundered through banks from Gibraltar and Hong Kong.[22] Johnson's wife, Amanda, fled for Dubai with their children. Dubai was also the hiding place for Craig's brother, Geoffrey, involved also in MTIC scams.

Stephen Hancock

Operation *Shoot*[23] took place in parallel with two other operations, *Shepherd* and *Emersed*. The group concerned four individuals led by Stephen Hancock, which was also charged as part of Operation *Emersed*. Hancock's gang controlled three main companies registered in the United Kingdom: Worldsoft (UK) Ltd., Lawley Technologies Ltd. and Calcon Industrial Supplies Ltd. Those companies either carried out 588 transactions with United Kingdom-based 'missing traders' or hijacked VAT-registered companies, resulting in 50 million pounds of unpaid VAT. The other members of the gang were Gerard Michael Forrest, Barbara Moran (Hancock's partner) and Shane Matthews.

Geoffrey Johnson

The tale of the Stoke-on-Trent connection surfaced in July 2017, when Geoffrey Johnson,[24] one of Britain's most wanted fugitives, was returned by Dubai's authorities. He was initially indicted in 2007 as a part of Operation *Vaulter*,[25] along with 17 other suspects. The trial that took place between 2012 and 2014 concerned him and his son Gareth Johnson, and a charge of money laundering 20 million pounds of criminal proceeds from an MTIC fraud with mobile phones. In 2014 the Johnsons fled Britain to a Tanzanian village called Iringa. They also had a Kenyan passport. When investors reached them in Tanzania, they fled for Kenya. Geoffrey managed to get a fake British passport and get to Dubai, where he was arrested by local authorities and deferred to the British justice system, which sentenced him to 24 years in prison; in his absence he was ordered to repay 109 million pounds worth of criminal proceeds.

21 www.telegraph.co.uk/news/uknews/law-and-order/5377725/Stately-home-Bentley-and-Ferrari-up-for-auction-after-crime-boss-jailed.html.
22 VAT fraudster jailed for 12 years (www.expressandstar.com/news/2008/09/27/vat-fraudster-jailed-for-12-years/#GedHw5IuqObHCVh1.99).
23 Sentencing in Worcester's £50 million fraud trial (www.worcesternews.co.uk/news/3708787. Sentencing_in_Worcester_s___50_million_fraud_trial/).
24 www.mynewsdesk.com/uk/hm-revenue-customs-hmrc/pressreleases/tax-fugitive-geoffrey-johnson-caught-and-jailed-2066980.
25 HMRC swoops on money laundering and VAT fraud gang (www.tax-news.com/news/HMRC_Swoops_On_Money_Laundering_And_VAT_Fraud_Gang___28334.html).

Gareth Johnson controlled Coast Logistics and Tectonics Holdings, two companies that laundered the proceeds of the fraud through offshore accounts, including those in Andorra, Dubai, Hong Kong, the United States, Switzerland and Portugal.[26] In 2017 he was still a fugitive. The Johnsons were supported throughout their criminal actions by the following associates:

- Albert Amritanand, a British citizen jailed for five years in 2013;
- Sarah Panitzke,[27] a British citizen from Yorkshire, based in Andorra and Spain, who helped the Johnsons in laundering big volumes of money through offshore bank accounts. She is currently a fugitive and sought internationally for laundering more than 1 billion pounds for various criminal groups; and
- Alison Elizabeth Samantha Shelton, a British citizen who worked for Coast Logistics and provided false paperwork.

A key finding of Operation *Vaulter* is the fact that MTIC fraudsters started to use specialized money launderers. This is the case with Sarah Panitzke, who not only worked closely with the Johnsons but also provided money laundering services to other groups.

Raymond Woolley

The MTIC gangs from Stoke-on-Trent were connected either to reputed crime figures or to known businessmen. The Ray Woolley case is an exception as he was a former pipe welder.[28] In 2003 Woolley and his crime associate Robert Garner were sentenced to imprisonment for scamming the taxman for 38 million pounds related to the trading of mobile phones. The two criminals established a carousel of companies based in Spain, Ireland and the United Kingdom. One of the main companies of the fraud, Roofsmart Ltd., had VAT liability in the third quarter of 2000 of more than 24 million pounds[29] but paid over its entire operating history less than 300 pounds of VAT.

At the time of the indictment in 2003, Woolley was living in Marbella, Spain. After refusing to reimburse HMRC he hid in Switzerland until 2008.[30]

Raymond Cox

One of the biggest carousels from Stoke-on-Trent was led by Raymond Cox.[31] His six-men gang managed to pocket 85 million pounds of VAT fraud on mobile phone

26 www.dailyrecord.co.uk/news/crime/scotlands-most-wanted-fraud-fugitive-10792863.
27 www.itv.com/news/calendar/2016-10-20/york-woman-convicted-of-laundering-1bn-thought-to-be-hiding-in-spain/.
28 www.theguardian.com/money/2005/mar/04/crime.scamsandfraud.
29 Two jailed for £38 million VAT fraud (www.wired-gov.net/wg/wg-news-1.nsf/54e6de9e0c383 719802572b9005141ed/6a807b67f130f13e802572ab004b7264?OpenDocument).
30 http://news.bbc.co.uk/2/hi/uk_news/england/staffordshire/8462274.stm.
31 £85 million phone fraudsters jailed (www.manchestereveningnews.co.uk/news/greater-manchester-news/85m-phone-fraudsters-jailed-995084).

sales. Cox's gang operated independently from the other three groups indicted in 2002 (Operations *Shepherd*, *Shoot* and *Emersed*). Cox, a former storeman in Stoke-on-Trent, owned two companies registered in Germany called Signal Telecom GMBH and Crystal Telkom GmbH, and was the director of two companies in Spain called Zeption Telecom SL and Nauti-Parts SL. The other members of this criminal enterprise were Brett Issitt and Michael McNeill, who served as sales executives for a company called Powertone B.V., a Dutch-registered company based in Amsterdam but with offices in Manchester. Powertone had a turnover of 49.5 million pounds.

Two other members were prosecuted: Paul Sweeney, arrested in Manchester but living in Amsterdam, and Colin Jones, director of a company called Data-cell Ltd. based in Sale. The gang controlled seven companies registered in four countries. HMRC started the investigation around the year 2000, but the court sentences were pronounced in 2007.

Compared to other gangs, Cox's group managed to operate a large-scale fraud with a limited crew. The gang put together a 'cookbook' for the formation of bogus companies. This textbook of crime written by McNeill would have helped the other members to deploy fraudulent trades more quickly. The Cox and Woolley cases are relevant with respect to two aspects. First, they underlined the beginning of a trend in which criminals were able to deploy massive operations with limited human resources. For comparison, the other gangs from Stoke-on-Trent counted dozens of members, thereby exposing the gang to bigger risks. This pattern showed its efficiency during the VAT fraud on CO_2 emissions, during which many groups counted less than five people. Second, the criminals became more cosmopolitan and started to use the advantages of the Single Market in their favour. Thus, they were able to register themselves easily to companies in other countries of the EU, without requiring strawmen in the respective locations.

Shehwad Ashraf[32]

The previous operations around the Stoke-on-Trent scene were not adding up to the total estimate of MTIC fraud in Britain, which accounted in 2003–2004 for a few billion. Under the media's pressure the British tax office launched in 2003 Operation *Euripus* to find the big fishes in the MTIC pond. The first target of that operation was the gang led by Shehwad Ashraf. After being charged for VAT fraud he fled to Dubai in 2004, but he was extradited from there in 2012.

Ashraf controlled three companies, including Imperium Corporation, a buffer company in the carousel, and Raj Trading Corporation and Alldech Ltd., import-export companies. Three other men were charged along with Ashraf: Javed Mohammed and his younger brother and Shoket Khan. All three managed to flee Britain at the time. By 2013 they were last known to be in Dubai and possibly in Pakistan. Ashraf's gang used offshore bank accounts in Hong Kong, Pakistan and Dubai.

32 www.mynewsdesk.com/uk/hm-revenue-customs-hmrc/pressreleases/ps250m-fraudster-jailed-843062.

Nasir Khan[33]

The second gang cracked down on by Operation *Euripus* in 2003 was led by Nasir Khan,[34] a well-respected entrepreneur in the accessories business. He was the owner and director of the accessories business The Accessory People (TAP), which sold products for 13 million pounds in 2001. After June 2001, his business entered into decline and opted for the fast money of the MTIC fraud on mobile phones. Khan quickly constituted a gang that counted amongst its ranks an ex-drug smuggler, a former used car salesman and a fish and chip shop owner. Khan used his firm, TAP, as one of the buffers in the carousel fraud. Thus, between 2001 and 2003, the revenue of his firm increased sharply from 13 to 219 million pounds.

Khan and his 14 associates controlled more than 200 companies in the United Kingdom, Spain and Holland as well as offshore bank accounts in Hong Kong, Dubai and Pakistan. Khan was sentenced to ten years of prison.

The trial took place in September 2008, and the gang members were sentenced to over 100 years in prison. The list of those imprisoned included Jo-Anne Halliday, Curtis Laurent, Dennis Hunter, Peter Arthur Ebbrell, Hashib Ansari Apabhai, Eisa Masihullah Apabhai, Adam Amani, German Castillo, Jonathon Baigent and Denise Westmoreland. Another four members of the gang – including Taher Majid, Abdul Koser, Quentin Reynolds and Marcus Hughes – were sentenced to prison.

Operation *Euripus* took over ten years and required hundreds of officers to work on the case. The two gangs led by Ashraf and Khan managed to defraud the HMRC of over a quarter billion pounds, thereby being the biggest fraud investigated in the Stoke-on-Trent circle. Operation *Euripus*, along with Operation *Vaulter*, pointed towards Dubai as a new hub for money laundering as well as a hiding place for fugitives.

Operation *Euripus* underlined that the MTIC fraudster moved forward in terms of complexity of their networks, the case itself accounting for not less than 200 companies used in the different stages of the carousel.

The Dubai Connection

The 'Dubai Connection' was mentioned in the British media for the first time in 2006.[35] This new avenue was an amplifier for the MTIC fraud across the EU. The European Commission estimated that the 'Dubai Connection's' represented 8 billion euros in pocketed taxes, accounting for almost three-quarters of the defrauded VAT between June 2005 and June 2006. This was also reflected in the evolution of trade balance between the United Kingdom and the United Arab Emirates. In June 2005[36] the British exports to Dubai increased to 529 million

---

33 www.bbc.com/news/uk-england-16262390.

34 www.mobilenewscwp.co.uk/2012/03/02/how-hmrc-finally-caught-nasir-khan/.

35 VAT scams hit UK taxpayers hard (http://news.bbc.co.uk/2/hi/business/5369776.stm).

36 The £30 billion money-go-round (www.telegraph.co.uk/news/1526770/The-30-billion-money-go-round.html).

pounds from 204 million pounds in the previous month. Those numbers had no economic justification. The increase was mainly due to the fact that the same items circulated several times back and forth between the two countries, sometimes in the same cargo flight. As a result, in Dubai an entire criminal industry has grown up to service carousel fraud in Britain. Underground factories, mostly operated by Pakistani businessmen, were forging the serial numbers of the electronic gadgets in order to trick the British customs upon the items' arrival in Britain (Frunza, 2015).

The fraud on electronic gadgets flourished across the EU. Most of the items were seemingly supplied from Dubai, but their initial origin was difficult to assess. Thus, the cases exposed in this section concern only those scams reported as part of the Dubai Connection. Many other VAT fraud cases concerning technology items could potentially be classified as part of the Dubai Connection. Despite the fact that the items circulated through other European countries, the United Kingdom seemed to be the preferred destination in the Dubai Connection.

The fraudsters from the Dubai Connection were in fact building carousels with both MTIC and MTEC mechanisms. One the one hand they were able to sell with VAT in the European countries goods imported VAT-free. On the other hand, they were claiming VAT reimbursements when items were sold to Dubai firms. Throughout the 2000s, the Dubai Connection concerned mainly mobile phones and computer parts. The late 2000s brought new opportunities with the missing trader fraud on services, mainly on CO_2 emissions.

Adam Umerji aka Shafiq Patel[37]

Adam Umerji aka Shafiq Patel appeared in 2012 on the list of Britain's most-wanted criminals. He fled to Dubai after being charged in a 56 million pounds VAT fraud. Umerji was the co-leader of the criminal group, along with Addullah Yusaf Allad, who was also a fugitive. Like most of their peers they planned a carousel between the United Kingdom and Dubai. In 2006 their enterprise claimed from HMRC VAT reimbursement of 56 million pounds. The group managed to launder 37 million pounds of evaded tax and to channel it towards Dubai. Adam Umerji, his older brother, and Muhammed Patel and Abdullah Yusuf Allad controlled three United Kingdom-based companies, Eurosabre Ltd., Vertu Telecoms Ltd. and Master Trading (UK) Ltd., which were part of the carousel. The gang included two other main associates which diverted the evaded funds towards offshore locations. Wai Fong Yeung and his partner Mohammed Mehtajee were involved with several businesses but principally with Armada UK, based in London. Yeung was also responsible for creating and operating Jai Hua International Ltd., a Hong Kong-based company, which was used to launder the proceeds of the crime.

---

37 www.wired-gov.net/wg/wg-news-1.nsf/0/196C319D9BC176AC80257906005AD5B6?
    OpenDocument.

Harjit Singh Takkar

A British court sentenced Harjit Singh Takkar[38] to seven years for VAT evasion. The crime was engineered between May 2004 and August 2004; Takkar controlled a company called Hi-Profile Ltd., which imported mobile phones and computer chips from sellers in France. The items were sold in the United Kingdom with VAT to other companies.

Those companies then exported the items to Dubai.[39] The investigation showed that from Dubai the items were shipped back to Continental Europe and back to Britain, thereby touring in the carousel. A German company was also linked to the carousel. Takkar's case shows that Dubai was not only the place from which items were imported into Britain or other countries but also a destination for exports.

Jasbinder Bedesha[40]

A major case of the 'Dubai Connection' involving companies trading mobile phones and computer processing units (CPUs) was busted in 2011, following Operation *Elemi*. The group, led by Jasbinder Bedesha and Daamin Kaif,[41] managed to steal 38 million pounds of VAT in 2005. The items were imported from Dubai via Europe and the sold in the United Kingdom. Daamin Kaif controlled two companies that constituted the core of the carousel: Sky Computers UK Ltd. and Maxro Technology Ltd. The money from the crime was laundered through overseas companies in Dubai and Spain. The following associates were involved at different levels in the gang: Stephen Stark, Duminda Thantrimudali, Baljinder Singh Sandhu, Mario Vocaturo, Iqbal Singh Gandham, Harnaik Singh Sandhu and Malcolm Edwards-Sayer.

Chaudry Ali[42]

The Dubai Connection was not dealing only with gadgets. Gold was also an option that seemed to be profitable for Chaudry Ali, a British jeweller. He has stolen 7 million pounds from the British taxpayers. The gold was bought in Dubai and brought into Britain via Frankfurt.

---

38 www.wired-gov.net/wg/wg-news-1.nsf/0/5FC2FCDC36C1DDC0802577070040C12B? OpenDocument.

39 Man jailed for £4.5 million VAT fraud (https://commsbusiness.co.uk/features/man-jailed-for-4-5-million-vat-fraud/).

40 www.mynewsdesk.com/uk/hm-revenue-customs-hmrc/pressreleases/extra-10-years-in-jail-for-ps38-million-fraudster-842376.

41 www.mynewsdesk.com/uk/hm-revenue-customs-hmrc/pressreleases/ps2-4-million-payback-for-high-life-fraudster-904156.

42 www.mynewsdesk.com/uk/hm-revenue-customs-hmrc/pressreleases/gold-smuggler-behind-bars-822392.

Chaudry Ali used two couriers who collected a large amount of gold from Dubai. The courier would then fly to Frankfurt and hand over the gold to Ali, who took it back to the United Kingdom. In case he was stopped by customs he carried documents concerning his VAT-registered business and indicating that the gold was originally from Frankfurt, thereby being exempt of taxes upon arrival in the United Kingdom.

The Iberian Connection

Portugal and Spain were harbouring, throughout the 2000s, numerous gangs involved in the MTIC fraud. Many cases signalled in Great Britain pointed towards companies or individuals based in Spain. As shown in Chapter 3, Spain is one of the European countries with the biggest VAT gap and the largest losses due to MTIC fraud. The geographical proximity of Spain and Portugal was leveraged by fraudsters in organizing VAT carousels. Moreover, Spain is a meetup place for most groups in the world of organized crime. Places like Marbella are a hotspot for major criminal figures, thereby facilitating the sharing of information and best practices in criminal enterprises.

Spain was also one of the starting points of the VAT fraud on CO_2 emissions that propagated afterwards to all European countries. In recent years Spanish police arrested individuals allegedly linked to terrorist organizations which were also involved in VAT fraud.

Portugal, along with Spain, faced some particular challenges in prosecuting the first cases of VAT fraud. For instance, in the case 'Carré & Ribeiro' in Portugal, the national tax offices struggled with the legal framework of the assets confiscation.

Valter Aleixo

One of the earliest cases of carousel[43] fraud in Portugal concerned the case 'Carré & Ribeiro' and the Portuguese entrepreneurs Valter Aleixo and Joaquim Ribeiro. The 'Carré & Ribeiro' case brought to court in 2005 had indicted 23 individuals and companies. The tax-evading activity took place between 1999 and 2002, when Carré & Ribeiro was one of the most important retail companies in Portugal in the electronic devices sector. The scammers defrauded the local tax office of 33.9 million euros.[44] The investigation revealed a carousel scheme that encompassed Spanish, English and American companies. Many of these companies never had commercial activity, and the electronic equipment was declared as sold to Spain or England but in reality was sold in Portugal.

In the Carré & Ribeiro case, two paths of VAT frauds were identified. A first pattern was the classic carousel with import from other countries of the EU. The second pattern involved fictitious purchases from other Portuguese

---

43 www.dn.pt/arquivo/2005/interior/quatro-empresarios-detidos-por-fraude-em-carrossel-no-iva-631893.html.
44 www.cmjornal.pt/exclusivos/detalhe/estado-fica-a-arder-com-339-milhoes.

companies, the products being resold domestically without any VAT being paid to the taxman.

Juan Díaz García

In 2009, the Spanish court charged and condemned a group led by Juan Díaz García[45] for a VAT evasion scheme that inflicted 40 million euros of losses to the tax office.

Five of García's accomplices were indicted and imprisoned: Juan Delgado Pulgar, Andrés Cano Rodríguez, Juan José López Asensio, Joaquín Tafur Fernández and Natalia Soldevilla. The fraud was committed between 2000 and 2002, and the Spanish authorities started the investigation in 2004.

García's case[46] is a perfect example of how the Iberian Connections worked in practice. Between August and December of 1997, Juan Díaz García and Juan José López Asensio bought three Portuguese companies: Cartaxo, Montagens e Material Eléctrico and Anibel Comercio Artesano.

The Portuguese companies purchased computer equipment from the Spanish companies controlled by García's gang. The Portuguese companies would then resell the merchandise to Spanish companies, thereby forming a carousel structure. The sale of computer equipment was made to the Spanish companies: Villanueva SL, Sistemas Informáticos Gomiz and Kno Quatro. Other companies controlled by García which were part of the fraudulent scheme included Ailicis SL, Microelvas, Touchsisten, Anibel e Montagen Electrical, Informatica Lda, Nanotecnología Integrada and Zipes.

The Spanish companies would claim VAT refunds from the National Treasury. All bank accounts of the companies involved with the carousel scam were controlled by García and Pulgar.

Mohan and Annand Chatlani

A more recent case in the Iberian Connection is related to Mohan and Annand Chatlani.[47] The two Indian citizens were charged as part of a broader investigation in Operation *Dreams*.

In 2018, after two years of investigation at the European level, law enforcements arrested 58 persons in Spain, Germany, Belgium and Portugal.

The Chatlani (father and son), alleged leaders of the criminal enterprise, became fugitives when the wave of arrests started to crack down on their gang. The gang managed to defraud around 250 million euros using fraudulent trades of

45 www.elperiodicoextremadura.com/noticias/badajoz/audiencia-ratifica-integramente-condenas-fraude-iva_435596.html.

46 www.elperiodicoextremadura.com/noticias/badajoz/penas-9-meses-15-anos-prision-8-condenados-fraude-iva_399479.html.

47 https://cronicaglobal.elespanol.com/vida/audiencia-nacional-mayor-fraude-iva_138857_102.html.

computer parts and luxury cars. The backbone of the scam was built on a hundred mercantile companies, mostly fictitious or on behalf of frontmen settled in Spain, Hungary, Germany, Italy, Romania, Bulgaria, Belgium, the United States, Portugal and Cyprus. The electronic devices were sold through various chains of companies organized in a carousel and ended up on the Spanish market, where they were sold at abnormally low prices. The criminals managed to establish trading relationships with large multinational retailers. These global retailers were the end point here; the items were sold at a big discount. They also legitimized the fraudulent trades vis-à-vis the Spanish Treasury, which was reimbursing VAT based on the invoices of those corporations.

In 2014[48] as a result of pressure from the Spanish authorities, the Chatlani moved to the United States, from which they oversaw their criminal activities in Europe. The proceeds of the crime were laundered with real estate investments, luxury vehicles, lines of bank loans and investments in companies related to the audiovisual sector in Spain, the United States and Hungary. The Chatlanis moved more than 140 million euros in two years between the companies they controlled using a 'funnel system'[49] through Hungary or Bulgaria.

Other significant connections

Daniel O'Connell

One of the earliest VAT frauds with computer processors took place between April 1996 and February 1999. It was orchestrated by the flamboyant Irish businessman Daniel O'Connell,[50] who managed to defraud the HMRC of 20 million pounds, a record amount at that time. During the period of the crime, O'Connell paid only 32,000 pounds in VAT to the British tax office. In order to gain credibility with his counterparts, he associated with Michael Keating, a former minister in the Irish government.

O'Connell controlled two firms, Irish Semi-Conductors and Anglo Irish Merchants, which were at the centre of the scam. He bought computer processors from London suppliers for almost 100 million pounds without VAT as he claimed that the chips were to be exported in Ireland. The items were sold to British companies controlled by O'Connell's associate, the Irish businesswoman Bernadette Devine. O'Connell managed to launder 4.2 million pounds of his criminal proceeds to offshore accounts in the Bahamas, Belize and the Turks and Caicos.

O'Connell's case was not technically an MTIC and was more a basic VAT fraud. This makes the size of the scam look outstanding. Fraud accounting for tens of millions of pounds was generally orchestrated through the carousel, which amplified the size of the fraud.

---

48 www.laverdad.es/murcia/detenidos-operacion-internacional-20180504114641-nt.html.
49 The funnel system is a version of Multilevel Marketing.
50 Playboy jailed for eight years in £20 million tax fraud (www.telegraph.co.uk/news/uknews/1352125/Playboy-jailed-for-eight-years-in-20m-tax-fraud.html).

Syed Ahmed[51]

Operation *Devout* was one of HMRC's most successful investigations from the 2000s. A 21-strong gang led by Syed Ahmed was charged with evading 37.5 million pounds of VAT. Compared to other investigations Operation *Devout* led to one of the largest confiscation orders at that time. HMRC managed to locate a few luxury properties of the gang and to freeze the assets.

HMRC started looking into Ahmed's affairs in April 2002 and his import-export business of CPUs. Ahmed and his associates imported CPUs from Ireland and sold them in the United Kingdom to companies controlled by the gang. The goods were sold with VAT, which was not reimbursed to the tax office. A few companies from the carousel exported the items back into Ireland. The exporter company claimed to be reimbursed for VAT. Part of the evaded funds was used to buy a third of a tonne of bullion gold. The gang also used gold trades to evade VAT.

Syed Mubarak Ahmed, Somasuntharam and Shakeel Ahmad were the masterminds of the scam and controlled MST Associates (UK) Ltd., a company which acted as buffer in the carousel. A VAT-registered business was used by the 'missing trader' to distance themselves from the shipper (or exporter).

Two other members of the gang, Stephen Farrell[52] and Mark Frederick Sheasby, both controlled a Birmingham-based company, GW 224 Ltd., used as a buffer in the carousel. Mark Sheasby was a respected figure in Birmingham's business world and a former commercial manager of a rugby club and a company that provided tickets for major sport events in Great Britain. One of the 'missing traders' used was Shivani (Ltd.) – an anagram of 'I Vanish'. Peter John Pomfrett and Timur Mehmet controlled Globalactive Technologies Ltd., a company which acted as an exporter in the carousel.

The following members controlled companies that acted as buffers in the carousel: Pravin Jogia with Aurum Jewellery (Wholesale) Ltd. and Aurum Jewellery 2000 Ltd., Jonah Adali-Mortty with Lightcare Ltd., Babak Cherazi and Khaled Hamidi with Beronvine Ltd. and Mustapha Mehmet with Globalactive Technologies Ltd.

Stuart Emilios Angelides coordinated most of the members of the gang in running companies for laundering the stolen tax: Jaswender Singh Chahal with Acorn Trading and Woodland Supplies, Harbans Singh Kohli with GK Telecommunications PLC, Martin Watmough with Gardham Ltd., Leslie Pummell with Glaston Ltd., Sukhdave Singh More with Rapid Distribution Ltd., Christopher Traverse with NCT Training Ltd. and Peter Newey and Tariq Kamal with Betta Solutions Ltd.

Stephen Pigott

Pigott's case stands out from the rest because it involved high-profile individuals. The individuals caught in the web of the MTIC were generally small- and

51 www.mynewsdesk.com/uk/pressreleases/hm-revenue-customs-crime-lords-92-3-million-payback-436307.
52 http://www.mynewsdesk.com/uk/pressreleases/hm-revenue-customs-london-37m-tax-crime-gang-jailed-415252.

medium-sized business owners who looked for shortcuts towards success. By the time he entered the MTIC scene Pigott was a reputed music producer who worked with pop stars, including Rob Stewart, Pet Shop Boys and Celine Dion. The changes in technology made his skills redundant, and this oriented him towards the MTIC fraud with mobile phones.

Stephen Pigott[53] formed a group with Joanna Harris (a former fitness instructor), Stacey Haber-Hofberg (a music lawyer and former New York law judge) and Theresa Igbanugo (a record label director).[54] Piggtt's associates were in charge of laundering the money. The group evaded tax of 40 million pounds, the money being diverted towards Hong Kong and Dubai, where Pigott was residing. The group had established in Hong Kong clones of their British companies to mislead their clients.

Zafar Baidar Chisthi[55]

Chisthi's name appeared on the 2012 list of the most-wanted British fugitives. He had previously been involved in MTIC fraud on mobile phones that entailed a prejudice to the British taxpayers of almost 150 million pounds. After being released on bail he fled for Dubai, where he seemingly resided for a while before fleeing for Pakistan.

The alleged leader of the gang was Dilawar Ravjani, director of Future Communications (UK) Ltd. and owner of Unique Distribution Ltd. At the centre of the fraud was Future Communications (UK) Ltd., part of the Ravjani's corporation called Innovative Global Business Group Ltd. (IGB), owned by his father. Nevertheless, the carousel encompassed no less than 50 companies in the United Kingdom and Belgium, 20 of which were directly controlled by Ravjani's corporation.

Ravjani's right-hand man was Tamraz Riaz, who managed Ravjnai's companies, including car sales businesses Prestige Cars and Crystal Cars Ltd., which served to launder the stolen tax money. The laundering was also done through Property and Management Services, a company controlled by gang associate Roshan Hussain, Ravjani's sister.

The gang traded in a carousel, over a few years, four million devices, consisting of high-end Sony Ericsson and Samsung phones, allegedly representing 1.7 billion pounds of turnover. From November 2005 to June 2006 HMRC reimbursed the companies involved in Ravjani's group 107 million pounds from a total of 176 million pounds claimed as VAT credit. During the mentioned period, Unique Distribution Ltd. reported sales of 2.2 billion pounds,[56] but paid less than 20 pounds in VAT.

53 Pop stars' ex-producer in VAT fraud gets nine years of prison (www.yorkshirepost.co.uk/news/pop-stars-ex-producer-in-vat-fraud-gets-nine-years-1-2482006).
54 www.wired-gov.net/wg/wg-news-1.nsf/54e6de9e0c383719802572b9005141ed/86ce5ba115d31682802572ab004bbc8b?OpenDocument.
55 www.dailymail.co.uk/news/article-2654296/Britains-wanted-tax-fraudster-involved-176million-VAT-swindle-thought-living-luxury-Dubai-pay-5million-hes-found.html#ixzz5DWr6f8dQ.
56 www.theguardian.com/uk/2012/jul/08/carousel-tax-fraud-mobile-phones.

198 *Who is who in the VAT milieu?*

Initially, the items were imported from Belgium and entered Britain through a ghost company, then went through other buffers before being bought by Future Communications (UK) Ltd., which sold them back into Belgium. Over a few months in 2005 more than 5,700 individual trades were realized by Future Communications (UK) Ltd., in some cases the items needing just one day to pass the carousel. Later, Future Communications (UK) Ltd. interposed Unique Distribution Ltd. into the carousel. Future Communications (UK) Ltd. sold the phones to Unique Distribution Ltd. and to other companies, which resold them to Belgium.

Chishti was the financial director of the Ravjani companies, including those which were part of the IGB. His role was to engineer the fraudulent trades in mobile phones between Future Communications (UK) Ltd. and Unique Distribution Ltd. Another key individual in the gang was Rajesh Gathani, a salesman for the Ravjani companies and the sales manager of Future Communications (UK) Ltd. and Unique Distribution Ltd.

Ravjani also controlled two freight companies, A1 Freight in Great Britain and Boston Freight in Belgium. The companies were in charge of transporting the phones back and forth across the channel.

Ravjani and his gang understood that the key in the carousel scam was the speed of trades and deliveries. Therefore, the gang controlled not only the missing trader and the buffers but also the freight companies.

This episode brought a valuable lesson to MTIC fraudsters and a paradigm shift in the 'low-volume and big-value' concept. The speed of the trades started to become a key factor, thereby explaining why many missing traders from the technology era moved into VAT fraud services.

Shahid Ramzan[57]

The MTIC fraud on mobile phones and computer parts touched mainly England, but cases were highlighted at the time in other regions of Britain. In Scotland, Shahid Ramzan, an aspiring actor, orchestrated a one-man carousel show, resulting in a 20.5 million pound VAT fraud. Ramzan owned Cortachy Wholesalers Ltd., Happyhillock Ltd. and Glam Entertainments Ltd., companies incorporated in Scotland, and two Spanish-registered firms,[58] Ibiplace SL and Treesandland SL. From January 2003 to July 2004 Ramzan traded millions of mobile phones through a number of companies he incorporated in Scotland and Spain. The majority of the trading was fraudulent, and the Spanish companies were in reality being run from addresses in Scotland. The funds were laundered through the Spanish companies.

---

57 www.mynewsdesk.com/uk/hm-revenue-customs-hmrc/pressreleases/dundee-dj-sentenced-for-ps20m-phone-fraud-827405.
58 A 'would-be' actor has been found guilty of a massive series of scams which cheated the government out of more than £26 million in VAT (www.dailyrecord.co.uk/news/scottish-news/wannabe-actor-shahid-ramzan-faces-1490918).

Ardip Singh Hayre[59]

A gang accused of stealing 17 million pounds was brought down by the HMRC in 2006. The MTIC carousel involved the import of mobile phone accessories and electronic media, including memory and subscriber identity module (SIM) cards, from other EU countries, including Italy, Denmark, Germany and Belgium.

Harbinder Singh Samra and Ardip Singh Hayre were the masterminds of the fraud. They controlled Goldfree Ltd., a Birmingham-based company, the exporter within this fraud.

The importers in the carousel were Cameron Charles Thurston, a dual South African/British national who controlled Synergy Services Ltd., and Diljan Saggar, aka Jon Soni, who controlled The Working Group Ltd. The logistics and freight side were dealt with by Terence Thomas Broad and Russell Crowther.

Syed Faraz Hussain[60] engineered a set of sham businesses that acted as buffers in the carousel, including Morganrise Ltd., controlled by Shabir Anwar Ahmed; K&M Supplies Ltd., controlled by Muhammad Al-Numairy Raza; and Synergy Services Ltd., controlled by Bharat Muriji Odedra.

Gurjit Singh, Karnail Singh Samra[61] (Harbinder's father) and Mandish Singh Hayre (Ardip's father) laundered the criminal proceeds through offshore bank accounts in China, Taiwan and India. The case revolved around two families, Samra and Hayre, which were at the core of the carousel and managed to control, through various associates, the entire crime.

Nasser Ahmed[62]

Nasser Ahmed appeared in 2013 on HMRC's 'Most Wanted' hotline after he fled Britain to avoid convictions related to a VAT fraud case. He was a fugitive for over a decade, first hiding in Dubai and then in Pakistan.

He was convicted in 2005 by a British court for defrauding HMRC of 156 million pounds. Between 2001 and 2005, he engineered an MTIC fraud with the illegal sale of CPUs, which he bought in big quantities from a company in Luxembourg.[63]

Nasser Ahmed, along with his partner in crime Urfan Ahmed, put together the entire infrastructure for companies for such a large-scale fraud. The pocketed

59 www.mynewsdesk.com/uk/hm-revenue-customs-hmrc/pressreleases/payback-time-continues-for-west-midlands-vat-fraudsters-856042.

60 www.igt.cc/news/further-four-jailed-in-17-million-vat-fraud.

61 www.mynewsdesk.com/uk/pressreleases/hm-revenue-customs-london-berkshire-money-launderer-jailed-573324.

62 www.flickr.com/photos/hmrcgovuk/7787502198/in/album-72157631087785530/.

63 www.dailymail.co.uk/news/article-2688940/Britain-s-second-wanted-fraudster-run-156million-tax-scam-t-hand-authorities-won-t-collect-Middle-East-hideout.html#ixzz5DWq5Uznq.

funds were channelled through British banks, including the Royal Bank of Scotland (RBS), and through bank accounts in the Cayman Islands and Spain.[64]

Michael Voudouri

In May 2014, one of Britain's most-wanted fugitives was returned to his homeland after being a fugitive for almost two years. In 2012, he was charged with VAT evasion on computer components. Voudouri[65] had previously been jailed for four years in 2004 for his involvement in a different VAT fraud. But in 2012 HMRC discovered another scam centred around Q-Tech Distribution, a company controlled by Voudouri. Over a period of three years he managed to defraud the HMRC of 11.6 million pounds. The money resulting from the fraud was diverted towards the British Virgin Islands and Swiss bank accounts. Voudouri was finally tracked down in the Turkish Republic of Northern Cyprus where he had hiding.

Voudouri's case underlines the fact that criminals and especially economic criminals look to hide in regions of the globe with unclear political situations, the 'no man's land' referred to in Chapter 6. The Turkish Republic of Northern Cyprus is a sound example and is a destination of predilection for many crooks of Greek or Turkish descent looking to avoid potential extradition.

Jens Kudahl Christensen

In 2015, a Danish businessman, Jens Kudahl Christensen,[66] was arrested in a case of VAT carousel fraud. The case, investigated since 2007, revealed that Kudahl and his associates controlled many companies in Denmark, Holland, the United Kingdom, Germany, the Czech Republic and Poland. The companies were trading electronic devices. Jens Kudahl had been involved with several limited companies as a founder, director or board member. At the time of the investigation most of his companies were either insolvent, liquidated or bankrupt.

Jens Kudahl Christensen served on the Executive Board of Dubai Commercial Investment, which had Carsten Robert Jensen as chairman. Carsten Robert Jensen was arrested in Germany in 2012 in a VAT fraud case with CO_2 emissions.

This transnational fraud entailed a 100 million euro loss to the Danish taxpayers. The carousel defrauded not only Denmark's Treasury but also the Dutch tax office, which suffered a loss of at least 30 million; the Czech Republic and Poland each lost at least ten million. The total loss due to VAT evasion reached 150 million euros.

This case was one of the few cases of carousel fraud which was tackled by the European agencies, including Europol and Eurojust. Therefore, the case delivers

64 www.accountingweb.co.uk/tax/business-tax/a-case-of-vat-fraud-ps151-million-lost-without-trace.
65 www.mynewsdesk.com/uk/hm-revenue-customs-hmrc/pressreleases/most-wanted-crime-cash-launderer-pays-the-price-1013812.
66 http://borsen.dk/nyheder/avisen/artikel/11/106592/artikel.html.

a global picture of fraud's impact at a European level. It appears clear that carousel fraud not only inflicts losses to one country but manages to defraud the taxpayers in all of the several countries where the carousel operates. Also, the VAT evaders involved in different markets, like electronics or the CO_2 emissions, are connected at certain level. This valuable information underlines the fact that VAT fraud requires transnational investigation taskforces, an idea developed in Chapter 13.

Nikolai Kitov

Bulgaria was highlighted as one of the countries with big losses due to VAT fraud (Poniatowski, 2017), but until recently fewer major cases came into light of public opinion. In 2015, Italian prosecutors launched a European arrest warrant against the Bulgarian businessman Nikolay Kitov,[67] who controlled Bulgarian companies Technomarket and K&K Electronics, which specialized in commerce with electronic devices. Kitov had founded Technomarket in 1992 as one of Bulgaria's top retail chains for household electronics, and he planned to expand his business into Romania. The fraud, involving trades on television sets, netted 70 million euros of pocketed tax.[68]

The investigation started in Italy, called Operation *Flat Screen*, with arrests and assets frozen. The scam consisted of exporting electronic items from Bulgaria to various regions of Italy, where they were sold at lower prices, sometimes 30% lower than the real price, through big retailers like Esselunga, Auchan and Mediaworld. The VAT collected in Italy was channelled into the carousel through other companies which never paid their liabilities.

The Bulgarian law enforcements arrested Kitov along with 26 other associates. He was the mastermind behind a huge carousel fraud deployed over nine European countries, including Bulgaria, Croatia, the Principality of Monaco, Poland, the Czech Republic, Romania, Spain and Switzerland. Kitov appeared in 'Panama Papers' as the owner of Vela Holdings Investments Ltd. in the British Virgin Islands.

The age of 'Aquarius': VAT fraud on services

The *Carbon Connection* (2008–2010)

The fraud on the carbon emission market was one of the most disruptive events of crime on a financial market in terms of losses and propagation speed. The issue with the emission allowances (EUA) was that under the EU Directive they were considered supplies (services) and therefore submitted to VAT. Thus the EUA were at that time instruments traded on exchanges (i.e., BlueNext), but each trader was liable for VAT in his(her) country. It is the main reason why the

---

67 Bulgarian entrepreneur detained over tax fraud probe in Italy (www.novinite.com/articles/
169725/Bulgarian+Entrepreneur+Detained+over+Tax+Fraud+Probe+in+Italy).
68 www.monzatoday.it/cronaca/arresto-kitov-dirigente-supermercato-bulgaria-evasione.html.

CO_2 emissions market attracted criminals from all walks of life: the glittering the dream of fast money. And indeed the promise was true for most of them. The law enforcements tried to dig into the frauds in the years after, but most of the funds defrauded were never recovered. The total amount of VAT defrauded reached over 10 billion euros, of which 1.9 billion were defrauded only through the online platform BlueNext. The list of the main operations carried out by the national and European investigators in relation to the *Carbon Connection* includes:

- Operation *Tulipbox*, Mirage in the United Kingdom;
- Operation *Crepuscule* in France;
- Operation *Dreyfus* in Denmark;
- Operation *Vertigo*, carried out by the Europol;
- Operation *B2 Euro* in Belgium;
- Operation *Blue Sky* in Spain;
- Operation *Green Plus AG Energy* in Norway;
- Operation *Hardware* in the Netherlands; and
- Operation *Odin* in Germany.

The *Carbon Connection* had a few main branches, including the French-Israeli, the French-Corsican, the German-Asian and the British-Asian branches. Other branches in the connection included the Nordic countries – Holland, Belgium and Dubai (Frunza, 2015).

The point where all the branches reunited was the Danish registry, an electronic infrastructure serving as a custodian for the CO_2 emissions permits. In fact, most criminals opened an account with the Danish registry. The account deposited CO_2 emissions permits, which were bought or sold on exchanges or over the counter. The Danish registry did not background-check or check the KYC for the individuals and companies applying for membership.

French-Israeli branch

The French-Israeli branch of the *Carbon Connection* was made up of a few dozen French citizens of Jewish Sephardic descent. They operated in a few major groups which were connected and shared their knowledge and connections. This branch was the most sophisticated, the best organized and the most aggressive group involved in this fraud. Most of its members were also Israeli citizens, thereby benefitting from the non-extradition policy that Israel had at that time. Moreover, most of them had already been initiated into the VAT fraud with mobile phones. What made the French-Israeli branch special compared to others was the fact that its members managed to register a few of the companies they controlled on the BlueNext, the biggest environmental exchanged at that time. Therefore, the size of the crime of this branch was bigger compared to other branches, given the short period of time of the fraud. Major conflicts amongst the various groups of this branch entailed a series of violent crimes that ended up with a few murders.

GREGORY ZAOUI

The central figure of the Parisian carbon ring is Gregory Zaoui. A low-profile character of the French carbon milieu, Zaoui is considered the genius mastermind behind the entire French VAT ring, which used mainly the Paris-based BlueNext exchange. The other groups, as well as the French-Corsican branch, had direct or indirect ties with him. Coming from a modest family in Seine-Saint Denis, one of Paris' most dangerous districts, he left school at the age of 16, began to import Cadillacs before having a licence, then began trading in jeans. He tried also to get close to the world of show business. He had his picture taken alongside French political figures like François Hollande and Bernard Cazeneuve.

Zaoui had had experience in mobile phone trading and was in contact with the British-Asian community in London. He was under surveillance in Operation *Euro Canyon*, concerning suspicions of VAT fraud on mobile phones. Zaoui's name did not figure as a director or nominee on the companies involved in the fraud. Zaoui worked closely with Kévin El Ghazouani, who helped with recruiting the strawmen for the companies involved in the fraud.

As early as 2006, Zaoui became interested in the market for carbon quotas. He incorporated a company, Marceau Trade, and became a broker on Powernext, the ancestor of BlueNext. Marceau Trade only served to test the fraudulent mechanics while waiting for the market to increase its turnover.[69] This happened in 2008 when CO_2 emissions prices reached the 30 euro level. By then Zaoui controlled, through strawmen, four companies, including Crepuscule V&A Corporation et Energy Stock Market and Coer2 Commodities.

Coer2 Commodities exhibited a total turnover of 156.4 million euros, corresponding to a total volume of carbon trades of 11.9 million tonnes of EUA, with an average brute margin of 12 cents per tonne, a margin slightly higher than the industry's average. Crepuscule, the other company which had ties with Zaoui, was one of the biggest players on BlueNext. In terms of volumes traded on BlueNext Crepuscule was as big as the main players: Societe Generale or Deutsche Bank.

Interestingly Crepuscule and another suspect company, V&A Corporation, were officially members on BlueNext until late 2009. In the aftermath, it is believed that Crepuscule traded CO_2 permits for a value of 827 million euros, which represents the sale of 65 million tonnes, accounting for half of the allowances allocated to the entire French industry. The proceeds of crime were transferred to banks in Hong Kong, Cyprus, Montenegro and Latvia.

Suspicions of contagion of the VAT fraud started when a number of companies with ties to the VAT fraud on carbon markets diversified their activity to other energy markets. For instance Coer2 Commodities, one of the companies linked to the visionary Zaoui, announced in 2010 that it had started trading crude oil, natural gas, gold and base metals.

---

69 www.nouvelobs.com/justice/20170529.OBS9978/gregory-zaoui-cerveau-ou-second-couteau-de-l-escroquerie-du-siecle.html.

FABRICE SAKOUN

Fabrice Sakoun was a close friend of Zaoui and another rising star of the French carbon milieu. The two men later shared the same detention cell during the first trial that targeted the VAT fraud in France.

Nathanael was the name of the carbon trading company with ties to Sakoun. The company was created by Sid Foudil as an enterprise specializing in clothing business and dissolved in late 2010. Nathanael entered the VAT fraud business towards the end, trading between March and June 2009. Sakoun's background was in textile wholesaling in the Parisian district 'le Sentier', which harboured in the early 2000s a massive scandal of money laundering between France and Israel.

The Sakoun group was the target of the first VAT trial in France that came to an end in January 2012, and the five defendants took sentences from one to five years of prison; they were obliged also to pay the French government 43 million euros of tax evaded. Prosecuted for the same acts, a sixth person was not convicted on the component carbon tax and convicted for money laundering to a one-year suspended sentence.

Fabrice Sakoun was given the longest sentence: five years in prison and a million euro fine. During the trial, which started in September 2010 and took several months, Sakoun pointed to the French state, Caisse des Dépôts et Consignation (CDC), Voltalia and BlueNext as also being big players in the scam.[70] Called as a witness by the defence, Gregory Zaoui, cellmate and friend of Fabrice Sakoun during his detention in 2010, questioned the prosecutors by drawing a parallel with the investigation in Belgium, where the Belgian State has filed a complaint against Fortis. The four accomplices of Fabrice Sakoun were also punished: Haroun Cohen, who fled to Israel, was sentenced to four years in prison and a million euro fine. Elie Balouka was sentenced to 30 months in prison, along with a six-month suspended sentence and a fine of 100,000 euros. David Illouz, the trader hired by the company to execute the trades, pointed during the process towards Voltalia, saying that he had cleared his orders through this company, which had had at that time other ventures with CDC. Illouz was sentenced to three years in prison and a fine of 100,000 euros. Sid Foudil, the founder of Nathanael, was sentenced to one year in prison.

CYRIL ASTRUC[71]

Born in a Paris suburb, Cyril Astruc worked in an insurance firm before opening his own. Amongst his clients were a group of old-timers from the *French Connection* who introduced him to the criminal trade.

In February 2001 Astruc was arrested, with his new friends, in a case of international cocaine trafficking. He was accused of supplying the network with telephones and fake car insurance certificates. He received three years in prison and a ban on practising in the insurance business.

---

70 www.20minutes.fr/france/857560-20120111-fraude-tva-marche-carbone-justice-prononce-lourdes-peines.
71 www.lexpress.fr/actualite/societe/alex-khann-l-homme-qui-valait-100-millions_1570979.html.

In November 2003, Astruc had already left France when the Paris Court of Appeal increased his initial sentence on drug trafficking, bringing it from three years of detention to four. With his wife and children, he left France to settle in Israel, where he opened a nightclub, the Excite, in the seaside resort of Eilat. He had chosen a new identity as Alex Khann.

In November 2005, Astruc aka Alex Khann went to Los Angeles to escape an extortion attempt by one of the Israeli mob families to produce a remake of a French TV movie, according to him. He founded a production company called ZEN group, through which he aimed to get into the movie production business, and started a real estate venture.

In 2006, the American justice system arrested him in his house in Beverly Hills with charges of money laundering. In 2007, he was extradited by Switzerland to France to serve his four-year prison term. While on parole at the end of the year, he escaped to Israel. He got acquainted with the Russian community and befriended the oligarchs Michael Cherney and Boris Berezovsky.

After his second return to Israel he bought several luxury brands very popular with the Russian clientele; started trading commodities and diamonds between Europe and the countries of the East; and founded ZEN Carbon Management, a company specializing in reducing CO_2 emissions in Africa. In the fall of 2008, the American magazine *Global Vision* (Forbes supplement) presented Alex Khann as the solution provider for developing countries in their fight against pollution.

In 2010 Khann was investigated by French and Belgian prosecutors for his involvement in VAT fraud with CO_2 emissions. They had records of telephone trades made to the broker Dubus, accused of being a buffer broker for VAT fraudsters. The calls were made to a phone number registered under the name of a Franco-Israeli citizen, Avi Ben Ezra, Alex Khann's friend. But for most calls it was Astruc who picked up Khann's phone several times.

Benoît Smagghe, commercial director of Dubus, made a quick trip to Tel Aviv on August 2009 on a private jet paid for by Alex Khann. Khann claimed to have a meeting to discuss the CO_2 emissions reductions in Africa. In the following week, Avi Ben Ezra contacted the defunct Belgian Fortis Bank (now BNP Paribas) on behalf of Dubus. Astruc aka Khann would have pocketed 146 million euros from the French and Belgian taxpayers.

The French justice system has also suspected him of being involved in a VAT fraud on sales of mobile phones, which defrauded the French taxpayers of 15 million euros between 2001 and 2003. He was not prosecuted in that case.

After the *Carbon Connection* episode, Astruc had at least four arrest warrants and allegedly a few crime groups chasing him. He resided in a huge mansion in Herzliya, Israel, with reinforced security. In September 2013, the French customs department attempted to arrest him in Israel without success. In January 2014, Astruc arrived in Paris. His return is explained by deteriorating relations with the Israeli crime boss Amir Mulner. In 2017, the French justice system could not reach him, rumours saying that he had escaped again for Dubai or Panama.

STÉPHANE VILLENEUVE

A group less known in the French milieu of tax scammers was formed by Morgan Erulin, Stéphane Villeneuve and Mickaël Kolkowicz.[72] They controlled a company called Power Trade which was involved in CO_2 trading. In May 2016, the three were sentenced by the Paris Criminal Court to ten months to three years of imprisonment for defrauding 2.4 million euros of VAT. They pocketed the sum during the last days of June 2009 before the French government introduced the VAT exemption on the CO_2 emissions trades. Stéphane Villeneuve had already been convicted in one instance, having defrauded companies by selling them false advertising panels.

The group of three was also suspected of having reinvested part of the funds to continue the scam in Spain from June to August 2009 via a company called 'Top Expansion', whose manager was actually Villeneuve. The fraud in Spain was estimated to be 18.3 million euros.

Kolkowicz was linked to Cyril Astruc, who was involved in other cases in France and Belgium. Kolkowicz spent a few months in 2014 in a luxurious apartment in Tel Aviv owned by Astruc.

Kolkowicz attended in the summer of 2009 a meeting held at the hotel Martinez in Cannes, along with other personalities implicated in CO_2 fraud, including the Touil brothers. One of them controlled Euro Trade Energy, a company which provided CO_2 emissions allowances to Power Trade. Another company present at that meeting was Coer2, managed by Grégory Zaoui. In July 2012, Kolkowicz was kidnapped and extorted by two figures of the Parisian-organized crime: a former robber of the 'Dream Team'[73] and the henchman of Samy Souied, another figure of the VAT fraud milieu, who was shot in 2010.

YANNICK DACHEVILLE

Dacheville is, in many ways, the prototype of the new generation of criminals. Dacheville, nicknamed '*Big*' because of his well-rounded face, spent his life between Miami (the United States), Israel, Panama and the United Arab Emirates, where he invested in real estate. He had false papers in the name of *William Pernot*. In 2016, Dacheville was arrested in Dubai, after being sentenced in his absence to 12 years in prison and a fine of 1 million euros by the Paris Criminal Court for trafficking 111 kg of cocaine.

Yannick Dacheville was reportedly seen with Khann in Tel Aviv in 2009. But Dacheville was also involved in VAT fraud on the carbon allowance market. Dacheville' case led to the indictment of Michel Neyret, the former deputy of Lyon's criminal police. Wiretapping caught a conversation between Gilles Benichou, friend of Alzrra, and Yannick Dacheville. In the discussion Benichou red to Dacheville his Interpol file, obtained from Neyret.

---

72 www.challenges.fr/economie/la-chute-d-un-petit-prince-de-la-fraude-au-co2_19482.
73 Famous gang of French bank robbers that acted during the 2000s.

Dacheville entered into VAT fraud using a frontman. Claude Bauduin, a retired 66 year old, was a senior citizen who opened a company in Germany called Bauduin GMBH and started to trade carbon and pocket VAT in a circuit between Germany, Luxembourg and France for a total amount of 10.8 million euros in only a few months of activity. Claude Bauduin knew Dacheville as *Marco*, and he had never met him physically, communicating with him only by telephone. For tens of thousands of euros, Dacheville persuaded Bauduin to create a company in Hamburg in September 2009, three months after the ban of the VAT on CO_2 emissions in France.

MARCO MOULY

Mardoché 'Marco' Mouly was a figure of the French-Israeli gang with extensive experience in VAT fraud with mobile phones. Mouly was born in Tunis and grew up in one of Paris' poorest districts. He was a close friend of Mimran, who invested around 800,000 euros in IGA Électronique, a mobile phone trading company based in France, Dubai and Hong Kong.[74] Later the two men entered into CO_2 emissions trading. Mirman was in charge of logistics in the carousel fraud engineered by the Mouly-Mimran group.

Mouly fits the profile of old-style crook that remained faithful to his criminal principles. He helped the Souied family after the death of his friend Samy and cut ties with the posher and more flamboyant Mimran, when he became suspicious. Mouly was a fugitive for 18 months until November 2016, when he was arrested in Geneva, where he allegedly was attempting to get funds from several accounts opened with HSBC Bank.[75] These accounts were controlled by companies registered in Panama, named Phantomas, one of Mouly's nicknames.

ARNAUD MIMRAN

Mimran was condemned in 2017 by a French court to eight years in prison for participating in the VAT fraud. He disclosed to the French court that he had invested 8 million euros in the CO_2 emissions operation but was not aware at any moment that the trade involved tax evasion.

Born in an upper-class French family, he started his career as a stock broker, where he got in trouble for insider trading. In the early 2000s, he made the acquaintance of Marco Mouly, a known figure of the Parisian milieu. With Mouly, Mimran entered the mobile phone business, financing one of Mouly's enterprises. Through Mouly, Mimran was also introduced to the CO_2 business. Mimran had many contacts in the show business as well as in politics, being a close friend of the former Israeli Prime Minister Benyamin Nétanyahou.

74 www.vanityfair.fr/pouvoir/politique/articles/comment-marco-mouly-et-arnaud-mimran-ont-monte-le-casse-du-siecle/47276.
75 www.nouvelobs.com/justice/20161116.OBS1309/escroquerie-a-la-taxe-carbone-fin-de-cavale-pour-marco-mouly.html.

Samy Souied, a close friend of Mouly, was introduced to Mirman and gave him a consistent amount for investment. Souied died in September 2010, and Mimran was one of the main suspects in the milieu for commanding the killing.

STEPHANE ALZRAA

Stephane Alzraa was a flamboyant figure of the *Carbon Connection* based in Lyon. He had ties with local crooks as well as police officers. The first arrest warrant was issued for Alzraa in September 2011 for corruption and bribery. The investigation showed that Alzraa was the person offering expensive gifts to a police inspector named Michel Neyret in exchange for confidential information about the foreseeable moves of the law against his friends involved in the VAT fraud. Under interrogation Alzraa disclosed that Neyret was his friend. It is supposed that Alzraa asked Neyret to grease his case in order to avoid indictments of the Zaoui-Astruc-Mouly group.

From the carbon fraud Alzraa had allegedly made over 50 million euros over 18 months between 2008 and 2010. Beyond the VAT fraud the financier started a new venture by brokering confidential police information concerning the Lyon milieu implicated in drug traffic. Thus Alzraa played the role of an intermediary between the mob and Neyret, providing them with police info. Alzraa's indictment brought to the frontispiece his links with other figures, like his cousin Giles Benichou and Michael Zaragoza, a former bank robber. He exercised legal activity as an insurance broker, and he had connections to the artistic world, criminal milieu and police. Benichou made the liaison with the controversial young venture capitalist Yannick Dacheville. Benichou accompanied Neyret on holiday to Morocco, paid at Benichou expense, in order to try to ease Dacheville's situation. Dacheville and Zaoui, two prominent VAT scammers based in Paris, profiled in the previous section, had close relationships with Alzraa.

JAROSLAW KLAPUCKI[76]

Consus, a company specializing in green energy, and his charismatic leader Jaroslaw Klapucki were targeted by the French justice system. Despite many allegations and suspicions, starting in 2010, none of the audits were able to find any trace of fraud in the financial statements of Consus. Certain elements raised many questions around the company, mainly related to its financial performance.

But after six years, in 2016 a French court found Consus, a Polish brokerage firm, guilty of involvement in a case of VAT fraud committed against the EU carbon market.

The court sentenced Klapucki, the director of the Consus brokerage, to seven years in prison for VAT fraud and money laundering.

---

76 www.euractiv.com/section/energy/news/polish-broker-faces-seven-year-prison-sentence-for-vat-fraud-on-eu-carbon-market/.

Imprisoned in France, Klapucki has also been handed a fine of 1 million euros and a five-year management ban. Together with the other members of his gang, the Polish broker was ordered to pay a total of 283 million euros in damages and interest. One year later,[77] a higher court of justice in France released Klapucki and dismissed all charges against his company.

The 'carbonized' branch

The complex network of companies and strawmen in the French-Israeli branch generated quickly discontent amongst the groups. This led to threats and disputes between the various factions, which ended up with a few murders. The timeline of four of the murders allegedly linked to the *Carbon Connection* are detailed in the following:

*   **April 2010:** Amar Azzoug, an ex-thief known as 'Amar Blue eyes', was shot dead in a brewery in Saint-Mandé in the Val-de-Marne, France. Azzoug was aware that a price had been put on his head by the Mimran-Mouly group.
*   **September 2010:** Samy Souied, born in Belleville, was publicly executed in Porte Maillot in Paris, few hours after arriving from Tel Aviv. Souied was close to Mouly, being involved with him in a business with advertising panels. He was known the boss of the racetracks.
*   **October 2011:** Claude Dray, the father of the ex-wife of Arnaud Mimran, a rich businessman, was murdered in his villa in Neuilly-sur-Seine, France.
*   **May 2014:** Albert Taïeb, driver of Cyril Mouly, a well-known poker player who had trouble with the law for scams with advertising panels.

French-Corsican branch

Most anthropologists claim that organized crime is born in the Calabrian Peninsula, but very few point to the Isle of Beauty as the cradle of organized crime. Corsica is without doubt the first provider of talent for serious organized crime in France. The Corsican clans juggling nationalist groups and criminal gangs are present at all levels of the French underworld. The *Carbon Connection* was no exception. The trail of the Marseille group involved in the *Carbon Connection* underlined the involvement of the Corsican milieu with alleged ties to the Neapolitan Camorra.[78] It should be underlined that the trial started in 2018, ten years after the actual fact took place. It emphasizes once more the many obstacles faced by the legal system to prosecute complex VAT cases. The French-Corsican branch is responsible for defrauding 380 million euros of tax.

77 www.nouvelobs.com/topnews/20170628.AFP6197/fraude-sur-le-marche-du-co2-jusqu-a-8-ans-de-prison-en-appel.html.
78 www.lepoint.fr/societe/au-proces-du-carbone-marseillais-code-d-honneur-et-trous-de-memoire-06-02-2018-2192860_23.php.

CHRISTIANE MELGRANI

The investigation of the Marseille group showed that the group was organized around the Corsican-born Christiane Melgrani, a former math teacher. All evidence pointed back to Zaoui, who seems to have put his know-how of VAT scams in the service of Christiane Melgrani, a colourful character of the Corsican milieu in Marseilles. Another character of the Corsican milieu connected to Zaoui is Jacques Santoni, leader of the crime gang 'Petit Bar' in Ajaccio. In February 2013, Grégory Zaoui met Mickaël Ettori, Santoni's henchman, in Paris, proposing money laundering services for the Corsicans.

A sulphurous businessman of Israeli origin, residing in Monaco before his arrest, Gérard Chetrit was suspected of having been with Christiane Melgrani, one of the main perpetrators of the fraud, mainly by bringing the initial funds.

JEAN-RENÉ BENEDETTI

Jean Benedetti, born in August 1942, is a known figure of the Mareille's milieu with a heavy criminal record. Benedetti spent more than 25 years in the correctional system and was part of the French Connection during the 1960s and 1970s. He was employed by Melgrani to be the director of a few of the companies involved in fraud. Thus, Benedetti was the managing director of the Energie Groupe, a limited company registered in Marseille in January 2007, but he claimed that a certain 'Raël Moyal' had asked him to front the business on his behalf. Benedetti received informal instructions from Moyal via letters passed through intermediaries across bars in Marseille (Frunza, 2015). He received large amounts of cash from Melgrani. During the trial he denied all facts, saying that he did not remember the events.

ANGELINA PORCARO

Melgrani's partner in crime was Angelina Porcaro, a former owner of a strip bar in Marseille who allegedly controlled the prostitution underworld in the Phocaean city. She was officially the owner of a restaurant, 'Saveurs d'Italie', used to launder part of the funds of the crime. Porcaro helped Melgrani with recruiting and organizing the strawmen for the companies involved in the fraud. The prosecutors suspect that she had ties with the Neapolitan Camorra.

German branch

Germany is EU's first producer and exporter of goods. VAT refund is a structural strategy for Germany's industrial and commercial sector, and the German tax office is used to reimburse considerable amounts of VAT to small- and medium-sized enterprises. This makes the German tax office an easy target for the VAT fraudsters that will take advantage of this governmental policy. This was the case with CO_2 emissions, Germany harbouring a few of the big cases of tax evasion.

CLAUDE BAUDUIN[79]

The first wave of indictments in Germany occurred in March 2011, with an initial group of 150 suspects, mostly CEOs and other businessmen; four of them were kept in detention, some for almost a year. On this occasion German prosecutors charged six individuals, aged 27–65, with accusation of having conspired from September 2009 to April 2010 to evade 230 million euros in VAT. The defendants were originally from Germany, France and Britain, and did not take any plea initially. One, holding a degree in Economics, in his hearing admitted that it had been an open secret that the cross-border trading offered quick money; he underlined that he did not realize he was committing fiscal fraud under the German law, but he knew that it was ethically and morally wrong. Another defendant, said that he initially did not understand the difficult nature of carbon trading and nevertheless accepted an annual salary of 170,000 euros and a 1 million euro bonus for passing trading orders in the market. He passed carbon exchanges' trader exams shortly before the indictment in April 2010.

Claude Bauduin, a retired Frenchman, was arrested in March 2011 in Milan and imprisoned in Germany. His lawyer underlined that his client was a victim as he came only twice to Germany, and he knew nothing of how the VAT carousel worked Bauduin was in the first maxi-trial in the VAT carbon fraud in Germany with five other defendants. Nevertheless, the police knew that Dacheville was the man pulling the strings in the affair.

FAISAL ZAHOOR AHMAD

In 2014 Frankfurt prosecutors issued arrest warrants for Faisal Ahmad, a British national, in connection with a VAT fraud of 58 million euros. It is believed that Ahmad fled for Dubai. German authorities charged Faisal Zahoor Ahmad for his role as general manager of a Munich-based company called Roter Stern Gmbh, which evaded VAT. Roter Stern was suspended from trading on the Munich-based Bayerische Boerse's carbon platform in 2010 and was closed after insolvency proceedings the same year.[80]

MOHAMMAD GOHIR[81]

The United States Secret Service arrested in Las Vegas in 2014 Mohammad Gohir, a British citizen living in Dubai. Gohir had travelled to Las Vegas to see boxer Amir Khan and was then extradited to Germany. German prosecutors

---

79 www.reuters.com/article/us-germany-carbon-fraud/six-stand-trial-in-carbon-fraud-case-in-germany-idUSTRE77E1Y920110815.

80 https://uk.reuters.com/article/us-carbontrading-germany/germany-seeks-arrest-of-briton-in-carbon-trading-scam-idUKBREA3915F20140410.

81 www.mirror.co.uk/news/uk-news/how-missing-trader-vat-fraud-7898489.

described Gohir as 'the Pope' of EU tax fraud, having stolen an estimated 180 million euros of VAT through CO_2 fraudulent trades from the German taxpayers. Virdee posed with high-profile figures like Amir Khan, a British boxer, and David Cameron, former British Prime Minister.

MOHSIN USMANGANI SALYA

Another British national involved in VAT fraud in Germany was Mohsin Salya.[82] He had been sentenced in 2016 by a German court to three years and three months in prison. Salya turned himself in to German authorities in 2017. He, with two other Brits, Ashraf Muhammad and Mobeen Iqbal, had stolen 125 million euros worth of tax.

Salya owns three apartments in the Discovery Gardens development in Dubai. He said that the properties were bought long before his involvement in the fraud that led to his jail term.[83]

Salya[84] was not a novice in the VAT troubles. In 2002, his accident claims and mobile telephone import business, Continental Claims Consultants, went into liquidation, owing more than 600,000 euros in VAT.[85]

The two other British and Pakistani citizens, Ashraf Muhammad and Mobeen Iqbal, remain wanted by German police. It is believed that they are hiding in Dubai or in Pakistan.

PETER SINGH VIRDEE[86]

Peter Singh Virdee, a British businessman known as 'Batman', was arrested in 2016 at Heathrow Airport and faced extradition to Germany for a VAT fraud of 125 million euros. German court charged him with a possible 15 years' jail sentence for VAT fraud on CO_2 trades. The German prosecutors alleged that he had extensive contacts abroad, especially in India, Pakistan, Dubai (UAE), Antigua, St. Kitts and Nevis. Prosecutors in Germany alleged that Virdee was one of the 'central organizers' of a criminal network of fraudsters. Mr Virdee appeared before Westminster Magistrate's Court in 2016and was released on 160,000 euro bail.

Mr Virdee is the founder and director of B&S Property, which claims to have global assets worth more than 4.6 billion euros. The company is registered at an address in Mayfair, along with the Peter Virdee Foundation, which describes itself as a philanthropic organization. He was profiled in the *Evening*

---

82 https://carbon-pulse.com/29736/.

83 www.theguardian.com/world/2018/jun/24/fraudsters-turn-dubai-new-costa-del-crime.

84 www.redd-monitor.org/2017/03/28/mohsin-salya-has-been-jailed-aadiel-salya-faces-jail-for-fraud/.

85 www.mirror.co.uk/news/uk-news/how-dare-you-defame-innocent-10034021.

86 www.telegraph.co.uk/news/2017/01/13/british-businessman-peter-virdee-arrested-heathrow-german-police/.

Standard in 2008 as one of London's rising property stars. Virdee posed with high-profile political personalities like Alex Salmond, the former leader of the Scottish National Party. He claims to participate in many charitable and philanthropic acts.

In 2017, there was no follow-up on Virdee's extradition, and the charges were seemingly dropped.

DEUTSCHE BANK

Deutsche Bank was one of the first institutions pointed out by the authorities for its alleged ties with the VAT scam ring. Deutsche acted as an intermediary on the market and provided banking services to fraudsters or to companies linked to fraudsters. Nevertheless, the bank did not commit itself to any funds extortion.

In 2010, German prosecutors investigated 25 bank staff on suspicion of severe tax evasion, money laundering and obstruction of justice. Police and tax inspectors searched Deutsche Bank's headquarters as well as staff's private residences in Berlin, Düsseldorf and Frankfurt. They also arrested five Deutsche Bank employees in the investigation linked to a tax scam involving the trading of carbon permits.

In 2012, the Frankfurt prosecutors started to investigate Jürgen Fitschen, the former co-CEO of Deutsch Bank, and Stefan Krause, the CEO.[87] In 2009, Fitschen was in charge of Deutsche Bank's operations in Germany. The two senior managers had signed the VAT return statements for 2009, the year when the tax crime peaked on the CO_2 markets.

In 2016, the Frankfurt Regional Court convicted six former employees of Deutsche Bank for tax fraud in a case worth 145 million euros. Helmut Hohnholz, formerly a regional sales manager with Deutsche's global markets division,[88] was sentenced to three years in jail.

British-Asian branch

The Asian community in Great Britain was active during the early 2000s in the VAT fraud with mobile phones and computer components. They built a network of companies that spread into Dubai and other offshore countries. The British Asians specializing in VAT had ties with the French-Israeli branch from those times. When the opportunity came on CO_2 emissions, they reactivated the network.

---

87 www.spiegel.de/international/business/deutsche-bank-co-ceo-juergen-fitschen-under-investigation-in-tax-probe-a-872563.html.
88 www.reuters.com/article/us-deutschebank-court/former-deutsche-banker-jailed-for-carbon-trading-fraud-idUSKCN0YZ1S6.

SANDEEP SINGH DOSANJH[89]

The first trial against criminals from the British branch of the *Carbon Connection* took place in 2012. Sandeep Singh Dosanjh was the leader of the criminal gang. He was condemned to 15 years in jail for defrauding a 38 million pound VAT. The court has been ordered to pay back nearly 13 million pounds to HMRC or face ten further years in prison.

Dosanjh worked with his business partner Dhanvinder 'Dan' Singh Basra in a company called KO Brokers. KO's website (www.kobrokers.com) was registered in Dosanjh's name. Dosanjh is also listed in company documents as being a director at the firm, while Basra's email signature said he was an environmental product trader at KO. Both men were identified by at least three traders from other companies as having approached them looking to trade emissions permits on behalf of KO in 2009. The peer traders underlined KO's insistence on having VAT paid on each transaction. KO's website said the firm specializes in 'trading within energy and foreign exchange markets, as well as dealing with financial global futures and options', despite not being regulated by the United Kingdom Financial Services Authority.

THE CITY

The major banks from the *City* had CO_2 emissions trading desk. The most active banks on the market were Barclay, Citigroup and Royal Bank of Scotland. These banks did not defraud VAT but were directly or indirectly in contact with brokerage companies involved in tax-evading acts. Therefore, HMRC set out cases against a few of the banks mentioned earlier for allegedly being responsible for the massive VAT fraud.

In 2013 Britain's tax authority[90] set out a case against Citibank over a tax liability of 13 million euros related to Citibank's CO_2 allowance trades and allegedly connected with fraud. HMRC thought that the American bank 'knew or ought to have known that … its transactions in these carbon credits were connected with fraud'. HMRC invoked arguments related to the rapid growth of carbon trading, superficial due diligence of its counterparties and reselling of the same allowance in short trading windows. Citibank contested HMRC's assessment and appealed to a British Tribunal. The court ruled in 2014 that HMRC needed to bring more clarity into its allegations.

RBS[91] was brought into court in 2016 by liquidators at Grant Thornton acting for the creditors of a number of fraudulent companies engaged in a VAT carousel fraud in which carbon credits were being traded. The state-owned

89 www.mynewsdesk.com/uk/hm-revenue-customs-hmrc/pressreleases/multi-million-pound-carbon-credit-vat-fraudster-to-pay-back-ps13-million-918542.
90 https://carbon-pulse.com/13009/.
91 www.scottishfinancialnews.com/8931/grant-thornton-sues-rbs-for-145m-in-vat-carousel-fraud-action/.

Scottish bank was being sued for 15 million euros. The allegations pointed out that a few traders from RBS Sempra, RBS's commodities division, had carried out transactions which helped fraudsters to evade VAT. Thus, between 8 June and 6 July 2009, the RBS traders bought 43 million carbon credits linked to VAT evaders.

The *VoIP connection*

In March 2010, the Italian law enforcements started the prosecution in a VAT fraud case, concerning telecommunication companies. All the evidence was pointing towards Telecom Italia and its chairman Silvio Scaglia, one of Italy's richest men and the owner of Telecom Italia Sparkle, a subsidiary of the Italian giant.

The fraud was conceived as a carousel, with both MTIC and MTEC features; was developed between 2003 and 2006; and is considered by specialists as the state of the art in terms of MTIC fraud (Ainsworth, 2010). The Italian prosecutors managed to identify not only the individuals but also the companies, the bank accounts and the transfers. Most important they managed to rebuild the full architecture of the fraud, including the emails and the communication between the various individuals involved in the scam.

The prosecution file of the operation, called *Operazione Phuncards-Broker*, includes more than 1,500 pages, is very rich information and points out the deep implications of the fraud. The criminal enterprise spread over many jurisdictions in Europe, the Unites States, the Caribbean, Central America and Russia. The group had ties to the Italian political arena as well as to organized crime, including the Calabrian clans ('Ndrangheta') and the Rome-based group ('Banda della Magliana').

The fraud was organized around two major Italian telecommunication companies: Fastweb S.P.A. and Telecom Italia Sparkle, both linked to the Italian tycoon Silvio Scaglia. The fraud had two interrelated mechanisms:

- Operation *Phuncards*, which was constructed around trade with cards offering access to online premium adult content, and
- Operation *Traffico Telefonico*, which concerned trades with Voice over Internet Protocol (VoIP).

Operation Phuncards

The fraudulent activity behind Operation *Phuncards* started in 2003 and was based on fictitious commercial transactions with 'cards'. A 'card' allegedly gave to its buyer the access right for a limited time to adult digital content protected by copyright, which was made available by the seller on dedicated servers.

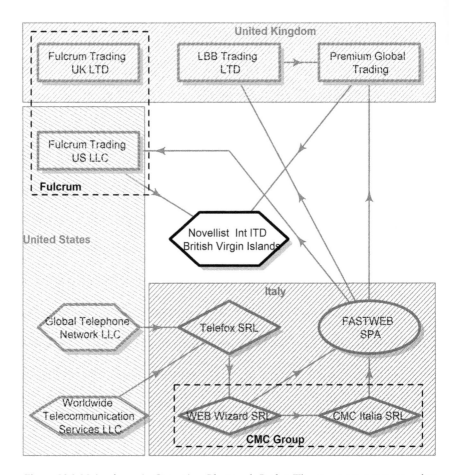

Figure 10.1 Main players in Operation *Phuncards-Broker*. The grey arrows correspond to the commercial transaction, with 'cards' given the right to access premium online content.

The investigation, carried out by the Italian economic police 'Guardia di Finanza' and supported by a forensic audit made by KPMG in 2007, showed that the entire scheme was fictitious and was engineered and implemented with the full complicity of Fastweb's senior management. The big picture of the fraud is presented in Figure 10.1, underlining the central role of Fastweb. The main companies involved in the fraud were:

- Global Telephone Service LLC, a company registered in Florida, United States, in 1993.
- Worldwide Telecommunication Services LLC (WTS), a company registered in Delaware, United States. WTS was legally represented by another Delaware-based company, Incorporative Service Ltd., and by Christophe Moudenc, a French citizen.

- CMC Italia Srl, a company with a key role in the fraudulent scheme exerting control over other companies. The company was initially based in Italy from 2000 to 2003, when it was transferred to London. The managing director of the company was an Italian citizen, Ferreri Antonio. The company structure of CMC Italia Srl, at the time of the constitution, was formed by three Italian citizens: Maurizio Cannavao (60% of the capital), Chiara Bovalino (20% of the shares) and Antonio Ferreri (20% of the shares). Since April 2001, the CMC Italia was wholly owned by the Dutch company Sworiba B.V., headquartered in Amsterdam, the Netherlands, and established in January 2001. The people who were really in charge of conducting the day-to-day business of CMC included:
  - Carlo Focarelli, who served as marketing director for CMC Italia Group. It is assumed that Focarelli engineered the whole *Phuncards* business. He appears to have received 90,000 euros in remunerations from CMC Italia Srl.
  - Giuseppe Cherubini, advisor to the company, received 26,000 euro in 2002.
  - Marco Toseroni, acting as advisor for CMC, received 26,000 euros in 2002 and 34,000 in 2003. He worked closely with Focarelli and was one of the main financial advisors for the head of the criminal gang Mokbel Gennaro.
- Web Wizard Srl, an Italian company based in Rome and controlled by CMC Italia Srl, that moved its office in December 2003 to the United Kingdom after being sold to Sworiba B.V. At the time of its incorporation in 2001 the capital structure was composed of CMC Italia Srl with 90% of shares and Sworiba B.V. with 10%. The legal representative of the company, from 2001 until the relocation of the headquarters, appears to have been Antonio Ferreri.
- Telefox Srl, based in Rome, Italy, was transferred in December 2003 to Panama. The corporate structure at the time of incorporation was composed of Fabio Arigoni, with a share equal to 95% of the share capital, and Daniele Priori, with a share of 5%. In December 2003, Arigoni and Priori sold all the shares to Giovanni Succu, which transferred them in December 2003 to JVA Corporation S.A., a company incorporated in Panama. A series of suspicious activity reports concerning transactions made by Telefox were raised in 2003. The key people of the company were:
  - Fabio Arigoni, from November 2002 to December 2003. Moreover, Arigoni appeared to have been a legal representative, since July 2003, of Telefox International Srl, sharing the same headquarters of Telefox Srl and of Trading Italia Srl, which was involved in suspicious transactions with CMC Italia Srl.
  - Giovanni Succu, who was a simple frontman of the company.
- LBB Trading Ltd., located in London, Great Britain. The individuals taking care of business within the company were:
  - Robert James Kenworthy, who acted as advisor from 1999 to 2004;
  - Pietro Musillo, who acted as advisor from June 2004;
  - Adam Roger Buckley Kenworthy, who acted as director from 1999;
  - Jason Short, who acted as head of sales since March 2000;

- Mrs. Nirmali, who was responsible for administrative tasks; and
- Mark Henley, who was in charge of logistics, and who also worked for Acumen (UK) Ltd., a key player in Operation *Traffico Telefonico*.

The company was the object of a suspicious transactions report that was sent by the Italian Exchange Office.

- Premier Global Telecom Ltd. (PGT Ltd.), located in London, United Kingdom, and represented by:
  - Robert Nicholas James Kenworthy, who was the sole shareholder and acted as Administrator from September 2003, and
  - Adam Roger Buckley Kenworthy, who has been company's secretary since September 2003.
- Fulcrum Trading US Inc., an American company represented by:
  - Paul Anthony O'Connor, who acted as company director;
  - Andrew David Neave from Great Britain, who acted as secretary, treasurer and director; and
  - James Edward Roberts, who was head of operations.
- Fulcrum Electronics UK, formerly Fulcrum Trading Company UK Ltd., based in London, United Kingdom. The company was delisted from the British VAT registry in December 2003. Neave Andrew David and O'Connor Paul Anthony were the directors of Fulcrum Electronics UK. DINES Emma Louis served as secretary in 1998.
- Suade Management Ltd., a company based in Barcelona, Spain, with a current account at Banco Bilbao Vizcaja. The account holder, as well as the person delegated to operate, is Augusto Murri, an Italian citizen. The Spanish Judicial Authority reported that the firm did not submit VAT declarations or financial statements for 2004 and 2005. The company was also the object of Suspicions Activity Reports.

The key role in Operation *Phuncards* was played by Fastweb S.p.A., which extracted the VAT from the Italian treasury and transferred it to the CMC Group, encompassing CMC Italy and Web Wizard Srl. Fastweb was placed in the centre of the operations by Focarelli, who conceived and planned the full fraudulent scheme.

Fastweb S.p.A. ceased its activity in December 2004 after being absorbed into its parent company, e.Biscom S.p.A., and was sold by its majority shareholder, Silvio Scaglia, to Swisscom AG, a Swiss major telecommunications provider. The main people involved with Fastweb S.p.A. during the *Phuncards* period were:

- Silvio Scaglia, who was, in 2003, majority shareholder, managing director and chairman of the board of directors for e.Biscom S.p.A. and the chief executive officer and chairman of the board of directors for Fastweb S.p.A.
- Mario Rossetti, who was a member of Anphora Srl majority shareholding company and Chief Financial Officer of e.Biscom S.p.A. until 16.04.2003. Also in 2003 he was advisor for Fastweb S.p.A.

- Bruno Zito, who was responsible for big clients and in particular for relations with CMC Italia Srl and Web Wizard Srl. It was he who proposed the business to Fastweb S.p.A. to take care of the qualitative evaluation of the product and the reliability of CMC Italia Srl and Web Wizard Srl. In this specific case, Zito took care of the contractual details of the operations in collaboration with the legal department.
- Giuseppe Crudele, who played the role of presale and sales support. For the period of January 2005–June 2006 Crudele held the position of manager of the VoIP services.

The *Phuncards* business was initiated by Carlo Focarelli in November 2002, who proposed this new project to his management in the CMC Group. His idea was to print and produce prepaid cards for the foreign market, mainly in the adult segment. At the time he had already secured the rights for three million PIN codes. The licence to issue the *Phuncards* was owned by Global Telephone Service LLC and Worldwide Telecommunication Services LLC. WTS had a distribution agreement signed in January 2003 with Telefox and Web Wizard Srl.

The *Phuncards* were in fact cards with a scratch-off section containing a unique code, which, when entered into a dedicated site, should have allowed end users to be identified as having the right to access protected contents through a reference website (www.phuncards.com). From the beginning, Focarelli indicated that there might be some negative cash flows for Fastweb S.p.A. due to VAT that needed to be paid to suppliers but was not recovered from the foreign clients. Nevertheless, he pitched the deal with a very profitable margin for Fastweb.

Some of Fastweb's managers were alerted by the VAT compliance issues raised by the *Phuncards* project. Therefore, they hired two consultants, '*Studio Maisto e Associati*' and '*Vitali Romagnoli Piccardi e Associati*'. The consultants recommended that Fastweb S.p.A. acts as proxy without representation of CMC revenue in its financial statement, and accounts only the margin of the operation, thereby acting more like a broker for CMC Group.

The *Phuncards* prospect indicated that the cards granted access to content on some websites. These websites were proven later not to exist. Subsequently, Focarelli changed the prospect in the later months of 2003.

In July 2003, e.Biscom, the owner company of Fastweb, started to get interested in the *Phuncards* business and Fastweb's role in the scheme. The main question was why the CMC Group did not sell the cards to the American and British clients directly.

An audit was mandated by Fastweb on the British clients towards the end of 2003. The due diligence concluded by Beverly Farrow pointed out the first elements, highlighting the likelihood of a fraud. When the due diligence was launched the commercial ties between the British companies and Fastweb ceased.

The CMC Group did not make direct sales to the British and American companies because it would have run through a VAT deficit between the moment they purchased the rights with VAT and the moment the cards were sold abroad without VAT. Only a big company like Fastweb was able to finance the deficit until the moment the Italian tax office reimbursed the VAT. Therefore, the main function of Fastweb S.p.A. was to pre-finance the pocketed VAT, a service that granted a steady 7% margin.

The British customers with whom CMC would not have been able to negotiate prepayment conditions were CMC's customers and not Fastweb's customers, introduced by Focarelli.

At the endpoint of the *Phuncards* scheme organized around the CMC Group and by Fastweb S.p.A. in 2003 were Suade Management Ltd., Novellist International Ltd. and Telefax Srl, companies managed by Murri Augusto and Arigoni Fabio. These companies were in fact the missing traders.

The dynamic of the trades in Operation *Phuncards-Brokers* can be summarized as follows:

- The 'CMC Group', encompassing CMC Italia Srl and Web Wizard Srl, purchased rights related to the 'paid services' accessible by card. They were allegedly purchased from WTS – Worldwide Telecommunication Services LLC or Global Telephone Service LLC. These transactions were proven to be fictitious.
- The CMC Group engaged in physically producing the cards (so-called *Phuncards*) and in issuing the access codes. The production work was done with two other Italian companies: Plastic Division Graf 3 Srl and Print Media Srl.
- The CMC Group subsequently sold the cards to British buyers (LBB Trading Ltd. and Premier Global Telecom Ltd.) and American buyers (Fulcrum Trading US Inc.) through Fastweb S.p.A., which took a 7% margin on the transactions.
- The British and American buyers transferred the (*Phuncards*) to Novellist International Ltd. Kenworthy Group (LBB Trading Ltd. and Premier Global Telecom Ltd.) delivered the cards to a few PO boxes in Geneva.
- Based on a bilateral agreement from November 2003, LBB Trading Ltd. sold to Web Wizard Srl a credit of 49.2 million euros against Novellist International Ltd. for the sale of the *Phuncards* to offset a debt of 49.1 million euros of LBB Trading Ltd. towards Web Wizard Srl.
- Similarly Fulcrum Trading US Inc. transferred to Web Wizard Srl a credit of 111.7 million euros owed to Novellist International Ltd. for the sale of the *Phuncards* to offset a debt of 116.4 million euros accrued by Fulcrum Trading US Inc. towards Web Wizard Srl.

The main financial flows in the *Phuncards* scam occurred between February and November 2003, and can be classified as following:

- Flows representing payments relating to *Phuncards-Broker* invoices:
  - LBB Trading Ltd. UK made payments to Fastweb S.p.A. for a total of 36.6 million euros from February to June 2003.
  - PGT Ltd. made payments to Fastweb S.p.A. for a total of 33.9 million euros from April to June 2003.

- Fulcrum Trading US Inc. made payments to Fastweb S.p.A. for a total of 111.9 million euros from September to November 2003.
- Fastweb S.p.A. made payments to CMC Italia Srl for a total of 167.1 million euros from February to November 2003, of which 165.2 million euros would represent payments for *Phuncards* invoices.
- Fastweb S.p.A. made payments to Web Wizard Srl for a total of 38.4 million euros from April to June 2003.
- CMC Italia Srl made payments to Web Wizard Srl for a total of 167.7 million euros from March to November 2003.
- Web Wizard Srl made payments to Telefox Srl accounting for 35.9 million euros from March to November 2003
- Telefox Srl made payments to Suade Management for a total of 35.6 million euros between April and November 2003.
- Flows related to the financing agreement granted by the CMC Group to the Kenworthy's Group:
  - Web Wizard Srl made payments to CMC Italia of 7.6 million euros between April and November 2003.
  - CMC Italia Srl transferred an amount to LBB Trading Ltd. UK of 2.5 million euros from February to July 2003.
  - LBB Trading Ltd. UK transferred to CMC Italia Srl 1 million euros in May 2003.
  - Web Wizard Srl transferred to LBB Trading Ltd. UK a total amount of 57.7 million euros between May and November 2003.
  - LBB Trading Ltd. UK transferred to Web Wizard Ltd. a total amount of 11.2 million euros in August 2003.
- Flows related to financing contracts stipulated in September 2003 between the CMC Group and Fulcrum.
  - Web Wizard Srl transferred to Fulcrum Trading US Inc. a total amount of 118.9 million euros between September and November 2003.
  - Fulcrum Trading US Inc. transferred to Web Wizard Srl a total amount of 3.4 million euros between October and November 2003.
- Flows related to Novellist International S.A.
  - Suade Management Ltd. paid to Novellist International S.A. 15.5 million euros between August and October 2003. Novellist International Ltd. made a payment of 23 million euros to LBB Trading Ltd. between April and August 2003.

The commercial and financial transactions were circular, thereby constituting a typical carousel fraud. The circuit was also leveraged to launder money by issuing false invoices and distributing the proceeds deriving from tax fraud among the participants of the criminal association. The core companies of the carousel were constituted by Novellist International Ltd., Suade Management and Telefox Srl.

Novellist is also the customer which purchased the *Phuncards* from Fulcrum Trading US Inc., and similarly to what happened with LBB Trading Ltd. the repayment of the loan to Fulcrum by the CMC Group was formally settled with a clearing of receivables and payables from Novellist. From the commercial and financial transactions it is clear that Novellist was an offshore shell company used for accounting purposes by the American and British clients. They reimbursed the debt towards the CMC Group with receivable from Novellist. Novellist was also the last piece that closed the carousel. The reports relating to commercial contracts and financing the agreement of Novellist International Ltd. showed that there were no real end customers, all transactions being fake.

The real aim of the *Phuncards* business was to pocket the VAT from Fastweb, which had a 7% operational margin that cannot be explained by its real revenues. The total loss of VAT for the Italian government is estimated to be 33.9 million euros corresponding to a turnover of 169.7 million euros of Fastweb between 2002 and 2005 for the 'cards'-related transactions. Table 10.2 shows the total revenue generated by Fastweb in 2003 from transactions with CMC Group.

It is clear that the American and British clients did not have the funds to pay immediately for the cards purchased from Fastweb. Thus, CMC Group arranged some loans to Fulcrum and LBB which would allow trade with Fastweb. Table 10.3 presents the main financing agreements and the fees (interests) paid by the beneficiary of the loans. The two debt assignments accounted for a total of 162.2 million euros, representing the equivalent of the value of the *Phuncards* produced by CMC Group.

Table 10.2 Fastweb recovered 33.39 million euros of VAT from the Italian tax office and sent it to Web Wizard and CMC Italia

Payer	Receiver	Amount (million euros)
Fastweb	CMC Italia Srl	165.2
Fastweb	Web Wizard Srl	38.4
	Total	*203.6*
	Value without VAT	*169.7*
	Including VAT	*33.93*

Table 10.3 Financing loans of Fulcrum and LBB Trading from Web Wizard Srl

Payer	Receiver	Amount (million euros)
Web Wizard Srl	Fulcrum Trading US Inc.	118.9
Web Wizard Srl	LBB Trading Ltd. UK	57.7
	Nominal loan	*176.7*
Fulcrum Trading US Inc.	*Web Wizard Srl*	3.4
LBB Trading Ltd. UK	*Web Wizard Srl*	11.2
	Interest on loan	*14.6*
	Net transfer	**162.1**

The funds obviously came from the sale of cards to Fastweb. Thus, Fastweb acted also as the banker for the companies involved in the fraud.

Operation Traffico Telefonico

Operation *Phuncards*, presented before, is linked to another operation that took place between 2005 and 2007 called Operation *Traffico Telefonico*. The severity of the losses in this scam is ten times bigger than in Operation *Phuncards-Broker*. This increase in magnitude is explained by the following features of the fraud:

- The scam was more complex and involved a large number of companies.
- The fraud took place over three years, the time amplifying the losses.
- The experience from Operation *Phuncards-Broker* was leveraged by the individuals involved.
- Two big companies were involved in the fraud, Fastweb being paired by Telecom Italia Sparkle S.p.A.

The underlying in Operation *Traffico Telefonico* was the sale of VoIP services. The aim was to purchase and resell foreign and satellite numbers that were not usually commercialized by the big operators. One example of such a product is the capacity to call numbers in Tuvalu.

Such services would allow clients from foreign countries to access, through international numbers, various services. The telephone traffic generated by those customers is collected by an access operator from a given country and transported by telecommunications operators up to the operator who has the international call destination numbers.

The following companies were involved in the Operation *Traffico Telefonico*:

- I-Globe Srl, registered in Rome, Italy, in April 2004 and transferred to Moscow in September 2006. In order to perform the interconnection activity, technical equipment were made available by Ubique Tic Italia Srl. The founding team included Riccardo Scoponi (95% of shares) and Manlio Denaro (5% of the shares). Carlo Foccareli acted as a consultant for the company. The directorship of the company was insured by:
  - Riccardo Scoponi until September 2006 and
  - Mikhail Ninkitin, Russian citizen. He succeeded in this function to Scoponi.
- Telefox International Srl, registered in Rome, Italy, since July 2003. Fabio Arigoni was the sole director and the main shareholder, with 95% of shares; Antonio Ricci had 5% of shares.
- Planetarium Srl, incorporated in Rome, in July 2006. The company was owned by Welco Holding AG, a Swiss company incorporated in 1991. The sole director of the company, from the date of incorporation, was Dario Panozzo. Like I-Globe Srl, Planetarium Srl has made use of the technical

equipment of Ubique Tic Italia Srl. Focarelli acted also as consultant for Planetarium Srl.

- Global Phone Network Srl, registered in Rome, Italy, since January 1993. Gionta Aurelio was the sole shareholder and company director.
- Diadem UK Ltd., based in Great Britain, incorporated in 2003 with a capital of 2 pounds split equally between two British citizens, Colin Edward Dines and Andrew Charles Edward Dines. Both shareholders were also company directors.
- Accrue UK Ltd., registered in London, United Kingdom, and represented by Andrew David Neave, Paul Anthony O'Connor and Harry Barclay.
- Accrue Telemedia OY, incorporated in Helsinki, Finland, since 2004 and represented by Neave Andrew David and O'Connor Paul Anthony.
- Acumen UK Ltd., registered in London, United Kingdom, since 1999, with a capital of 2 pounds controlled by the very same Neave and O'Connor. The auditor of Acumen (UK) Ltd. was Fallows & Company, a firm that had the same headquarters as Diadem (UK) Ltd.
- Acumen Europe OY, registered in Helsinki, Finland, in 2004 with a capital of 12 euros was managed by Neave Andrew David and O'Connor Paul Anthony.
- Ubique Italia Holding Srl, registered in Rome in 2004 and owned by another Dutch company called Ubique Europe B.V. The list of directors included Maurizio Salviati, Paul Anthony O'Connor and Andrew David Neave. The employees of Ubique Italia Holding Srl, were employees or self-employed persons working for CMC Italia Srl.
- FCZ Srl, registered in Milan, Italy, in 2004 and controlled by Francesco Fragomeli.
- Ubique TLC Italia Srl (P.I. 08103861004), registered in Rome, Italy, in 1999 and owned by Ubique Italia Holding Srl, represented by Salviati Maurizio. I-Globe Srl and Planetarium Srl used technical routing material from Ubique. The technical lead of Ubique was Massimo Ronchi, who was introduced to Ubique by Carlo Focarelli.
- Broker Management S.A., with headquarters in Panama City, established in 2003. The directorship was insured by other companies: First Executive Directors Inc., The First Company Directors Inc. and the First Overseas Nominees Inc. The company had a current account at Banco Bilbao Vizcaya Argentaria (BBVA). The company was controlled by Augusto Murri, who also controlled the bank account of Suade Management and Coriano Capital.
- Coriano Capital S.A., registered in 2003 in Panama. Coriano was managed in fact by firms: First Executive Directors Inc., First Company Directors Inc. and First Overseas Nominees Inc. The company had a bank account with BBVA controlled by Augusto Murro.
- Crosscomm Ltd., a British company, represented by Sean Hogan.
- Carlo Focarelli, as a sole trader, received fees from I-Globe Srl, Planetarium Srl, Acumen UK, Accrue Telemedia and Ubique TLC Italia Srl. He had close relationships with the senior management of Fastweb S.p.A. and Telecom Italy Sparkle S.p.A.

The main companies that legitimized to a certain extent the fraudulent scam were Fastweb S.p.A. and Telecom Italia Sparkle S.p.A. Individuals involved with Fastweb were the same as those highlighted for Operation *Punchards*. Thus, the key people were:

- Silvio Scaglia, main shareholder in Fastweb S.p.A. through the SMS Finance S.A. until the company was absorbed by Swisscom in 2007.
- Stefano Parisi, CEO since 2004. Two key figures in the scheme reported to Parisi: Roberto Contin, responsible for big clients, and Giovanni Moglia, director of the legal department.
- Mario Rossetti, member of Anphora Srl, majority shareholding company of e.Biscom S.p.A., the company that took over Fastweb. Also in Fastweb S.p.A. he has held the position of director since 2003.
- Roberto Contin, who reported directly to the CEO, Stefano Parisi, and was in charge of marketing premium numbers to big clients. His responsibility encompassed the wholesale clients managed by Fabrizio Casati (Giuseppe Crudele's manager) and the corporates managed by Bruno Zito.
- Bruno Zito, responsible initially for corporate clients and transferred in 2006 to the marketing department.
- Giuseppe Crudele, working under Fabrizio Casati, was head of sales for the wholesale clients until 2006, when he moved to the marketing department along with Zito.

Telecom Italia Sparkle S.p.A. (TIS S.p.A.) was a wholly owned subsidiary belonging to the Telecom Italia group S.p.A. and started its activity in 1997. The individuals associated with TIS that were involved in Operation *Traffico Telefonico* are:

- Amandino Pavani, Chairman of the Board of Directors from April 2003 to April 2006.
- Riccardo Ruggerio, chairman of the board of directors after April 2006.
- Stefano Mazzitelli, chief executive officer since June 2004, responsible for the regulatory matters related to the company. Carlo Baldizzone, director of the business control department, and Massimo Comito, responsible for the European area, were directly reporting to Mazzitelli.
- Massimo Comito, responsible for sales in the European area (EU TIS) and the direct superior of Antonio Catanzariti.
- Antonio Catanzariti, head of carrier traffic sales for Italy, reporting directly to Comito Massimo. The following persons were working in his department:
  - Elisabetta Secchi was a manager, following the commercial relationship with Acumen and I-Globe Srl from December 2004 to June 2005 and with Accrue from January 2006 to May 2007.
  - Simona Maga was a manager, following the commercial relationship with I-Globe Srl from July 2005 to September 2006, Acumen from July 2005 to May 2007 and Diadem and Planetarium Srl from September 2006 to May 2007.

The investigation was carried by the Special Operative Grouping of the Carabinieri. The investigation was initiated due to Vito Tommasino's allegations (owner of a company called Ase Technology) in April 2006 concerning his role in bringing 1.5 million euros from overseas into Italy for Luca Berriola. Berriola was at that time an officer with Guardia di Finanza, in charge of the investigation concerning public finances. Tommasino told Italian investigators that he had a close relationship with Berriola, and intermediated transactions with an offshore company through his own company. Tommasino disclosed the name and the address of Broker Management S.A. in Panama as one of the sources of funds channelled to Berriola. This was the point that unwound the investigation and was the starting point that allowed the Italian police to trace the full operation. The fact that Berriola was working for Guardia di Finazia could explain why this operation was conducted by a 'Carabinieri' special unit and not by Guardia di Finacaizia, as in Operation *Phuncards-Broker*.

Two main schemes used in the VAT fraud from Operation *Traffico Telefonico* are represented in Figures 10.2 and 10.3. The main difference between the two

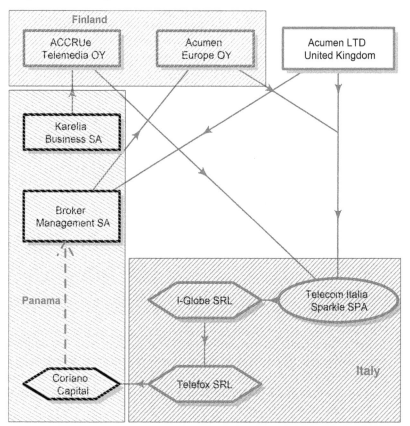

Figure 10.2 Operation *Traffico Telefonico* scheme involving I-Globe Srl and Telefox Srl (Ainsworth R., 2010; Ainsworth R. T., 2010).

Source: Tribunale Ordinario di Roma: Operazione *Phuncards-Broker*.

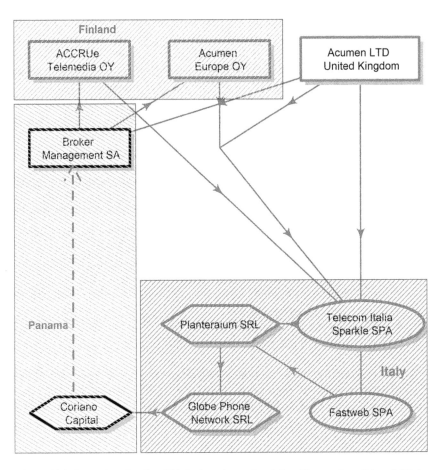

Figure 10.3 Operation *Traffico Telefonico* scheme involving Planetarium Srl and Globe
Phone Network (Ainsworth R., 2010; Ainsworth R. T., 2010).
Source: Tribunale Ordinario di Roma: Operazione *Phuncards-Broker*.

schemes is that in one the link with Coriano Capital is insured through I-Globe
Srl and Telefox Srl (Figure 10.2), while in the other it is insured through Planetarium Srl and Global Phone Network Srl (Figure 10.3).

The main operations that were part of VAT fraud on VoIP traffic can be summarized as follows:

- Coriano Capital S.A., a company based in Panama, transferred rights on
  adult content to Telefox International Srl and Global Phone Network Srl.
  Neither Italian company fulfilled their VAT liabilities in Italy. These companies were the missing traders in the scam. Arigoni Fabio, who acted as director for Telefox International Srl, was already involved in the 2003 Operation
  Phuncards-Broker as a representative of Telefox Srl.

- Telefox International Srl and Global Phone Network Srl sold the rights to I-Globe Srl and to Planetarium Srl; the latter companies took in concession from Crosscomm Ltd., a British company, a numbering range for VoIP terminations. In particular I-Globe Srl managed the numbering range for Tuvalu,[92] whilst Planetarium Srl managed both the Tuvalu numbering range (the ones of I-Globe Srl) and the Iridium satellites numbers.
- Fastweb S.p.A. and Telecom Italia Sparkle S.p.A., both Italian companies, acquired VoIP termination on the numbers accessing the adult content from a few companies, including Acumen (UK) Ltd., Accrue Telemedia OY, Acumen Europe OY- Finland (which took over from Acumen (UK) Ltd. in December 2005) and Diadem UK Ltd. These companies acted officially as aggregators of international traffic, while in reality they were buffers in the VAT carousel. Planetarium Srl took over I-Globe Srl on September 2006. In this regard, it is reported that:
  - Diadem Ltd. (client of Fastweb S.p.A. and Telecom Sparkle S.p.A.), Acumen Ltd., Acumen Europe OY and Accrue Telemedia OY (clients of Telecom Italia Sparkle S.p.A.) aggregated traffic from third parties.
  - Fastweb S.p.A. and Telecom Italia Sparkle S.p.A. acted in theory as connectors between the origin of the telephonic traffic and its destinations, thereby being carriers of traffic.
  - I-Globe Srl and Planetarium Srl had equipment for the VoIP termination from Ubique TLC Italia Srl.

Table 10.4 shows the evolution of the TIS's performance of the VoIP traffic business in terms of revenues and operating margins from 2005 to 2007. The operating margin grew from 4.4% in 2005 to 7.9% in 2007. In 2005, the VoIP sales showed a margin of 12.2 million euros, but interestingly enough, until August 2005, the margin figured only 2 million euros. It was the turnover generated

Table 10.4 Operational margins of TIS S.p.A. between 2005 and 2007

Year	Revenue (million euros)	Cost (million euros)	Operating margin (million euros)	Operating margin/ revenue (%)
2005	275.8	263.6	12.2	4.4
2006	751.1	704.2	46.9	6.2
2007	166.5	153.3	13.2	7.9
Total	1,193.3	1,121.1	72.2	6.1

Source: Tribunale Ordinario di Roma: Operazione *Phuncards-Broker*.

92 These telephone numbers, if called by a user (telephone or internet), provide for the application of a higher rate compared to an ordinary call as they provide access to a paid service (likely content for adults). These telephone numbers, despite being enumerated with the name of the country Tuvalu or with the name 'Iridium', do not constitute geographic numbering in the sense that they can be active in any State or better geographical point where the licencees decide to activate them.

Table 10.5 Operational margins of Fastweb S.p.A. between 2005 and 2007

Year	Revenue (million euros)	Cost (million euros)	Operating margin (million euros)	Operating margin/revenue (%)
2005	70.4	66.2	4.3	6.1
2006	122.3	116.3	6.0	4.9
2007	11.0	10.5	0.5	4.5
Total	203.7	192.9	10.8	5.3

Source: Tribunale Ordinario di Roma: Operazione *Phuncards-Broker*.

with the British firm Acumen Ltd. that provided the remaining 10 million euros of margin until the end of the year.

Danesi Arturo, in charge of the wholesale business with TIS S.p.A., reported in August 2005 to the CEO, D. Stefano Mazzitelli, that the VoIP business with Acumen UK Ltd. and I-Globe Srl helped with reaching the corporate objectives for that year. For the period 2005–2007 Acumen, Accrue and Diadem were overall amongst TIS's top ten clients, thereby underlining the strong dependence of TIS on the VoIP business.

Table 10.5 shows the operating margins of the VoIP business for Fastweb S.p.A. between 2005 and 2007. The margin was between 4.5% and 6.1%, and was mainly explained by the revenue driven by the fraudulent operations.

Given the huge impact of the VoIP business generated by the 'clients' from the carousel, it is obvious that the senior management of Telecom Italia Sparkle and Fastweb were aware to a certain extent of what was going on.

Moreover, Fastweb S.p.A. and Telecom Italia Sparkle S.p.A., as mentioned earlier, acted as traffic carriers, thereby providing connection services of VoIP traffic between two operators. The two Italian carriers connected two types of operators:

- On the one hand there were the foreign telephone aggregators, including Diadem, Accrue and Acumen. They were clients for Fastweb S.p.A. and Telecom Italia Sparkle S.p.A.
- On the other hand there were two Italian companies, I-Globe Srl and Planetarium Srl, which terminated the VoIP traffic from the specific numbering ranges, which they purchased from the Panama-based company Cariano Capitai S.A. through two buffers: Telefax International Srl and Global Phone Network Srl. The latter two companies were the missing traders in the carousel.

From a purely economic point of view, the scheme presented here involved a large number of intermediaries. The profitability of this business decays with the number of buffers in the scheme. This aspect is not confirmed by the margins of the Fastweb S.p.A. and Telecom Italia Sparkle S.p.A., presented in Tables 10.4 and 10.5. Thus, the origin of this margin is questionable and cannot be explained in fact by anything else other than the VAT fraud. A common feature in the carousel frauds is the fact that the margin of intermediaries is much higher than the benchmark of the regular companies.

Such an intermediary is Telefox International, which, along with its manager, Fabio Arigoni, was a key element in both Operation *Phuncards-Brokers* and Operation *Traffico Telefonico*. Telefox International played the role of the missing traders that pocketed the VAT in both cases. As mentioned earlier I-Globe Srl acquired premium content available through Tuvalu number from Telefox. When I-Globe Srl was raided by the police in November 2006 no contract with Telefox was found. Only an electronic version of the contract was available. Arigoni ordered shortly before the police raid that all documentation be withdrawn from Telefox's headquarters.

Another intermediary was Planetarium Srl, later replaced in the carousel by I-Globe Srl. Planetarium Srl purchased premium content available through the Tuvalu numbers, from Global Phone Network Srl, a company managed by Gionta Aurelio. A contract between the parties was found during a police raid in the headquarters of the two companies in May 2007. The contract is, interestingly enough, dated February 2005, way before Planetarium Srl was registered in July 2006. The first invoice issued by Global Phone Network Srl towards Planetarium Srl was in September 2006.

Additionally, there are no technical details concerning the interconnection between the two companies, with respective IP addresses, internet communication protocols and network characteristics concentring the Tuvalu numbers. There were some technical documents making reference to a number unrelated to the premium content. The server used by Global Phone Network Srl was provided by the company BT Italia S.p.A. starting in May 2007. The investigation of the Italian police showed that technical connection issues were raised in relation to BT Italia S.p.A. A solution was brought by Ubique TLC Italia Srl, a company introduced to Gionta by Carlo Focarelli. Global Phone Network Srl was the other missing trader in the scheme, and all its claimed business with VoIP termination was not even feasible from a technical point of view.

The investigation of the Italian police provided useful elements concerning the financial flows between the various players involved in Operation *Traffico Telefonico*. The examination of the banking accounts of Fastweb S.p.A., TIS S.p.A., I-Globe Srl, Planetarium Srl and Telefox International Srl confirmed the carousel nature of the fraud. The financial flow is synthesized in Table 10.6, underlining the main roles of each company:

- Fastweb S.p.A. and TIS S.p.A. played the role of 'bankers' and collectors of VTA from the Italian tax office.
- Broker Management and Karelia Business were offshore buffers in the carousel.
- Acumen, Diadem and Accrue acted as overseas clients for Fastweb and TIS, selling traffic without VAT.
- I-Globe Srl and Planetarium Srl acted as Italian suppliers of termination traffic to Fastweb and TIS, thereby being paid with VAT.

Table 10.6 Main financial flows between the companies involved in Operation *Traffico Telefonico*

Date	Payer	Receiver	Amount (million euros)
May 2005 to March 2007	Diadem UK LTD	Fastweb S.p.A.	203.7
February 2006	Acumen Europe OY	Acumen Ltd.	7.9
May 2005 to February 2006	Broker Management	Acumen Ltd.	370.1
April 2005 to February 2006	Acumen Ltd.	TIS S.p.A.	359.7
March 2006 to August 2007	Broker Management	Acumen Europe OY	267.3
August 2006 to May 2007	Broker Management	Acumen Europe OY	311.5
February to July 2006	Acumen Europe OY	TIS S.p.A.	586.4
January 2007	Broker Management	Accrue Telemedia OY	3.7
August 2006 to April 2007	Karelia Business SA	Accrue Telemedia OY	330.8
March 2006 to June 2007	Karelia Business SA	Accrue Telemedia OY	132.4
March 2006 April 2007	Accrue Telemedia OY	TIS S.p.A.	464.2
September 2006 to April 2007	Diadem UK Ltd.	TIS S.p.A.	151.8
May 2005 to September 2006	Fastweb	I-Globe	182.9
September 2006 to March 2007	Fastweb	Planetarium Srl	48.7
April 2005 to September 2006	TIS S.p.A.	I-Globe	977.8
September 2006 to May 2007	TIS S.p.A.	Planetarium Srl	809.5
May 2005 to August 2006	I-Globe	Broker Management	845.1
April 2005 to August 2006	I-Globe	Crosscomm	5.2
April–May 2005	I-Globe	Acumen Ltd.	8.3
August 2005	Acumen Ltd.	I-Globe	8.3
March 2006 to August 2006	I-Globe (IT account)	I-Globe (AT account)	10.9
September 2006 to May 2007	Planetarium	Global Phone Networks SRL	848.3
October 2006 to May 2007	Planetarium	Crosscomm	2.5

Source: Tribunale Ordinario di Roma: Operazione *Phuncards-Broker*.

The top-down analysis of the information exhibited in Table 10.6 requires a closer look at the cumulated outflows concentring the VoIP business from Fastweb S.p.A. and TIS S.p.A.

Table 10.7 shows that the two Italian companies have sent funds to Planetarium Srl and I-Globe Srl for a total of 2,018.9 million euros. This corresponds to the total amount of defrauded VAT, estimated to be 333.9 million euros. The total sum of the purchases for the two companies, excluding VAT, represented 1,682.4 million euros.

The total revenue of Fastweb and TIS from the British and Finnish clients between 2005 and 2007, as computed in Table 10.5, accounted for 1,765.8 million euros. Therefore the total margin for the two companies for the considered period was 83.4 million euros, underscoring an operating margin of 4.7% confirmed by the previous analysis.

The payment received from Diadem, Accrue and Acumen by the two Italian companies needed to be channelled from I-Globe Srl and Planetarium. These transfers took place through two companies: Broker Management S.A. and Karelia Business.

Table 10.7 Cash outflows from Fastweb and TIS towards Planetarium Srl and I-Globe
between 2005 and 2007

Date	Payer	Receiver	Amount (million euros)
September 2006 to March 2007	Fastweb S.p.A.	Planetarium Srl	48.7
May 2005 to September 2006	Fastweb S.p.A.	I-Globe Srl	182.9
September 2006 to May 2007	Telecom Italia Sparkle	Planetarium Srl	809.5
April 2005 to September 2006	Telecom Italia Sparkle	I-Globe Srl	977.8

Source: Tribunale Ordinario di Roma: Operazione *Phuncards-Broker*.

Table 10.8 Financial flows of Broker Management S.A.

Period	Amount (+ inflow/– outflow) (million euros)	Counterparty
May 2005 to September 2006	947.2	I-Globe Srl
September 2006 to April 2007	523.3	Global Phone Network Srl
January 2007	-3.7	Accrue Telemedia OY
May 2005 to February 2006	-370.30	Acumen UK Ltd.
January 2006 to May 2007	-590.9	Acumen Europe OY
May 2005 to April 2007	-359.7	Diadem UK Ltd.
August 2006	-2.2	Secondary broker management account

Source: Tribunale Ordinario di Roma: Operazione *Phuncards-Broker*.

A key role in closing the carousel was played by Broker Management S.A., a Panamanian company controlled by Augusto Murri. The main financial flows corresponding to the bank accounts of the company are presented in Table 10.6. Broker Management S.A. received 1,470.5 million euros from I-Globe Srl and Global Phone. Broker Management S.A made payments accounting for 1,320.9 million euros to the European companies: Accrue, Acumen and Diadem. This represented more than 75% of the total sum involved in the carousel, the remaining being channelled through Karelia Business (Table 10.8). The account showed also fund transfers in favour of Tommasino Vito.

Table 10.9 resumes the main payments and reimbursements of the Italian companies involved in Operation *Traffico Telefonico* related to the VoIP transactions. The total amount of VAT lost in this scam is 333.9 million euros, corresponding to the economic and the financial elements exposed before.

Aftermath

The turnover entailed by the commercial transactions in both operations was critical for TIS S.p.A. and Fastweb S.p.A. The transactions increased the turnover of both companies and showed that they achieved their objectives, an

Table 10.9 Synthesis of the VAT inflows and outflows made towards the company involved in the fraud

Company	Reimbursed VAT (million euros)	Paid VAT (million euros)	Balance (million euros)
Fastweb S.p.A.	38.6		38.6
ITS S.p.A.	297.9		297.9
I-Globe Srl		1.7	–1.7
Planetarium Srl		0.9	–0.9
Total	336.5	2.7	333.9

Source: Tribunale Ordinario di Roma: Operazione *Phuncards-Broker*.

essential fact for the analysts, for the banks that financed the company and its development, and for the financial markets (Fastweb was listed on the Milan stock exchange and was subject to a merger with e.Biscom in December 2004).

The fraud investigated in Operation *Phuncards-Broker* caused 33.9 million euros of VAT loss, while the VoIP business entailed 333.9 million euros in defrauded tax for the Italian taxpayers. But the total amount of pocketed VAT could be much bigger, especially for Operation *Traffico Telefonico*. The estimates of the frauds do not include the potential VAT fraud in other countries and through companies other than TIS S.p.A. and Fastweb S.p.A. The prosecutors identified fund transfers which did not have any economic justification representing 2.2 billion euro.

Table 10.10 synthesizes the sentences given by the Italian courts during the initial 2013 trial and the revised sentences in appeal. The top management was acquitted in both instances, while the court of appeals reduced the sentences for the other individuals.

The core group

The Italian prosecutors charged over 50 individuals in both cases *Phuncards* and *Traffico Telefonico*. Only a small number of people and company representatives were finally condemned. The top representatives of Fastweb and TIS were acquitted. Arigoni, head of Telefax, was initially charged but not condemned in the end, probably due to his help to the Italian investigators.[93] Crudele from Fastweb collaborated with the prosecutors. The directors of Web Wizard did not seem to have been prosecuted. Web Wizard seemed more like a shell company controlled by CMC Italy.

The core group of people condemned by the court were Gennaro Mokbel, Nicolo di Girolamao, Carlo Focarelli and Bruno Zito. Another key person in the group, Silvio Fanella, was killed after the first court gave the first verdict.

93 www.ilsole24ore.com/art/finanza-e-mercati/2010-09-21/svolta-inchiesta-fastwebtelecom-sparkle-090308.shtml?uuid=ADpZ0H&refresh_ce=1.

Table 10.10 Sentences for the persons charged in Operation *Phuncards-Broker*

Name	Initial sentence (2013)	Court of appeal (2018)
Silvio Scaglia	Acquittal	Acquittal
Stefano Mazzitelli	Acquittal	Acquittal
Antonio Catanzariti	Acquittal	Acquittal
Massimo Comito	Acquittal	Acquittal
Mario Rossetti	Acquittal	Acquittal
Roberto Contin	Acquittal	Acquittal
Manlio Denaro	Acquittal	Acquittal
Gennaro Mokbel	15 years of prison	10.5 years of prison
Carlo Focarelli	11 years of prison	9 years of prison
Luca Berriola	7 years of prison	5 years of prison
Luca Breccolotti	7 years of prison	4.5 years of prison
Giorgia Ricci	8 years of prison	4 years of prison
Paolo Colosimo	5 years of prison	5.3 years of prison
Giuseppe Cherubini, Francesco Fragomeli, Aurelio Gionta and Massimo Micucci	6.5 years of prison	4 years of prison
Nicola Paolo Di Girolamo		5 years of prison
Giuseppe Crudele		5 years of prison
Riccardo Scoponi	4 years of prison	3.5 years of prison
Bruno Zito	6 years of prison	6 years of prison
Luigi Marotta	3 years of prison	3 years of prison
Giovanni Gabriele	3.5 years of prison	3.5 years of prison

Augusto Murri, another key person in the organization, committed suicide. He had had a big conflict with Mokbel since 2008, related to money due to Murri.

GENNARO MOKBEL

Mokbel was portrayed by the Italian prosecutor as the head of the criminal group, technical promoter and organizer of the criminal gang. He had links with the far-right circles from Rome, with the political circles represented by Senator Di Girolamo and with the Calabrian mob.

He was charged with money laundering, corruption of officials, attacks on citizens' political rights and abuse on elections. His plan was to leverage the funds from the VoIP connection and buy in to the Italian political system. For that he pushed for the election of Di Girolamo, a Roman senator from the far-right political spectrum. In order to get the necessary votes, Mokbel got in contact with the 'Ndrangheta clan from Capo Rizzoto. The 'Arena' family, through its ties in Germany, was supposed to push Di Girolamo's election for a seat representing the Italian community living abroad. This was supposed to take place during the 2008 election.

With respect to the fraud itself Mokbel did not hold positions in any of the companies identified in the entire financial circuit linked to the illicit operations.

In 1994 he was arrested, together with Antonio D'inzillio, exponent of the former *Banda della Magliana*.

NICOLA DI GIROLAMO

Once upon a time a prominent Roman political personality, Di Girolamo resigned from his functions in March 2010 and was sentenced for money laundering to five years' imprisonment and a repayment of 4.2 million euros.

Nicola Paolo Di Girolamo was involved with the fraud as legal and financial consultant, thereby being fully aware of the illegal activities. In his role he worked closely with Toseroni Marco in building the intricate financial network that served as backbone for the carousel.

He mediated with Mokbel and Colosimo the purchase of a boat for Pugliese Franco through a company called Adv & Partners Srl. The boat served as compensation for helping with getting elected in Germany.

Di Girolamo did not figure as director in any companies involved in the carousel. He had ties with companies that received funds from companies linked to the carousel. He was the director of the British company Managest Ltd. Di Girolamo together, with Toseroni, controlled an Italian company called Amon Capital LLC, which received funds from offshore accounts linked to the VAT fraud.

CARLO FOCARELLI

Focarelli was neither employed nor director in any of the companies involved in the fraud. He acted in his capacity as business consultant and de facto manager of the companies that came into contact with the Fastweb and Telecom Italia Sparkle, including CMC Italia Srl, Web Wizard Srl, I-Globe Srl and Planetarium Srl. From this point of view he was the creator and the manager of the VAT carousel. He was one of the few people involved in all steps of the scam in both *Phuncards-Broker* and *Traffico Telefonico*. Focarelli spoke a few foreign languages fluently, thereby facilitating contact with the British and Panamanian firms.

In each operation he was following very closely the details. For example, in Operation *Phuncard* he:

• prospected and negotiated on behalf of the CMC Group *Phuncards* business with Fastweb S.p.A.;
• tried to influence within Fastweb the people concerned with the potential issues with VAT;
• got involved in the graphic development of the actual *Phuncards* cards;
• introduced the British purchasers LBB Trading Ltd., PGT Ltd. and Fulcrum Trading US Inc. to Fastweb S.p.A.; and
• negotiated the contract between the Brits and Fastweb S.p.A.

Towards the end of 2004 Focarelli proposed a new business to Giuseppe Crudele and Bruno Zito, sales managers with Fastweb. The aim of this was to replicate the

Phuncards business with VoIP. The business was too big for Fastweb, and so they got in contact with Telecom Italia Sparkle. In fact it was not the size of the business but the capacity to get big VAT refunds that made TIS appealing for Focarelli.

LUCA BRECCOLOTTI

Luca Breccolotti and Silvio Fanella were operating heads of the organization structured by Gennaro Mokbel. Breccolotti made a few trips to Honk Kong, Switzerland and Nice (France) to meet with other members of the gang and to oversee the money movement from and to the offshore accounts of the group. Therefore, he was charged for being organizer, promoter and head of the criminal association, and for providing technical support to Toseroni Marco (one of the individuals that engineered the scam) and the lawyer Di Girolamo. He personally worked to hire security boxes in England to hide the proceeds of the illicit activity (cash and diamonds), a part of which was seized by the British Police.

GIUSEPPE CHERUBINI

Giuseppe Cherubini was the director of Globestream Ltd. which had the same address in England as Diadem Ltd. Globestream was owned by Giuseppe Cherubini and Luigi Cantarini, who held also the position of secretary. Silvio Fanella, Breccolotti, Focarreli and Cherubini made a trip to England in 2004 to meet with the Neave-O'Connor group.

Globestream Ltd. has been the company to transport a substantial sum of money to credit institutions in Hong Kong and Dubai in favour of corporate and personal accounts attributable to Carlo Focarelli, Bruno Zito, Giuseppe Crudele and others.

Between November 2005 and December 2007 Globestream received transfers from the offshore firm Broker Management S.A. and from FCZ Srl, a company managed by Fancesco Fragolmelli. At the end of 2007 Globestream had in its account over 42 million euros split amongst a few banks in Hong Kong, Dubai and Italy.

FRANCESCO FRAGOMELI

Fragomeli was charged for laundering the proceeds of the crime in his capacity as sole director of the company FCZ Srl. The company transferred big sums received from Broker Management in favour of Globestream Ltd.

The telephone intercepts have shown that Francesco Fragomeli, Bruno Zito and Giuseppe Crudele were using 'sim' cards registered to non-EU citizens, thereby not being able to be traced by the Italian investigators.

GIUSEPPE CRUDELE

Crudele worked for Fastweb as head of retail business and as head of marketing. He was charged with unfaithful declaration through the use of invoices for non-existent transactions as part of Operation *Traffico Telefonico*. Focarelli indicated that Crudele was informed about the commercial operations of Fastweb. Crudele Giuseppe has materially supervised and allowed, as manager of Fastweb S.p.A, the realization of the commercial Operation *Traffico Telefonico*.

Crudele Giuseppe was a friend of Zito Bruno, a Fastweb manager also involved in the fictitious transactions. Zito was hired by Crudele to help him with supervising the whole framework. Zito had no share or had seemingly not received the proceeds of the VAT fraud. Nevertheless Operation *Traffico Telefonico* allowed him to reinforce his position in the company and to reach his commercial targets for 2005 and 2006.

BRUNO ZITO

Zito was the head of big accounts with Fastweb S.p.A. and was seen to facilitate the fraudulent trades. Bruno Zito was involved in both Operation *Phuncards* and Operation *Traffico Telefonico*. Zito tried to justify himself in front of the prosecutor by pointing out that he was just conducting business for Fastweb, and he was not aware of what was really going on as a full picture.

But the relationship between Bruno Zito and Carlo Focarelli was beyond the relationship that should be between two managers/employees of companies that carry out a business and of a normal friendship. In fact they were linked by economic interests that were not transparent to all stakeholders. For example Zito concealed his offshore accounts in Hong Kong and Switzerland.

During the investigation Zito tried to hide part of the document related to the businesses involving Fastweb. He also did not disclose at all his connections with Focarelli, who in fact was not hired by the company involved in the carousel, acting as a sole agent. The phone conversations intercepted by the police exhibited the connection between the two managers.

The acquitted link

The Italian prosecutors in the initial indictment underlined that given the sizes of the operations and the governance of the involved companies, the senior managers in Telecom Italia Sparkle and Fastweb were surely aware and in control of what was really going on. In the aftermath the senior management was acquitted in the first instance, a fact confirmed also by the appeal in the higher courts.[94]

SILVIO SCAGLIA

Scaglia was accused of aggravated transnational criminal association and unfaithful tax declaration. His main roles during the VoIP connection were as CEO and Chairman of Fastweb S.p.A. as well as CEO and majority shareholder of e.Biscom S.p.A.

94 www.ilfattoquotidiano.it/2017/09/27/riciclaggio-telecom-sparkle-fastweb-assoluzione-anche-in-appello-per-scaglia-e-mazzitelli/3881605/.

Silvio Scaglia declared in 2007 that his role in the company was to organize its functioning and that he was not involved with the commercial activity. He declared also that he had never known or heard of Focarelli or Ferreri. Moreover, since April 2003 Emanuele Angelidis became the managing director and the person who interacted with Scaglia. Thus, Scaglia declared he was not aware of what was going on in the firm besides what Angelidis reported. He underlined that the contract relating to the *Phuncards-Broker* was initiated by the commercial office and verified by the tax and legal departments, and no one communicated any kind of problems regarding the *Phuncards-Broker* contract stipulated with CMC Italy Srl.

STEFANO MAZZITELLI

Mazzitelli was also not convicted in court, but initially he was charged for participation in the criminal association in his capacity as CEO of Telecom Italia Sparkle. TIS's role was identified following the investigations carried out on the bank accounts of Arigoni Fabio, Telefox International Srl and I-Globe Srl. The companies were involved in Operation *Traffico Telefonico*. In that operation, TIS's role was to interpose between suppliers I-Globe Srl/Planetarium Srl and customers Diadem UK, Acumen (UK), Acumen Europe OY (Finland) and Accrue Telemedia OY (Finland) by signing interconnection contracts with these companies in order to generate telephone traffic.

Mazzitelli signed tax declarations and financial statements for the years 2005 and 2006, presented by Telecom Italia Sparkle S.p.A., from which the company obtained a reimbursement from the Italian tax office of 298 million euros in VAT. A chunk of 72 million euros from the reimbursed VAT was considered by TIS 2007 as operating margin, for the year 2007.

ANTONIO CATANZARITI

Antonio Catanzariti emerges as the head of the carrier clients with Telecom Italia Sparkle. Catanzariti was charged for using invoices for non-existent transactions issued by I-Globe. Antonio Catanzariti and his superior Comito Massimo (sales manager at Telecom Italia Sparkle S.p.A., Europe region) dealt with the commercial and pre-contractual activities of the telephone traffic business. Both Comito and Catanzariti were in contact with Carlo Focarelli, who presented the opportunities with I-Globe Srl/Planetarium Srl) and made the contacts with the customers Acumen/ Accrue Telemedia Ltd./Diadem UK. The indictment stated that Catanzariti was fully aware of the fictitiousness of the operations. At the end of 2004, Catanzariti was contacted by Giuseppe Crudele from Fastweb at the recommendation of Carlo Focarelli. Focarelli offered Catanzariti a business opportunity with Fastweb S.p.A. which became later the fraud undercovered in Operation *Traffico Telefonico*.

ROBERTO CONTIN

Contin was charged for the role played within Fastweb with respect to Operation *Traffico Telefonico*. Roberto Contin served as Director of the Large Account

Division and member of the Steering Committee of Fastweb S.p.A., and he supervised the realization of the commercial Operation *Telephone Traffic*.

The Italian prosecutors assumed initially that Roberto Contin, top manager of Fastweb S.p.A., was in possession of all the useful elements concerning the involvement of Fastweb S.p.A. in the VAT fraud and was therefore aware of the essential role played by Fastweb S.p.A. within the supply chain of the companies involved as well as the reimbursements received from the Italian treasury. Roberto Contin appeared to be involved in the negotiations, the preliminary phases and the 'feasibility plan' of Fastweb S.p.A. related to the *Telephone Traffic* business. In theory, the traffic resell was a low-margin business, with negative effects on cash flows. Nevertheless Fastweb S.p.A. made 10 million euros of income which impacted positively on its profitability indices.

MANLIO DENARO

Denaro was charged with participation in a criminal association and issuance of invoices for inexistent operations. He, together with Riccardo Scoponi, owned I-Globe Srl, a company actually managed by Focarelli. I-Globe Srl had numerous fund transfers with Telefax International.

The Italian prosecutors accused initially Denaro for acting as a frontman for I-Globe, being responsible, with Scoponi, for issuing invoices for non-existent transactions and, with Mikhail Nikitin, for concealing the accounting books.

The dead link

Two people were murdered in the VoIP connection, two others were gravely wounded and two more were wounded. Two individuals were seriously beaten in 2012: Giovanni Battista Ceniti, a far-right militant, and Marco Iannilli, an accountant (ex-far-right militant) involved in the relationship between Mokbel's group and the Calabrian organized crime. Iannilli testified in the trial and cooperated with the investigators, offering details on funds transferred from Singapore and Hong Kong to a San Marino account.

SILVIO FANELLA

Fanella, Mokbel's treasurer, was killed in July 2014 with a gunshot by a group of criminals disguised as policemen. The attack took place in Fanella's residence in Via Gandolfi at Camilluccia. The real aim of the criminals was to seize cash and precious stones that Fanella kept in his house, representing part of the proceeds of the VoIP connection. One of those indicted with the murder was the far-right militant Giovanni Battista Ceniti.[95] Fanella worked closely with Augusto Murri, also in charge of executing money transfers.

---

95 www.romatoday.it/cronaca/omicidio-fanella-assoluzione-mandanti.html.

AUGUSTO MURRI

Augusto Murri was one of the central figures in Mokbel's group. His main role was to execute fund transfers from and to the Italian firms in connection with offshore firms. He worked closely with Mokbel and Panozzo, director for Planetarium Srl. Murri was key in both Operation *Phuncards* and Operation *Traffico Telefonico*, thereby making him one of the few that had a full picture of what was going on.

He was in charge of operating on the current account in Spain of Suade Management Ltd. He delivered Mokbel's money to Switzerland and brought funds from Switzerland back to Italy, often to Rome, to deliver them to Fanella.

After the investigation started, Murri had a clash with Mokbel. Augusto Murri decided to return to Italy to try to discuss, without success, with Gennaro Mokbel his position and to request the other sums of money previously agreed upon, which he claimed were not paid. The sit-down created new tensions within Mokbel's group, which forced Murri to take refuge first in Spain and then in Panama. In May 2007 a conversation between Panozzo and Mokbel pointed out that both were aware of the Murri problem and that they were looking for a solution.

In May 2012, at the beginning of the Sparkle trial Murri took his own life with a shotgun in his family estate in the countryside of Siena.

The 'Ndrangheta link

The involvement of the 'Ndrangheta was related to the potential support for the election in the Italian senate of Di Girolamo. Gennaro Mokbel intermediated the connection between Girolamo and the Calabrian clan 'Arena' through Paolo Colosimo, a lawyer close to the crime gang.

'Ndrangheta was in charge of insuring that the Italian Federalist Party, having Di Girolamo on its list, could gather enough votes from Italians living in Germany for the Italian elections of 2008.

FRANCO PUGLIESE

Born in Isola Capo Rizzuto the Calabrian businessman Pugliese was the son-in-law of the current chief of the 'Arena' family of Isola Capo Rizzuto, Arena Fabrizio. Arena was at that time fugitive for serious crimes, such as murder and mafia association. Pugliese was in charge of accomplishing the electoral project of the Roman gang headed by Mokbel. Pugliese also had the responsibility of facilitating the cooperation between the 'Arena' family and the Nicoscia family, required to insure the votes in Germany. Gabriele Giovanni, Pugiese's henchman, had taken the responsibility of the procurement of blank ballot papers from the Calabrian community in Germany for the purpose of votes in favour of Di Girolamo. Pugliese asked Mokbel to be compensated for his services with a boat which was supposed to be built in a shipyard in Trappani.

The British link

In 2012, four British citizens were extradited from England to Rome in relation to the investigation on the VoIP connection. Officers from the Serious and Organised Crime Agency requested their arrest in February 2010,[96] but the four appealed the warrant. The appeal was refused, and the Brits were deferred to the Italian justice system.

The companies managed by the Brits in the United Kingdom played a key role in both scams. They acted as buyers of services from outside Italy. Their companies represented the critical link in the carousel, connecting the offshore companies with the Italian ones.

PAUL O'CONNOR AND ANDREW NEAVE

Fulcrum Electronics UK and Fulcrum Trading Inc. were controlled by Paul O'Connor and Andrew Neave. O'Connor and Neave were charged with completing financial operations to hinder the identification of the criminal origin funds and to favour the re-employment of the funds in both legal and illicit activities. The Fulcrum Group received on its accounts with Banca Antonveneta and Bank of America a total of 1,119 million euros from the companies CMC Group and Web Wizard. The Fulcrum Group paid 112 million euros to Fastweb, justifying the aforementioned financial transactions with the fictitious purchase of *Phuncards-Broker*, and with a financing transaction apparently carried out in their favour by the companies CMC Ltd. and Web Wizard Srl.

After being extradited to Italy, O'Connor and Neave did not appear in the final court judgement. In the aftermath of the trial, the Brits were not convicted for their ties with the Italian fraudsters.

COLIN AND ANDREW DINES

Colin Dines was an English retired criminal barrister who, along with his son Andrew, was concerned by the initial indictment. Andrew and Colin Dines were charged for having a 50% share in the company Diadem UK Ltd. Colin Dines also director of the company, was responsible for billing for non-existent transactions as part of the 'telephone traffic reselling' operation.

The role of the Dines was linked to the pair Andrew Neave and Paul O'Connor, who were charged for their contribution to realizing the financial transfers in the carousel. Diadem UK received between 2005 and 2007 more than 360 million euros from the offshore firm Broker Management S.A. Colin and Andrew Dines also had managerial responsibilities with Fulcrum.

---

96 www.telegraph.co.uk/news/uknews/crime/9366573/Retired-judge-among-Britons-facing-extradition-to-Italy-on-Mafia-money-laundering-charges.html.

ADAM AND ROBERT KENWORTHY

The Kenworthys controlled the companies LBB Trading Ltd. and Premier Global Telecom Ltd., both registered at the same address in London. Pietro Mussilo, an Italian citizen based in Rome, acted as advisor for LBB Trading Ltd. and introduced the Kenworthys to Focarelli. Both firms were suppliers for Fastweb S.p.A. in the *Phuncards* business. LBB was also a supplier for CMC Italia. The Kenworthys were not subjected to indictments entailed by the Italian investigations.

The Russian link

The VoIP connection involved mainly Italian and British citizens. A small group of individuals with ties in ex-Soviet countries appeared in the investigations. Their roles were to launder the proceeds of the fraud through offshore companies.

EUGENE GOUREVITCH

In 2008, the Information Unit of the Bank of Italy started to dig into Gourevitch, a Kirgiz-born man residing in the United States and controlling numerous offshore companies. Gourevitch's name came from analyzing an account with the Anglo Irish Bank in the name of Broker Management S.A., where Virage Consulting, controlled by Gourevitch, was the beneficiary of credit transfers for 1.2 million euros.

The Unit for Combating Money Laundering of the Republic of Cyprus reported that Wolstin Ltd. and Crown Era Investments Ltd., both controlled by Gourevitch, were used to launder the proceeds of criminal activities from carousel fraud and trafficking in tobacco and drugs. The funds were transferred to Wolstin Ltd., probably from Italy, in the form of loan contracts, and then they were subsequently transferred to other accounts, including that held by Crown Era Investments Ltd.

Global Phone Network Srl, a company controlled by Gionta Aurelio, transferred periodically funds to Wolstin Ltd. Gourevitch and had a fundamental role in the establishment of Welco Holding S.A., a company governed by Swiss law which was specifically set up for Planetarium Srl.

I-GLOBE AND MIKHAIL NIKITIN

I-Globe was one of the companies that defrauded VAT on VoIP in Operation *Traffico Telefonico*. I-Globe Srl and Planetarium Srl were the companies that provided termination traffic to Telekom Italia Sparkle. Carlo Focarelli acted as advisor for the company, and Ricardo Scopioni was the sole director. The firm moved its headquarters to Moscow in 2006. A Russian citizen, Mikhail Nikitin appeared to be controlling the Russian office. The move is justified by fraudsters' intention to make the investigations as complicated and long as possible.

The 'Hollywood' connection

Recently, national tax offices have started to be more careful when making VAT reimbursements. The increasing number of VAT frauds raised the alert level of tax offices. Therefore, tax evaders started to experience increased difficulty in claiming VAT credit refunds. Consequently, criminals used out-of-the-box methods in order reach their shady goals. On principle, tax offices aim to serve the businesses and to help them with credit tax refunds in those areas of the economy that generate growth and jobs. Tax offenders are aware of these aspects and use creative control in order to give the impression that their businesses are contributing to the economy. Thus, many fraudsters moved into new markets, which would not be suspected of any ties with the VAT fraud scene. One of these markets is the movie production business. The budget for producing a movie is generally consistent, and any tax claim representing a few million dollars (euros) would not surprise anybody. Being essentially a services business, the purchases are mainly related to actors' salaries and to hiring professional moviemakers. A few relevant cases are exposed in the following.

Bashar Al-Issa[97]

In 2013, a gang led by Bashar Al-Issa was dismantled in Great Britain after an investigation of the HMRC. The gang was pretending to make a film and asked for a 2.8 million pound tax relief. The gang claimed they were shooting a film called *A Landscape of Lives* staring Hollywood A-list actors. HMRC found that the whole plot was a sham production, the real goal of the gang being to defraud the taxpayers of 1.5 million of VAT and almost 1.3 million pounds in tax film credit.[98]

Gang leader Bashar Al-Issa, along with his associates Aoife Madden, Tariq Hassan and Osama Al Baghdady, controlled a film company called Evolved Pictures. The gang claimed that their movie project was backed by a Jordanian company with a budget of more than 19 million pounds.

The gang also informed HMRC that their company, Evolved Pictures, spent millions of pounds on the film-making, including paying actors and film set managers, claiming a consequent VAT repayment. After HMRC investigations started the gang tried to quickly shoot a movie with some C-list personalities.

Al-Issa's case shows that VAT fraud can be orchestrated in a relatively flexible manner. The cargo filled with electronics is replaced with actors' names and fake invoices.

97 www.mynewsdesk.com/uk/hm-revenue-customs-hmrc/pressreleases/a-landscape-of-lies-film-tax-fraudsters-jailed-for-over-22-years-850016.
98 In Great Britain, HMRC accords film tax relief to legitimate film-makers for British films that are intended to be shown commercially in cinemas whose total production cost accounts for at least 25% of activities in the United Kingdom.

Anish Anand[99]

Between 2007 and 2011, Anand defrauded the HMRC by pretending he was producing big-budget movies. Based on these fake claims, Anand applied for VAT and film tax credit of 6 million. He controlled a few companies involved in the fraud. He was helped by three Londoners, Amit Kumar, Afsana Karim and Sanjeev Mirajkar. One of their bogus productions was called 'Billy'[100] and was an animated story about a Beagle dog escaping London Zoo to undertake a journey in London. Thus, the costs for which the gang claimed VAT reimbursement were not related to actors or moviemakers.

Richard Driscoll[101]

Not all VAT frauds in the movie business involved fictitious or sham productions. A highly respectable British producer, Richard Driscoll, who contributed to the first modern 3D British film, was charged in 2011 with VAT evasion.

Driscoll was the director of a few companies based in Cornwall, including Higher Nanpean Film Studios Ltd., House of Fear Ltd., House of Fear Film Production Ltd. and Grindhouse Films Ltd.

In his studios, he produced horror movies, some starring reputed actors. In 2009 he produced *Eldorado*, starring David Carradine, Daryl Hannah and Peter O'Toole, and in 2008 he produced *Evil Calls*, starring Norman Wisdom, Rik Mayall and Jason Donovan.

Between January 2009 and September 2011 Driscoll falsified invoices for the cost of making films in order to get a VAT refund. He claimed that the production cost of his movies represented more than 9 million pounds when in reality they accounted for less than 1 million pounds. Based on these false claims he defrauded HMRC of 1.5 million pounds.

Compared to other VAT frauds on services, the frauds in the moviemaking sector consisted of smaller gangs with a reduced number of companies involved in the criminal process. The key of such VAT frauds was to mislead the tax offices into believing that the inflated cost of moviemaking was actually real. Indeed, in Driscoll's case, the cost of a few million pounds would not appear as exaggerated for a movie starring A-list actors.

Other connections

The range of services touched on by VAT fraud is very wide, two cases of VAT fraud on data acquisition and accounting services being presented in the following.

---

99   www.coventrytelegraph.net/news/coventry-news/coventry-man-part-6m-bollywood-5262294.

100   Coventry man part of £6 million Bollywood scam on the run (www.coventrytelegraph.net/news/coventry-news/coventry-man-part-6m-bollywood-5262294).

101   www.mynewsdesk.com/uk/hm-revenue-customs-hmrc/pressreleases/film-producer-guilty-of-vat-fraud-873946.

Jason Butler[102]

The recent case related to the British businessman Jason Butler[103] exposes a rather unusual VAT fraud with the purchase of data. Butler controlled a United Kingdom-based company called Multi Level Media. Through this company he claimed trades of Payment Protection Insurance (PPI) customer data from nine British companies via an international agency which he also controlled. The investigation revealed that no trade of PPI data occurred, and Butler had created hundreds of fake invoices. In reality, he traded cheap raw data with United Kingdom-based firms. The data was then sold to a respectable data company in Gibraltar, which resold it to a company in the United States, controlled also by Butler. These trades generated significant VAT liabilities that Butler paid to the HMRC. But it was the fake trades that generated the loss for the British taxpayers.

The fake trades were engineered between November 2011 and January 2015. Butler claimed that the total turnover of Multi Level Media throughout that period was around 60 million pounds and entailed a 9.8 million pound loss for the British tax office. The proceeds of the tax evasion were sent through offshore accounts.

VAT fraud on data is similar in many ways to the fraud on CO_2 quotas, in both cases the entire trading infrastructure being internet-based. Data can easily be circulated from one server to another at a very fast pace. The advantage of data over CO_2 quotas from a fraudster perspective is the fact that the price of data has a strong subjective component, while in the case of CO_2 quotas the price was quoted on the market.

Geoffrey Copp[104]

In 2017, the Copp family appeared in the British media after being charged with a 45 million pounds VAT fraud. Geoffrey Copp, his brother Andrew and his son Joshua ran a payroll business for low-wage temporary workers, the majority of which were migrants. The family controlled a company called Central Payroll Specialists, later rebranded as Quality and Premiere Services. They provided payroll services to recruitment companies, VAT being charged to their customers. It is a common practice in the United Kingdom for big companies to employ temporary workers. The workers are paid either through their limited company or through a payroll company (called an umbrella). In theory, a payroll company invoices the big firm with VAT for the services of the temporary workers, pays the salaries of the workers and reimburses quarterly the VAT to HMRC.

---

102 www.mynewsdesk.com/uk/hm-revenue-customs-hmrc/pressreleases/ferrari-driving-fraudster-jailed-for-ps9-dot-8m-international-tax-fraud-2459740.

103 www.dailymail.co.uk/news/article-5548449/Yorkshire-businessman-masterminded-9-8m-VAT-fraud-fund-lavish-lifestyle.html.

104 www.dailymail.co.uk/news/article-4589048/Family-stole-45m-VAT-scam-jailed-27-years.html.

The Copps declared a 20 million pound turnover of their business, when in reality it was more than 250 million pounds. Thus, the Copps never declared the VAT for all the business they made, a fact that entailed a 45 million pound loss in tax for HMRC. Moreover, the Copps paid between 2009 and 2015 just 16,000 pounds in tax income.

The Copp brothers had had previous troubles with the law. Geoffrey had been convicted of acting as a company director while being banned from taking such a position after a bankruptcy. His brother Andrew had been indicted for handling stolen goods and possession of cocaine.

Payroll companies do process big sums of money, and in the payroll services a VAT fraud would not be easy to spot. It was Joshua Copp's activity on social media, showing his lifestyle, that brought the attention of authorities.

In the United Kingdom and across the EU, payroll companies (umbrella companies) play a big role in providing temporary workforces for big public and private companies. These companies work closely with recruitment agencies of low-skilled workers, most of them coming from Eastern European countries. These companies operate in areas with murky regulation as the European law for the temporary workers within the EU is not genuine. Some of these firms are causing not only VAT fraud but also income tax fraud and benefit frauds.

11 How the VAT fraud reshaped the criminal underworld

I knew that the Indians held the VAT business in England. So I looked for my Indian. I was in the lobby of the hotel, I had tea. He was sitting in front of me. We looked at each other; he approached me. I cannot tell you why but he immediately trusted me. All my life, I've had meetings like this. I must have something extra, right? Five minutes later, we talked business. He unblocked me on the spot a cargo of mobile phones. There was 5 million pound.[1]

Cyril Astruc, VAT fraudsters

The fall of 'old moustache Petes'

The term *'old moustache Petes'* is the name given by members of the American 'La Cosa Nostra' to traditional and conservative older members. The term originated in the 1920s, during the *Castellammarese* war amongst the old-school faction of the New York Sicilian mafia and the newer wave of more Americanized mobsters, *the Young Turks*.

During the 1990s the various crime syndicates suffered a profound mutation from 'blue-collar' rackets into more sophisticated 'white-collar' economic crimes. In the midst of this transformation, the organized crime changed in terms of structure and configuration. The profits from traditional criminal activities involving 'street-type' gangster crimes shrunk significantly and brought a lot of attention from both media and investigators. The economies of developed countries migrated gradually from predominantly manufacturing-type to services-oriented. The manufacturing-type economies have a few characteristics that allowed the flourishing development of organized crime. The presence of a blue-collar population segment with low wages, the massive use of cash transactions and the strong dependency of material facilities and infrastructures (building, factories and transportation) were proper conditions for illegal activities like racketeering, loan sharing, gambling or unions' greasing. The migration towards services-oriented economies declined the power and influence of the old generation of massive criminals.

1 www.vanityfair.fr/pouvoir/politique/articles/cyril-astruc-lescroc-du-siecle/27006.

DOI: 10.4324/9781315098722-11

Therefore, the old crime syndicates either died slowly or were massively re-shaped. The new economic crimes, including tax evasion, profited some factions or groups that managed to increase their power.[2] In Europe, for example, the Sicilian syndicates from Italy lost supremacy to their Calabrian neighbours, 'Ndrangheta. With the increased pressure of law enforcement the Sicilians did not manage to get a proper stake in the new economic crime. This, despite the fact that they were amongst the pioneers of financial crime during the 1980s, with the scandals involving Michele Sindona and the Bank of Vatican (Instituto per gli Opere Religiose).

The same thing happened with thieves in law (*'vhor-v-zakone'*) in the ex-Soviet zone. If, in the 1980s, the *vhors* sat at the top of the criminal trophic chain in the USSR, during the 1990s their power faded away and was replaced by gangs formed by the small crooks, sportsmen and war veterans who formed the *'bratva'* or the brotherhoods, with less rules and the old *vhor* system. The most reputed were Solnsevo, Tambovskaya and Ismailovskaya. But, after the 2000s, the 'brat-vas' were slowly replaced by the Russian-speaking organized crime. The same trend was observed in the ex-Yugoslavian organized crime that lost slowly its influence in the European crime world.

In the United Kingdom the traditional organized crime was slowly replaced by foreign groups, a fact also explained by the gentrification of cities and the attrition of the working class.

The large amount of funds defrauded through Value Added Tax (VAT) empowered new groups that emerged in the transition described earlier.

Emergence of new crime groups

'Ndrangheta: a stronger group

Italy is one of the countries with the biggest losses in the European Union (EU). Table 11.1 shows a few examples of operations of the Italian police against VAT fraudsters. An unadvised reader would be tempted to believe that behind all these frauds is one of the four crime syndicates from Southern Italy. But surprisingly, traditional organized crime is less present than expected in VAT fraud. The only exception is the Calabrian 'Ndrangheta.

'Ndrangheta was in the centre of two frauds that struck the financial markets in the EU during the late 2000s: the Voice over Internet Protocol (VoIP) and the CO_2 allowance tax fraud. Both frauds accounted for billions of euros in criminal profits. The Calabrian clans benefitted largely from those funds, thereby putting them in a stronger position in the globalized world of crime.

2 The classification of the following groups is done depending on a number of factors, including country of origin, ethnicity, language, political views or religious orientation. This association does not reflect in any way a causality between these factors and the occurrence of these new criminal groups. Thus, the taxonomy would be more accessible and easier to understand for readers with less expertise in the criminality.

Table 11.1 Summary of main operations of Italian law enforcement against VAT fraudsters

Operation	Year	Fraud underlying	Amount
Phuncards	2003	Cards	34
Traffico Telefonico	2004–2006	VoIP	330
Round Trip[1]	2016	Technology devices	200
IVA bevuta[2]	2016	Beverages	20
Forlì[3]	2017	Electronic products	60
Sharp[4]	2018	Plastic packages	1.7
Green Fees[5]	2010	CO_2 emissions	500
Car Jumping[6]	2018	Luxury cars	10
Good Platts[7]	2018	Fuel	25
Sogni d'Oro[8]	2018	Gold	10
Rambo[9]	2017	Electronic products	60
Paper-one[10]	2018	Paper and office consumables	14

1 www.fiscooggi.it/dal-mondo/articolo/italia-sulle-frodi-iva-truffasi-fa-ancora-piu-sofisticata.
2 www.padovaoggi.it/cronaca/frodi-fiscali-finanza-padova-operazione-iva-bevuta-arrestata-lady-fatture-false.html.
3 http://bologna.repubblica.it/cronaca/2017/07/21/news/forli_scoperta_maxi_frode_da_60_milioni-171319446/.
4 www.tarantinitime.it/2018/03/15/operazione-sharp-scoperta-frode-iva-per-17-milioni-di-euro-nei-guai-un-imprenditore-barese-ed-i-suoi-due-prestanome/.
5 www.blitzquotidiano.it/cronaca-italia/truffa-co2-frode-500-milioni-684994/.
6 https://roma.corriere.it/notizie/cronaca/18_febbraio_05/frosinone-vendevano-auto-lusso-frode-fisco-16-denunciati-704f0a7e-0a69-11e8-aeb9-f008c9e7034a.shtml.
7 www.gdf.gov.it/stampa/ultime-notizie/anno-2018/marzo/operazione-good-platts-associazione-per-delinquere-finalizzata-alla-frode-fiscale.
8 www.ilmetapontino.it/index.php/component/k2/item/32586-operazione-sogni-d-oro-si-ipotizza-maxi-frode-iva.
9 www.gonews.it/2017/02/08/frode-carosello-nel-settore-hi-tech-fatture-false-per-60-milioni-di-euro/.
10 http://giornaledimonza.it/attualita/fatture-false-ed-evasione-delliva-lideatore-della-frode-e-un-monzese.

Israeli groups

The VAT fraud on the CO_2 emissions markets exposed the international dimension of Israeli organized crime. The Israeli mafia had been reputed since the 1980s for its involvement in drug trafficking, extortions and other violent crimes. The Israeli underworld is dominated by a dozen families, most of them being of Sephardic descent from Northern Africa. Indeed, in the '*Carbon Connection*' most of the French-Israeli criminals were originally from Tunisia. The *Aliyah* of the Jewish community from the ex-Soviet countries that started in the 1980s added new features to the Israeli milieu. Russian and Georgian criminals of Jewish descent, reputed in the ex-Soviet space (especially in the Odessa region), found in Israel the promised land for deploying their new operations. The ex-Soviets did not attempt to move into the territory of the already-established Israeli families but used their new country as a platform for deploying global economic crimes.

Throughout the 2000s, the Israeli technology sector boomed, and the supply of qualified technology experts was leveraged by the criminal groups. Thus,

Israeli criminal groups moved towards a new type of white-collar crime, including VAT fraud, card skimming and social engineering.[3]

Russian-speaking Organized Crime

The widely spread term 'Russian Mafia', or 'Red Mafia' or 'KGB Mafia', is as misleading as a term can be. Russian Mafia is not an accurate term due to the fact that within criminal groups from ex-Soviet spaces Russian ethnics were and are not the majority. Moreover the top positions in power are detained by non-Russians.

After the fall of the traditional criminal structure from the ex-Soviet Union (*vhor-v-zakone*), a new amorphous criminal system took over. It is constituted of different criminal groups of different ethnicities that have in common the use of the Russian language and some kind of belonging to the ex-Soviet (sub)culture. Georgian, Chechenian, Azerbaijani, Armenian, Ukrainian or Dagestani groups are in many cases misclassified as 'Russian Mafia', while in reality they are different crime groups. In fact, the criminals of Russian ethnicity are a minority in this new picture of post-Soviet crime. Most Russian criminals who were part of the old traditional crime milieu left Russia for Europe or the United States, being chased by the newer groups or by the Russian Federal Security Service (FSB) since the early 2000s. These groups are in many cases allies but in other instances are rivals.

One of the hubs of intersection of all those Russian-speaking groups is Spain. Georgian criminals and some Russians from the old guard have found refuge there since the late 1990s. Spain is one of the countries with the biggest VAT loss entailed to fraud, and the ex-Soviet groups cut their piece of illegal proceeds.

In 2017, after a long investigation the National Court of Justice of Spain indicted prominent figures of the Russian crime groups for VAT fraud and money laundering.[4] Among those accused were Gennady Petrov (one of the leaders of the '*Tambovskaya*' crime group) and Alexander Malyshev (the leader of the '*Malyshevskaya*' group). The Spanish court accused also high-ranking Russian officials, including Vladislav Reznik, State Duma deputy, and his wife, Diana Gindin; Igor Sobolevsky, former Deputy Head of the Federal Drug Control Service; Nikolai Aulov, State Duma deputy; Yury Salikov; and Leonid Khristoforov. In 2009, Yuri Salikov was already sentenced in Spain to 2.5 years in jail for VAT fraud of over 20 million euros.

Romanian and Bulgarian groups

Romania and Bulgaria appear with the biggest VAT losses in the EU. The laxity of justice in both countries, along with the systemic corruption, was pointed out as the main reason why tax evasion reached those proportions. While this might be the reason why the VAT fraud is a serious phenomenon, the proliferation of the fraud has its origin in the structural issues of the society in both countries.

---

3 https://fr.timesofisrael.com/le-sentier-larnaque-au-president-au-co2-forex-et-les-call-centers-en-israel/.

4 https://en.crimerussia.com/organizedcrime/investigative-committee-and-federal-drug-control-service-management-ex-deputies-served-with-spanish-/.

First, both countries were far from having the success of the Baltics or the Czech Republic in their European journey. The economic growth in Romania and Bulgaria is fragile, despite having the biggest figures in the EU. The taxation policies have observed massive fluctuation over the years, and the taxation codes of both countries are presented in a cryptic language. These structural factors push in many cases the entrepreneurs towards tax evasion. The region experienced an unprecedented phenomenon of population dislocation, between 30% and 50% of the workforce having migrated to other countries, mainly in the EU. Therefore many families have multiple residences and have tax liabilities in multiple countries, thereby making any assessment relative to their status difficult. The migratory effect is a serious enabler for VAT fraud as tax authorities in one country would have a hard time investigating a family with business in few jurisdictions. Sectors like transportation, construction and caregiving services are structurally exposed to VAT fraud.

Romania and Bulgaria are also a hub of intersection for various criminal groups from the ex-Soviet Union, Southern Italy, Israel and the Middle East. These versed criminals can easily leverage their experience for defrauding the local taxpayers.

The last, but not the least, important factor contributing to the VAT fraud is the minority Romani population, representing more than 10% of the population in both countries. This ethnic group is organized in big clans and has a semi-nomadic way of life. Their traditional wing lives in almost a parallel society, with its own justice system and set of laws. The people from these groups divide their life amongst a few European countries and in their majority master at least two or three languages from a very young age. They have a strong position in the organized crime in both countries, specializing in racketeering, extortion, prostitution and tax evasion.

Many companies investigated for tax evasion in Romania or Bulgaria have as director or legal representative a Romani ethnic with no fixed address living below the poverty level. Indeed, there are many cases in which criminal groups specializing in VAT fraud are profiting from the fact that some individuals from this minority are undocumented or live a nomadic lifestyle by using them as strawmen for companies defrauding tax. Thus, Bulgarian and Romanian law enforcements have a hard time investigating most VAT frauds and an even more complicated task in prosecuting the guilty persons.

The use of Romani[5] ethnics or socially disadvantaged citizens from Romania, Bulgaria and Greece has been extensively reported in the Bulgarian media since the late 2000s. Organized VAT fraud groups have registered, Romanian or Greek companies in the names of Bulgarian Romani. The other way works too, with Bulgarian companies being registered in the names of Romanian directors from a disadvantaged background. More than 50% of the companies with Romanian directors registered in Bulgaria fall under this configuration. Also a third of the companies registered for VAT in Bulgaria in 2011 have no real address. The loss in VAT for the Bulgarian taxpayers caused by these types of frauds was estimated to be 1 billion euros.

5 www.24chasa.bg/Article/836449.

One of the first cases was signalled in 2012, when the Romanian Agency for fighting organized crime (DIICOT)[6] raided companies controlled by members of the reputed '*Bratianu*' clan in Southern Romanian counties. Those companies were suspected of tax evasion of 10 million euros from selling oil products and sugar. The indictment aimed to dismantle a 28-strong group, which controlled 20 firms involved in VAT fraud. The group imported petroleum products (gas oil, petrol and oils) from Bulgaria, which they introduced and sold in the territory of Romania without paying the related taxes and duties. The fraudsters produced false documents stating that the goods had either been returned to Bulgaria or exported to Hungary to various companies controlled by the members of the group. In the same way, large amounts of sugar and sunflower oil were claimed to be exported, while in reality the goods were produced at different factories in Romania and were sold in supermarkets across the country.

In 2012, four members of the '*Stanescu*'[7] clan active in the northern counties of Romania were investigated by the police for tax evasion and money laundering. Members of the clan had set up 14 trading companies, and based on fictitious invoices they generated a turnover of 11 million euros and a VAT loss of 1.7 million euros for the taxpayers. The companies were also used to launder the proceeds of the fraud.

The 2012 crackdown on Romanian VAT gangs hit also the '*Butoane*' clan,[8] and several employees of the Romanian Economic Police were arrested for tax fraud, representing nearly 25 million euros of unpaid VAT. The criminal network consisted of 120 individuals and 25 companies grouped into suppliers, beneficiary firms and intermediary firms. Most companies did not fill tax returns, did not justify the origin of their goods, did not pay VAT and did not operate at their declared premises. Sixteen companies of the criminal network had 'normal behaviour', giving the impression of real economic activity. Nevertheless, they recorded unrealistic purchases from vendors who did not recognize those transactions and made fictitious sales to other companies. The criminal activity was supported by Octavian Grecu, head of the '*Butoane*' clan. The activity of the criminal group was aimed at intra-Community trade in sugar and was surrounded by companies or groups of companies Lemarco SA Bucharest (represented by Tudor Constantin), Ductil Rom SA Bucharest (represented by Sorin Stuparu), Novicio Food & Beverage SRL Ilfov (represented by Nicole Saikaly), Vega Trade Comodities SRL Giurgiu (represented by Sorin Adrian Găzdac) and Livia Ioana Găzdac. Another businessman, Viorel Bulearca, owner of the companies Bunbusinesselite BBE Ltd. and Stefaris cigarette SRL, provided to the criminal network consumer goods (sugar, rice, vinegar and sunflower oil) used

6 www.antena3.ro/actualitate/evaziune-fiscala-de-10-000-000-euro-clanul-bratianu-din-valcea-a-fost-destructurat-188539.html.
7 adevarul.ro/locale/iasi/membri-clanului-stanescu-dati-urmarire-evaziune-fiscala-spalare-bani-foto-1_50aef2e77c42d5a663a1da43/index.html.
8 www.gandul.info/stiri/reteaua-clanului-butoane-cum-functiona-si-cati-bani-a-rulat-grupul-de-evazionisti-protejati-de-anaf-exclusiv-9902245.

in the tax evasion. The goods were acquired by SC Novicio Food & Beverage SRL. Representatives of the tax office and of the treasury were also indicted by prosecutors.

Another relevant example is an investigation that took place in 2015 in the Timis county in Romania involving the notorious criminal clan '*Novacovici*'. Between 2013 and 2015, 12 persons associated with the clan served as legal representatives of the four companies with headquarters declared in Timis county and never paid the VAT liabilities. They would have recorded in the companies' accounts several tax invoices issued on the basis of commercial fictitious transactions, representing purchases and deliveries of ferrous and non-ferrous materials for which they artificially diminished the tax liabilities.

The Romanian Economic Police[9] dismantled in 2017 a network of 72 companies that were involved in fictitious trading circuits of meat and meat products with the final aim of defrauding VAT, resulting in a 10 million euro loss for the Romanian taxpayers. The companies were suspected of having purchased livestock from private farmers but recorded fictitious invoices from ghost companies. The group has simulated intra-Community trade operations consisting of deliveries of meat and meat products to clients from Bulgaria, Hungary and Poland. The legal representatives of the investigated companies were in fact strawmen from a disadvantaged background.

The Bulgarian prosecutors dismantled in May 2017 a nine-strong crime group for tax crimes with luxury cars. Seven members of the group were employed in a vehicle insurance company, MM Insurance Broker Ltd.[10] The group stole 0.8 million euros of tax between 2015 and 2017.

The luxury cars were imported from Germany and were registered in Bulgaria in the name of companies controlled by the gang. In order to avoid paying the VAT due for a car, the hollow company took fictitious purchases of other goods at approximately the same price and thus deducted the VAT. Thereafter, the cars were transferred several times to fake firms or to individuals and ultimately to leasing companies which sold them to final buyers.

The Varna region, at the shore of the Black Sea, has harboured since the early 1990s a high concentration of criminal figures. Many VAT fraud cases are investigated and prosecuted in the Varna region, as exemplified by the following:

- Four defendants[11] were prosecuted at the Regional Prosecutor's Office in Varna for avoiding the payment of 0.3 million euros in VAT. The gang leader Raycho Il. already had 11 convictions behind him, including tax crimes and even human trafficking across borders.

---

9 www.vrancea24.ro/antifrauda-descoperit-o-retea-de-evaziune-fiscala-de-zeci-de-milioane-de-lei-domeniul-procesarii-carnii/.
10 https://news.bg/crime/sadyat-zastrahovateli-za-izmama-s-milioni-dds.html.
11 https://news.bg/crime/osadiha-4-ma-za-650-hil-lv-dds-izmama-vav-varna.html.

- In 2016, another VAT fraud investigation ended with three convictions[12] and six acquittal convictions for VAT offences at the Varna District Court. The court convicted Yanko Yanev for defrauding 1 million euros of VAT between 2006 and 2008 as representative of EuroCommerce 01 Ltd. The court also convicted Daniel Naydenov and Gancho Ganev from Varna for VAT crimes. They were tax inspectors in Varna and worked in complicity with Yanev.
- In 2016, the Bulgarian Prosecutor's Office in Varna[13] condemned Chavdar P. to five years in prison and Theodor K. to three years in jail for VAT evasion and illegal possession of fire guns. The two defrauded 250,000 euros of VAT, the funds being laundered through a third person, Plamen Ang., sentenced to 1.5 years imprisonment and to avoiding the establishment and payment of VAT in particularly large amounts.

Baltic groups

After the fall of the Soviet Union, the Baltic countries followed an accelerated track of integration into the EU. They became success stories in the EU adopted the Euro and joined the International Monetary Fund's (IMF's) list of advanced countries. Despite being in the EU the Baltic countries still have strong economic ties to the ex-Soviet zone. Since the fall of the Soviet Union, the Baltic region has been confronted with an increasing threat of organized crime. After the three countries joined the EU the presence of organized crime increased massively due to the fact that the Baltics served as a buffer between ex-Soviet countries and the EU. Indeed, these small countries have a significant Russian minority which accounts for between 30% and 40% of their populations, and members of which have ties to the Russian Federation. In the 2000s the Russian-speaking organized crime used the position of the Baltics to transfer funds from and to the EU. Until recently Latvia was on the list of tax-havens with limited cooperation with respect to money laundering.

The VAT losses due to fraud for the Baltic countries are above the average of the EU. VAT scammers were attracted by the unique position of the Baltics, and over the past years tax evasion has become a serious issue. Moreover, Baltic countries have strong harbour infrastructures, being an important hub for maritime trading at the Baltic Sea. The import/export activities offer many opportunities for VAT fraudsters, as shown in the following examples.

---

12 www.monitor.bg/bg/a/view/73418-%D0%9E%D1%81%D1%8A%D0%B4%D0%B8%D1
   %85%D0%B0-%D1%83%D1%81%D0%BB%D0%BE%D0%B2%D0%BD%D0%BE-%D0%B
   1%D0%B8%D0%B7%D0%BD%D0%B5%D1%81%D0%BC%D0%B5%D0%BD-%D0%B8-
   %D0%B4%D0%B2%D0%B0%D0%BC%D0%B0-%D0%B4%D0%B0%D0%BD%D1%8A%D
   1%87%D0%BD%D0%B8-%D0%B7%D0%B0-%D0%94%D0%94%D0%A1%D0%B8%D0%B
   7%D0%BC%D0%B0%D0%BC%D0%B0/.
13 https://novavarna.net/2016/11/28/2-%D0%BF%D1%80%D0%B8%D1%81%D1%8
   A%D0%B4%D0%B8-%D0%B7%D0%B0-%D0%B4%D0%B4%D1%81-%D0%B8%D0%
   B7%D0%BC%D0%B0%D0%BC%D0%B0-%D0%B7%D0%B0-%D0%B1%D0%BB%D0%B8%
   D0%B7%D0%BE-600-000-%D0%BB%D0%B5%D0%B2%D0%B0/.

The increase of the VAT fraud during the late 2000s in Lithuania was so sharp that law enforcement set up a Risk Analysis Centre which joined analytical capacities and available data in order to identify instances of tax fraud and organize their investigation.

Additionally, Lithuanian law enforcement increased its cooperation with European agencies like Europol and Eurofisc, and completed between 2010 and 2014 nine joint investigations with tax administrations from various EU Member States, conceding VAT frauds of more than 25 million euros. As a result, in the first month of 2013 the Lithuanian tax office[14] dismantled VAT scam rings that had caused losses of 20 million euros and indicted 76 people. One of the biggest cases involved a VAT fraud network of more than ten Lithuanian companies specializing in importing sugar, which defrauded 10 million euros.

Being a hub trading and an international financial platform Lithuania attracted international criminal groups associated with the Italian mafia who developed VAT scams and money laundering activities. In 2013[15] the Vilnius Regional Prosecutor's Office concluded investigations on a carousel fraud scheme initiated by Italian companies with activities in Lithuania. Two Italian companies established in Lithuania specialized in the international trade of precious metals. The investigation started due to suspicious transactions of very large amounts of cash from domestic banks to overseas accounts as well as funds received from foreign countries on behalf of companies registered in other countries.

Companies operating in Lithuania, Bulgaria, the Netherlands, Italy, Slovenia and the United Kingdom, allegedly dealing with metals, were involved in laundering the proceeds of the VAT fraud. The Italian masterminds were also involved in drug trafficking and used the network of companies to launder the proceeds of narcotics sale. A total of 1.4 million euros were seized by the Lithuanian police from the two Italian citizens. The turnover of the carousel was 150 million euros, and VAT was defrauded mainly in Italy, Great Britain and Bulgaria for 30 million euros, while the Lithuanian taxpayers lost 100,000 euros.

Other transnational investigations of the Lithuanian police revealed VAT rings with interesting geographic geometries as follows:

- Lithuania, Latvia, Poland and Cyprus, with VAT fraud in the sale of petroleum products;
- Lithuania and Sweden VAT fraud in the sale of second-hand cars;
- Lithuania, Finland, Estonia, Latvia and Germany, with VAT fraud on clothes;
- Lithuania, Latvia and Estonia, with VAT fraud on household electrical goods;
- Lithuania and Holland, with VAT carousel on flowers and 'second-hand' cars, causing 1.5 million euros of losses between 2008 and 2012; and
- Lithuania and Poland, where an organized gang defrauded VAT through a carousel made up of tractors reselling for a total of 3 million euros.

14 www.15min.lt/verslas/naujiena/finansai/vmi-atskleidzia-kokius-didziausius-tyrimu-atlieka-siuo-metu-ir-kokios-sumos-nesumoketos-i-biudzeta-662-345933.
15 www.respublika.lt/lt/naujienos/lietuva/nusikaltimai_ir_nelaimes/italiska_mafija_sustabdyta_lietuvoje_atnaujinta_0819/,print.1.

The sector of luxury car[16] dealers was also affected by VAT fraud, as shown by reports from Latvia. Latvia is used as a platform for importing luxury cars (i.e., Bentley, Ferrari, BMW) from Germany for clients in the Russian Federation. In many cases this process involves smuggling, fake documents and VAT fraud. A car valued at 70,000 euros of VAT would account for 14 thousands euros. Avoiding the VAT payment would make a luxury much cheaper for the final client. A typical fraud on luxury cars has the following steps:

- A Lithuanian car dealer buys a car from a German supplier in Germany.
- A temporary registration of a car issues transit numbers to export a car to Lithuania in the name of a Lithuanian company. The technical documents of the car are easily forged because the technical passports issued by Lithuanian authorities have no validity date. This scheme is used to disguise the fact that the machine has not been sold to Lithuania as a destination because VAT would then be applied.
- The car dealer has a parent company in Estonia, for example, which resells the car to a car dealer in Latvia.
- The car is registered to the Latvian company.
- The car is re-registered in Latvia in the name of another Latvian company. The car registration does not appear in the books of the firm. Later this company will have a new director in a citizen from Moldova, Belarus or Tajikistan.
- Finally, the car is sold to its final owner – a physical or legal person from the Russian Federation. The last company in the circuit can be reimbursed of VAT from the Latvian government. The time gap between resales of the car in the circuit is one or two days, and the number of the resale is around seven.

Over the past five years the number of cases of VAT fraud investigated in Latvia significantly increased, as proven by the following examples:

- In 2014, the Latvian Financial Police stopped a VAT fraud scam that stole 11 million euros. The scam involved more than 60 fictitious companies, mainly involved in construction, trade in petroleum products and trade in various goods and services.
- In July 2015[17] the Latvian Financial Police dismantled a VAT fraud and money laundering ring. Between 2014 and 2015, the group obtained unjustified VAT refunds of more than 3 million euros. The groups used 35 companies, both real and fictitious, representing different fields of activity – international freight transport, retail and wholesale. The individuals from the groups were already asked to prosecute and have a criminal past.

---

16 http://nra.lv/latvija/191115-nra-atmasko-bledibas-premium-klases-automobilu-tirgunoziedzigas-pvn-shemas-un-naudas-izkrapsana.htm.
17 www.delfi.lv/news/national/criminal/63-kratisanas-35-uznemumi-9-aizturetie-aptur-verienigu-krapsanas-shemu.d?id=46199325.

- In 2016, a VAT fraud scandal erupted with two Latvian environmental companies – E-Daugava and Eko Ltd. – specializing in recycling used tires, suspected of fictitious economic activity. The most interesting thing in this case is that the tire recycling project received about half a million euros of EU financing.
- In November 2017 the Financial Police Department[18] dismantled a criminal group which had defrauded 900,000 euros of VAT since April 2016. More than 20 Latvian companies and several companies from Lithuania, Great Britain, the Czech Republic and Poland, the main activity of which was the sale of office equipment and office supplies, were involved in the activity of the criminal group.

Tax administration representatives were involved in many cases in VAT frauds. For instance in 2016,[19] an employee of the Latvian tax office was arrested for organizing a fraudulent VAT that resulted in a 1.6 million euro loss. He was essentially the brain of a criminal group specializing in large-scale VAT carousel scams. Another example was signalled in 2013, when Agnese Leimane, a Latvian tax office employee, was arrested for organizing VAT fraud with three entrepreneurs.

Asian English-speaking groups

The evolution of VAT fraud in Great Britain from the 1970s until recently underlined a massive dislocation in the criminal underworld. English and Irish criminal groups were slowly replaced by British-Asian groups of Pakistani and Indian descent. The turning point occurred in the late 1990s. If, in the early years of the *Hatton Garden Connection* and the Stoke-on-Trent, the tax evaders were mainly English or Irish, in the early 2000s, Asian groups became the major stakeholder of the VAT fraud in the United Kingdom. This trend was underlined during the *Carbon Connection* when the British-Pakistani groups pocketed a big share of the total defrauded VAT. The groups used the various ties in Dubai and Pakistan or India in order to launder the proceeds of crime. The Asian English-speaking crime groups are the fastest-growing criminal network in the United Kingdom, Europe and worldwide.

18 www.lsm.lv/raksts/zinas/latvija/vid-pieker-biroja-tehnikas-un-kancelejas-precu-tirgonus-pvn-izkrapsana.a258849/.
19 http://procesilatvija.lv/lv/vertejumi-un-analize/pazudusa-tirgotaja-karuselis-vai-pvn-shemotaji/.

12 Investigating the VAT fraud

Vint'un anni lavoraru sutt'a terra
Pi fundari li reguli sociali
Leggi d'onore, di sangue, di guerra
Leggi maggiori, minori e criminali[1]

Calabrian folk song

'Anthropological' approaches

'Anthropological' approaches or ground investigations are the most straightforward ways of digging into most types of crimes. Value Added Tax (VAT) fraud is no exception from this postulate. The parallel with anthropology is grounded in the fact that in the recent past fraudsters specializing in VAT have had particular features and ways of organizing their scams. Therefore, VAT fraud cannot be treated like any other type of tax evasion. The banking systems and tax offices are massively overwhelmed with a multitude of white-collar crimes, and VAT frauds are not always on the top of their pile of investigations. Moreover, VAT fraud occurs in markets with a high level of technicality, including rights to pollute, telecommunication traffic, cloud computing capacity, etc. Investigating VAT in those markets would require a cutting-edge knowledge of the respective technologies. Therefore, law enforcements are, in many cases, overpassed by the complexity of the frauds, and the simple surveillance of VAT fillings or bank transfers do not provide useful alerts.

Thus, many investigations of VAT frauds start with whistle-blowers, informants, or even journalists. 'Anthropological' techniques require first a good understanding of the VAT fraud milieu encompassing the main groups and their main operative areas. Fighting traditional organized crime in countries like Italy, Russia and the United States required paradigm shifts in the way law enforcement was dealing with the crime spree. Traditional approaches needed to be adapted to the way organized crime functioned. A deep understanding of the 'cultural' aspect of the organized crimes was needed in order to build a framework able to stem those groups.

---

1 Twenty years they worked underground to found the social rules, Laws of honour, blood and war, Big, minor and criminal laws.

DOI: 10.4324/9781315098722-12

The VAT fraud groups will surely not develop into religious mysticisms like the groups from Southern Italy, parallel social systems like the Russian 'vhors' or even political whims like 'Gokudos' in Japan. But what makes VAT fraudsters unique is their capacity to absorb in real time financial and economic information from different regions of the globe, from different strata of society and from various silos of economy. Moreover, VAT fraudsters are in fact a true global community which exchanges tips and criminal best practices, bypassing the barriers related to race, political view, religion or ethnicity.

Therefore, the investigation techniques based only on data and analysis have limited success and need in fact to complement the ground investigation. Ground investigation does not guarantee success in tackling the VAT fraud. The various agencies and ruling bodies of the fight against tax evasion have still a limited range of cooperation and information exchange. If regionally some efforts are taken to improve this aspect at the global level law enforcements are still way behind tax evaders in terms of cooperation.

Interestingly enough, journalists have achieved significant success in uncovering major VAT frauds. Indeed, traditional investigative journalists are more connected to the streets than law enforcements. Also, they are less regulated and may have more freedom in their approaches compared to governmental bodies, including police or customs officers. Journalists also have a more solid international community, the members of which are capable of working together and sharing information. In many cases, whistle-blowers prefer journalists to law enforcements, judging that the awareness of the public will have a bigger and quicker impact than alerting the official investigators.

Structural approaches

The VAT fraud is estimated to be over 200 billion euros in the European Union (EU) only. The VAT evasion is linked to many other epiphenomena, including the informal economy, money laundering and terrorism financing. Thus, its impact on the mainstream economy is not negligible. VAT fraud can bring distortions in completion and alter the efficiency of markets. Analyzing the sectorial trends and the stability supply/demand equilibrium for different products can provide useful signals, thereby constituting a valuable complement to the ground investigations.

Lower retail prices in some regions or an increase in the number of transactions or deliveries can be valuable indicators for potential VAT fraud. Also, statistics of VAT balances in different regions or for different industries can provide indicators of ongoing VAT scams. Complex markets like CO_2 allowances or Voice over Internet Protocol (VoIP) are not easy to investigate, and the analysis of macro data from those markets can indicate abnormal behaviours. The sudden increase of CO_2 emissions allowances volumes traded on the *BlueNext* platform in 2009 is just an example underlining the importance of structural approaches.

Structural approaches are relevant beyond the scope of VAT fraud investigations. They can indicate trends in other areas of economic crime. VAT fraudsters are also involved in social benefit fraud, credit card scams, insurance fraud, application fraud and social engineering. The proceeds of all those crimes need to be laundered or transferred to safe harbours. Structural analysis of the trends in this sector can lead to crucial strategic intelligence on the avenues taken by criminal groups.

Data mining techniques

The use of technology-based solutions is the fastest-growing trend in fighting financial crime. If the analysis of structured data is well covered by most specialized providers, the unstructured data still has a few hurdles to jump. Information contained in text originated by humans is without any doubt richer and with a broader range than traditional numeric data sets. Crime investigation in a broad sense does rely massively on unstructured data from various sources: paper, electronic message, audio and video. If traditionally the exploration of unstructured data was done by attorneys and compliance officers, technology started to play a growing role, mainly with the increase of data volumes and with the need for speed in detecting signals about illegal acts. The amount of data embedded in the court documentation of *Operazione Phuncards-Brokers* is a relevant example of this aspect.

Financial crime investigation is one of the first areas of application for unstructured data mining. Information extraction allows investigators to assess quickly and in a structured manner data from emails, chats or other electronic documents. Sentiment analysis provides an additional feature by categorizing the documents in various classes (positive or negative sentiments, bullish or bearish market views, etc.) (Frunza, 2015).

The challenge of the unstructured data analysis is linked to the fact that documents, audio and video tracks have a high number of features and require an a priori background knowledge of the topic addressed in the language of the supports. Numeric structured data can be easier subjected to free mining or analysis without specific information about the set. Even a small set of documents (e.g., emails or tweets) contains a large number of patterns, hence the need for interactive informational exploration. The science dealing with the interpretation of human language, as it appears in written documents, emails, web pages or conversations, is called natural language processing and has been developing since the 1950s.

Two topics relevant for VAT fraud investigations are discussed hereafter:

- text mining principles and
- multilingual name matching.

Text mining

Text mining can be defined as a process aiming to extract useful information from a collection of unstructured data sources through the identification and exploration of interesting patterns (Feldman, 2007). The text mining approaches aim to transform the information embedded in a document or conversation into a structured (numeric) frame.

With the increase of computing power, the methods for unstructured data exploration are able to leverage statistical and machine learning algorithms. Information extraction and sentiment analysis are the application of text mining relevant for crime investigations.

The aim of information extraction is to identify a set of objects and features contained in a text and the relationship between those objects. A simple way to achieve this is through text classification on the base of a predetermined set of categories: for instance, determining in a document the names of individuals, locations, phone numbers or quantitative info. For example in the following email excerpt, reproduced from the court documents for Operation *Phuncards-Broker*, text processing would be able to extract the numeric objects and tag their relations with the other objects:

(All-in) in 2005 we collected from Correspondents and Other Licensed Operators € **867M** compared to € **596m** in 2004 (+271) and paid € **881 M** compared to € **540m** in 2004 (+341). In the final analysis of third-party sales we should close **+ 5M** € approx. above Forecast2 of which approximately **-27M** € for traffic management (proportionally we paid more) and **+ 32M** € on Opex / Capex.[2]

From this email, an algorithm of information extractions would ideally tag 867 million euros as an incoming flow and 881 million euros as an outgoing flow.

Classification can be done through the rule-based approach or with (supervised) machine learning techniques. The machine learning algorithms are trained on initial datasets, which are already classified.

A frequently used information extraction technique is Part-of-Speech tagging (POS Tagging). POS tagging is a method that has as input a source of text written or expressed in a language and that assigns grammar parts of speech to each word, such as noun, verb, adjective, adverb, numerals, etc. POS tagging is generally the first step in analyzing supports containing human language.

Before tagging the text preprocessing is necessary to obtain a set of words (tokens) to process. Two steps are generally implemented: sentence detection and tokenization. Sentence boundary detection requires marking the start and the end of a sentence, a simple task that is complicated in documents containing abbreviations and titles. Tokenization is a process of converting sentences into chain words or tokens (word, punctuation) within a sentence. A straightforward example of preprocessing is given in the previous excerpt:

---

2 *(All- in) nel 2005 abbiamo incassato tra Corrispondenti e OLOs 867M€ contro i 596M€ del 2004 (+271) e abbiama pagato 881M€ contro i 540M€ del 2004 (+341). In ultima analisi sui saldi commerciali terzi dovremmo chiudere +5M€ ca. sopra il Forecast2 di cui circa -27M€ per gestione traffici (proporzionalmente abbiamo pagato di più) e +32M€ su Opex/Capex.* (Original in Italian, Source: *Operazione Phuncards-Brokers* PROCEDIMENTO N. 6429/2006, page 721).

In 2005 we collected from Correspondents and Other Licensed Operator € 867M compared to € 596m in 2004 and paid € 881 M compared to € 540m in 2004.[3]

A POS algorithm would recognize that *we* is a pronoun, *collected* is a verb, *paid* is a verb.

Nevertheless, some words can be assigned to various POS tags. The word *paid*, for example, can be easily (and wrongly) tagged as an adjective. The role of an appropriate POS tagging process is to assign the right tags given the context. Given a set of N words $\{w_1, w_2, ..., w_N\}$ the POS tagging should find the corresponding set of possible tags $\{t_1, t_2, ..., t_N\}$. There are a few approaches to doing this: rule-based and machine learning methods. Machine learning techniques are either generative or discriminative. Generative methods are based on models of probability distributions. Discriminative methods estimate posterior probabilities based on observations. Logistic regression and conditional random fields (CRFs) are examples of discriminative methods, while Naive Bayes classifiers and hidden Markov models (HMMs) are examples of generative methods (Nadkarni, 2011).

Sentiment and opinion analysis is a specific type of classification which aims to assess the opinions, sentiments, evaluations, preferences, choices, review, views, emotions, etc., expressed in a set of documents. For example in the following email excerpt from the court evidence in Operation *Phuncards-Broker*, the sentiment analysis would indicate a negative opinion.

The information on the Acumen company is incorrect, as they reported news about Acumen Group and not about Acumen Ltd.[4]

Multilingual name matching

When investigating VAT frauds one big challenge is to establish links between people who have businesses or bank accounts in various countries and use variations of their names. The variations are explained in many cases by fraudsters' intention to create multiple identities. But name variations can be easily created when names are transposed in languages with different alphabets. Examples of name variations are presented in Table 12.1, encompassing examples of individuals investigated for alleged crimes in the *Carbon Connection*.

Name variations can also originate from versions of the same name in different languages. For example the Persian name Rostam has variations like Rustem and Rustam; it becomes Rüstem in Turkish, Röstäm in Tatar, مٽسور in Arabic, מתסור in Hebrew and Рустем in Kazakh. Name variations can be due to differences in pronunciation and differences in spelling. For example, the Russian name Михаил has a Ukrainian counterpart Міхайло. A person with such a name,

---

3 nel 2005 abbiamo incassato tra Corrispondenti e OLOs 867M€ contro i 596M€ del 2004 e abbiama pagato 881M€ contro i 540M€ del 2004 (Original in Italian, Source: *Operazione Phuncards-Brokers* PROCEDIMENTO N. 6429/2006, page 721).

4 Le informazioni sulla società Acumen sono errate, in quanto hanno riportato notizie su Acumen Group e non su Acumen Ltd. (Original in Italian, Source: *Operazione Phuncards-Brokers* PROCEDIMENTO N. 6429/2006, page 721).

Table 12.1 Name versions in several languages for some individuals investigated in the Carbon Connection

Language	Yannick Dacheville	Gregory Zaoui	Jaroslaw Klapucki
Russian	Янник Дачевиль	Грегори Зауи	Ярослав Клапуцки
Hebrew	ליבשד קיני	יוז ירוגרג	יקצופלק בלסורי
English (transliteration from Russian)	Yannic Dashevilli	Gregory Zauy	Yaroslav Klapucky
English (transliteration from Hebrew)	Yinik Deshvil	Gregory Zoy	Yarslov Klaputzky

born in Ukraine during the Soviet era would have both of these names printed in their passports; the English spelling would be Mikhail, but nowadays the name would be spelled as Mykhailo (Erimolovici, 2001). In this way, one person can have two very different names both in spelling and in pronunciation.

Name matching can be defined as the process of determining whether two name strings are instances of the same name (Thompson, 2003). Given a name represented by String A in one language (possibly unspecified) and a name represented by String B in another language (possibly unspecified), a name matching algorithm would provide the likelihood that both names, A and B, represent the same person.

One approach is to convert name strings to some phonetic representation of how the name is actually pronounced, not written. The basic method of identifying whether two names are instances of the same name is comparing codes of the names. If the codes are equal, then the names match. If the codes are not equal, then the names do not match. A few of the popular phonetic matching methods are:

- 'Soundex' algorithm (Russell, 1918), which is the ancestor of phonetic name matching algorithms. Soundex maps names to a special code consisting of a letter and three digits. The letter is the first letter of the name, and the digits describe approximatively the consonants of the name. The initial aim of Soundex was to be easily manually computed and to be applied to paper documents. Its performance is relatively poor compared to more recent development.
- Match Rating Approach (MRA) (Moore, 1977), which employs a very basic process that transforms the string by deleting the vowels and double letters, thereby reducing the name to a maximum of six characters by retaining the first and the last three characters. After the two names are encoded the MRA compares the two strings. This approach can work for strings in multiple languages.
- Daitch-Mokotoff Soundex approach (Mokotoff, 1997), which consists of an alternation of the original Soundex for German and Slavic languages. In this algorithm names are given to six digit codes. The first letter is coded too (contrast to original Soundex, where the first letter was retained as it was). Names can have multiple codes, which is different from the original Soundex, where names are mapped to only one code.
- Beider-Morse Phonetic Matching (2008) (Beider, 2008), which is a modification of Daitch-Mokotoff Soundex aiming to work with multiple languages. One of the differences is that the first step is to identify the language, then language-specific rules are applied.

An alternative to phonetic analysis is the comparison of names as sequences of characters. The string-based analysis is generally formalized in terms of the distance between characters and their positions, without any phonetic information applied. Two popular distances used to name matching are:

- Levenshtein's distance (Levenshtein, 1966) between two strings, which is a metric representing the number of one character changes (substitute a character with another character, remove a character, insert a character) needed to change one word into another.
- Guth's algorithm (Guth, 1976), which was specifically designed to compare names. It takes two names as an input and as an output provides the probability that the two names are variants of the spelling of one name. Guth's algorithm compares two strings character by character, sometimes skipping or backtracking one or two characters.

Deep learning algorithms using the trained recurrent neural network 'Seq2seq', developed by Sutskever (2004), are providing promising results, especially for converting names from one language to another and assessing their matching probability.

13 Avenues of countering VAT fraud

He looks like he has been graduated from a correctional facility.

Sandra F., banking auditor

Over the past ten years authorities became aware of the threat represented by Value Added Tax (VAT) fraud and tried all kinds of measures to reduce the fraud. Yet the main view is that VAT fraud is inherent to global trade and is more like a 'cost of doing business' or an acceptable loss. The solutions exhibited in the following are based upon empirical observations from the recent cases of VAT fraud and are not classified in a comprehensive manner. A more structured approach to classifying the avenues of tackling VAT fraud is proposed by Bukhsh (2014), which distinguishes between: extended verification, disruption of criminal activity, cross-border cooperation, Reverse Charge, scrutiny of new VAT registration, real-time logging of trades and verification of counterparties, and collection of VAT in real time.

Quick fixes

Whenever a VAT fraud endemic hits a market, governments try to curb it with quick fixes aiming to reduce the incentive to pocket the VAT. Quick fixes do not solve the core issues because they are entailed by the laxity of the taxation systems and by the involvement of serious organized crime in tax evasion. Two types of quick fixes are discussed hereafter:

- the VAT exemption or zero rate and
- the reverse VAT charge.

VAT exemption

When the CO_2 emissions allowance market was touched by a massive VAT fraud in 2009, France and Great Britain opted to exempt CO_2 emissions permits from VAT. Thus, at that time, no reimbursements of VAT related to CO_2 allowances were possible. The number of transactions plummeted quickly after that measure, and the fraudsters moved to other countries where the VAT was still applicable (i.e., Italy).

DOI: 10.4324/9781315098722-13

VAT exemption or the zero rate VAT is an efficient short-term solution, aiming to curb tax evasion on a market heavily touched by fraud. But, from an economic perspective, VAT exemption could distort the competition amongst companies and markets. There is no sustainable rational in not taxing a product just because that market is targeted by fraudsters. Moreover, if the VAT exemption is not applied in all countries of an Economic Union, it could act as a catalyst of the fraud. For example if a country exempts VAT on a product, but another country keeps it, the first country will be in fact supplying cheaply that product in the second country where the VAT can still be defrauded. Therefore, the application of such a measure would require good coordination amongst the members of an Economic Union (i.e., European Union) in order to avoid a situation like that encountered in 2009 at the time of the *Carbon Connection*.

Reverse VAT charge

The domestic reverse VAT charge is the second measure undertaken by governments when massive VAT scams strike a sector. For instance, when the VAT carousel struck the CO_2 emissions market in July 2009 the Dutch government opted for a 'Reverse Charge', requiring all traders, including the domestic firms, to account for VAT at the time of purchase.

In practice, the domestic Reverse Charge mechanism means that no VAT is charged by the supplier to taxable customers who become liable for the payment of the VAT. The liable company with the right to deduct VAT on that specific transaction would declare and deduct VAT without charging it to its client and without paying it to the domestic Treasury (Kogels, 2010). Lind (2013) points out that in the context of the missing trader fraud the reverse taxation seems to be the most effective and easily applicable measure of the existing proposals which would considerably reduce tax fraud.

Originally, the concept of VAT Reverse Charge was introduced by the European Union (EU) in order to simplify trade within the Single Market. The Reverse Charge moves the responsibility for the reporting of a VAT transaction from the seller to the buyer of a good or service. This reduces the requirement for sellers to register for VAT in the country where the supply is made.

When a transaction is subject to Reverse Charge, the recipient of the goods or services reports both their purchase (input VAT) and the supplier's sale (output VAT) in their VAT return.[1] These two VAT fillings offset each other from a cash payment point of view, thereby involving no payment of VAT towards each other or towards their national Treasuries. Nevertheless the authorities have full visibility of the transactions.

Most sales between companies incorporated in different Member states are subject to a Reverse Charge for both goods and services. Additionally, there are many instances in which a domestic Reverse Charge rule exists in certain

1 www.vatlive.com.

Member states. The domestic VAT reversed charge is used to tackle VAT fraud when law enforcements cannot control the phenomena in real time.

Indeed, despite its many drawbacks, the Reverse Charge is currently the most effective weapon against fraud. It has the advantage upon other approaches (like VAT exemption) due to the fact that it keeps the accounting of the VAT on transactions without involving a reimbursement or payment of VAT. In fact there is a minimal lag between the time a fraud appears and the time when the customs and tax officers became aware. This lag is due to the fact that the VAT fillings are done in most cases on a quarterly basis. From the moment a filling is remitted to the tax office until some signals of alarm start ringing there is a minimum additional lag of six to nine months. Therefore, investigators will always start the work one year after the beginning of a fraud. Under these constraints, the Reverse Charge is the quickest and most effective tool to cut a VAT fraud that corrupts a market.

The Reverse Charge mechanism is not applicable at the free will of each Member state. It should pass through a dedicated framework called the Quick Reaction Mechanism (QRM). QRM is a special measure of the European Commission embedded in the VAT Directive, consisting of the option to apply for a short period of Reverse Charge, following appropriate notification by the Member State concerned. In order to ensure the appropriateness of exercising the option, the European Commission is notified by the concerned Member state of the relevant information and has a short period in which to appraise the notification and confirm whether it objects to the QRM special measure. Therefore, the European Commission amended in 2013 the VAT Directive by introducing Article 199b, which states that

> a Member State may, in cases of imperative urgency [...]designate the recipient as the person liable to pay VAT on specific supplies of goods and services by derogation from Article 193 as a Quick Reaction Mechanism ("QRM") special measure to combat sudden and massive fraud liable to lead to considerable and irreparable financial losses.

Pursuant article 199a[2] and Article 199b of the VAT Directive, a Member State can apply the Reverse Charge mechanism on a given set of products or services

---

2 Member States may, until 31 December 2018 and for a minimum period of two years, provide that the person liable for payment of VAT is the taxable person to whom any of the following supplies are made:

   a) the transfer of allowances to emit greenhouse gases as defined in Article 3 of Directive 2003/87/EC of the European Parliament and of the Council of 13 October 2003 establishing a scheme for greenhouse gas emission allowance trading within the Community, transferable in accordance with Article 12 of that Directive;

   b) the transfer of other units that may be used by operators for compliance with the same Directive;

   c) supplies of mobile telephones, being devices made or adapted for use in connection with a licensed network and operated on specified frequencies, whether or not they have any other use;

   d) supplies of integrated circuit devices such as microprocessors and central processing units in a state prior to integration into end user products;

as part of the QRM. Currently Article 199a encompasses the CO_2 emissions allowance, high technology product and gas and electricity trades.

A first example of the application of the Reverse Charge prior to the QRM occurred with the eruption of cases of VAT frauds on electronic products in the early 2000s, referred to in the previous chapter. That event produced a chain reaction among the concerned Member countries. Thus, Austria requested in October 2005 that the European Commission allow the reverse VAT charging for domestic transactions with high technology products. Austria was followed by the United Kingdom in January 2006 and Germany in April 2006.

A recent example of the use of the reverse VAT charge is in relation to the construction sector in Great Britain. Thus, in March 2018, Her Majesty's Revenue and Customs (HMRC) started discussion with various stakeholders prior to finalizing the draft legislation for its anti-fraud measure that seeks to tackle organized tax fraud on labour in the construction sector.[3] The construction sector in Great Britain has experienced a sharp increase since 2010, and its growth is fuelled by temporary staff, which is remunerated through many intermediary companies. These intermediaries or umbrella companies are billing the services of the workers with VAT, thereby allowing the development of VAT fraudulent schemes. The application of the domestic VAT Reverse Charge in the building sector is complex because it relies on the concept of 'final customer'. Putting the responsibility of the VAT liability on the 'final customer' could introduce additional distortions as many development projects are public or public-private partnerships. Therefore, HMRC intends to propose a modified version of the Reverse Charge where the main contractor will act as the 'final customer'.

The challenge of implementing the domestic Reverse Charge in the United Kingdom comes along with the impact of Brexit on Britain's taxation. In fact, HMRC would probably need to mirror or replicate part of the QRM in order to maintain the consistency and efficiency of its own version of VAT Reverse Charge.

Controls of cash payments

Measures aimed to curtail the VAT fraud are addressed mainly to the 'Missing Trader' typology. The informal economy is a big contributor to losses caused by

---

e) supplies of gas and electricity to a taxable dealer as defined in Article 38(2);

f) supplies of gas and electricity certificates;

g) supplies of telecommunication services as defined in Article 24(2);

h) supplies of game consoles, tablet PC's and laptops;

i) supplies of cereals and industrial crops including oil seeds and sugar beet, that are not normally used in the unaltered state for final consumption;

j) supplies of raw and semi-finished metals, including precious metals, where they are not otherwise covered by point (d) of Article 199(1), the special arrangements for second-hand goods, works of art, collector's items and antiques pursuant to Articles 311 to 343 or the special scheme for investment gold pursuant to Articles 344 to 356 (Source: https://eur-lex.europa.eu/legalcontent/EN/ALL/?uri=COM%3A2018%3A0118%3AFIN).

3 www.taxadvisermagazine.com/article/anti-fraud-measure-vat-domestic-reverse-charge-construction-sector.

VAT evasion. The fears of commingling the VAT evasion in the informal economy with terrorism financing and money laundering pushed European governments to take radical measures for the business-to-client (B2C) businesses. The risk in the B2C sector, encompassing retail, taxi services, food and catering hostelry, is linked to unregistered transactions paid in cash by customers. Traditionally, the tax inspectors were checking the balance of credit cards payment, but the cash settled trades were always in the dark grey area. The unregistered transactions conferred to the business a stream of revenues, which was invisible to the tax collectors. The cost associated with these 'invisible' sales is deductible for VAT and corporate tax purposes, thereby enabling the tax evasion. Governments put pressure on businesses to use a software that registers all transactions, regardless of the nature of the payment.

In France,[4] for instance, from 1 January 2018, taxable persons subject to VAT who record their customers' payments via accounting or management software or cash register systems were required to use certified secure software or systems that meet conditions of data inalterability, security, retention and archiving. This legal requirement concerning taxable persons subject to VAT on the transactions that they perform (i.e., restaurants, mini-shops, clothes retailers taxi drivers and hotels) is not limited to cash payments softwares. It concerns all softwares that register transactions and payments made by customers, whether they be private individuals or businesses: cash, checks, transfers, etc. Few cases of 'altering' the sales software for facilitating the VAT evasion were reported in Eastern European countries. A patch was installed on the machine emitting the sales receipts. The role of the patch was to give the possibility to the manager to register a sale in the accounting system. For example if a sale is paid in cash the manager has the option to emit a sale receipt but not to register it in the accounting system for VAT purposes. The French law aims to eliminate this avenue and to offer a traceable environment for both payment and sales orders.

Kittel principle

In most of the carousel frauds, there are intermediary firms that are not missing traders but do trade directly with the missing traders. These companies are often reimbursed by their national treasuries for the VAT amount corresponding to their transactions with rogue counterparts. The intermediary traders involved in a Missing Trader Intra-Community (MTIC) carousel do deduct the input VAT, despite the fact that somewhere along the chain that VAT will be pocketed. In some cases the intermediaries or the third parties are aware of the whole picture of the carousel, but in other cases they act as honest parties.

4 www.ey.com/Publication/vwLUAssets/France_implements_anti-fraud_measures_requiring_certain_VAT_registered_businesses_to_use_certified_software_or_systems_to_record_payments/$FILE/2017G_03276-171Gbl_Indirect_FR%20implements%20anti-fraud%20measures%20re%20VAT%20businesses%20to%20use%20certified%20software%20or%20systems%20to%20record%20payments.pdf.

Therefore, some companies were denied input tax relief when their activities were connected with MTIC fraud. One of those cases, involving a Belgian trader called Axel Kittel, ended up in front of the European Court of Justice in 2006.[5] Thus, the 'Kittle principle', known as the 'knowledge principle', was introduced in order to address the right of parties involved in MTIC schemes to deduct VAT and to be reimbursed. The principle states that a trader of goods or services cannot deduct input tax if 'that trader knew, or should have known', that the corresponding transactions were linked to a VAT loss generated by a fraud.

De La Feria (2016)[6] exposes an in-depth analysis of third-party liability related to VAT fraud. This research points out that the question of the 'knowledge principle' arose in the context of three cases – 'Optigen', 'Fulcrum',[7] and 'Bond' involving British companies between 2003 and 2009. In those cases, HMRC had denied recovery of input tax, despite the fact that concerned companies were not missing traders but were indeed participants in a carousel VAT fraud scheme by buying goods or services from other companies involved in an MTIC. At that time, the British tax office argued that despite the taxpayers being unaware of the carousel fraud, the transactions did not constitute an economic activity for the purposes of VAT (Article 9(1) of the VAT Directive)[8] and consequently did not give rise to the right to deduct input tax.

---

5 On those grounds, the Court (Third Chamber) hereby rules,

> Where a recipient of a supply of goods is a taxable person who did not and could not know that the transaction concerned was connected with a fraud committed by the seller, Article 17 of Sixth Council Directive 77/388/EEC of 17 May 1977 on the harmonisation of the laws of the Member States relating to turnover taxes – Common system of value added tax: uniform basis of assessment, as amended by Council Directive 95/7/EC of 10 April 1995, must be interpreted as meaning that it precludes a rule of national law under which the fact that the contract of sale is void – by reason of a civil law provision which renders that contract incurably void as contrary to public policy for unlawful basis of the contract attributable to the seller – causes that taxable person to lose the right to deduct the value added tax he has paid. It is irrelevant in this respect whether the fact that the contract is void is due to fraudulent evasion of value added tax or to other fraud.
>
> By contrast, where it is ascertained, having regard to objective factors, that the supply is to a taxable person who knew or should have known that, by his purchase, he was participating in a transaction connected with fraudulent evasion of value added tax, it is for the national court to refuse that taxable person entitlement to the right to deduct.
>
> (Source: https://eur-lex.europa.eu/legal-content/EN/
> TXT/?uri=CELEX%3A62004CJ0439)

6 http://eprints.whiterose.ac.uk/101748/1/RdlF_RB-Italmoda-3May2016_CLEAN.pdf.
7 Fulcrum was a key player in the VoIP (Voice over Internet Protocol) connection.
8

> 1. 'Taxable person' shall mean any person who, independently, carries out in any place any economic activity, whatever the purpose or results of that activity. Any activity of producers, traders or persons supplying services, including mining and agricultural activities and activities of the professions, shall be regarded as 'economic activity'. The exploitation of tangible or intangible property for the purposes of obtaining income therefrom on a continuing basis shall in particular be regarded as an economic activity.

In 2016, HMRC[9] launched a consultation on VAT fraud, aiming to assess the possibility of inflicting penalties based upon the 'Kittel principle' to traders which 'knew or should have known their trades were linked with VAT fraud'. The main question behind the knowledge principle is under what circumstances should a company have known that its counterparties were involved in some kind of VAT wrongdoing?

A few potential answers to these questions could be:

- Can a price lower than the market for a given product be the result of a VAT fraud?
- Could a big trading volume, which does not have any economic rationale, be explained by a VAT carousel?
- Does wiring or receiving payment form offshore companies represent a sign of tax evasion?

On the one hand, these are legitimate questions that should be addressed by a trader before going into a transaction. On the other hand, a small-/medium-sized company would not have the capacity to enter into this type of reasoning or analysis. Big firms, involved in the *Carbon Connection* or the *VoIP connection* that had big compliance departments, fell in the claw of the missing traders. Therefore, the application of the 'Kittel principle' should be apprehended cautiously and analyzed depending on the circumstances of the concerned company.

Distributed ledger technologies

One of the main issues with the current VAT system is the traceability of the transactions and the assessment of the accuracy of VAT fillings submitted periodically by concerned economic agents. The VAT fillings are currently based on a self-assessment, and any consistency check can be made only a few quarters after their submission. One way of addressing these issues is by leveraging technology into the VAT compliance. Technology-based solutions have the potential to provide a better and closer view upon the level of VAT compliance. The main challenge here is to structure data from companies with VAT liabilities and to make the data accessible as fast as possible to customs and tax officers.

Two types of technology-based solutions are currently proposed by specialists:

- data warehouse based solutions and
- blockchain solutions.

---

2. In addition to the persons referred to in paragraph 1, any person who, on an occasional basis, supplies a new means of transport, which is dispatched or transported to the customer by the vendor or the customer, or on behalf of the vendor or the customer, to a destination outside the territory of a Member State but within the territory of the Community, shall be regarded as a taxable person (Source: https://eur-lex.europa.eu/legal-content/EN/ALL/?uri=CELEX:32006L0112).

9 www.gov.uk/government/consultations/penalty-for-participating-in-vat-fraud.

The data warehouses based solutions aim to centralize information relative to invoices or shipments concerning domestic and cross-border transactions. A data warehouse based solution for centralizing VAT information has a three-tier architecture:

- a front-end application available for end users which are companies that have VAT liabilities;
- a back-end database where all information collected from the end users is centralized; and
- a computation engine, which maps the transactions and search correspondences and targets potential issues.

Data warehouse based solutions include the real-time VAT system and the Digital VAT (D-VAT) discussed in the seminal paper of Ainsworth R. T. (2010). Real-time VAT aims to collect the right amount of tax in real time and to transfer it directly to the tax authorities. The real-time system of all Member states should be interconnected in order to assess whether the payments are coherent, especially for the cross-border trades.

A real-time VAT system has been implemented since 2018 in Hungary.[10] The system, which is named Kobak, concerns all VAT-registered businesses, which must submit domestic business-to-business (B2B) sales invoices with a VAT amount equal to or more than 320 euros to the Hungarian tax office in a window of 24 hours. Businesses not complying with the 24-hour rule face a penalty. The main issue with the real-time VAT is that it is focussed only on the invoices and not on the supply chain of the goods or services. To combat MTIC, the information concerning shipments and deliveries is a key piece of the puzzle.

A solution that englobes both invoicing and deliveries in a centralized system was proposed by Ainsworth (2006) and is called the D-VAT. That proposal was the precursor to the current digital framework of the VAT system that the European Commission aims to implement in Member States by 2020.

The implementation of D-VAT systems would eliminate carousel fraud. A company engaged in the trading of goods with another company in another Member state would need to register with the D-VAT applications and to submit the features of the trade. Its counterparty in the trade would be required to do the same and submit the trade in the D-VAT system. The system would match the trades and would approve the use of the Reverse Charge on VAT on that trade.

The second type of solution is based on a decentralized ledger, also known as blockchain, detailed in recent research papers (Ainsworth, 2015). The principles of blockchain were already presented in Chapter 9. Blockchain has the advantage that information is distributed and accessible to all users of the system. In the case of VAT all transactions will be distributed on a ledger that is accessible to all members of the system. Moreover, the chain of transactions of goods or services

---

10 https://sovos.com/blog/hungary-real-time-vat-reporting-july-2018/.

can be easily followed by blockchain technology. A distributed ledger would require that each trade/payment/delivery is to be validated by the other members. Blockchain validation solutions, including the proof-of-work or proof-of-stake, are already available.

The next step in the use of the blockchain would be the smart contract already implemented in platforms like Ethereum. If the VAT system relied on the backbone of the smart contract, the payment of VAT would be automatic, and no compliance failure would be possible. The governments or the national treasuries would therefore need to be part of this system. Ainsworth (2016) even proposed a dedicated token VATCoin that would facilitate this.

The Gulf countries opted to implement a blockchain-based system in order to have better control of the newly introduced VAT (Ainsworth, 2017). The main drawback of a blockchain VAT system is that the government will not have the upper hand anymore. National tax offices will be users of this distributed ledger, with the same rights and responsibilities as other VAT-liable companies.

Transnational investigation agencies

VAT fraud is by its nature transnational, and the groups that are behind the main VAT scams are multinational, involving individuals of various nationalities and companies involved in different jurisdictions. The early transnational VAT frauds were investigated by national law enforcement agencies, the degree of cross-border cooperation being relatively reduced. This issue is particularly problematic for the MTIC cases, which took, in many cases, as many as ten years to be investigated and to appear in court due to the lack of cross-border cooperation between the Members of the EU. This lack of an European agency that could respond effectively to VAT cases spanning several countries is one of the main reasons that MTIC fraud developed at a big scale took such amplitude within the EU. The United States, which is also a union of states, has several well-defined federal investigation agencies, the best known being the Federal Bureau of Investigation (FBI). The EU does not have such an agency, but there are signs of convergence in the field of sharing the knowledge and experience of European investigators.

One of the first examples of cooperation[11] in tackling VAT fraud occurred in 2006, when combined teams of British and German customs officers stopped a cross-border VAT fraud worth as much as 116 million pounds. The operation, called *Sunrise*, uncovered a carousel of mobile phones based in Germany, the United Kingdom and Switzerland. During that operation the teams seized more than 30,000 mobile phones at Frankfurt Airport and on the German-Swiss border.

The key to Operation *Sunrise* was a computer database that had been operated by HMRC since 2005, called Nemesis. It contained the identification

---

11 http://news.bbc.co.uk/2/hi/business/5305074.stm.

numbers of all mobile phones imported and exported from the United Kingdom. When the phones seized in Germany were scanned into the database it revealed those which appeared to have been previously moved around the EU for no apparent commercial purpose, thereby raising suspicions of a carousel fraud. At that time Operation *Sunrise* was the first cross-border cooperation between HMRC and its European counterparts to combat carousel fraud.

The European Commission created in 1998 Europol, the first agency aiming to centralize intelligence concerning serious organized crime from the Member States. A second agency was created in 2002, Eurojust, aiming to improve and assist in the coordination of investigations and prosecutions between the law enforcement bodies in the Member States when dealing with cross-border crime. Eurojust also aims to facilitate the execution of international mutual legal assistance and the implementation of extradition requests.

An example of such a coordinated effort occurred in March 2015,[12] when law enforcement and prosecution authorities from Germany and the Netherlands, supported by Eurojust and Europol, dismantled a gang responsible for defrauding approximately 150 million euros of VAT. The investigation, named Operation *Vertigo*, concerned companies and individuals from the Czech Republic, Germany, the Netherlands and Poland.

A more recent investigation took place in 2016, when the Spanish Tax Agency, supported by Europol and Eurojust, dismantled a big VAT fraud involving 100 companies across Belgium, Bulgaria, Cyprus, Germany, Hungary, Italy, Portugal, Romania, Spain and the United States.

Another part of the operation were the Bulgarian authorities,[13] which assisted by investigating the Bulgarian bank accounts used to launder the proceeds of the crime. The loss caused to the Spanish taxpayers due to the VAT fraud reached 60 million euros.

In June 2017,[14] the Member states of the EU made decisive progresses in establishing the European Public Prosecutor's Office (EPPO) by agreeing upon legislation setting out the details of its functioning and role. Based in Luxembourg, the EPPO will have the authority in certain circumstances to investigate and prosecute fraud and other crimes affecting the EU's financial interests. EPPO aims to unite the efforts of European and national law enforcements to tackle fraud within the EU. The creation of EPPO is a huge step forward that could be decisive in tackling cross-border crime like the VAT fraud.

If the EU is searching for convergence of its national law enforcement agencies the newly created Eurasian Economic Union (EAEU) is still at its beginning with regards to cross-border cooperation. The Eurasian Economic Commission (EEC) is a permanent body regulating the issues within EAEU's competence. The Department of Customs Legislation and Law Enforcement Practice is one of the 25

12 www.eurojust.europa.eu/press/pressreleases/pages/2015/2015-03-03.aspx.
13 https://sofiaglobe.com/2018/05/04/bulgarian-connection-as-eu-wide-vat-fraud-organised-crime-group-busted/#.
14 www.consilium.europa.eu/en/press/press-releases/2017/06/08/eppo/.

departments of the EEC. The role of this department is to oversee EAEU's issues related to security and trade, encompassing the VAT fraud. But, its powers and responsibilities are very limited. The main issues related to the security of the Eurasian Union rely on the Russian Federal Security Services, which has an extensive presence in the Members of the Eurasian Union and in some of the countries, the Eurasian Union has free trading agreement with. This cooperation centred around the Russian security agency encompasses also the economic crime.

A similar problem is faced by the Gulf countries that adopted the VAT from 2018. The economic crime in each Emirate is dealt with by the local law enforcement. The cooperation between Emirates in terms of law enforcements that would potentially address the VAT fraud is currently limited.

The role of KYC in financial institutions

KYC is an uncharted area...

With the recent big scandals related to tax evasion and the information disclosed to the public in 'Panama Papers' and 'Paradise Papers', regulators and investigators have an increased focus of compliance. One of the main tools of the compliance function in a financial institution is the Know Your Customer (KYC). KYC is the process of a business identifying and verifying the identity of its clients. The term is also used to refer to the bank and anti-money laundering regulations which govern these activities.

Parra-Moyano (2017) underlined that the KYC due diligence process is outdated and generates costs of up to 500 million dollars per year per bank. The cited research proposed a new system, based on distributed ledger technology that reduces the costs of the core KYC verification process for financial institutions and improves the customer experience. In their proposed system, the core KYC verification process is only conducted once for each customer, regardless of the number of financial institutions with which the customer intends to work. Thanks to distributed ledger technology, the result of the core KYC verification can be securely shared by customers with all the financial institutions that they intend to work with. This technology should allow for efficiency gains, cost reduction, improved customer experience and increased transparency throughout the process of onboarding a customer.

...with many limitations

The cognitive biases exposed in Chapter 9 not only exist amongst individuals but are also present in many processes and systems deployed across corporations. KYC being a topic poorly covered by research, many biases are reflected in the compliance processes, thereby making them less comprehensive and vulnerable to external threats which are aware of this flaw.

Prior to the 2008 crisis many companies based their credit risk assessment on the concept 'too big to fail'. This pattern persists today in the way banks deal with compliance issues. Amongst the common biases encountered in the KYC framework and in the derived processes, the following require a closer look:

- **Too big to fraud**: '*A big financial institution or corporation will never enter into a scheme that could be deemed non-compliant*'. Big organizations tend to be perceived as better from a compliance perspective than smaller ones. If a fraud occurred, a small company would appear more suspicious than a bigger one. This reasoning proved to be wrong in most of the carousel frauds in which big firms were involved. The examples of Deutsche Bank in the VAT fraud on the carbon market and Telecom Italia Sparkle in the VoIP connection are relevant in this context.
- **(I) Moral hazard**: '*The big company will never be investigated or liable for compliance issues*'. A common belief found in the KYC processes is that a big company is less liable from a compliance perspective if it is involved in a fraud. Big corporations are seen as having an equal weight with regulators and investigators in the complex play of financial crime. Despite being Europe's first investment bank, Deutsche Bank was targeted by arrests when the German authorities investigated the German branch of the carbon connection.
- **Eschatology**: '*If this big corporation is involved in wrongdoings we will have bigger issues at that time*'. The eschatological belief is another reason why many compliance processes lower their assessment standards with regards to big clients.

When analyzing credit ratings (S&P, Fitch, Moodys), big companies appear to have a better creditworthiness than small companies. In a similar manner, compliance officers tend to overlook big clients, thereby implying a biased KYC outcome. This type of bias is particularly relevant in the VAT fraud, resulting in honest companies' and individuals' being commingled in a scam due to a wrong judgement of their clients/suppliers. A few of the biases hindering a reasonable assessment of a big corporation are:

- **Size bias**: '*A big organization has better means for corporate transparency and investors communication*'. Therefore, in most of the cases big corporations are perceived as less exposed to compliance issues. This bias is exploited by fraudsters on numerous occasions. For example big retailers are targeted by VAT fraudsters on electronics. Some cases showed that gangs used reputed global retailers as an endpoint for the VAT carrousel.
- **Reputation bias**: '*If a company has bonds with a reputed institution, it is perceived as safer*'. Examples include start-ups backed by reputed funds, subsidiaries of major corporations or even companies audited by The Big 4. For instance in the VoIP connection, Telecom Italia Sparkle and Fastweb, companies linked to the giant Telecom Italia, were perceived as less risky with regards to tax evasion.

- **Geographic bias**: '*A company incorporated in a developed country is considered safer than a company from an emerging country*'. Currently compliance systems deem companies incorporated in the EU to be safer than those incorporated in the Eurasian Union. This could hold true in many aspects of financial crime, but concerning the VAT fraud this hypothesis is not always true.
- **Safe harbour bias**: '*Some markets and products were wrongly perceived as safe harbours*'. That was one of the main reasons that the VAT fraud on carbon markets took place. The authorities did not suspect that a market aimed at solving the world's stringent issues, such as global warming, could harbour a huge criminal operation. Therefore, there are no markets or products safe from VAT fraud.

The compliance technique went to the next level due to the advantage of technology. Currently within organizations most KYC processes are automatized, and clients receive scores depending on their risk levels with regards to financial crime. Moreover, the clients' transactions are monitored through dedicated systems. Despite adopting various technological solutions, fallacies persist in the compliance world. A few of the biases entailed by the use of technology are:

- *A customer not being assessed as non-compliant is compliant.* This is a common fallacy resulting from the inappropriate use of statistics. The fact that a hypothesis is rejected does not mean that this alternative is true.
- *Onboarding is the main focus of compliance.* KYC as a process should not consist only in assessing a client at the beginning of a commercial relationship with an organization. KYC should be an ongoing process over the entire life span of the relationship with that customer.
- *A high number of 'false positives' is a good thing for a compliance methodology.* One of the big drawbacks of the KYC systems currently employed by financial institutions is the fact that they generate a large number of false positive. This aspect is seen as a good thing by compliance officers, as a way to cope with the main fear that they might miss something. In fact, this induces another bias, where, in some complex cases, the compliance might need to search for the needle in the haystack.

Know Your Network, a sound alternative

The obsolete KYC needs to be replaced with a tool based on the disruptive set of methods and tools. The backbone of such a new method should be a hyper-network of objects composed of both individuals and organizations. The connections and linkages between the nodes of the network are established through a semi-supervised learning algorithm trained on various databases, including the national registries of people and companies.

This technique provides a fully fledged picture of an individual or a company, with their corresponding transnational networks. We introduce a change of paradigm by replacing the static and one-dimensional concept of KYC with the dynamic, multidimensional and forward-looking concept of 'Know Your Network' (KYN).

The KYN environment serves both investigation and compliance professionals in their quest for deep-dive analytic tools. On the one hand investigators will be able to assess the hidden connections within a criminal network and explore the dynamic of the network in the near future. On the other hand, compliance officers will be able to quantify the risks of their clients' portfolio with respect to various drivers, including Anti-Money Laundering, Counter Terrorism Financing, Sanctions and Tax evasion.

When implementing KYN the backbone should be a hyper-network, whereas its nodes are the hyper-objects. A hyper-object is a general concept that can include both legal and physical persons, single and multiple elements.

The connections between the various nodes of the network, required for the KYN framework, are built through data linkage. Data linkage is the process of finding records in one or a few data sets that refer to the same person or entity across those data sources. The process is necessary when joining data sets based on entities that may or may not share a common identifier (e.g., database key, national identification number), as may be the case due to differences in record shape, language or national registry.

The following types of data linkages are relevant for building a hyper-network:

•   Deterministic data linkage: link by first name, last name and date of birth.
•   Probabilistic data linkage: match only parts of the names/translate in various languages.
•   Machine learning data linkage: train the links on a sample data set and apply the rules to full set.

KYN is a tool that would provide superior results when assessing companies involved in VAT scams. A VAT fraud is generally based upon a multitude of companies in many jurisdictions. The cases presented in Chapter 10 showed that most companies shared director or some individuals having powers over the bank accounts. In the cases of the VoIP connection and the *Carbon Connection* the firms involved in the same carousel had accounts opened with the same bank. Therefore, through a KYN approach a financial institution could have easily reconstituted a least part of the fraud and raised comprehensive alerts.

APPENDIX

Interview: Chris Perryman, Europol

Chris Perryman is a senior specialist with Europol.[1] His work focusses on Missing Trader Intra-Community (MTIC) fraud in the European Union. Previously, he worked for Her Majesty's Revenue and Customs (HMRC).

MARIUS-CRISTIAN FRUNZA (MCF): **What are the major challenges faced by law enforcement agencies when investigating VAT fraud cases?**
CHRIS PERRYMAN (CP): One of the first challenges is that invariably the law enforcement agencies aren't the tax administrations. I'm originally from HMRC in the United Kingdom, which is both the tax administrator and the competent law enforcement agency that investigates VAT fraud. Within HMRC the investigators have actually got full and unfettered access to traders' details, traders' records, etc. In many member states that isn't the case. The tax administrations will obviously administer the personal day-to-day affairs of a VAT-registered trader. And then once an offence has been identified, a package is handed over to the law enforcement agents, who then have to investigate that package. The law enforcement agents generally have no direct access to material to identify whether there are actually other VAT registrations that might be involved, for example, or whether the persons of interest have got previous connections with other areas. That's at a national level, of course. You can multiply that by the fact that there's 28 countries in the European Union at the moment. Invariably MTIC fraud is involving by its very nature more than one member of state, so clearly this cross-border dimension and cooperation becomes an issue.

You probably are aware that the European Commission is trying to look at improving the cooperation between tax administrations and law enforcement agencies. The European Commission had set up something called EUROFISC[2] in 2012.

---

1 Europol is the European Union's law enforcement agency. Europol's main goal is to achieve a safer Europe for the benefit of all the EU citizens. Headquartered in The Hague, the Netherlands, Europol supports the 28 EU Member States in their fight against terrorism, cybercrime and other serious and organised forms of crime. (Source: www.europol.europa.eu/about-europol).
2 EUROFISC is a mechanism provided for Member States to enhance their administrative cooperation in combating organised VAT fraud and especially carousel fraud. EUROFISC

EUROFISC is a platform which exists for tax administrations to exchange data in certain aspects of irregularities within VAT. I say that because theoretically the information's meant to be administrative as opposed to criminal, although in many instances of course it's bordering on criminality. But in those meetings what has been exchanged is completely prevented from reaching the likes of ourselves. We at Europol have no, or indeed, law enforcement agencies have no access to these EUROFISC meetings. One of the reasons for that is that when the regulation was created, and EUROFISC was set up, it did say that the Commission would have no access to that data. Europol is an agency of the Commission, and some member states by extension have included Europol in that.

But it's all tied up with taxpayer secrecy, and some Member States are more rigorous in defending that than others. From a personal perspective I cannot see why non-taxpayers, i.e. criminals, benefit from taxpayer secrecy. That's something which I've sort of been banging my head against the wall about for a long time. The European Commission I think are seeing that there is value in having much more, certainly at the strategic level, data shared between law enforcement and tax administrations. The current Commission initiatives launched on the 30th of November last year are very much in keeping with that. That's one of the things we have. Another problem we have is that in some member states, which will remain nameless, there are several law enforcement agencies that are charged with tackling MTIC fraud. And they are not joined up at a national level; in fact some of them are not even joined up at a regional level. That creates a bit of a difficulty to look at who is looking at who, whether there is duplication being undertaken and whether things are being prioritized in the right way.

Obviously the solution to that would be to ensure that cases and intelligence are centralized in one area: at Europol. I'm the project manager of the MTIC team at Europol, and we are the only area that centralizes intelligence and knowledge of who's been looked at across Europe at a criminal level. But there is no compulsion by the member states to actually advise us of what cases they're working on. Although out there now, and certainly since the time of the carbon credits frauds, I think people and prosecutors have recognized the expertise we have, the knowledge that we have and the assistance we can bring to their cases, that still doesn't enforce people to actually give us all the things that they're working on. We are unsighted in certain areas, and if people come to us as the fount of all knowledge, or at a point at which they can get some access to this, but the database and the knowledge isn't shared with us, then obviously it creates a bit of a problem. It's ensuring that the fight is coordinated, and there is somewhere centralized that knows what is going on or can be asked to find out what is going on to enable others. And I think that's the biggest problem we've got, at least at the moment.

allows for quick and targeted sharing of information between all Member States on fraudulent activities (Source: https://ec.europa.eu/taxation_customs/sites/taxation/files/docs/body/2011-02-07_eurofisc_pressrelease_en.pdf).

MCF: Do you think the investigation techniques used by law enforcement at a local/national level are fit for whatever happens currently in the VAT fraud area?

CP: I don't think there's anything special about the techniques that relate to MTIC fraud that might relate to any other type of fraudulent activity. All of the techniques that you would normally associate with law enforcement agencies would be open to those investigating VAT frauds, I mean it's a criminal offence. The whole toolbox of what is used to tackle criminality is used.

MCF: In many MTIC cases, time and speed are key factors. Can national law enforcements have an appropriate response?

CP: It depends on who might be carrying out the frauds, the size of the group, the threatening nature of the criminality, whether there is a well-known history of those conducting it. Obviously, the groups with a well-known history have a continual monitoring by law enforcement agents. Also, law enforcement would be looking to see which areas those groups are moving to and paying them closer attention. If you had, for sake of argument, a brand-new group from a brand-new area that was coming out of left field from somewhere, that would probably go a bit unnoticed, and you wouldn't know that frauds have occurred until you get past evidence. And if you think of the VAT system itself and the very nature of the thing, in normal circumstances the norm would be to submit a VAT return every quarter, with a month's delay to make that payment, etc., Therefore, brand-new frauds potentially could operate for four months before the tax administrations recognize there is actually an irregularity. And then the tax administrations, if they are not charged with actually criminally investigating that, have processes which they need to go through before the cases come over to the law enforcement agencies. So, that's again further delaying there.

Quite often these MTIC cases are investigated historically. But as I say, if you've got active groups that have a very, very close attention, then there's an opportunity to try to prevent the frauds from happening. I'm a customs officer from the United Kingdom, and our ethos is prevention is better than cure. But in some of these countries, as I say, that receive the package to investigate, they are investigating the complaint, and the complaint is something that's occurred in the past. That has affected recovery; it's affected who has been prosecuted because invariably missing traders are literally that, they are no longer there. They've moved to another jurisdiction, for example, and if they move to another jurisdiction, it could be that that receiving law enforcement agency then really sort of puts the case to one side and doesn't have anything to do with it anymore because they've chosen one of the other 27 member states in which to start perpetrating their frauds. This is the problem we've got.

The other thing is, unless you've got a specialized entity that investigates these things, and if they have competing crimes to start investigating, then quite often the very technical and arduous, long-winded nature of investigating MTIC frauds can put off people actually starting an investigation. We were talking initially about this Marseille case,[3] which is being at trial now, in 2018; it involves criminality conducted in 2009, nine years down the line. Stories like that put people off investigating. They think I do not want to have my officers tied up in a case that's going to take seven, eight, nine years before it actually comes to trial. There are other things that some law enforcement agencies can tackle, and probably will, to actually get the throughput. In an ideal world with loads of resources you'd investigate everything. But sometimes you've got to choose what you can do and what you can actually realize realistically.

MCF: **How do you see the geographical spread of the VAT fraud? Is this a global crime?**
CP: We are the European Union's law enforcement agency, which is mandated to deal with serious organized crime and terrorism. Quite clearly, our priority therefore is to look at threats to the European Union. However, those threats are being orchestrated in many instances by entities which operate from outside the European Union. Certainly the money that is generated, the proceeds that emanate from these frauds are immediately sent outside the European Union, so we need to liaise with partners there. Increasingly, techniques which have used in frauds against the European Union are now being examined, sometimes by the same groups that perpetuate in crimes against the European Union to see if they can actually fit with some of the GST[4] systems, in the world.

You've only got to look at open sources to find out that there have been collaborations with the United Kingdom's customs and the Canadian revenue authorities; for example, last year there was a big operation concerning false claims to do with GST credits in identical fashion to false input claims in VAT within the European Union. Australia last year again reported similar issues related to the gold sector. Gold was one of the first areas that was looked at by criminals in the European Union as a means of conducting VAT fraud. They're looking at where those things are being traded elsewhere, and Australia's got a problem with that. With the carbon credit system, obviously we had massive problems back in 2009. That trading system was looked at by other areas of the world as a model to how they could use that to try to help tackle CO_2 emissions. And obviously if those models are actually implemented elsewhere, it could provide an opportunity for fraudsters to undertake similar sorts of frauds there. A lot of these things are transportable across the world. And they have been and are being transported across the world.

MCF: **VAT was recently introduced in the Gulf countries from 1st of January 2018. How this will affect the VAT fraud picture?**
CP: I found that quite interesting, to be honest. And I think I'm correct in saying they're going to try to underpin it with blockchain technology, which is

3 A VAT fraud on carbon emissions allowances operated in 2009 by a group based in Marseille, France.
4 Goods and Services Tax.

meant to be quite transparent to all parties. I just find that quite interesting. Because, as you know, that is one of the bases for some of the organized crime groups that are perpetrating, it's no secret. And those groups have set up businesses in the region to legitimize the transfer of funds or to try to legitimize the transfer of funds there. It's very interesting that that area has opened up this VAT field, and those businesses will have to come into that area. We are watching that to see how this develops.

MCF: **Are there criminal groups that specialized in VAT fraud over time?**

CP: Criminal groups specialize in VAT, but they're not limited to VAT. The crime groups will look at any opportunity for the frauds themselves to make some money. If we go back to the carbon credit frauds, that was a very well-identified opportunity by the fraudsters who maximized their opportunity in it, in the very short time span. It was a massive VAT fraud, in an area in which nobody thought there would be VAT fraud because the purpose of the system was to create a mechanism to reduce harmful elements, CO_2 being reduced into the atmosphere. The administrators then decided to charge VAT on domestic transactions with that. But those administrators of course had nothing to do with the tax authorities necessarily. This disconnect allowed this to happen. Similarly, with a lot of the gas and electricity sectors, de-regulated industries trying to stimulate competition have had a knock-on effect, allowing fraudsters to enter a market which is a very specialized market and a difficult market to understand for police officers and customs offices. Fraudsters have got the wherewithal to either employ specialized help or corrupt those that operate in those areas for the purposes of fraud. They look at these opportunities coming along, and they enter into these markets.

A few groups specialized in VAT fraud on the carbon emissions market; they are now operating not only in VAT circles but also in social engineering frauds. Now that's nothing to do with VAT. But it's everything to do with the techniques of how businesses operate, where money could be made. They are specialists in VAT. But they're not siloed or ring-fenced by VAT. If suddenly VAT was removed from everywhere, we wouldn't get rid of them; they'd be doing something else somewhere; they'd be looking for an opportunity.

MCF: **What are the potential links of VAT fraudsters with money laundering circles?**

CP: You've only got to look at some of the enablers that have created opportunities in the banking and parallel banking sectors to assist the VAT fraudsters. Obviously the purpose of committing VAT fraud is to get money, and when you get that money you've got to try to get access to that money. One of the big weapons that of course was used by law enforcement to detect MTIC fraud schemes was the suspicious transaction reporting (STR) system. But it was quite obvious to the fraudsters what was going on there. And there are obvious telltale signs as to what looks suspicious. I mean in the commercial world, if I was to buy some goods from you, I would negotiate a 60-day payment term for example and probably wait till 70/80 days until I actually physically paid you. In the world of VAT, money hits the bank account and literally in the space of ten minutes goes out of that same bank account, even before the goods have moved, if they ever move at all, of course.

Alternative banking platforms (Abps) were used by MTIC fraudsters because the transactions between them actually happen below in a specially predesigned, bespoke designed accounting mechanism. A correspondent bank is used, money is paid into it, and then there are subaccounts set up by the fraudsters for them to move the money. They set up their own websites, to which access is only allowed to those in the circle. A regular person can't join this website to set up an account. We all know about that, they know that we all know about that. But it's an area nevertheless that is a bit of cat and mouse for us to try to detect these things and take action against these things. The whole story has involved New Zealand, Panama and the Caribbean. The ABPs are set up in Hong Kong, the Far East, Seychelles, not in the European Union. The difficulty for the prosecutions is, well, persuading a prosecutor to go after money in those jurisdictions that house those platforms. It is the geographical spread and diversity outside the European Union which is making the control and enforcement of this phenomenon so difficult for us. Again it's a question of trying to detect, trying to close down engagement of open authorities.

MCF: Could the growth of global trading through online marketplace platforms play a role in VAT fraud?

CP: Well, with the electronic communication services, that would include *VAT*; of course the United Kingdom brought in a reverse charge on that. That was an interesting fraud because the traditional way of looking at intercommunity VAT fraud is that it would involve two or more Member States. But with that of course you were having companies set up in North America that would supply telephony services to British companies but have a couple of missing traders, or a buffer and then a broker, who then of course supply the airtime services down to places not normally covered by big companies like British Telecom. Fraudsters would set up mechanisms to create or to falsify records, which suggests that real trade was going on. Some real trades might have gone on, but clearly what fraudsters created exaggerated the trade and created some more opportunities for refunds. Basically the fraud only involved one Member State, hence being MTEC[5] fraud. This is the first thing.

The second thing is concerning the e-commerce. Indeed, there's a lot of concern at the moment about how that might work. People generally associate sole traders selling from home goods on eBay or Amazon, etc. But of course it's more than that; it's a big business, and it can be generated from anywhere. It's something which is a bit problematical to examine now. As things stand of course, the tax administrations are looking at ways to tax all this. It's not law enforcement, and it's not the job of Europol to actually facilitate the gathering of revenue. We

5 Missing Trader Extra-Community.

are here to support criminal investigations and develop criminal intelligence that suggests how groups are orchestrating this. Certainly we have got a couple of criminal investigations and a bit of intelligence around this. But once again, it is the organized crime group which is identifying how the system works, identifying the vulnerability and exploiting the vulnerability. It is an area which is showing some concern, and there's a lot of press coverage about that at the moment again.

MCF: **What do you think about the universe of cryptocurrencies? Is it something that could enable VAT fraud?**

CP: There is an explosion in these things; we all heard of Bitcoin and Ethereum, and there seems to be another one every moment cropping up. One has got to question why these things need to be created, if they're not for nefarious purposes. Quite clearly it's another opportunity that fraudsters might have to actually use or put law enforcement off the scent of where this money is moving, etc. The role of the cybercrime units now has to probably step up to a degree to assist the law enforcement efforts into this. I'm sure that the organized crime groups are looking at this and they've got things going on. We all hear about the Dark Web and what goes on in there. VAT fraud is probably one of the least threatening things that go on in there.

It's probably not the major concern, and again, because of that sheer potential of more virulent and threatening forms of criminality, the VAT fraudsters have got a chance of somewhere to hide because the investigators will have different priorities. If the role of your team is to actually have a multitude of competencies, something is always at the bottom of that multitude of competencies, something is always at the top. That either reflects your chances of getting something done, or it reflects your understanding of how things work, or it reflects the ability to actually take some action and actually easily do it. Anything that falls into the too difficult box adds to where you sit in the bottom of that pile.

MCF: **How do you see the role of technology in tackling VAT fraudsters?**

CP: I think there has to be a place for it, obviously. If you look at how some of the VAT frauds have been working in recent years, the carbon credits fraud, for example, was all done through registers with an online account, which can then be accessed anywhere in the world. In the old and early days of MTIC fraud, the adage used to be that the commodities of choice would be small volume, high value because quite clearly you could get more things in your container, which then needed to be physically shipped across a border, then they needed to be stored, and then moved on. Of course we're looking at intangible goods and increasingly intangible goods that are traded online through registries, some of which are public registries. It gives us the chance to find out who might be registering.

And quite clearly there is a need, and there is a reality that law enforcement agencies will work closely with market surveillance teams, for example, for industries.

Because industries have seen what happened to the carbon credits sector. You've only got to look at *BlueNext*; it had a 32 million euro fine from the French government as well for its part in the fraud. And its part in the fraud was merely providing the marketplace where the fraudsters then abused the system. The BlueNext exchange doesn't operate anymore. Other sectors have seen what's happened there. Therefore, they doubled up on their Know Your Customer efforts and their willingness to collaborate with law enforcement agencies and to provide law enforcement agencies with intelligence. But when you start looking at some of these other areas, these dark net areas, for example, you don't seem to have the same sort of degree of policing going on. There are some exceptions obviously, and obviously some of the guys that work in our dedicated unit know and do collaborate with those markets. But the pool of knowledge decreases; there's only a certain number of specialists. The hope is that we've got more specialists than the opposition, but they have probably got more money than we've got.

MCF: **Would it be foreseeable that private intelligence agencies get involved in tax evasion or in VAT frauds?**

CP: It's not unusual for cases to involve former law enforcement officers. We've had some cases where people that were previously in the police, for example, are now working for the organized crime groups. They of course will be aware of the techniques that are used by law enforcement officers and will be aware of the vulnerabilities of those techniques and, you know, might be…or would be aware of how interception tools are deployed, for example. I mean none of this is rocket science. That does happen. Similarly, as I mentioned before, the sheer pool of money these fraudsters have got away with over the years. If they invest in acquiring expertise, or taking over certain and current areas that effectively turn people to working towards them, then of course they've got the ability to make more money.

There will also be those that will be horizon scanning as to how tax authorities and the European Commission, for example, might be taking action in relation to preventing frauds. One good example would be when the United Kingdom brought in the reverse charge on the mobile phones in 2006 or so. At that time, the United Kingdom had to make representations to the commission to get a derogation for the reverse charge. I think it was on the third attempt that they made this proposal to the European Commission. The European Commission eventually gave them the green light to bring in the reverse charge. But the reverse charge wasn't brought in the next day. The reverse charge was brought in with some delay. The fraudsters can just read the newspapers and find out what was going on with this. They then recognize that their opportunity to conduct VAT fraud in mobile phones against the United Kingdom was going to be limited. But it gives them sufficient time to then say, 'Right, we're going to now move the markets'.

The carbon credits fraud was dealt with by reverse charge, but not all countries brought this in together. We had a number of Member States who brought it in, in 2009, including France, Spain, the Netherlands, Belgium and the United Kingdom. The Italians brought it in on the 1st of January 2015. That's six years after the other member states. The fraudsters have a playground of 28 member states. If a Member State has decided to change the legislation to prevent or reduce the effects of the fraud, but the member state next door doesn't, then all they've got to do is change operations to that area. I'm sure that decision-making by the organized crime groups isn't reactionary; I'm sure it's anticipated beforehand. They know that there is very little new unanimity in how the member states bring in countermeasures. Because of that they can set up the countermeasures themselves to actually probably do frauds elsewhere. They will be employing people to do that. You only really need to have the ability to read the newspapers and just keep up-to-date with what's happening on the Commission's website and to actually work that out for yourself.

MCF: **What do you think about the degree of awareness of European authorities (i.e., the European Commission, European Parliament) concerning VAT fraud?**

CP: The European Commission is very aware. I mean you've only got to look at the legislation that they've brought in, so, the quick response mechanism and the reverse charge. With the reverse charge they specify the number of traditional areas where VAT fraud has been carried out (i.e., the mobile phones, etc.). And then the quick response mechanism was an acceptance that if there's a sudden spike in fraudulent activity in another sector, then this gives the Commission's blessing for the member states to bring in a reverse charge or any other measure that the member state wishes to do in response to that. Thus, that's an anti-fraud measure.

I mentioned before about the proposals on the 30th of November, where the Commission is looking at rewriting the VAT regulation (Council Regulation (EU) No 904/2010 of 7 October 2010), which actually eventually established the EUROFISC platform. The original wording was quite convenient to some of the member states who might not wish to share with law enforcement, and that there's an opportunity to say, 'Well, it does say in the regulation that we can't share stuff with the commission, or intelligence with the commission, therefore Europol'. By rewording that, that takes that excuse of non-cooperation away; Member States have to cooperate. At least they can no longer hide behind the regulations. The Commission is doing all they can to try to create the environment that allows the member states to start cooperating more between themselves and between different regimes if they want to do so. But at the end of the day it's the Member States themselves who make that decision about what they do and how they will do it. Some are more progressive than others, and some, as I say, quite rightly, are protecting taxpayer data. Certainly, as far as we're concerned we're not interested in the taxpayers, we're interested in the non-taxpayers.

Interview: Bo Elkjaer, a pioneer journalist in VAT investigation

Bo Elkjaer is a Danish investigative reporter. He has worked on subjects such as terrorism and extremism, organized crime, fraud, intelligence and surveillance, and environment issues. He has published three books and two e-books. He won the Danish Cavling award in 2003 and the FUJ (Foreningen for Undersøgende Journalistik) award for investigative journalism in 2010, 2014 and 2015. He graduated from the Danish School of Journalism in 1997.

MARIUS CRISTIAN FRUNZA (MCF): **How did you get involved as a journalist in investigating VAT fraud cases?**
BO ELKJAER (BE): I first got involved in covering VAT fraud in 2009. That year Denmark was host of the UN Climate Conference COP 15. At the time I worked at the Danish newspaper *Ekstra Bladet*. My colleague John Mynderup and I were assigned to investigate the climate change issue and see if we could find stories that *Ekstra Bladet* could bring up to the conference. We looked into several different paths of possible stories. One focus was on how a Danish farmer (married to a minister) got Danish government funds to set up a biogas plant in Poland. He was funded through a carbon offsetting program but would subsequently be able to trade off carbon credits from the government-funded project. It was part of the story that the plant was constructed to clean up after huge, scandalous pollution on a pig farm he owned and had set up under Danish government development funds.

So, he got paid to build a farm. This developed into a huge pollution scandal, which he got paid to clean up, and he could sell off the credits. Also his wife was minister of the department that funded both the initial project and the subsequent clean-up.
    I digress. We never got around to writing this story because in our research we found out that Denmark held the single largest carbon trading registry of its kind in the world. The energy authority was extremely proud of this fact. I downloaded the entire registry, and we looked into the traders registered in Denmark. No matter which one we looked into they were all full of false information, anonymous brass plate companies, addresses that ended blindly (one parking lot in London, another non-existing address in Copenhagen, etc.). Very quickly it was obvious that the Danish carbon platform was the centre of some sort of enormous scam, attracting

people from all over the world. (I plotted the traders on a map. They literally came from all over the world to trade carbon through the Danish registry.)

Initially we had no idea what the scam could be. But it was obvious that some sort of scam was under progress – real time as we looked into it.

After some research we found out that it was a VAT scam, that the accounts were used for carousel fraud with the credits. So, we dug in, trying to wrap our heads around the extent of the fraud. The Danish authorities initially denied any wrongdoing was in the works. They stated that everything was under control. After we ran our first story, Europol confirmed in a press release our findings, assessing that the fraud extended 5 billion euros in the 18 months leading up to the COP15 conference in December 2009.

Mynderup and I travelled to the Netherlands, Belgium, France and the United Kingdom looking for companies involved in the fraud. Later we also visited Sweden where we found online payment platforms that were used to hide transactions. Of course, we also visited the Danish traders registered in kiosks, used car dealers, worn down housings, etc. We went looking for lots of scammers.

MCF: **What are the major challenges faced by journalists when investigating the VAT fraud cases?**

BE: The largest challenge is that VAT fraud is a very hard sell to the editors. It is extremely unsexy. You're working uphill in your own editorial department, even before you're out there, looking for the details to uncover the fraud. (Same thing applies to police departments, several sources tell me.) VAT fraud is just too abstract to comprehend, and you have no real victims to identify with to make it real for the readers.

That aside, you also face the difficulty of documenting the fraud. Basically, the VAT fraud is extremely easy to perform – it is certainly not rocket science – and very difficult to investigate.

The carbon fraud was a boon because the EU ETS registry showed the movement of every single credit. You can track all transactions literally down to milliseconds. That is a main challenge: You need to document the movement of the goods used for the fraud – and you need to document the movement of funds.

In a later investigation I looked into VAT fraud with soft drinks, candy, food. Here the bankruptcy filings of the companies involved in the fraud became extremely useful. They sometimes contained receipts, bank transfers, etc., documenting payments and transfers of different goods. In the matter of the company Q Transport ApS the files showed how electronics were bought in Germany, and cheese and chicken meat were bought in the Netherlands – all without VAT due to intra-EU regulations, and the documents showed how these goods were traded at exactly the same price – now with VAT included. Thus the next company in the chain would have legitimate receipts on the goods with VAT included, so they could trade it on – and Q Transport ApS could be left for bankruptcy whenever the VAT was due for payment.

You need a lot of brass plate companies for this kind of fraud. That fact is also very useful in the investigation of the fraud. You look for imported strawman directors and companies set up on suspicious addresses. I found a company trading in temporary workers with a registered main office in a meter cabinet, and I found several companies listed on an empty lot in Copenhagen. Directors were Romanian citizens travelling to Denmark, setting up addresses in hotels, student lodgings, etc., and leaving again within weeks or months.

MCF: **In many cases journalists had more insights than the authorities. Is there a reason for that?**

BE: Journalists sometimes happen to have better insight due to several reasons. Among them:

- Journalists do not have jurisdictions. I have investigated VAT fraud in Denmark, Germany, Sweden, the United Kingdom, Poland, Belgium, the Netherlands, France, etc., looking for criminals in places like Hong Kong, Pakistan, Russia, Israel, etc. Single cases span several countries. This is an essential part of both MTIC and MTEC fraud. Authorities are bounded by borders and jurisdictions, and need to establish cooperation on different levels of formality to follow these leads.
- Some of the tools available to journalists are unavailable to law enforcement. For instance, I have tracked mails by incorporating hidden links and, by this method, been able to identify when and where these emails were opened. (Check out readnotify.com.) By doing this I was able to identify in the CO_2 fraud that a lot of the accounts spanning Latvia, Hong Kong, etc. all originated in the same village in Israel. Law enforcement would not be able to do this.
- Sources might also trend towards trusting journalists more than law enforcement and give better access to information and validation of information than what they would give to authorities.

MCF: **Do you think investigation techniques used by journalists can be more effective than the techniques used by the criminal justice system?**

BE: In some situations, I think that journalists can be more effective than the criminal justice system. But in the overall picture it is definitely the other way round: law enforcement works over greater time spans than media, and investigative reporters are always blocked in by deadlines and other projects, so the attention span of media is very short.

MCF: **How do you see the geographical spread of the VAT fraud? Is it a global crime?**

BE: Since VAT fraud now has popped up in Kenya in Africa at the latest, yes this is most definitely a global crime. One thing is that the markets for this fraud are expanding, as with Kenya. Another thing is that the criminals are coming from all different places, and, finally, the 'tools of the trade' (i.e., goods, brass plate companies, directors, etc.) are also global.

MCF: **Are there groups or crime circles that specialized in VAT fraud over time?**

BE: Several networks have grown that are specialized in VAT fraud. I have had a lot of focus on the Pakistani networks where a lot of funds have been moved to the Middle East and Pakistan, and where the Pakistani diaspora in Europe plays an important part. But France, for instance, has had serious trouble with Israeli-based networks. If you look into the frauds taking place you also find other kinds of organized crime. Italian organized crime groups, biker gangs and Eastern European networks are just few examples. There is just too much money available – and the crime is too easy to commit and too hard to investigate.

MCF: **What are the potential links of VAT fraudsters with terrorism, especially with Islamic terrorism? Are authorities aware of these links?**

BE: In our investigation in Danish Broadcasting Corporation (DR) we found several hard, direct links between VAT fraud and terror funding. We identified a Danish-Spanish network where a group of Danish jihadists radicalized a Spanish mosque. This group took part in major VAT fraud in Denmark and has several links to a similar fraud in Sweden. Members of the Spanish group travelled to Denmark to register as directors in several companies, and the group also recruited foreign fighters that have travelled to Syria, Mali, Libya and Iraq to fight. This was all orchestrated under the umbrella of the Sharia network that spans several European countries. We found German foreign fighters that were recruited to the fight in Spain, travelled to Denmark to to work as companies as directors and travelled on towards Syria.

A conservative estimate is that the total fraud of these groups in Denmark is around 80 million DKK, and in Sweden it is 100 million SEK.

The authorities are aware and very nervous about these links. The Spanish group was arrested. But unfortunately it is not very well coordinated, so in Denmark the fraud was allowed to go on for years, even though several members of the group were monitored by the intelligence services.

MCF: **What do you think about the degree of awareness of the European Union's authorities with regards to the VAT fraud?**

BE: It has been a hard journey since 2009, but now the European Commission is fully aware of the extent of the problems with VAT fraud and has declared that they want to stop it. I have had talks with EU commissioner Moscovici on the subject, and it is my understanding that they now take this problem very seriously and urgently want to stop it.

Interview: Dr Mike Cheetham, VAT fraud expert

Dr. Michael Cheetham is a fraud expert based in Dubai. He was the former managing director of Bond House Systems, which was one of the largest computer component distributors in the United Kingdom. Bond House Systems had been trading for approximately ten years and was appointed as an official AMD[6] processors reseller for the United Kingdom just before being confronted by the HMRC in an MTIC case in the early 2000s. His company was unwittingly involved in a missing trader fraud chain in 2002. It won a European Court of Justice appeal against HMRC. In 2007 Mike presented in front of the British Parliament a set of facts depicting the gravity of the MTIC VAT fraud, there being one of the first experts triggering the alarm about this crime. Over the past decade Mike served as expert witness in more than 40 criminal cases involving VAT carousel fraud in the European Union and Great Britain.

MARIUS-CRISTIAN FRUNZA (MCF): **How has the VAT fraud evolved over the past 25 years?**
MICHAEL CHEETAM (MC): One of the first[7]-ever VAT frauds in the United Kingdom involved the smuggling of gold, which at that time, 1996, was subject to normal VAT at 17.5%. Ironically this case was based around a serving United Kingdom police officer who drove across to Belgium and then collected the gold from Luxembourg. He was only spotted by chance when customs officers noted that his car looked particularly heavy as it unloaded from the cross-channel ferry. The team smuggled a total of three tonnes of commodity gold from Europe into the United Kingdom in their cars, worth around 20 million pounds.

If the United Kingdom and European lawmakers had stopped at this point to properly consider just how easily the VAT system, with its cross-border 0% interest community supply, had been exploited, then they should have realized that the 'temporary interim VAT system' was not going to work. From that first

---

6 Advanced Micro Devices, Inc. (AMD) is an American semiconductor company.
7 www.independent.co.uk/news/pc-convicted-of-gold-smuggling-1316659.html.

significant case, the policy of the United Kingdom and European authorities was, in principle, to remove affected items from being subject to VAT.

In the early cases, such as the bullion gold, the proposed solution was to make it exempted from VAT.[8] In later cases, the European Commission authorized the use of the reverse charge mechanism as an anti-fraud tool, and thereafter this was used extensively across the European Union in an effort to remove potential fraud where it was identified in particular markets.

In not seeking to address the causative underlying problem of cross-border MTIC at the very start, they began an elaborate cat and mouse game between the criminals and policing tax authorities. The criminals exploited gold. The governments made gold exempt. The criminals move to mobile phones. The governments applied reverse charge to mobile phones. The criminals moved into computer chips. The governments applied reverse charge to computer chips. The criminals moved into carbon emissions fraud. The government attacked the United Kingdom banking system by forcing mainstream banks to close accounts held in at-risk trade sectors. The criminals exploited offshore banks like FCIB[9]. The governments closed down FCIB. The fraudsters created non-European online banking companies – termed 'trading platforms'. The governments applied reverse charge to carbon emissions. The criminals moved into those countries that did not apply the reverse charge... And so the story continues.

As the authorities tried to strike a deeper wound into the arteries of fraud, the criminals were forced to make even deeper vessels that carried more blood and were harder to find. Authorities failed to tackle the root cause of VAT fraud, namely the capacity to buy goods at 0% intra-community without any kind of controls or monitoring (other than an EC sales list or Intrastat which can be submitted (or not) up to four months later).

Each weapon devised by the criminals became more lethal. Forcing the criminals to use banking outside of the European Union, where transactions could be monitored and flagged by non-corrupt banking officials, meant that billions could be moved in a matter of weeks without any alarm bells being sounded. Pushing the fraudsters out of gold through mobile phones and into carbon trading meant that tangible goods that needed to be stored and transported (hence slowing down the fraud process) were replaced with digital certificates that could be traded three or four times a day online. No need for a warehouse. No need for customs documentation. No need for transportation costs. It was a fraudsters dream.

When carbon emissions were subjected to sporadic staged 'reverse charge', the fraudsters simply moved around Europe, exploiting those countries that had not introduced the preventative measure. From France to the Netherlands to the United Kingdom to Germany to Italy to Poland, on their merry way they rode, raking in billions upon billions as the authorities took many years to even identify the fraud.

8 www.gov.uk/government/publications/vat-notice-70121-gold/vat-notice-70121-gold.
9 First Curaçao International Bank.

Likewise, VoIP[10] fraud proved a perfect forum for the fraudsters to exploit all of their ill-gotten, ultra-productive tools of a non-tangible, digital crypto-market coupled with distant trading platforms based in banks that appear to turn a blind eye to the billions rolling in and out of the accounts.

Even worse is the scenario where the mainstream fraud markets are supposedly eliminated. In reality the fraud simply breaks into 1,000 pieces. These people are not deterred by custodial sentences or superficial fines. They have seen the rich rewards of their crimes and understand that the benefits of operating in any market where you can generate 15% to 25% per day in returns far outweigh anything that can be dealt in punishment.

One could draw a parallel to the use of antibiotics. Whilst they appear to work in the short term, the bacteria mutate and migrate to new cell types and develop immunity to the antibiotics being used to attack them.

Those are the key phrases that I would use in describing the evolution of VAT fraud over the last 25 years – mutation and migration in reaction to the foolhardy measures applied by the authorities. You need to tackle the disease itself, not the symptoms.

MCF: **What are the major challenges faced by authorities and investigators?**

MC: Apart from the aforementioned defensive weapon of removing particular commodities and markets from being subject to VAT, the primary tool which has been repeated time after time, publication after publication and in every European anti-fraud policing conference is cross-border cooperation. This involves the exchange of intelligence and central bodies to communicate between the European states and their tax intelligence sources so that the fraud can be prevented if possible or at best shut down soon after it commences. There are now between six and eight pan-European bodies charged with this very task. The preventative aspect sounds good on paper, however, with the exception of de-registering the potential fraudulent companies (which underwent a moderate degree of success in the early days); most of the intelligence is retrospective and after the event. Tax police authorities race to try and identify individuals before they flee to safe havens and secure paperwork necessary for conviction. The challenge is that this always involves massive cross-border cooperation with cases involving hundreds of officers and millions of euros of investigation costs. Rarely is the money recovered, and financial penalties imposed by the majority of European courts are primitive in striking at the huge cash reserves obtained by the criminals. Only the United Kingdom, which operates a catch-all 'proceeds of crime' process, seems to be able to recover sizeable amounts in proportion to those that are stolen. Even in the United Kingdom, the ill-gotten proceeds are often so rich in their pickings that the criminals will ignore a Judge's instruction to return the funds or face a longer period in prison. They choose the prison option, knowing that the process per year still runs into the millions, far more than they would be able to make on the outside doing legitimate work.

10 Voice over Internet Protocol.

MCF: **What is the role of expert witnesses? Can they help prosecutors? Can you share your views on this?**

MC: This is an interesting question. Rarely have the prosecutors or tax authorities sought the assistance of real experts regarding the fraud. Occasionally large blue-chip accountancy firms like KPMG and PWC are brought in to construct the most fabulous of reports and market summaries, but nobody really addresses the repeated theme of my response to these questions, namely that we have to find a solution to the underlying problem of cross-border VAT fraud, and that is the VAT system itself and how it operates. Experts like Prof. Richard Ainsworth have long since published detailed technical solutions to the root problem of MTIC fraud. In one paper alone he explored 13 different technical solutions, all of which, in my opinion, would have probably served the European Community better than the cat and mouse of reverse charge and increased intelligence swapping.

I remember the famous case of the IT programmer within the bank who altered the interest calculations, rounding up to his own account and rounding down to the clients' accounts. When he was caught, he was chastised, and the stolen funds were returned, but the bank recognized that his skills could be used to their benefit, and he became the ultimate head of IT security. Whether this story is in reality a work of fiction is not important. The prosecutors and tax authorities need to stop thinking like prosecutors and tax authorities, and understand how the criminals will exploit and counter their measures.

We repeatedly see the fraud escalating; one time I recall estimated levels of European VAT fraud in excess of €200 billion. Even now, despite all of the aforementioned methods being implemented, the fraud is still operating in excess of €100 billion. The sums, free-falling into organized crime's pockets, are greater than many European countries' national debt.

The ivory tower approach of tackling MTIC fraud is simply not working, and it is time for the authorities to adopt a new panel of experts and be prepared to embrace technology to take away the capacity to steal these vast sums. These ideas have been on the table since 2006. Can you imagine how much has been lost in the last 12 years? The sad thing is that I see that the general direction of the solutions to VAT fraud is finally meandering slowly in the direction of our suggested digital controls, but why is it taking so long?

MCF: **What is your view on UAE[11] countries implementing VAT?**

MC: Living and working in the UAE as I do, I was excited to see the birth of the VAT system, which had the chance to be shaped in its pre-embryonic growth sac into a robust anti-fraud baby and later adult. Experts like Prof. Richard Ainsworth and I wrote to the highest officials in the country, offering our opinions for free and explaining how easy it would be to introduce digital controls from the outset. Not only would this lessen the burden of

11 United Arab Emirates.

administration upon the domestic companies (who have no experience of any form of tax regime), but the introduction of a crypto-based digital currency such as 'VATCoin' would remove the negative cash flow implications of such a scheme. With the exception of zero rating bullion gold, it appears that the Federal tax authority ignored our warnings. They appear to have introduced a near carbon copy of the European system, along with all of its inherent flaws, but they failed to implement some of the lessons learned in Europe within the base system. In essence the UAE system is wide open for fraud, albeit at 5% for now. Nobody believes that the tax will remain at this low level since this will generate only 1% of GDP[12] for the country. Ultimately we may see rates stepped up slowly but ending as high as 15%. Corporation tax will also need to be added to supplement these essential non-oil-based revenues. Prior to 2017, the country didn't even have a tax authority or a single tax officer. Plans are underway to recruit and train up to 6,000 VAT inspectors, but can you imagine how they will fare in comparison to the European officers who have 25 years' experience trying to combat the advanced fraud techniques? In my opinion, it will be a fraudster's paradise for many years to come, and it will take the authorities a long time to get a grip on what is happening with their newborn tax systems. As the VAT rate rises, the motivation to develop the fraud in the region will increase accordingly. Let us not forget that many of the European fraudsters moved to the UAE and surrounding countries as a safe haven. We therefore have a cocktail of criminals with a PhD in VAT fraud and a tax officer equipped, if he or she is lucky, with a bachelor degree.

Quite why the GCC[13] system has not been designed to be anti-fraud proof is a deeply worrying puzzle to me, especially as many of the advisors sitting on the right hand of the Arabic tax ministers are blue-chip European VAT firms who surely understand the vulnerabilities that they are allowing to be built into this primitive legislation.

I will go down on record as saying that this was perhaps the greatest opportunity missed in not implementing GCC VAT as a digital currency from the very start. The UAE in particular has a state-funded Blockchain centre which develops, along with IBM, state-of-the-art blockchain solutions to government administration challenges. I can think of no greater challenge for that centre.

MCF: **Have they learned the EU lessons on VAT fraud?**
MC: As I have entered, absolutely not. The system is wide open to fraud and without the advanced cross-border detection systems that the European Union proudly boasts it operates. Having studied the GCC legislation released to date, I can see at least half a dozen routes through which VAT fraud can be implemented. Perhaps the simplest example is that goods can be imported

---

12 Gross Domestic Product.
13 Gulf Cooperation Council.

into the country with the VAT deferred to the VAT return, simply by providing the VAT number. That allows goods to enter the local market at 0%. The goods can be sold at +5%. VAT return periods are quarterly, with a 28-day window after that, so the criminals would have four months in which to exploit the import, fold the company and disappear. We have calculated that, even after discounting the imported goods by 1% under the market value (to enable a quick sale), the fraudulent return of 4% spread over five days in a week and across four months would quickly turn $1 million into $26 million. That is with one deal a day. The fact that they have only removed bullion gold means that all of the European suspects can be exploited, including diamonds, mobile phones, electronics and all the rest of the commodities and markets in the experienced European fraudsters' arsenal.

It appears that the GCC system actually unlearned the lessons of the European Union on VAT fraud.

My greatest concern is that the terrorist organizations around the world, but in particular in the Middle East, where they have many a home, will begin to use VAT fraud as a two-pronged weapon against these legitimate states. First they will strike economic damage into the very heart of the countries as they seek to move away from an oil-dependent economy. Second, they will derive great income from the fraud, which will be used to further finance their beliefs, weapons and recruitment. Whilst I have seen a few small examples of terrorist exploitation of VAT fraud in Europe, I believe that the scope for this to happen is much greater in the GCC.

MCF: **How do you see the VAT fraud arena in the following years?**
MC: The pickings of VAT fraud are so rich that the criminals can make billions of euros in a year. A prime example of this was the Italian fraud in VoIP, which was thought to be in the region of $2.7 billion stolen over a nine-month period:

Prior to that paper there was very little (if any) public discussion of VoIP MTIC. There were no assessments, no arrests, and not a hint of litigation. Fifteen days later, and before final publication, the financial press exploded with coverage of a massive VoIP MTIC fraud (the *Operazione Phuncards-Broker* investigation). The Wall Street Journal reported: An [Italian] judge...ordered the arrest of 56 people, including one of Italy's richest men as part of an international probe into an alleged $2.7 billion money-laundering and tax-evasion scheme involving two major Italian telecommunications providers.

In 2014 a second VAT fraud was discovered that had taken place in Italy around carbon trading in 2010. It seemed that the Italians had lost over €1 billion and didn't even know about it until a laptop was discovered in a terrorist hideout in the Middle East. One has to ask how our country did not know that it had lost €1 billion.

I see the fraud continuing to mutate and migrate, and occasionally being broken into 1,000 smaller pieces, all of which make it hard to monitor and detect. The authorities will continue to play retrospective catch-up until we implement a fraud-proof VAT system. I become more concerned when I don't see exploited markets being reported in the VAT cases. That does not mean the fraud has gone away but merely that it has gone underground into some new market as yet undiscovered by the tax authorities.

MCF: **Are the current solutions to tackle the fraud efficient?**
MC: VAT fraud in the European Union continues to operate at levels in excess of €100 billion. By its very nature, the calculations of lost revenue are only hypothetical, and, whilst these estimations are very useful, lump sum cases like the Italian job example illustrate that our best guess is far from that.
MCF: **What solution would be the best alternative?**
MC: There are only two effective solutions:

1   You change the underlying legislation and remove the capacity to have 0% goods sold within the member states.
2   You remove the VAT from a tangible currency to an inert monopoly-style cryptocurrency.

MCF: **How can blockchain technology be leveraged to VAT?**
MC: Blockchain is nothing more than a global time and date stamp, which certifies anything to which it is applied as authentic. Blockchain mining is currently a notoriously slow process, and I see no reason why the European or GCC tax authorities could not themselves generate a digital certificate for a fictional VAT currency which can be securely verified by all taxpayers as authentic. Whether this digital tax currency which we have termed 'VAT-Coin' is generated and certified by the wider blockchain community or the governments themselves is irrelevant. What matters is that it can only be cashed by the relevant tax authority. Each currency base in the European Union would need to have its own crypto-tax currency.
MCF: **Can blockchain tackle the VAT fraud? What are its strengths over other current foreseeable solutions?**
MC: Whilst you technically could steal 'VATCoin' from third parties, the core principle is that it can only be utilized by governments. To the criminals it would be a worthless digital 'monopoly style' transaction. Even if it were stolen and used as fraudulent input tax, the traceability and inheritance of blockchain mean that it can be easily identified and returned to its rightful owner. I cannot see a flaw in something that cannot be turned into real money being stolen.

When the original VATCoin concept was devised in 2006, it was suggested that the handshaking would be conducted by accountancy software, which would obtain certified lot numbers for each transaction from government servers.

Blockchain was not in existence as we know it today. The accelerated development of the blockchain principle means that the authentication of a crypto-tax currency is now more secure than ever, and to me this seemed the perfect solution. It was just a matter of time before one of the governments tried such a scheme. It is a shame that the GCC did not embrace such a revolutionary idea and set the gold standard for other VAT-based countries around the world.

Bibliography

Ainsworth, R. (2010a). MTIC (VAT fraud) in VoIP—Market Size $3.3b. *57 Tax Notes International*, 57, 1079.

Ainsworth, R. (2010b). *VAT fraud: MTIC & MTEC—The tradable services problem.* SSRN.

Ainsworth, R. T. (2006). Carousel fraud in the EU: A digital VAT solution. *Tax Notes International*, 443.

Ainsworth, R. T. (2010a). *VAT fraud-Technological solutions.* SSRN.

Ainsworth, R. T. (2010b). VoIP MTIC—The Italian Job (Operazione 'Phuncards-Broker'). *58 Tax Notes International*, 721.

Ainsworth, R. T. (2015a). *A VATCoin proposal following on The 2017 EU VAT Proposals-MTIC, VATCoin, and BLOCKCHAIN.* SSRN.

Ainsworth, R. T. (2015b). *VAT fraud and terrorist funding—The Azizi extradition allegations Part I*, Boston University School of Law Law & Economics Working Paper No. 15–24

Ainsworth, R. T. (2016). *Blockchain (distributed ledger technology) solves VAT fraud.* SSRN.

Ainsworth, R. T. (2017). *The first real-time blockchain VAT-GCC solves MTIC fraud.* SSRN.

Albert, M., & Ball, R. J. (1983). *Towards European economic recovery in the 1980s.* European Parliament Working Documents 1983–4.

Arner, D. W. (2016). FinTech, regtech and the reconceptualization of financial regulation. *Northwestern Journal of International Law & Business*, 37(3), 371.

Babiak, P. (1996). Psychopathic manipulation in organizations: Pawns, patrons, and patsies. *Issues in Criminological and Legal Psychology*, 24, 12–17.

Bai, J., & Perron, P. (1998). Estimating and testing linear models with multiple structural changes. *Econometrica*, 66(1), 48–78.

Baltagi, B. (2008). *Econometric analysis of panel data.* Chichester, UK: John Wiley & Sons.

Barbone, L., Belkindas, M., Bettendorf, L., Bird, R. M., Bonch-Osmolovskiy, M., & Smart, M. (2013). *Study to quantify and analyse the VAT Gap in the EU-27 member states.* CASE Network Reports No. 116/2013.

Barbone, L. (2014). *2012 Update report to the study to quantify and analyse the VAT Gap in the EU-27 member states.* CASE Network Reports No. 120/2014.

Barbone, L., Bonch-Osmolovskiy, M., & Poniatowski, G. (2015). *Study to quantify and analyse the VAT GAP in the EU member states.* CASE Network Reports No. 124.

Basalisco, B., Wahl, J., & Okholm, H. (2016). e-*Commerce imports into Europe: VAT and customs treatment.* UPS.

Beider, A., & More, S. P. (2008). Beider-morse phonetic matching: An alternative to soundex with fewer false hits. *Avotaynu: The International Review of Jewish Genealogy*, Summer 2008.

Borselli, F. (2011). *Organised Vat fraud: Features, magnitude, policy perspectives*. Bank of Italy Occasional Paper No. 106.

Bryans, D. (2014). Bitcoin and money laundering: Mining for an effective solution. *Indiana Law Journal*, 89(1), 441.

Bukhsh, F. A., & Weigand, H. (2014). *VAT fraud: Possible technical and ontological solutions*. Madalmaad: *Tilburg* University.

Burniske, C. W. (2017). Bitcoin: Ringing the bell for a new asset class. *Ark Invest*.

Buss, D. M., Gomes, M., Higgins, D. S., & Lauterbach, K. (1987). Tactics of manipulation. *Journal of Personality and Social Psychology*, 52(6), 1219–1279.

Campos, N. F. (2014). Economic growth and political integration: Estimating the benefits from membership in the European Union using the synthetic counterfactuals method. IZA Discussion Papers, No. 8162, Institute for the Study of Labor (IZA).

Chaum, D. F. (1990). *Untraceable electronic cash. Proceedings on advances in cryptology*. Santa Barbara, CA: Springer-Verlag, 319–327.

Chugani, S. H. (2008). Benevolent blood money: Terrorist exploitation of zakat and its complications in the war on terror. *North Carolina Journal of International Law and Commercial Regulation*, 34(2), 601.

Coase, R. H. (1974). Choice of the institutional framework. *The Journal of Law and Economics*, 17(2), 493–496.

Croissant, Y. M. (2008). Panel data econometrics in R: The plm package. *Journal of Statistical Software*, 27(2), 1–43.

De La Feria, R., & Foy, R. (2016). Italmoda: The birth of the principle of third-party liability for VAT fraud. *British Tax Review*, 2016(3), 270–280.

De Smet, D., & Mention, A. -L. (2011). Improving auditor effectiveness in assessing KYC/AML practices: Case study in a Luxembourgish context. *Managerial Auditing Journal*, 26(2), 182–203.

Dickey, D. A. (1979). Distribution of the estimators for autoregressive time series with a unit root. *Journal of the American Statistical Association*, 74(366), 427–431.

Dion, M., Weissstub, D., & Richet, J. -L. (2016). *Financial crimes: Psychological, technological, and ethical issues*. Switzerland: Springer.

Efron, B. (1987). Better bootstrap confidence intervals. *Journal of the American Statistical Association*, 82(397), 171–185.

Ella, V. G. (1973). Multi-level or pyramid sales systems: Fraud or free enterprise. *South Dakota Law Review*, 18, S. 358–393.

Erimolovici, D. (2001). *Имена собственные на стыке языков и культур. Р.Валент*.

European Commision. (2013). *Vat rates applied in the member states of the European Union*.

European Commision. (2017). *On the follow-up to the action plan on VAT towards a Single EU VAT area—Time to act*.

EY. (2015). *Assessment of the application and impact of the VAT exemption for importation of small consignments*. European Commsion, TAXUD/2013/DE/334.

Fechner, G. T., Howes, D. H., & Boring, E. G. (1860). *Elements of psychophysics [Elemente der Psychophysik]*. New York: Holt, Rinehart and Winston.

Feldman, R., & Sanger, J. (2007). *The text mining handbook: Advanced approaches in analyzing unstructured data*. Boston, MA: Cambridge University Press.

Fernandez, R., & Sanger, J. (1991). Resistance to reform: Status quo bias in the presence of individual-specific uncertainty. *The American Economic Review*, 81(5), 1146–1155.

Franzese, M. (2009). *Quitting the mob*. Miami Gardens, FL: St. Thomas University School of Law.

Frunza, M. (2014). The cost of non-Europe of an incomplete economic and monetary union to prevent future crises. Labex ReFI , European Parliament Reports .

Frunza, M. (2016). *Cost of the MTIC VAT fraud for European Union members.*

Frunza, M., & Guegan, D. (2018). Is the bitcoin rush over? University Ca' Foscari of Venice, Department of Economics Research Paper Series No. 10/WP/2018.

Frunza, M.-C. (2013). Aftermath of the VAT fraud on carbon emissions markets. *Journal of Financial Crime*, 20(2), 222–236.

Frunza, M. -C. (2015a). *Introduction to the theories and varieties of modern crime in financial markets.* Cambridge, MA: Academic Press.

Frunza, M.-C. (2015b). *Fraud and carbon markets.* Routledge, United States.

Frunza, M.-C. (2015c). *Solving modern crime in financial markets: Analytics and case studies.* Cambridge, MA: Academic Press.

Frunza, M.-C., Guégan, D., & Lassoudière, A. (2010). Forecasting strategies for carbon allowances prices: from classic arbitrage pricing theory to switching regimes. *International Review of Applied Financial Issues and Economics*, 576.

Frunza, M.-C., Guégan, D., & Lassoudière, A. (2011). Missing trader fraud on the emissions market. *Journal of Financial Crime*, 18(2), 183–194.

Geng, Z., & Lu, X. (2014). *Implicitly-coordinated stock price attack and exploitation of retail investors' behavioral biases: Widespread evidence in the chinese stock market.*

Gradeva, K. (2014). VAT fraud in intra-EU trade. Goethe University, 33.

Grinberg, R. (2012). Bitcoin: An innovative alternative digital currency. *Hastings Science & Technology Law Journal*, 41, 159.

Gustafsson, L., & Ranstorp, M. (2017). *Swedish foreign fighters in Syria and Iraq: An analysis of open-source intelligence and statistical data.* Forsvarshogskolan (FHS).

Guth, G. J. (1976). Surname spellings and computerized record linkage. *Historical Methods Newsletter*, 10–19.

Haigh, M. S. (2005). Do professional traders exhibit myopic loss aversion? An experimental analysis. *The Journal of Finance*, 523–534.

Harrington, C. (2017). Why fintech could lead to more financial crime? *CFA Institute Magazine*, 28.

Haselton, M. G. (2005). The evolution of cognitive bias. *The handbook of evolutionary psychology.* Wiley Online Library.

Hiller, W. (2017). *Mapping the cost of non-Europe, 2014–2019.* European Parliament.

HMRC. (2010). *Measuring tax gaps 2010.* HM Revenues and Customs.

HMRC. (2016). *Fulfilment house due diligence scheme.* HM Revenues and Customs.

Hofer, P. (1989). The role of manipulation in the antisocial personality. *International Journal of Offender Therapy and Comparative Criminology*, 33(2), 91–101.

Keen, M. S. (2007). *VAT fraud and evasion: What do we know, and what can be done?.* International Monetary Fund No. 7–31.

Kidd-Hewitt, D. (2002). *Crime and the media: A criminological perspective. Criminology: A Reader.* London, UK: Sage, 116–129.

Kogels, H. (2010). VAT fraud with emission allowances trading. *HeinOnline.*

Kozmetsky, G. & Yue, P. (2005). *The economic transformation of the United States, 1950–2000: focusing on the technological revolution, the service sector expansion, and the Cultural, ideological, and demographic changes.* Purdue University Press.

Lane, J.-E. (2017). *Globalization and politics: Promises and dangers.* Routledge, United Kingdom.

Lashmar, P., & Hobbs D. (2017). Diamonds, gold and crime displacement: Hatton garden, and the evolution of organised crime in the UK. *Trends in Organized Crime*, 21(2), 1–22.

Laure, M. (1955). *Revolution: Derniere chance de la France.* Presses universitaires de France.

Lee, D. (2015). *Handbook of digital currency: Bitcoin, innovation, financial instruments.* Cambridge, MA: Academic Press.

Levenshtein, V. (1966). Binary codes capable of correcting deletions, insertions and reversals. *Soviet Physics Doklady*, 707, Soviet Union.

Lim, S. S. (2006). Do investors integrate losses and segregate gains? Mental accounting and investor trading decisions. *The Journal of Business*, 79(5), 2539–2573.

Lind, K. (2013). Reverse charging: The best possible solution for preventing VAT fraud. *World Journal of VAT/GST Law*, 2(2), 97–115.

Martin Gill, G. T. (2004). Preventing money laundering or obstructing business? Financial companies' perspectives on 'know your customer' procedures. *The British Journal of Criminology*, 44(1), 582–594.

Miers, I., Garman, C., Green, M., & Rubin, A. D. (2013). Zerocoin: Anonymous distributed E-Cash from Bitcoin. *IEEE Symposium on Security and Privacy (SP)*, 397–411.

Mitnick, K. D., Simon, W. L., & Wozniak, S. (2002). *The art of deception.* Hoboken, NJ: Wiley Publishing.

Mokotoff, G. (1997). *Soundexing and Genealogy.* www.avotaynu.com/soundex.html.

Moore, G. B. (1977). *Accessing individual records from personal data files using non-unique identifiers.* US Department of Commerce, National Bureau of Standards.

Mourao, P. J. (2012). The weber-fechner law and public expenditures impact to the win-margins at parliamentary elections. *Papers, Prague Economic*, 21(3), 291–308.

Muncy, J. A. (2004). Ethical issues in multilevel marketing: Is it a legitimate business or just another pyramid scheme? *Marketing Education Review*, 21(1), 47–53.

Nadkarni, P. M.-M. (2011). Natural language processing: an introduction. *Journal of the American Medical Informatics Association*, 541–551.

Normark, M., & Ranstorp, M. (2015). Understanding terrorist finance. Modus Operandi and National CTF-Regimes. Stockholm: Swedish Defence University.

Normark, M., Ranstorp, M., & Ahlin, F. (2017). *Financial activities linked to persons from Sweden and Denmark who joined terrorist groups in Syria and Iraq during the period 2013–2016: Report commissioned by Finansinspektionen.* Finansinspektionen.

Olson, D. T. (2012). *Tactical counterterrorism: The law enforcement manual of terrorism prevention.* Springfield, IL: Charles C Thomas Publisher.

Park, J., Konana, P., Gu, B., Kumar, A., & Raghunathan, R. (2013). Information valuation and confirmation bias in virtual communities: Evidence from stock message boards. *Information Systems Research*, 24(4), 1050–1067.

Parra-Moyano, J., & Ross, O. (2017). *KYC optimization using distributed ledger technology.* SSRN.

Peter, C. (2001). Pricing and hedging in incomplete markets. *Journal of Financial Economics*, 62(1), 131–167.

Phillips, P. C. (2011). Explosive behavior in the 1990s nasdaq: When did exuberance escalate asset values? *International Economic Review*, 52(1), 201–226.

Phillips, P. C. (2015). Testing for multiple bubbles: Historical episodes of exuberance and collapse in the S&P 500. *International Economic Review*, 56(4),1043–1078.

Pigou, A. C. (1912). *Wealth and welfare.* France: Macmillan and Company, Limited.

Poniatowski, G., Bonch-Osmolovskiy, M., & Belkindas, M. (2016). *Study and reports on the VAT Gap in the EU-28 member states: 2016 Final Report.* CASE Research Paper No. 483.

Poniatowski, G., Bonch-Osmolovskiy, M., & Belkindas, M. (2017). *Study and reports on the VAT Gap in the EU-28 member states: 2017 Final Report*. DG TAXUD Project 2015/CC/131.

PWC. (2013). *Study on the feasibility and impact of a common EU standard VAT return*, Brussels.

Reckon, L. (2009). *Study to quantify and analyse the VAT Gap in the EU-25 Member States*. Report for DG Taxation and Customs Union.

Richard, A. (2013). VoIP MTIC–The Italian Job (Operazione 'Phuncards-Broker'). *58 Tax Notes International 721.*

Russell, R. (1918). *Patent No. US Patent 1261167.* United States Patent Office.

Said, S. E. (1984). Testing for unit roots in autoregressive-moving average models of unknown order. *Biometrika*, 71(3), 599–607.

Schneider, F. (2003). *The shadow economy. Encyclopedia of public choice*. Dordrecht: Kluwer Academic Publishers.

Schneider, F. (2005). Shadow economies around the world: What do we really know? *European Journal of Political Economy*, 21(4), 598–642.

Schneider, F. (2010). The influence of public institutions on the shadow economy: An empirical investigation for OECD Countries. *European Journal of Law and Economics*, 6(3), 441–468.

Schneider, F. (2011). *Handbook on the shadow economy*. Cheltenham, UK: Edward Elgar.

Schneider, F. (2015). Schattenwirtschaft und schattenarbeitsmarkt: Die entwicklungen der vergangenen 20 Jahre. *Perspektiven derWirtschaftspolitik*, 16(1), 3–25.

Schneider, F., & Enste D. (2000). Shadow economies: Size, causes, and consequences. *The Journal of Economic Literature*, 38(1), 77–114.

Schneider, F., & Enste D. (2002). *The shadow economy: Theoretical approaches, empirical studies, and political implications*. Cambridge: Cambridge University Press.

Selgin, G. (2015). Synthetic commodity money. *Journal of Financial Stability*, 17, 92–99.

Sutskever, I., Oriol, V., & Le, Q. V. (2004). Sequence to sequence learning with neural networks. *Advances in neural information processing systems*, vol. 1, 3104–3112.

Tagkalakis, A. O. (2014). Tax arrears and VAT revenue performance: Recent evidence from Greece. *Economics Bulletin, AccessEcon*, 34(2), 1141–1155.

Thaler, R. H. (1999). Mental accounting matters. *Journal of Behavioral Decision Making*, 12(3), 183–206.

Thompson, P. F. (2003). Names: A new frontier in text mining. In R. M. Chen H., *Intelligence and security informatic* (pp. 27–38). New York: Springer Berlin Heidelberg.

Vander Nat, P. J. (2002). Marketing fraud: An approach for differentiating multilevel marketing from pyramid schemes. *Journal of Public Policy & Marketing*, 21(1), 139–151.

Van der Veen, R. A. (2016). The electricity balancing market: Exploring the design challenge. *Utilities Policy*, 43, 186–194.

Williams, C. C. (2016). *Measuring the global shadow economy: The prevalence of informal work and labour*. Cheltenham, UK: Edward Elgar Publishing.

Yang, X., Liao, H., Feng, X., & Yao, X. (2018). Analysis and tests on weak-form efficiency of the EU carbon emission trading market. *Low Carbon Economy*, 9(1), 1–17.

Zeileis, A., Leisch, F., Hornik, K., & Kleiber, C. (2002). strucchange: An R package for testing for structural change in linear regression models. *Journal of Statistical Software*, 7(2), 1–38.

Index

A1 Freight 198
Abu Hamzah 124
The Accessory People (TAP) 190
Acciaieria Riva 16
accounting shenanigans 4, 12–13
Accrue Telemedia OY 224, 228, 231–2, 238
Accrue UK Ltd. 224
Acorn Trading 196
Acumen Europe OY 224, 228, 231–2, 238
Acumen Ltd. 228–9, 231
Acumen UK Ltd. 224, 229, 232
Adali-Mortty, Jonah 196
Advanced Petroleum Services 30
Agency for Combating Economic Crimes 110
Ahmad, Faisal Zahoor 211
Ahmad, Shakeel 196
Ahmed, Hasnat Siddique 123
Ahmed, Nasser 199–200
Ahmed, Niaz 123, 125
Ahmed, Shabir Anwar 199
Ahmed, Syed Mubarak 196
Ahmed, Yakub Imran 121
Ailicis SL 194
Ainsworth, R. 14, 70–1
Ainsworth R. T. 272
Airbnb 140
al-Andalusi, Abu Nur 126
Al Baghdady, Osama 243
Al-Issa, Bashar 243
Aleixo, Valter 193–4
Ali, Chaudry 192–3
Alibaba 134, 140
Allad, Abdullah Yusuf 191
Alldech Ltd. 189
Almeida, Joaquim de 97
Al-Qaeda 113–14, 124
Altcoins 5; BaFin and 169; legal status of 167; mixing/tumbling and 165; as virtual goods or services 162

alternative banking platforms (ABPs) 96–9; BlueNext 97–8; Deuss, John 99; Nexor One 98–9; Swefin (Danish internet bank) 97
Alzraa, Stephane 208
Amani, Adam 190
Amazon 71, 73, 134, 135, 137–8, 140
Amazon.com 134
Amritanand, Albert 188
Anand, Anish 244
Angelides, Stuart Emilios 196
Anglo Irish Merchants 195
Anibel Comercio Artesano 194
Anibel e Montagen Electrical 194
Antonio, Ferreri 217
Apabhai, Eisa Masihullah 190
Apabhai, Hashib Ansari 190
Apple Pay 160
application-specific integrated circuit (ASIC) 174
Arigoni, Fabio 217
artificial demand 18–19; see also demand
Arturo, Danesi 229
Asensio, Juan José López 194
Ase Technology 226
Ashraf, Shehwad 189
Asian English-speaking groups 257
Astruc, Cyril 204–5, 206, 247
Auchan 201
Aulov, Nikolai 250
Aurum Jewellery 2000 Ltd. 196
Aurum Jewellery (Wholesale) Ltd. 196
Australian Crime Commission 16
avenues of countering VAT fraud: controls of cash payments 268–9; distributed ledger technologies 271–3; Kittel principle 269–71; KYC, a sound alternative 277–8; quick fixes 265; reverse VAT charge 266–8; role of KYC in financial institutions 275–7;

transnational investigation agencies 273–5; VAT exemption 265–6
Axpo Italia 121
Azizi, Samir 116
Azzoug, Amar 209

B-2-B (business to business) companies 2
BaFin (Bundesanstalt für Finanzdienstleistungsaufsicht) 169
Baghdadi, Benaissa Laghmouchi 123
Bai, J. 89
Baigent, Jonathon 190
Baillie, Stuart 185–6
Baillies Ltd. 185
Balcom LLC 107
Balouka, Elie 204
Baltic groups 254–7
Banda della Magliana 215, 235
Bank of Italy 242
Bank of Vatican 248
Barclays 151, 214
Baretsky, Stas 77
barter trading 6
Basra, Dhanvinder 'Dan' Singh 214
Bauduin, Claude 207, 211
Bauduin GMBH 207
Bedesha, Jasbinder 192
Beider-Morse Phonetic Matching 263
Belgian Fortis Bank 205; *see also* BNP Paribas
Belle Gray 157
Benali, Mohamed Mohamed 123
Benelux Connection: and the birth of MTIC 181–4; first cases 182; Gilmore, Lucie 182–3; Gilmore, Michael 182–3; Karim, Shabir 183–4; Mann, Geoffrey 183; reloaded 184
Benichou, Giles 206, 208
Berezovsky, Boris 205
Berlin Wall, fall of 46, 100
Beronvine Ltd. 196
Betta Solutions Ltd. 196
Bhatti, Imran 184
Bhatti, Kamran 184
bias: confirmation 150; expectation 150; geographic 277; reputation 276; safe harbour 277; size 276
bilateral extradition agreements 158
Bilunov, Leonid Mackintosh 103
bin Laden, Osama 121
Bitcoin 5, 174; accounting treatment of 160–2; BaFin and 169; birth of 160; crypto-exchanges and 165–6; crypto-flipping and 166; enhancing the VAT

fraud 162–3; Ether and 175; financial criminals and 162; gains and losses incurred on 170; in Israel 172; legal status of 167; mining machines for 174; as popular cryptocurrency 160; surfaced in 160; in Switzerland 172–3; in United Kingdom 169–70; in United States 171
Bitcoin Blender 164
Bitcoin Cash 160
'Bitcoin-mania' 158; *see also* 'Crypto-mania'
Bitcoin mixing 164; *see also* Bitcoin tumbling
Bitcoin (crypto) protocol 176
Bitcoin tumbling 164; *see also* Bitcoin mixing
Bitmain 174
BitMixer.io 164
Bitsquare 166
black market 5; *see also* shadow economy
Blockchain.info 164
blockchain technology 74, 158–9, 175, 273
'blue-collar' crime 178
BlueNext exchange 87–8, 90, 97–8, 131–2, 150–2, 202–4, 259
BNP Paribas 205; *see also* Belgian Fortis Bank
Boston Freight 198
Bourke, Robert 16
Bouygues Telecom 19
Bovalino, Chiara 217
Bowden, Raymond 184
Boykin, Gennady 108
'*Bratianu*' clan 252
Breccolotti, Luca 236
Breton Woods 160
Brexit 135, 155; customs clearance 80–1; enforcing the LVCR 82–3; 'Hard'-Brexit scenario 79; MOSS scheme and MTEC 81–2; 'Soft'-Brexit scenario 78–9; VAT and 'Brexit' negotiations 77–8; VAT fraud after 83–4; VAT scrapping scenario 80
BRFkredit 124, 126
British Asians 213
British Audit Office 71
British Parliament 82, 138
Broad, Terence Thomas 199
Broker Management S.A. 224, 232, 241
Brown, Wayne Stewart 211
Bruno, Zito 237
B&S Property 212
BT Italia S.p.A. 230
B-to-C (business to client) companies 1–2

Bufete Orfisa 30
Bulearca, Viorel 252
Bullion Bond 16
Bunbusinesselite BBE Ltd. 252
Bunge Ltd. 47, 93
Business Activities Tax 2
Business Email Compromise (BEC) 155
Butler, Jason 245
'*Butoane*' clan 252

Calabrian 'Ndrangheta 248–9
Calcon Industrial Supplies Ltd. 187
Cameron, David 212
Campos, N. F. 35
Cannavao, Maurizio 217
Carbon Connection 94, 201–15; Ahmad,
    Faisal Zahoor 211; Alzraa, Stephane
    208; Astruc, Cyril 204–5; Bauduin,
    Claude 211; Benedetti, Jean-René
    210; British-Asian branch 213–15;
    'carbonized' branch 209; Dacheville,
    Yannick 206–7; Deutsche Bank
    213; Dosanjh, Sandeep Singh 214;
    French-Corsican branch 209–10;
    French-Israeli branch of 202–9; German
    branch 210–13; Gohir, Mohammad
    211–12; Klapucki, Jaroslaw 208–9;
    Melgrani, Christiane 210; Mimran,
    Arnaud 207–8; Mouly, Mardoché
    'Marco' 207; Porcaro, Angelina 210;
    Sakoun, Fabrice 204; Salya, Mohsin
    Usmangani 212; Villeneuve, Stéphane
    206; Virdee, Peter Singh 212–13; VoIP
    connection 215; Zaoui, Gregory 203
carousel fraud 6, 8, 17, 20, 25, 47, 85,
    146, 153, 191, 200–1, 215, 242,
    269–72
car production, in France 91–2
Carradine, David 244
'Carré & Ribeiro' case 17, 193
Cartaxo 194
cash: dirty 96; financial asset as 160; as
    king 95; physical 95, 96
cash payments 268–9
Castillo, German 190
Catanzariti, Antonio 225, 238
Cazeneuve, Bernard 203
Ceniti, Giovanni Battista 239
CEO fraud 145, 155–6
Chahal, Jaswender Singh 196
Charlie Hebdo 113
Chatlani, Annand 194–5
Chatlani, Mohan 194–5
Chaum, David 160

Cheetham, Michael 292–9
Cherazi, Babak 196
Cherici, Estefano 30
Cherney, Michael 205
Cherubini, Giuseppe 217, 236
Chetrit, Gérard 210
Chevron 29
Chisthi, Zafar Baidar 197–8
Chogin, Fidel 108
Cian Plus 30
Citibank 214
Citigroup 214
clothes 18
CMC Group 218–22, 235, 241
CMC Italia Srl 217, 219, 220–4, 235
CMC Italy 218
CO_2 emissions 21–2
CO_2 emissions allowances 87–8
Coast Logistics 188
Coer2 Commodities 203
Cohen, Haroun 204
Coinmixer.se 164
Comito, Massimo 225
Committee of French Automobile
    Manufacturers 91
confirmation bias 149–50
Contin, Roberto 225, 238–239
Continental Claims Consultants 212
'contra-trader' 10–11
contratrading 6, 10–11
Copp, Andrew 245
Copp, Geoffrey 245–6
Copp, Joshua 245–6
Coriano Capital S.A. 224, 227
Corriere della Sera 121
Cortachy Wholesalers Ltd. 198
'The cost of non-Europe' 38
Council Directive 2006/112/EC 166, 168
Counter-Terrorism Financing systems 114
countertrade (barter) fraud 11–12
Cox, Raymond 188–9
Crepuscule 151–2
criminal underworld: Asian
    English-speaking groups 257; Baltic
    groups 254–7; Calabrian 'Ndrangheta
    248–9; emergence of new crime
    groups 248–9; fall of 'old moustache
    Petes' 247–8; Israeli groups 249–50;
    Romanian and Bulgarian groups 250–4;
    Russian-speaking organized crime 250
Crosscomm Ltd. 224
cross-invoicing 6, 9
Crown Era Investments Ltd. 242
Crownlink Networks Ltd. 186

Crowther, Russell 199
Crudele, Giuseppe 219, 225, 236–7
cryptocurrencies 158–60; blockchain and 158–9; enhancing the VAT fraud 162–3; liable to VAT 173
'Cryptocurrency Fairness in Taxation Act' (CFTA) 171
crypto-economy: VAT treatment of 166–7
crypto-flipping 166
'Crypto-mania' 158; *see also* 'Bitcoin-mania'
crypto-mixing 164; *see also* crypto-tumbling
crypto-tumbling 164; *see also* crypto-mixing
Crystal Cars Ltd. 197
Crystal Telkom GmbH 189
customs clearance 80–1

Dacheville, Yannick 206–7, 208
Daech *see* Islamic State of Iraq and Syria (ISIS)
Daitch-Mokotoff Soundex approach 263
Dane Elec 17
Dark Ronnie 180
Datacell Ltd. 189
data mining techniques 260
data preparation 61
decentralized exchanges 165–6
De La Feria, R. 270
demand: artificial 18–19; inelastic 26–7
Denaro, Manlio 239
Dentalloy and Stewart Nicol Solutions Ltd. 16
Deral Spa 16
deregulated commercial contracts 175–6
Deuss, John 99
Deutsche Bank 203, 213, 276
Devine, Bernadette 195
DHL 174
Diadem Ltd. 228
Diadem UK Ltd. 224, 241
DigiCash, Inc. 160
Di Girolamo, Nicola Paolo 235
digital economy 40
'digital nomads' 174
digital products 24–5; *see also* products
Digital VAT (D-VAT) 104–5, 272
DIICOT 252
Dines, Andrew 241
Dines, Colin 241
Dion, Celine 197
direct taxes 1, 31–2, 34

'dirty cash' 96
'dirty money' 95–6
distributed application platform 175
distributed ledger technologies 271–3
Donovan, Jason 244
Dosanjh, Sandeep Singh 214
DRl 116
Dray, Claude 209
Dreamweavers Theatre Company 157
Driscoll, Richard 244
Dris, Kamal Mohamed 123
Dubai Connection 84, 116, 178, 190–3; Ali, Chaudry 192–3; Bedesha, Jasbinder 192; Takkar, Harjit Singh 192; Umerji, Adam 191
Ductil Rom SA Bucharest 252
Dutch Reverse Charge 20

eBay 71, 73, 134, 135, 137–8
Ebbrell, Peter Arthur 190
e.Biscom S.p.A. 218
eCash 160
EcoDutch Carbon 123
Eco Logic Solutions 16
e-commerce 129–30; and Brexit 82; in the EU 134–5; peer-to-peer delivery services and 140
econometric models 57–61
economy of terror: case studies 120; low-cost modus operandi 114; operations 118–19; paradigm shift 113–14; Q-Transport 123–8; SF Energy Trading 121–3; uber-terrorism, financing of 115–16; uber-terrorism and low-cost terrorism as new directions of global terrorism 113; uber-terrorist 115; VAT fraud, reasons for 117–18; VAT fraud as source of financing of terrorism 116–17
E-Daugava 257
Edwards-Sayer, Malcolm 192
efficient-market hypothesis (EMH) 88, 150
e-gold 160
Eko Ltd. 257
Eldorado 244
electronic exchanges 130–3
electronic trading platforms 130–3
El Ghazouani, Kévin 203
Elkjaer, Bo 288–91
'Emirate of Caucasus' 113–14
Energie Groupe 210
Erulin, Morgan 95, 206
eschatology 276
Es-Kontrakstroy Ltd. 107

Esselunga 201
ethash encryption process 175
Ether 160, 174, 175
Ethereum 175
Ettori, Mickaël 210
EU Emissions Trading System (EU ETS) 21
Eurasia Economic Union 71
Eurasian Customs Union 104
Eurasian Economic Commission (EEC) 104, 274–5
Eurasian Economic Union (EAEU) 103, 274–5; digital VAT 104–5; estimates of VAT fraud in 111–12; examples 106–9; existence on 103; fully integrated framework, far from 105; mechanisms 105–6; sanctions: a new variable for the VAT fraud 110–11; VAT fraud in 105–6; VAT: new form of 'roof' 109–10; VAT rates in the Member states of 104
EUROFISC 94, 255, 279–80, 287
Eurojust 200, 274
European Commission 17, 21, 28, 31, 38–44, 48, 55, 57, 61, 64, 75, 77–8, 82, 93, 104, 119, 138–9, 151, 176, 181, 190, 267–8, 272, 274, 279–80, 286–287
European Common Market 15
European Court of Justice (ECJ) 168–9, 270
European Customs Union 78
European Economic Area (EEA) 78
European Federation of Accountants (FEE) 41–2
European Football Championship 26
European Parliament 38, 267
European Public Prosecutor's Office (EPPO) 274
European Single Market 78, 178
European Single Mechanism 182
European Union (EU): anti-fraud unit (OLAF) 77; estimation of shadow economy in 49–51; technology 168–9; VAT fraud as drawback to fully fledged integration of 35–41; VAT gap in 41–6
European Union Allowance (EUA) 21
European VAT Directive 177
Europol 96, 255, 274
Eurosabre Ltd. 191
Euro Trade Energy 206
Eurowire Finance Ltd. 99
EU's economy, and VAT fraud: data preparation 61; econometric models 57–61; estimates of MTEC VAT fraud 70–5; estimation of losses due to MTIC VAT fraud 57; estimation of shadow economy in the EU 49–51; model estimates 64–70; outlook 75–6; panel regression model 61–4; real figure of VAT fraud 46–8; relationship between VAT and GDP 51–4; role of collected VAT in national budgets 31–5; size of VAT loss due to shadow economy 54–7; VAT fraud as a drawback to fully fledged EU integration 35–41; VAT gap due to shadow economy 48–9; VAT gap in the EU 41–6
Evening Standard 212–13
Evil Calls 244
Evolved Pictures 243
expectation bias 149–50
externality: defined 85; negative 57, 85–7
Exxon Mobil 110
Ezra, Avi Ben 205

Facebook 20, 117, 155
Fanella, Silvio 239
Farrell, Stephen 196
Fast Petrol Company 30
Fastweb S.p.A. 215–16, 218–20, 221, 225, 228–9, 230
Fateh, Abdessamad *see* Abu Hamzah
FCZ Srl 224
Federal Bureau of Investigation (FBI) 119, 145, 273; Witness Protection Program 158
Federal Trade Commission (FTC) 142
FedEx 174
Fernández, Joaquín Tafur 194
Ferreri, Antonio 217
field-programmable gate array (FPGA) 174
financial asset: cryptocurrencies as 173, 175; defined 160–1
Financial Crimes Enforcement Network (FinCEN) 171
financial institutions: and Counter-Terrorism Financing systems 114; and KYN 278; non-banking 5; role of KYC in 275–7
First Curaçao International Bank Britain 99
Fitch 276
Fitschen, Jürgen 213
Florida Miami Gold 30
Focarelli, Carlo 217, 219, 224, 230, 233, 235–6, 238
food and beverages 27–8

food markets: competitive distortion of 93;
     domestic 93; in Hungary 47
formal economy 3–4; output products of 51
Forrest, Gerard Michael 187
Fragomeli, Francesco 236
Frankfurt Regional Court 213
Franzese, Michael 29–30
French Ministry of Finances 91
French National Federation of Automobile
     Workers 91–2
fuel 29–30
Fulcrum Electronics UK 218, 241
Fulcrum Trading Inc. 241
Fulcrum Trading US Inc. 218, 220, 221
Future Communications (UK) Ltd. 197–8

Galleon Holdings 29
Gandham, Iqbal Singh 192
Ganev, Gancho 254
Garbro, Anders 97
García, Juan Díaz 194
Gardham Ltd. 196
Garner, Robert 188
gas and electricity 22–3
Gathani, Rajesh 198
gbullion 160
GDP: European 38, 42, 49–51, 75, 104;
     nominal 52; ratio 53; 54–5and VAT
     51–4
geographic bias 277
German Ministry of Finance 169
Gilmore, Lucie 182–3
Gilmore, Michael 182–3
Gindin, Diana 250
Giralda Oil Services 30
Girolamao, Nicolo di 233
GK Telecommunications PLC 196
Glam Entertainments Ltd. 198
Glaston Ltd. 196
Globalactive Technologies Ltd. 196
Global Phone Network Srl 224, 228,
     230, 242
Global Telephone Service LLC 216,
     219, 220
global terrorism: low-cost terrorism as
     new directions of 113; uber-terrorism
     as new directions of 113
Global Vision 205
Globestream Ltd. 236
Gohir, Mohammad 211–12
Goldfree Ltd. 199
goods: high-value/low-weight 7, 27, 184;
     industrial 79; luxury 14; misclassification

of 106–7; purchase of 173–4; smuggled
     51, 81, 84, 111; virtual 14, 162;
     zero-rated 7
Goods and Services Tax (GST) 2–3,
     15–16, 80, 282
Google Voice 20
Google Wallet 160
GoShare 140
Gossamer Web 157
Gourevitch, Eugene 148, 242
government consumption: unrecoverable
     VAT on 42
Grabr 140
Great Train Robbery 180
Grecu, Octavian 252
Green, Mickey 180
gross fixed capital formation (GFCF):
     unrecoverable VAT on inputs to 42
Guardia di Finanza 25, 40, 121, 216, 226
The Guardian 135, 138
Guppy, Darius 181
Guth's algorithm 264
GW 224 Ltd. 196
Gyraland UK Ltd. 186

Haber-Hofberg, Stacey 197
Haccoun, David 17
Hackney, Charles 186
Hackney, Paul 26
Hague, Phillip George 186
Halliday, Jo-Anne 190
Hamed, Rachid Abdel Nahet 123–4
Hamidi, Khaled 196
Hancock, Stephen 187
Hannah, Daryl 244
Happyhillock Ltd. 198
'Hard'-Brexit scenario 79
Harris, Joanna 197
Hassan, Tariq 243
Hatton Garden 16, 180–1
Hawala transfer 6
Hawala-type systems 6
Hayre, Ardip Singh 199
Hayre, Mandish Singh 199
Hedqvist, Daniel 168
Helix 164
Henley, Mark 218
Herbalife 141–2
Her Majesty's Revenue and Customs
     (HMRC) 11, 17
hidden Markov models (HMMs) 262
high-value products 15, 25–6; *see also*
     products

Hi-Profile Ltd. 192
Hofer, P. 146–7
Hohnholz, Helmut 213
Hollande, François 203
'Hollywood' connection 243–4; Al-Issa, Bashar 243; Anand, Anish 244; Driscoll, Richard 244
Holvi 155
household consumption liability 42
HSBC Bank 207
Hughes, Marcus 190
Hunter, Dennis 190
Hussain, Roshan 197
Hussain, Syed Faraz 199

Iannilli, Marco 239
Iberian Connection 193–5; Aleixo, Valter 193–4; Chatlani, Annand 194–5; Chatlani, Mohan 194–5; García, Juan Díaz 194
Ibiplace SL 198
identities: multiple 153–4; synthetic 154–7; vanishing 157–8
identity engineering 153
IFT Food ApS 123
IGA Électronique 207
Igbanugo, Theresa 197
I-Globe Srl 223, 227, 229–30, 242
iGolder 160
Illouz, David 204
Imperium Corporation 189
Incorporative Service Ltd. 216
indirect taxes 1, 15, 31–2, 34, 159, 173
inelastic demand 26–7; *see also* demand
Infinity System 17
Informatica Lda 194
Initial Coin Offering (ICO) 175
Initial Crypto Offerings (ICO) 159
Innovative Global Business Group Ltd. (IGB) 197–8
Instagram 25
Interfin Trust & Finance Ltd. 97
intermediate consumption: unrecoverable VAT on 42
Internal Revenue Service (IRS) 29, 171
International Accounting Standards (IAS) 160
International Monetary Fund (IMF) 254
inventories 161
investigating the VAT fraud: 'anthropological' approaches 258–9; data mining techniques 260; multilingual name matching 262–4;

structural approaches 259–60; text mining 260–2
invisible dividend 90–1
Iorizzo, Larry 29
Iqbal, Mobeen 212
Irish Republican Army 113
Irish Semi-Conductors 195
Islamic State of Iraq and Syria (ISIS) 101, 113–17, 120
Islamist terrorism 113
Israel 172
Israeli-Arab Hariri crime organization 145
Israeli groups 249–50
Israel Tax Authority 172
Issitt, Brett 189
Italian Customs Office 40

Jai Hua International Ltd. 191
James, Roy 180
JD.com 134
Jensen, Carsten Robert 200
Jingdong Mall 134
Jogia, Pravin 196
Johns Hopkins University 164
Johnson, Craig 186–7
Johnson, Gareth 187–8
Johnson, Geoffrey 186–8
Jones, Colin 189
Jones, Craig Michael 186
Jon Soni 199
JSC 'Trade and Production Company (TPK)' Yashma 108
JVA Corporation S.A. 217

Kaif, Daamin 192
Kamal, Tariq 196
Kanda, Jeevan 183
Kappers Foods BV 126
Karelia Business 232
Karim, Afsana 244
Karim, Shabir 183–4
KB Jewellers 184
Keating, Michael 195
Kenworthy, Adam Roger Buckley 217–18, 242
Kenworthy, Robert James 217, 242
Kenworthy, Robert Nicholas James 218
'KGB Mafia' 250
Khan, Amir 211–12
Khan, Genghis 104
Khan, Nasir 190
Khan, Shoket 189
Khann, Alex 205

Khristoforov, Leonid 250
Kidd-Hewitt, D. 148
Kittel, Axel 270
Kittel principle 269–71
K&K Electronics 201
Klapucki, Jaroslaw 208–9
K&M Supplies Ltd. 199
Kno Quatro 194
'knowledge principle' 270
Know Your Customer (KYC): an
    uncharted area 275; limitations of
    275–7; role in financial institutions
    275–7; a sound alternative 277–8
'Know Your Network' (KYN) 278
Kobak 272
Kohli, Harbans Singh 196
Kolkowicz, Mickaël 96, 206
Koser, Abdul 190
KPMG 216
Krause, Stefan 213
Kray twins 180
Krugerrand 15
KUGA DATA SmbA 97
Kumar, Amit 244
Kumar, Surinder 183
Kyoto Protocol 21

A Landscape of Lives 243
Lansky, Meyer 31
Latvian Financial Police 256
Lauré, Maurice 2, 46
Laurent, Curtis 190
Lawley Technologies Ltd. 187
LBB Trading Ltd. 217, 220, 242
Lehman Brothers 98
LeKiosk (Bouygues) 19
Lemarco SA Bucharest 252
Levenshtein's distance 264
Lightcare Ltd. 196
LinkedIn 155
Litecoin 160, 174
Livia Ioana Găzdac 252
Liviz 108
Lloyd, Howard R. 116
London exchange Intercontinental
    Exchange (ICE) 150
low-cost terrorism: as new directions of
    global terrorism 113
Low Value Consignment Relief
    (LVCR) 135
Low Value Customs Relief (LVCR) 77–8;
    and Brexit 84; enforcing 82–3; as
    European setup 82–3

Ma, Jack 14
McNeill, Michael 189
Madden, Aoife 243
Maga, Simona 225
Magnusson, Carl Michael 98
Majid, Taher 190
Malyshev, Alexander 250
Mann, Geoffrey 183
Manson, Charles 113
Maranzano, Salvatore 85
Marceau Trade 203
María, José 30
market behaviour: structural breaks in
    88–90
markets and VAT fraud: artificial demand
    18–19; clothes 18; CO_2 emissions
    21–2; digital products 24–5; food and
    beverages 27–8; fuel 29–30; gas and
    electricity 22–3; high-value products
    25–6; inelastic demand 26–7; low-
    volume, high-value products 15;
    negative externality for 85–7; overview
    14; precious metals and stones 15–16;
    services 23–4; technology products
    16–18; telecom services 19–20
Markowitz, Michael 30
Marsden, James 'Bug Eye' 180
Martirosyan, Robert 108
Mash, Benedict 181
Massimo, Comito 238
Mastercard 96
Master Trading (UK) Ltd. 191
Match Rating Approach (MRA) 263
Matlub, Kaiser 27
Matthews, Shane 187
Mavlyanov, Igor 108
Maxro Technology Ltd. 192
Mayall, Rik 244
Mazzitelli, D. Stefano 229
Mazzitelli, Stefano 225, 238
Mediaworld 201
Meflur 17
Mehmet, Mustapha 196
Mehmet, Timur 196
Mehtajee, Mohammed 191
Melgrani, Christiane 210
MEM Catering 126
mental accounting 151
mental accounting bias 151–2
Microelvas 194
Mimran, Arnaud 207–8, 209
mining 176–7
Mini One-Stop-Shop (MOSS) 81–2, 105

Mir, Fraz 211
Mirajkar, Sanjeev 244
Mishustin, Mikhail 109
misrepresentation: of goods and services 4;
  of product type 13
missing trader 6–12, 179; carousel fraud
  8; contra-trading 10–11; countertrade
  (barter) fraud 11–12; cross-invoicing
  9; Missing Trader Extra-Community
  (MTEC) 12; Missing Trader
  Intra-Community (MTIC) scam 6–7
Missing Trader Extra-Community
  (MTEC) fraud 6, 12, 70–5, 81–2
missing trader fraud 4, 6, 14, 81, 176,
  191, 266
Missing Trader Intra-Community (MTIC)
  scam 6–7, 57, 181–4
Mitnick, Kevin 144
MM Insurance Broker Ltd. 253
Mohamed, Mustafa Al Lal 123
Mohamed, Zakaria Said 126
Mohammed, Javed 189
Mohand, Mustafa Zizaoui 123
Mokbel, Gennaro 233, 234–5
Mokbel Gennaro gang 217
Monero 160, 166
money laundering 95, 163–4
money rinsing 95
Montagens e Material Eléctrico 194
Moodys 276
moral hazard 276
Moran, Barbara 187
More, Sukhdave Singh 196
Morganrise Ltd. 199
Moscovici, Pierre 117
Moudenc, Christophe 216
Mouly, Cyril 209
Mouly, Mardoché 'Marco' 207
MST Associates (UK) Ltd. 196
Muhammad, Ashraf 212
Mulner, Amir 205
multilevel marketing (MLM) 140–4
Multi Level Media 245
multilingual name matching 262–4
multiple identities 153–4
Murri, Augusto 218, 232, 240
Musillo, Pietro 217
Myths and Mirrors Theatre Company 157

Naive Bayes classifiers 262
Nanotecnología Integrada 194
Nathanael 204
National Court of Justice of Spain 250

Nauti-Parts SL 189
Naydenov, Daniel 254
NCT Training Ltd. 196
'Ndrangheta 148
Neapolitan Camorra 209, 210
Neave, Andrew David 218, 241
negative externalities 57, 85–7
Neo 160
Nétanyahou, Benyamin 207
Newey, Peter 196
New York Sicilian mafia 247
New Zealand Companies Office 98
Nexor One 98–9
Neyret, Michel 206, 208
Nikitin, Mikhail 239, 242
Nimber 140
Ninkitin, Mikhail 223
Noriega, Manuel 29
'*Novacovici*' clan 253
Novellist International Ltd. 220
Novellist International S.A. 221
Novicio Food & Beverage SRL Ilfov 252
Novostroy LLC 107
Noya, Bernabé 17
Nykredit 97

O'Connell, Daniel 195
O'Connor, Paul Anthony 218, 241
Odedra, Bharat Muriji 199
OLAF 77, 81
'On Digital Financial Assets' 172
online marketplaces 24, 133–9
Openledger Dex 166
Operation *B2 Euro* 202
Operation *Blue Sky* 202
Operation *Burlao* 30
Operation *Car Jumping* 25
Operation *Crepuscule* 202
Operation *Devout* 196
Operation *Dreams* 144, 194
Operation *Dreyfus* 202
Operation *Elemi* 192
Operation *Emersed* 186, 187, 189
Operation *Euripus* 189, 190
Operation *Euro Canyon* 203
Operation *Fenix* 15
Operation *Finger* 180
Operation *Flat Screen* 201
Operation *Good Platts* 30
Operation *Green Plus AG Energy* 202
Operation *Hardware* 202
Operation *Medina* 17
Operation *Meeting* 28

Operation *Nosean* 16
Operation *Odin* 202
Operation *Phuncards* 215–23, 225
Operation *Phuncards-Broker* 148–9,
   226, 230
Operation *Shepherd* 186, 187, 189
Operation *Shoot* 187, 189
Operation *Shout* 186
Operation *Sith* 18
Operation *Sunrise* 273–4
Operation *Sweets* 28
Operation *Traffico Telefonico* 20, 215, 218,
   223–32
Operation *Tulipbox* 202
Operation *Vaulter* 187, 188, 190
Operation *Vertigo* 202, 274
Operation *Wheels III* 26
Operazione Phuncards-Broker 215, 260
Organisation for Economic Co-operation
   and Development (OECD) 49
O'Toole, Peter 244
output products: of formal economy 51; of
   shadow economy 51

Panama Papers scandal 155, 275
panel regression model 61–4
Panitzke, Sarah 188
'Paradise Papers' 275
Paris Court of Appeal 205
Parisi, Stefano 225
Parra-Moyano, J. 275
Part-of-Speech tagging (POS Tagging)
   261–2
Patel, Irfan Musa 211
Patel, Muhammed 191
Patel, Shafiq 191; *see also* Umerji, Adam
Pavani, Amandino 225
Payment Protection Insurance (PPI)
   customer data 245
PayPal 160
peer-to-peer delivery services 140
Peitzmeyer, Bjoern 211
Peitzmeyer, Robert 211
Perron, P. 89
Perryman, Chris 279–87
Peter Virdee Foundation 212
Petromiralles 3 SL 30
Petromiralles SL 30
Petrov, Gennady 250
Pet Shop Boys 197
PGT Ltd. 220
phonetic matching methods:
   Beider-Morse Phonetic Matching 263;

Daitch-Mokotoff Soundex approach
   263; Match Rating Approach (MRA)
   263; 'Soundex' algorithm 263
Phuncards-Broker case 19, 148
Pigott, Stephen 196–7
Planetarium Srl 223, 230
Pomfrett, Peter John 196
Porcaro, Angelina 210
Powertone B.V. 189
Power Trade company 96, 206
precious metals and stones 15–16
Precious Waste Recovery 16
Premier Global Telecom Ltd. (PGT Ltd.)
   218, 242
Prestige Cars 197
products: digital 24–5; high-value 15,
   25–6; technology 16–18
Promsvyazbank 108
Property and Management Services 197
psychological manipulation 146–7
Public Accounts Committee, of the House
   of Commons 83
public switched telephone network
   (PSTN) 20
Pugliese, Franco 240
Pulgar, Juan Delgado 194
Pummell, Leslie 196
purchase: of goods 173–4; of services
   174–5
pyramidal marketing companies 141

Qadri, Kashif Ghaus 97
Q-Tech Distribution 200
Q-Transport 123–8, 126
Quick Reaction Mechanism (QRM) 267–8

Raj Trading Corporation 189
Ramzan, Shahid 198
Rapid Distribution Ltd. 196
Ravjani, Dilawar 197
Raza, Muhammad Al-Numairy 199
RBA Trading 184
RBS Sempra 215
Red Brigades 113
Red Channel 18
'Red Mafia' 250
Regal Metals 184
relative differential sensitivity 152
reputation bias 276
reverse VAT charge 266–8
Reynolds, Alison 156–7
Reynolds, Quentin 190
Reznik, Vladislav 250

Riaz, Tamraz 197
Ribeiro, Joaquim 193
Richardson family 180
Richet, Jean Stephane 121
Ripple 160, 165
Roadie 140
Roberts, James Edward 218
Rodríguez, Andrés Cano 194
Romanian and Bulgarian groups 250–4
Romanian Economic Police 253
Ronnie Dark 180
Roofsmart Ltd. 188
Rossetti, Mario 218, 225
Roter Stern Gmbh 211
RouteCall 133
Routledge, David G. 186
Royal Bank of Scotland (RBS) 200, 214–15
Ruggerio, Riccardo 225
Russian Duma 172
Russian Federal Security Service (FSB) 250, 275
Russian Federation 3, 41, 95, 103–13, 110, 172, 176, 254, 256; Federal Law No. 39-FZ of April 22, 1996 "On the Securities Market"' 172; Federal Law of November 21, 2011 No. 325-FZ "On Organized Trading"' 172
Russian Mafia 250
Russian-speaking organized crime 250

Sabadash, Alexander 107–8
safe harbour bias 277
Saggar, Diljan 199
Sakoun, Fabrice 204
Salgsbutikken A/S 126
Salikov, Yuri 250
Salikov, Yury 250
Salmond, Alex 213
Salya, Mohsin Usmangani 212
Samra, Harbinder Singh 199
Samra, Karnail Singh 199
sanctions: against the apartheid regime 99; against the Russian Federation 110–1; new variable for VAT fraud 110–11
Sandhu, Baljinder Singh 192
Sandhu, Harnaik Singh 192
Santoni, Jacques 210
Sari Trading Consult Aps 126
Satoshi Nakamoto 160
Saunders, Clive 186
Sberbank 108
Scaglia, Silvio 215, 218, 225, 237–8

SC Novicio Food & Beverage SRL 253
Scoponi, Riccardo 223
Scout Energy Petrol 30
Secchi, Elisabetta 225
Second Chechen War 113
Second World War 113
September 11, 2001 attacks 114
services 23–4; in the crypto-universe 176–7; purchase of 174–5; telecom 19–20; VAT fraud on 201–46
Sesay, Osman 124
SF Energy Trading 121–3
SFR Presse 19
SHA^{72-}256 175
shadow banking 5, 97, 117
shadow economy 4–6; estimation of, in EU 49–51; output products of 51; size of VAT loss due to 54–7; VAT gap due to 48–9; *see also* black market
Sharm ElCheik 113
Sheasby, Mark Frederick 196
Shell 29
Shelton, Alison Elizabeth Samantha 188
Shivani (Ltd.) 196
Short, Jason 217
Siemens 111
Signal Telecom GMBH 189
simple differential sensitivity 152
Sindona, Michele 248
Singh, Gurjit 199
Sistemas Informáticos Gomiz 194
size bias 276
Skancom Finans AB 97
SKAT (Danish tax agency) 125
Sky ApS 123
Sky Computers UK Ltd. 192
Skype 20
Slack 20
Smagghe, Benoît 205
small and medium enterprises (SMEs): and scissor effect 39; simplifying VAT system for 41
Sobolevsky, Igor 250
social engineering 144–6
Societe Generale 151, 203
'Soft'-Brexit scenario 78–9
Soldevilla, Natalia 194
Souied, Samy 206, 208, 209
'Soundex' algorithm 263
South African Krugerrand 179
South African Revenue Service 3
Soviet Union: fall of 103
S&P 276

'*Stanescu*' clan 252
Stark, Stephen 192
status quo bias 150–1
Stefaris cigarette SRL 252
stereotyping: classic 148; form of cognitive
bias 147–8; and corporate world 149;
role of media in reinforcing 148;
technology 147–9; and white-collar
criminals 148
Stewart, Rob 197
Stoke-on-Trent connection 185–90;
Ashraf, Shehwad 189; Baillie, Stuart
185–6; Cox, Raymond 188–9;
Hancock, Stephen 187; Johnson, Craig
186–7; Johnson, Geoffrey 187–8;
Khan, Nasir 190; Saunders, Clive 186;
Woolley, Raymond 188
Stoyakov, T. 107
structural breaks, in market behaviour
88–90
Suade Management Ltd. 218, 220, 221
Succu, Giovanni 217
Suspicious Activity Reports (SAR) 163, 218
Swaab, Remy 98
Sweeney, Paul 189
Swefin AB (Danish internet bank) 97
SWIFT system 165
Swisscom AG 218
Swiss Federal Tax Administration 172
Switzerland 172–3
Sworiba B.V. 217
Synergy Services Ltd. 199
synthetic identities 154–7

Taher, Rawand Dilsher 124
Taïeb, Albert 209
Takkar, Harjit Singh 192
Taliban 120, 121
Taobao.com 134
tax, defined 1; *see also specific types*
tax arbitrage 3, 41
tax avoidance 3, 38, 43, 93, 143
tax fraud 2–3
tax-havens 99–102
tax optimization 2, 3
'Technologies Savings & Loans' 97
technology: accounting treatment
160–2; blockchain and cryptocurrencies
158–9; confirmation bias 149–50;
cryptocurrencies 159–60;
cryptocurrencies enhancing VAT fraud
162–3; cryptocurrencies liable to VAT
173; crypto-flipping 166; decentralized

exchanges 165–6; deregulated
commercial contracts 175–6;
e-commerce and trading infrastructures
129–30; electronic exchanges or
electronic trading platforms 130–3;
European Union 168–9; expectation
bias 149–50; identity engineering
153; Israel 172; mental accounting
bias 151–2; mining 176–7; money
laundering 163–4; multilevel marketing
(MLM) 140–4; multiple identities
153–4; online marketplaces 133–9;
peer-to-peer delivery services 140;
psychological manipulation 146–7;
purchase of goods 173–4; purchase of
services 174–5; role of the 'mixers/
tumblers' 164–5; Russian Federation
172; service in crypto-universe
176–7; social engineering 144–6;
status quo bias 150–1; stereotyping
147–9; Switzerland 172–3; synthetic
identities 154–7; United Kingdom
169–70; United States 171; vanishing
identities 157–8; VAT treatment of
crypto-economy 166–7; Weber's law
152–3
technology products 16–18; *see also*
products
Technomarket 201
Tectonics Holdings 188
Telecom Italia Sparkle S.p.A. (TIS S.p.A.)
149, 215, 223, 225, 228–9
telecom services 19–20
TelecomsXChange 133
Telefax Srl 220
Telefox International Srl 217, 223, 228, 230
Telefox Srl 217, 221, 227
Telemarket APS 126
Telepart Distribution 126
terrorism *see specific types*
terrorism financing: VAT fraud as source
of 116–17
Texaco 29
text mining 260–2
Thantrimudali, Duminda 192
Theatre Productions 157
Thurston, Cameron Charles 199
TIS S.p.A. 229–30
Tmall.com 134
Tommasino, Vito 226
Torrens, José María 30
Torrens, Pedro 30
Toseroni, Marco 217

Touchsisten 194
trading infrastructures 129–30
Trading Italia Srl 217
transnational investigation agencies 273–5
Transworld Oil 99
Traverse, Christopher 196
Treesandland SL 198

Uber 140
uber-terrorism: financing of 115–16; as new directions of global terrorism 113
uber-terrorist 115
Ubique Italia Holding Srl 224
Ubique Tic Italia Srl 224
Ubique TLC Italia Srl 224, 230
UFC Denmark Aps 126
Umerji, Adam 191; *see also* Patel, Shafiq
Unique Distribution Ltd. 197–8
United Kingdom 169–70
United Parcel Service (UPS) 139, 174
United States 171; Daech and 114; federal investigation agencies in 273; global investment vehicles in 99; legal status of Bitcoin and Altcoin in 167; sanctions against the Russian Federation 110; VAT acceptance in 2
United States Congress 171
United States Secret Service 211
unrecoverable VAT: on government consumption 42; on inputs to gross fixed capital formation (GFCF) 42; on intermediate consumption 42
US Treasury Department 110

V&A Corporation 203
Value Added Tax (VAT): accounting shenanigans 12–13; and 'Brexit' negotiations 77–8; cryptocurrencies liable to 173; digital 104–5; a European concept 1–2; fraud typologies 3–4; and GDP 51–4; misrepresentation of product type 13; missing trader 6–12; a new form of 'roof' 109–10; role in national budgets 31–5; scrapping scenario 80; shadow economy 4–6; tax fraud 2–3; treatment of crypto-economy 166–7
vanishing identities 157–8
Vantage Petroleum 29
VAT backlogs 39
'VAT brokers' 109
VAT evasion 3, 17, 22, 23, 25–8, 46, 71, 75, 77, 79, 84, 136–7, 146, 152, 156,
158, 179, 181, 192, 194, 200, 244, 259, 269
VAT exemption 265–6
Value Added Tax (VAT) fraud: after Brexit 83–4; competitive distortion of the food markets 93; cryptocurrencies enhancing 162–3; as a drawback to EU integration 35–41; in the EAEU 105–6; impact on the car production in France 91–2; impact on the CO_2 emissions allowances 87–8; invisible dividend 90–1; negative externality for markets 85–7; real figure of 46–8; reasons for 117–18; typologies 3–4; on services 201–46; as source of financing of terrorism 116–17; structural breaks in market behaviour 88–90
VAT gap: defined 38; due to shadow economy 48–9; in the EU 41–6
VAT losses: due to MTIC VAT fraud 57; size of, due to shadow economy 54–7
VAT milieu: acquitted link 237–9; aftermath 232–3, 233–7; age of 'Aquarius': British link 241–2; age of 'Cancer': Benelux Connection and the birth of MTIC (1993–1997) 181–4; age of 'Gemini': technology gadgets era (1998–2005) 184–201; dead link 239–40; 'golden' age (1979–1992) 179–81; Guppy, Darius 181; Hatton Garden 180–1; 'Ndrangheta link 240; Russian link 242; VAT fraud on services 201–46
VAT rate policy 41
VAT Reverse Charge 266–7
VAT Total Tax Liability (VTTL) 42–3, 70
VDL Duty Free Wholesale 123
Vega Trade Comodities SRL Giurgiu 252
Vela Holdings Investments Ltd. 201
Vertigo 97
Vertu Telecoms Ltd. 191
Villanueva SL 194
Villeneuve, Stéphane 95, 206
Virdee, Peter Singh 212
Visa 96
Vocaturo, Mario 192
Voice over Internet Protocol (VoIP) 8, 14, 20, 25, 70, 81–2, 117, 132–3, 149, 173, 215, 223, 228–42, 248–9, 259, 271, 276, 278
VoIP Business Forum 133
VoIPexchange 133

Vriesekoop BV 126
VTB 108
Vyborgskaya Cellulose LLC 107, 108

Wai Fong Yeung 191
Warner & Richardson 157
'war on cash' 96
Watmough, Martin 196
Waves Dex 166
Weber's law 152–3
Web Wizard Srl 217–22, 233, 235, 241
Welco Holding AG 223
Welco Holding S.A. 242
Wembley Mob 180
West, Michael 186
Westergaard, Kurt 124
Westmoreland, Denise 190
'white-collar' crime 178
Willoil 30
Wilson, Charlie 180
Wisdom, Norman 244
Witness Protection Program (FBI) 158
Wolstin Ltd. 242
Woodland Supplies 196

Woolley, Raymond 188
The Working Group Ltd. 199
Worldsoft (UK) Ltd. 187
Worldwide Telecommunication Services
    LLC (WTS) 216, 219, 220
World Wide Web 129

Yanev, Yanko 254
Yasin, Tariq 123
the Young Turks 247
YouTube 25
Yukatel 126

Zakaria Abbas el Hajj 124
Zakat 118
ZAO Rosmash 108
Zaoui, Grégory 203–4, 206, 210
Zaragoza, Michael 208
Zealand Financial Group 98
ZEN Carbon Management 205
Zeption Telecom SL 189
Zerocoin 164
Zipes 194
Zito, Bruno 219, 225, 233, 237

For Product Safety Concerns and Information please contact our EU
representative GPSR@taylorandfrancis.com
Taylor & Francis Verlag GmbH, Kaufingerstraße 24, 80331 München, Germany

www.ingramcontent.com/pod-product-compliance
Ingram Content Group UK Ltd.
Pitfield, Milton Keynes, MK11 3LW, UK
UKHW021018180425
457613UK00020B/976